The Moral Domain

The Moral Domain

Essays in the Ongoing
Discussion between Philosophy
and the Social Sciences

edited by Thomas E. Wren

in cooperation with Wolfgang Edelstein and
Gertrud Nunner-Winkler

The MIT Press
Cambridge, Massachusetts
London, England

© 1990 Massachusetts Institute of Technology

All rights reserved. No part of this book may be reproduced in any form by any electronic or mechanical means (including photocopying, recording, or information storage and retrieval) without permission in writing from the publisher.

This book was set in Baskerville by DEKR Corporation and printed and bound by Halliday Lithograph in the United States of America.

Library of Congress Cataloging-in-Publication Data

Zur Bestimmung der Moral. English.
    The moral domain: essays in the ongoing discussion between philosophy and the social sciences / edited by Thomas E. Wren.
    Rev. translation of: Zur Bestimmung der Moral.
    Based on a conference convened by the Max Planck Institute in 1984 in Germany.
    Includes index.
    ISBN 0-262-23147-6
    1. Ethics.   2. Psychology—Philosophy.   3. Moral development.
4. Kohlberg, Lawrence, 1927–.   5. Habermas, Jürgen.   I. Wren, Thomas E.
II. Title.   III. Series.
BJ1114.Z8713   1990
170—dc20   89-35726
                                                                        CIP

Contents

Introduction
Thomas Wren   vii

From the Introduction to the German Edition
Wolfgang Edelstein and Gertrud Nunner-Winkler   xvii

**I Charting the Moral Domain: The Relationship
between Philosophy and Psychology in Research
on Morality**

The Necessity for Cooperation between
Philosophical and Empirical Research in the
Clarification of the Meaning of the Moral "Ought"
Ernst Tugendhat   3

The Possibility of Convergence between Moral
Psychology and Metaethics
Thomas Wren   15

How Should Psychologists Define Morality? or, The
Negative Side Effects of Philosophy's Influence on
Psychology
Augusto Blasi   38

Against the Neglect of "Content" in the Moral
Theories of Kohlberg and Habermas: Implications
for the Relativism-Universalism Controversy
Rainer Döbert   71

Moral Relativism and Strict Universalism
Gertrud Nunner-Winkler   109

II Morality and Cognitive Development: Principled Thinking as a Developmental End State

The Study of Moral Development: A Bridge over the "Is-Ought" Gap
Dwight R. Boyd   129

The Return of Stage 6: Its Principle and Moral Point of View
Lawrence Kohlberg, Dwight R. Boyd, and Charles Levine   151

The Majesty and Mystery of Kohlberg's Stage 6
Bill Puka   182

Justice and Solidarity: On the Discussion Concerning Stage 6
Jürgen Habermas   224

III Morality and Personal Development: Moral Experience as Self-Transformation

The Emergence of Morality in Personal Relationships
Monika Keller and Wolfgang Edelstein   255

Moral Balance: A Model of How People Arrive at Moral Decisions
Mordecai Nisan   283

Moral Responsibility and Moral Commitment: The Integration of Affect and Cognition
Helen Haste   315

Beyond Freud and Piaget: Biographical Worlds— Interpersonal Self
Gil G. Noam   360

Contributors   401

Index   405

Introduction

Thomas Wren

This volume has its roots in a special working conference convened by the Max Planck Institute in 1984 at Ringberg Castle in Germany, with the purpose of examining the state of the conversation between moral philosophy and the social sciences. Although that conversation is a global one, its dominant voices are English and German, as the involvement of the Max Planck Institute indicates. The dozen or so scholars who came together under its auspices presented and responded to papers that were subsequently revised and published, first in German and now, after further editing and updating, in this book. As noted in the introduction to the German edition (whose thematic portion is reproduced below), the contributors are all intimately familiar, and generally in agreement, with the hermeneutic and reconstructivist paradigm of cognitive developmental theory as well as the nonrelativist tradition of moral and social philosophy. It is within these theoretical horizons that the present paradigm of moral development has itself developed over the last decades, primarily because of the one contributor to these pages whose chapter is, sadly, a posthumous publication: Lawrence Kohlberg, to whose memory this volume is dedicated. His chapter is the center of gravity for the whole book, partly because of the revisions that after his death were made in the other chapters: in it he presents the final formulation of his much-discussed Stage 6, which until now has only been available in its German version in spite of the fact that it was originally written (and then, working with his coauthors, painstakingly revised) in English.

Of course Kohlberg is not the only scholar who has worked in the interspace between moral philosophy and psychology: in addition to Jürgen Habermas—whose social science is even more interdisciplinary than Kohlberg's—all the other contributors are known for the research they have done outside the narrow limits of their home disciplines. In this respect they embody an openness of spirit that has come about over the last three decades, as social scientists investigating moral phenomena have become increasingly conscious of the philosophical issues inherent in their subject matter. Similarly, either by design or coincidence, moral philosophers have reciprocated, becoming more and more sensitive to the need for empirical research into the sociological and psychological dimensions of morality. To be sure, a perfect alignment of philosophy and the so-called moral sciences is as unlikely as ever, if only because of the divisions still to be found within each of the various disciplines: among psychologists, for instance, there is every reason to expect that social learning theorists will never fully accept the structuralism of cognitive developmental theory, that developmentalists will continue to regard the reinforcement paradigm as hopelessly inadequate where cognitive motivations are concerned, and that both groups will retain their profound misgivings about psychoanalytic theory as long as it continues to use the psychodynamic categories that are its hallmark. Similar conditions of mutual suspicion obtain in moral philosophy, where the old disputes between emotivists and naturalists, and later between prescriptivists and descriptivists, are now reiterated between the partisans of universalizability and the partisans of particularity, with their respective emphases on justice or love, principles or virtues, and so on. Nor are psychology and philosophy the only arenas of inner conflict where research on topics such as morality is concerned: sociologists, anthropologists, and educators continue to disagree among themselves about methods, contents, and even the autonomy of their own disciplines. It is, then, something of a wonder that there is any cross-disciplinary conversation going on at all.

Part One: Charting the Moral Domain

The essays contained in the first part of this book focus most directly on the relationship between philosophy and psychology (and cognate areas of the social sciences), in order to chart the moral domain. Ernst Tugendhat opens the discussion by challenging the tendency, found in cognitive psychology, to separate questions about the meaning of moral judgments from those about their motivational force. In contrast, he claims that empirical research and philosophical theory must complement each other in the analysis of the meaning of the moral "ought." As he points out, in moral contexts the word "ought" is not used simply as a short way of indicating what sorts of behavior are rational. Immoral action is behavior that one ought not engage in, not because it is irrational but rather because it merits sanctions. What is distinctive about moral norms is that they carry an "internal sanction," such that blame and praise are tied in with the moral agent's self-respect and self-affirmation, from which such norms derive their power to move the agent. Where this connection is absent, due to an unhappy socialization, we speak of "lack of moral sense." From this line of argument Tugendhat shows that the philosopher must rely on the empirical psychologist to clarify this "inner sanction," which constitutes not only the main motive for compliance to moral norms but also the very meaning of the moral "ought" and hence of morality as such.

The second chapter, which is my own contribution to this volume, continues Tugendhat's inquiry into the nature of moral motivation, but takes as its point of departure the distinction between internalist and externalist perspectives on the relation between motivation and meaning in moral judgments. Contemporary moral philosophers generally treat moral judgments as involving at least some minimal degree of moral motivation on the part of the subject who sincerely utters them. This is in marked contrast with most psychological treatments of morality, except for that of cognitive developmentalists such as Kohlberg. Thus the essay examines the possibility of a mutually illuminating convergence or "reflective equilibrium" between cognitive developmental psychologists and moral philosophers, with particular attention being given to the recently introduced construct of "responsibility judgments" that mediate judgments of rightness and decisions to act.

Blasi's chapter agrees with the first two that philosophy and psychology have much to offer each other in the discussion of morality, but warns against taking a pollyanna view of their interaction. He discusses three negative features of cognitive developmental research on morality that seem to be the result of an uncritical use of philosophy by psychologists. These baneful effects are that the domain of the moral has been unnecessarily restricted to justice; that philosophical considerations are frequently used as an intrinsic part of the empirical argument; and that developmental psychologists have failed to observe their own methodological postulate that morality must be defined from the perspective of the individual agent. To prevent these unwanted results, Blasi concludes, we must avoid confusing the psychologist's question (how is morality in fact experienced by different people?) and the philosopher's question (what should morality be like?) as well as the equally misguided tendency on the part of psychologists to answer the philosopher's question with empirical tools.

Döbert's chapter shares at least the first of Blasi's concerns, i.e., the tendency of philosophically informed social scientists such as Kohlberg and Habermas to restrict the moral domain to justice. He argues that the core of the moral sphere consists of universal basic rules of acting rightly and abstaining from acting wrongly, all of which are summarized in the formula "Do not do harm to other human beings." This formula provides a content-oriented criterion of morality that he believes distinguishes moral action from other forms of behavior in a way that purely structural considerations could never do. He also believes that it clarifies the true nature of the moral dilemmas used in Kohlberg's developmental moral psychology: in spite of the impression often given by Kohlberg and others who discuss his work, they are not really restricted to justice issues, if only because they reveal that there are competing theories of justice. Moral reasoning, Döbert concludes, must adjudicate the claims of justice, as well as correlate general principles with situational details in order to determine where exceptions must be made to those claims.

The last chapter in Part One, by Nunner-Winkler, directly addresses the topic of universality in moral thinking and moral development. She argues for a qualified universalism, which holds that while universalizability as a procedural criterion for moral judgment is rationally justifiable, universal concurrence about the solution of a concrete dilemma may very well prove unattainable even by the most open-minded interlocutors. When there is a question of allowing for exceptions to moral principles in order to avoid greater harm done to others, a weighting of evils is called for; and while there is normally rational agreement on what is bad, no general agreement on a hierarchical ordering of evils can be presupposed. This view is offered as a correction to the unduly strict universalism of Kant, which assumes that universal consent can be reached not only with respect to the procedural criterion but also to "right" solutions in moral conflicts. As Nunner-Winkler recognizes, Kohlberg also seems to hold a strict universalism in some of his writings, though his essay in the present volume seems closer to the qualified universalism that she has suggested.

Part Two: Morality and Cognitive Development

The preceding chapters by Döbert and Nunner-Winkler set the stage for Part Two since, as they themselves illustrate, the cognitive conception of the moral domain quickly leads to the philosophical and psychological question of whether principled thinking is an end state of moral development. Also, they show that it is virtually impossible to discuss this question in any serious way without reference to the work of Lawrence Kohlberg, especially his various views on the nature of Stage 6. Accordingly, the second part of this volume is the setting for what is literally Kohlberg's last word on that topic. However, even though his chapter is the featured essay in this section and indeed the entire book, it takes on additional significance when read in tandem with the other chapters in this section.

The first of these chapters, by Boyd, is a philosophical argument for the fundamental cognitive developmental suppo-

sition that the study of moral development requires the
construction of a bridge over the "is-ought" gap. Kohlberg's
general approach to the study of moral development is examined within this context in order to show that it *does* respect
the distinction between statements of fact and value, once that
distinction is properly understood. Boyd then focuses on what
more can be said within a developmental framework, in order
to provide an analysis and elaboration of the "complementarity" of psychology and philosophy that Habermas has claimed
exists within Kohlberg's approach to the study of moral judgment. In Boyd's view, this complementarity is best understood
in terms of the researcher's need to assume the "performative
attitude" with regard to questions of truth—the facts of developmental change—and, at the same time, with regard to questions of rightness—the morally appropriate direction of that
change.

Kohlberg's own essay is predictably apt as an illustration of
this complementarity. Using a combination of case studies and
philosophical analysis, he and his coauthors Boyd and Levine
demonstrate that the heart of Stage 6 is the attitude and principle of equal respect for human personhood and dignity, as
well as the need to engage in consensus-seeking dialogue from
the moral point of view. Although he continues to insist on the
importance of principled thinking and taking another's perspective, this final formulation of Stage 6 introduces a feature
that earlier formulations did not have, or at least did not emphasize, in their attempts to distinguish between it and the
lower stages (including Stage 5). This is the feature of consensus, whereby the ideal resolution of a moral dilemma is understood to be that which everyone involved agrees to as a result
of mutual review of the situation from everyone's perspective.
The willingness to undertake such a review is, Kohlberg concludes, the moral point of view itself. A look at the reasoning
of such great figures as Lincoln, Gandhi, and King reveals a
conviction on their parts that the core of morality is respect
for the other's dignity, a respect manifested in their willingness
to engage in dialogue even with those who were in deepest
disagreement with their specific social programs.

The other two essays in this section, by Puka and Habermas, take issue with Kohlberg even though they accept the general framework within which his final revision of Stage 6 was carried out. Puka feels that Kohlberg has not succeeded in working out the relationship, on the one hand, between justice and benevolence, and, on the other hand, between equality and individual merit or responsibility. He discusses these issues by reviewing both psychological controversies (e.g., the Kohlberg-Gilligan debate) and philosophical ones (e.g., the Rawls-Nozick debate). But Puka's deepest disagreement with Kohlberg is his belief that there are insurmountable empirical and conceptual problems in Kohlberg's claim that an end point in moral development defines the whole sequence of moral development.

Habermas, in contrast, shares Kohlberg's belief in a developmental end point, but not his trust that it can be articulated in the form of a system of philosophical ethics. In other words, Habermas denies that variations in conceptual content—in the present case, substantive differences between moral philosophies—reflect intrapsychic structures of human cognition. This assumption, which is typical of cognitive developmental theory, is criticized by Habermas as fallaciously naturalistic, notwithstanding his general agreement with Kohlberg's description of Stage 6 as the end point of moral development. The latter part of the essay attempts to replace that naturalism with what Habermas has elsewhere described as "discourse ethics," a philosophical model that he believes to reciprocally support and be supported by Kohlberg's own empirical work.

Part Three: Morality and Personal Development

Part Three of the book comprises four chapters that do not so much define or analyze the moral domain as they relate it to the equally complex domain of personal development, here understood for the most part as the development of that sense of commitment that is often simply called "responsibility." The first of these, by Keller and Edelstein, is an account of how morality emerges in the course of personal relationships, in particular, friendships. Using interviews and other empirical methods, they show that there are developmental transformations in the way one comes to have a sense of commitment within (and toward) personal relationships. Whereas most psychological research on the social cognitions involved in friendship considers only descriptive judgments, Keller and Edelstein focus on the prescriptive judgments involved, in particular those that spill over into the moral domain. Thus they consider two sets of standards whereby friendships are evaluated by moral agents: justice-oriented standards of what is right and reasonable in terms of fairness, and care-oriented standards of what is good in terms of ideals of self and the preservation of personal relationships. Contrary to what has sometimes been claimed, both sets of standards are used by moral agents, be they male or female, since each has its basis in the agent's understanding of personal interaction.

A rather different account of moral judgment and personal involvement is provided by Nisan, who develops the distinction drawn in the opening chapters between moral judgment and moral decision. In the first case the individual judges an act in light of absolute moral principles, without regard to the agent's own individuality and historicity. In the second case, that of moral decision, the individual decides whether or not to perform an act already judged to be morally relevant. Although cognitive developmentalists tend to treat moral decisions as moral judgments, and internalization theorists tend to treat moral judgments as moral decisions, Nisan regards these as two separate processes. He goes on to show that a moral decision has its origins in one's definition of oneself ("identity") and one's evaluation of one's "moral position" at the moment. The result of this evaluation Nisan calls the agent's "moral balance"; it is necessary for the maintenance of a person's identity, of which morality is an important constituent but not the only one. However, Nisan understands moral balance as a weighted summary of the moral values of the individual's separate acts, and believes that these moral values are themselves tied to the agent's own self-respect and respect for other persons. Hence it seems that personal identity also serves as a condition for moral decision and even moral judgment, especially (if we accept Kohlberg's account of Stage 6) at the post-conventional level.

Haste's chapter adopts, and then goes beyond, the cognitive approach to morality and moral development. She believes it has yielded a rich body of data about reasoning processes, but argues that it has missed an important dimension of the making of individual moral decisions. Employing concepts from other forms of social psychology, most notably schema theory, she outlines a model that incorporates the role of affect in the process of individual engagement in a moral decision, and shows how affect and personal responsibility are related to cognitive processes. She illustrates her model with several case histories, portraying varying degrees of moral commitment and moral responsibility.

In the final chapter, Noam combines psychodynamic constructs with the structuralism of Piaget and Kohlberg, in order to explore developmental patterns and clinical manifestations throughout the moral agent's life span. After reviewing some basic ideas of conflict, change, and moral action in Kohlberg's work, Noam concludes that the biographical dimension has been excluded from the study of moral conflict. However, he goes on to argue, clinical-developmental psychology, with its emphasis on forms in which people recreate the past in present situations, can enhance the study of moral judgment and moral action by introducing a dimension of personal history. In the theory of biography and transformation that he proposes, each developmental transition is seen as a reworking of earlier unresolved moral conflicts. Arrest or delay in moral development during adolescence and adulthood is thereby related to earlier, unresolved moral conflict.

As I noted above, a German version of this book has already appeared; its title was *Zur Bestimmung der Moral: Philosophische und sozialwissenschaftliche Beiträge zur Moralforschung* (Suhrkamp Verlag), and the editors were Wolfgang Edelstein and Gertrud Nunner-Winkler. Although the present volume is not a direct translation of that book (in the meantime some chapters were extensively rewritten, others added or subtracted), my debt to Edelstein and Nunner-Winkler is very great. They not only edited the German volume, but also organized the Max Planck conference at Ringberg that was the original forum for our conversation and graciously supported my own efforts to bring the conversation to the English-speaking world. For various reasons, not all the participants of that conference have a chapter of their own in these pages, but they were all crucial to the collective cognitive process whose external expression is this book. The "invisible contributors" include Ringberg participants Marvin Berkowitz and Jyotsna Vasudev (USA), Hans Bertram, Lutz Eckensberger, and Max Miller (Germany), Fritz Oser and Reto Fetz (Switzerland), and Thør Thørlindsson (Iceland); their catalytic and corrective influence is here gratefully acknowledged. Also to be included among the invisible contributors are those who helped with the tasks of translation and, often enough, retranslation: Shierry Weber Nicholsen translated the Habermas and Döbert chapters, and (in addition to the authors themselves) Hans Seigfried, David Ingram, and especially Tom McCarthy gave useful advice. Mary Lou Arnold prepared a comprehensive and much-appreciated index. Needless to say, my thanks also go to the visible contributors from the Ringberg conference. They patiently reworked their essays as requested for the English edition, so that it can serve as a memorial to our good friend Larry Kohlberg and as a resource for understanding what at the end of his life he meant by principled thinking. With this knowledge, philosophers and social scientists can all the more intelligently continue their conversation about the psychological structure of the moral domain.

From the Introduction to the German Edition

Wolfgang Edelstein and
Gertrud Nunner-Winkler

This book aims at clarifying the connection between philosophical theory and empirical psychological research in morality. It is authored by philosophers working in the nonrelativist tradition of moral and social philosophy and social scientists working within the hermeneutic and reconstructivist paradigm of cognitive developmental theory. This paradigm, which can be traced back to the writings of Piaget and eventually to Kant, has in our time been shaped most profoundly by Lawrence Kohlberg, whose philosophical as well as psychological views pervade the present volume in spite of the many differences between Kohlberg and the other authors, as well as the equally significant differences among the authors themselves. The controversies that are taken up in the following papers focus on problems that have remained controversial among philosophers and empirical psychologists. Some of the problems are due to the tendency of psychologists to base their work on ethical theories selected for their affinity to the researchers' personal biases; other problems originate in the tendency of philosophers to ignore the insights gained from empirical research. But these problems are not the main concern of the present volume. Rather it focuses on major and substantive differences that arise between psychologists and philosophers (or even members of each group) whose work is based on similar metatheoretical presuppositions. These issues will be outlined and specified in the following introductory remarks.

The first part of the book introduces a problem that recurs in the later parts as well, namely, the problem of defining morality. How are moral and nonmoral questions to be demarcated? Who is to determine the boundary—philosophers or empirical researchers? Is morality defined by an a priori conceptual decision or by inference from empirical evidence? For some, morality is to be defined from the top down, by deduction from a metaethical perspective or from the highest stage of moral development; for others, morality is to be defined from the bottom up, i.e., by induction from what the subjects interviewed actually say concerning their understanding of morality. For instance, Kohlberg takes the first position: along with his collaborators Boyd and Levine he regards universalizability and the perfect reciprocity of norms as the criteria of morality. However, Blasi, Puka, and Döbert take the opposite stance, holding that an empirically minded psychologist can only grasp the nature of morality by starting from an everyday understanding of morality, that is, by taking the subjective sense of obligation as the defining criterion.

This controversy can be resolved to some extent by integrating philosophical analysis with certain empirical studies that show that even young children are able to differentiate clearly between the domains of morality, convention, and personal preference (see Turiel, 1980, 1983). This they do using the same criteria that Kohlberg takes to be decisive, namely obligatoriness, generalizability, and impersonality. Conversely, Tugendhat holds in his essay that an empirical analysis of "respect," the inner sanction for norm conformity, is necessary for a philosophical understanding of the meaning of "ought." And also Wren and Boyd, whose respective essays can also be read as instances of the top-down position, conclude that morality will not be reducible to classificatory thinking but has to be defined from the perspective of the subjects. Thus deductive and inductive definitions of morality begin to converge. In defining morality, subjects themselves rely on universalizability and impersonal obligatoriness, i.e., they use the same criteria that philosophers accept as valid. The convergence, however, is limited to *formal criteria of demarcation*: the subject pays respect to those norms he or she considers universally valid. The *content* of these norms, however, remains controversial.

For Kohlberg and Habermas, questions of content are fundamentally related to justice, in that each of these theorists conceives as moral only those norms directed at providing just solutions to social conflicts. For Blasi, however, there is no warrant for defining morality in such restrictive terms. He points out that for many individuals (as well as for certain ethical traditions) a number of additional norms are considered morally binding. Among them are duties toward the self (which Kant also counted among the moral duties); altruistic duties; and religiously based duties toward God, nature, and life. Blasi thus obtains the contents of morality inductively, by listing phenomena that have been considered as "moral" by specific individuals or cultures.

Döbert takes a different view in his chapter, arguing that the core of morality is precisely delimited and universally given. Moral rules are not developed or constructed. Rather they are discovered like natural laws. Döbert claims that Kohlberg and Habermas misunderstand procedural ethics when they assume that norms are actually produced (and not merely justified) by procedures. According to Döbert the misunderstanding results from mistakenly identifying universally valid moral norms that stipulate the avoidance of harm and the promotion of welfare with issues of justice where, in principle, consensus cannot be reached about the competing criteria of equality, merit, and need. It is in these cases that consensus can only be reached procedurally. Thus, Kohlberg and Döbert agree on the contents of morality (avoiding harm, promoting welfare)—yet they do so for opposite reasons: Kohlberg deduces content from procedure, Döbert thinks that moral content is derived from basic anthropological conditions (and that the procedures are later constructions, made to fit the content given). Thus both stand in contrast to Blasi, who treats the topic of content as a purely empirical question.

The delimitation of the content of morality is not the only topic at issue in these pages. A further controversy refers to the exact meaning of the formal criterion of universalizability. Nunner-Winkler attempts to clarify the range of the claim of universalism. While she does not adopt a relativistic stance, she argues for a restrictive interpretation of the claim of universalism. It is the procedures for justifying norms or solving conflicts that lay claim to universal validity. Theoretical considerations and empirical data lead her to repudiate the claims advanced by Habermas and more recently by Kohlberg according to which universal consensus about the solution of moral dilemmas is possible as well.

The second part of the book deals directly with Kohlberg's theory of moral development, especially its highest stage. Boyd's essay provides a transition from the first part by analyzing the relationship between philosophy and empirical social science, discussing, in particular, the relationship between "is" and "ought" in Kohlberg's thought. Boyd concludes that theories based on a developmental logic are capable of tying together the causal thinking characteristic of empirical social sciences and the hermeneutic attitude characteristic of the philosophical approach.

Kohlberg provides just such a theory in a chapter that constitutes his final statement of the nature of Stage 6 thinking. In this essay he and his coauthors revisit the intensely disputed issue of whether the seemingly independent principles of justice and benevolence (Frankena, 1973; Gilligan, 1982) can be integrated. They tackle this issue on two levels of argumentation: First, they seek to demonstrate that the principles of justice and welfare can both be derived from the highest constitutive principle of morality, namely respect for persons. Second, they demonstrate how justice and welfare are coordinated in the application to concrete moral dilemmas of those operations that are characteristic of the highest stage of moral development (Stage 6): sympathy, ideal reciprocal role-taking, and universalization. Puka's essay critiques this endeavor on several grounds: he maintains that Kohlberg has failed to provide empirical support for Stage 6 reasoning as well as to convincingly demonstrate the need, on philosophical grounds, for constructing a highest stage. This criticism resembles Blasi's argument. Further, according to Puka, Kohlberg's individualistic approach to ethics prevents him from adequately considering problems of the good life and common welfare. Finally, an ethic postulating a universal obligation to supererogatory actions is overtaxing: in view of the conditions of the real world, no normative ethics could credibly declare that everybody's duty is to seek, beyond particular relationships, the realization of a "cosmic justice" of benevolence.

In his response to these contributions Habermas (agreeing with Kohlberg and disagreeing with Puka and, by implication, Blasi) claims that cognitivist developmental theories must define a normatively marked end point of individual development. The "highest stage of morality," however, should be regarded not as a natural stage but as a construct of moral philosophy. Much like Puka, Habermas calls attention to individualistic shortcomings in the autonomous morality of the modern natural rights position. The same holds true for that interpretation of Kantian ethics (also adopted by Kohlberg) that restricts the principle of benevolence to caring for "thy neighbor's welfare" and does not mention the question of the common good. In contrast, the discourse ethics of Habermas proceeds from the insight that it is only by way of socialization that persons can be individualized (Mead, 1934). Thus the welfare of the individual is linked not only to the welfare of others but also to the integrity of collective life. Principles of solidarity that refer to the common good replace the principles of benevolence that refer to individual welfare. Solidarity transcends all concrete (personal, ethnocentric) relationships so as to include all mankind, even potential members of a potential communicative commonwealth. Habermas rejects Puka's objection that an obligation to care morally overtaxes man—an argument that applies a fortiori to solidarity as a morally binding principle. In Habermas's view this is a pseudo-problem that confounds questions of morality with questions of law.

By way of summarizing these issues and positions discussed in the first two parts of the book, we can distinguish five controversial issues that have emerged in the course of working out the definitions of morality and moral development: (1) the criteria for demarcating moral and nonmoral issues; (2) the content of norms that satisfy these criteria; (3) the basic principles that enable us to deduce concrete norms; (4) procedures suited for justifying moral norms and for examining their validity; and finally (5) the question concerning universal validity of moral norms and principles, of procedures of moral justification and of specific solutions to moral conflicts. The authors address these issues quite differently. There are several points of disagreement and some points of convergence. The authors' positions with regard to the five issues can be summarized as follows:

1. *On the basis of what criteria* and in *what ways* can we differentiate moral from nonmoral issues? Possible answers:

• Morality is defined bottom-up, from the perspective of the subject. The criterion is the subjective sense of obligation.

• Morality is defined top-down, through philosophical explication. The criteria are objective characteristics of moral norms such as universality, impersonal authority, independent validity, independence from context.

Taking the empirical researcher's perspective, Blasi adopts the first position. Descriptive science has to define morality from the perspective of the subjects, through recourse to empirical inference. Kohlberg and Habermas, on the other hand, maintain that empirical investigation must be preceded by a definition of the object of study that can only be achieved on a theoretical level. Kohlberg assumes that this definition can only result from an explication of the highest stage of moral development (the empirical existence and theoretical necessity of which Puka doubts). According to Habermas this definition follows from reasons produced in philosophical argumentation, the validity of which cannot be decided on empirical grounds. A first solution to this problem is provided by taking into consideration empirical data (such as those of Turiel, 1983) that show that subjects (even young children), in demarcating the realms of the moral, the conventional, and the unregulated, make use of the same criteria that philosophers introduce, namely, a sense of subjective obligation toward rules that are granted universal and impersonal validity. Of course this only shifts the problem to the next question.

2. What *kinds* of norms (what normative contents) are marked as "moral" by the criteria of morality? Possible answers:

• Duties toward others, either negative duties (thou shalt not kill, steal, lie, etc.; in general, refrain from doing harm) or positive duties (help those in need, promote the interests of others, etc.; in general, prevent evil and do good).

• Duties toward the self.

• Duties based on religious imperatives (toward God, nature, life).

Döbert, Habermas, and Kohlberg agree that morality is restricted to positive and negative duties toward others. Blasi and Nisan disagree, holding that this delimitation is too narrow and that duties toward the self and even religious duties be included in the moral domain.

3. From which moral *principles* can we deduce concrete norms? Possible answers:

• Justice and equality as defined by fairness and impartiality.

• Benevolence (care for the welfare of others).

• Respect defined as an integration of justice and care.

• Solidarity defined as an integration of care for the welfare of others and care for the common good.

• Avoidance of harm and promotion of the interests of others.

Kohlberg has always identified morality with the formal principle of justice defined as impartial treatment and fairness. In his present paper he seeks to explicitly and theoretically integrate the principle of benevolence, which in fact has always been part of what he considered to be the "moral" solution to a dilemma (see Nunner-Winkler, 1984). Habermas, through a generalization of the principle of benevolence, generates the principle of solidarity and seeks to deduce the coherence of the two aspects of justice and solidarity from the logic of argumentative discourse. Döbert critiques procedural rules of justice for their aloofness from content. Following Gert (1973), he regards the avoidance of harm and the promotion of the welfare of others as constitutive principles of morality.

4. What are the *procedures for justifying* and *examining* the validity of moral rules? Possible answers:

• The categorical imperative.

• The original position under the veil of ignorance.

- Ideal reciprocal role-taking.
- Discourse.
- The analysis of basic conditions of human life.

Kohlberg claims that his method of ideal reciprocal role-taking is an analogue to Rawls's (1971) decision procedure "in the original position under the veil of ignorance"; he uses his method primarily for solving moral dilemmas. In contrast, Habermas claims that Kohlberg's procedure of ideal role-taking is a first step leading from Kant's purely monological position and from Rawls's predominantly monological stance toward his own discursive or dialogical procedure. Discourse for Habermas is less a method of solving moral problems than a procedure for the justification and examination of the validity of moral rules. Döbert reverses this logic of argumentation, claiming that rules are given a priori whereas procedures or justification are reconstructed with hindsight; that is, before they can be accepted, they have to stand the test of our moral intuitions.

5. How *general* are moral rules, principles, procedures of justification, or specific solutions to concrete moral dilemmas?

Döbert maintains that the moral principles of avoidance of harm and promotion of the interests of others, as determined by the basic conditions of human life, and thus their derivatives, positive and negative duties, are universally valid. Puka, following Nozick (1974), doubts that positive duties have any strict universalizability. Kohlberg and Habermas claim universal validity for their respective moral procedures as well as for the concrete solutions produced by applying these procedures to moral dilemmas, whereas Nunner-Winkler, who takes a qualified universalist position, rejects the universality of concrete solutions to conflicts.

The summary of these positions shows that several problems remain controversial among the authors: delimiting morality, the range of validity, and the range of universality. The positions they take cannot be attributed to the authors' backgrounds as either philosophers or social scientists. The controversies confirm Blasi's observation that behavioral scientists tend to be eclectic when they make use of philosophical arguments to back up their preferred type of demarcation (whereas philosophers hardly take notice of empirical research). Social scientists' resorting to philosophical argument may be explained by the fact (pointed out by Habermas and Boyd) that moral research in the hermeneutic-reconstructivist tradition must integrate the first-person perspective that is characteristic of the philosophical approach with the third-person perspective that is characteristic of empirical science.

In the third part of the book the goal of increased cooperation between philosophy and psychology becomes more concrete. This part of the book focuses on the problem of moral motivation that was raised in the first part, especially in the discussions by Tugendhat and Wren concerning the diverse motives for moral action that have been advanced by different ethical theories. Although their essays opened the discussion of the relation between philosophy and psychology, they also raised the motivational question of why people care about morality, a question whose answer or answers are the proper subject matter of the third part of the book. Besides the simple and obviously nonmoral fear of external sanctions, other motives such as sympathy, reason, and long-range interests are characterized as not meeting the specific meaning of the moral "ought." Instead, Tugendhat postulates an internal sanction, namely self-respect as mediated through the respect of others. This internal sanctioning process, of course, presupposes moral orientations. It must matter to a person whether he or she is valued as a person, i.e., as someone who follows moral rules. On this point Tugendhat concurs with Wren, who in explicating the metaethical perspective of internalism points out that understanding the meaning of a moral judgment implies perceiving its mandatory character and its grip on one's motivational system. That is, some antecedent moral core of identity must be presupposed if one is to grasp morality as such. However, how this core is constituted remains an open question for these two philosophers. A solution to this issue requires the cooperation of philosophy and psychology. In fact, the empirical studies reported in the third part of the book make some progress toward clarifying this question.

In their empirical study of interpersonal relations, Keller

and Edelstein analyze data from a longitudinal study of children aged 7 through 12, in order to show how an understanding of moral obligation gradually develops through reflecting on relations between individuals in friendship. Thus being part of close and emotionally based peer relations seems to represent an antecedent of emergent moral motivation such as Tugendhat and Wren had asked for. The claim that solidarity and positive moral commitment in friendship relations are necessary for the development of moral motivation casts doubt on Kohlberg's description of preconventional morality as basically oriented toward avoiding sanctions. This analysis provides an opportunity for bridging the gap between justice and care not by defining a highest stage but by giving an adequate description of the lowest stages.

Nisan and Haste in their respective analyses do not focus on universal conditions of the genesis of moral motivation but on the differential importance attributed to morality depending on specific forms of identity construction. Haste describes a model for the emergence of special moral commitment. It is triggered by an experience replete with high affective intensity. Later reflection then leads to cognitive reorganization that allows the moral relevance of the situation to be recognized. The sense of personal moral responsibility and efficacy develops as practical commitment is intensified. But not everybody follows this path of growing moral commitment. Some ignore the moral challenge, thus falling behind their moral insights in action (see Döbert and Nunner-Winkler, 1978; Keller, 1984). Others do not even recognize it. This corresponds to the "normal case" of a more or less conscious suppression of moral goals that Nisan analyses in his model of moral balance. Nisan points out that persons do not only pursue moral motives but also specific ego interests that appear legitimate to them and are weighted against moral obligations. In a moral conflict a person has to choose among moral interests and potentially conflicting ego interests (see Rest, 1983, 1984). The decision depends on which of the conflicting interests have greater relevance for the identity of the individual. Thus, while the motivational question raised by Tugendhat and Wren can now be formulated in a more precise fashion, it has not yet been answered. It is not clear why, or when, some people accord highest importance to the domain of morality in defining their identity, while others prefer other values such as truth or beauty. Further research, such as that of Noam that draws from both the cognitive developmental and psychoanalytic traditions, is needed in order to unravel the relations between self-concept, identity development, and the development of moral competencies (see Döbert, Habermas, and Nunner-Winkler, 1987; Kegan, 1982; Noam and Kegan, 1982; Noam, Kohlberg, and Snarey, 1983).

The discussion between philosophers and social scientists reported in this book has led not only to the reciprocal acknowledgment of different and even incompatible positions but to a more differentiated perception of these problems. Some will find it regrettable that scientists who work in a clearly circumscribed domain, and start from shared assumptions, entertain so many perspectives and unresolved controversies. For others, this is only what is to be expected. However, awareness of these differences among individual philosophers and between philosophers and social scientists is a necessary first step in the development of fruitful cooperation. The controversies show that merely appealing to one's favorite philosopher does not solve any theoretical problem. Such appeals may prove counterproductive as they burden research with externally generated questions. On the other hand, not all problems without clear-cut solutions have been shown to be pseudo-problems. Thus, the status of the highest stage of moral development remains unclear—despite the arguments exchanged between philosophers and social scientists. And yet it is clear that only cooperative endeavors of philosophers and social scientists will lead to a viable solution to this dilemma.

Possibly the range of cooperation between philosophers and social scientists has been somewhat overestimated. Even under the assumption of a more modest role for philosophy as a stopgap for empirically unsolvable problems, as Habermas (1983) has elsewhere claimed, cooperation between philosophy and social sciences may prove difficult. Nevertheless, the net result of this cooperation does not appear altogether negative: controversial issues can only be clarified by confronting different aims and positions. Several issues stand out where cooperation between philosophers and social scientists appears particularly promising. Among these are: the relationship between structure and content; function and type of moral motivation; structure and genesis of the self; the role of experience in the development of morality. Therefore we trust that philosophers and social scientists will maintain this cooperation, perhaps with added skepticism, lest the core issues of reflexive social science remain unresolved forever.

References

Döbert, R., Habermas, J., and Nunner-Winkler, G. (Eds.). (1987). The development of the self. In J. M. Broughton (Ed.), *Critical theories of psychological development*. New York: Plenum Press.

Döbert, R., and Nunner-Winkler, G. (1978). Performanzbestimmende Aspekte des moralischen Bewußtseins. In G. Portele (Ed.), *Sozialisation und Moral*. Weinheim and Basel: Beltz.

Frankena, W. K. (1973). *Ethics*. Englewood Cliffs, NJ: Prentice-Hall.

Gert, B. (1973). *The moral rules: A new rational foundation for morality*. New York: Harper and Row.

Gilligan, C. (1982). *In a different voice: Psychological theory and women's development*. Cambridge, MA: Harvard University Press.

Habermas, J. (1983). Die Philosophie als Platzhalter und Interpret. In J. Habermas, *Moralbewußtsein und kommunikatives Handeln*. Frankfurt: Suhrkamp.

Kegan, R. (1982). *The evolving self: Problem and process in human development*. Cambridge, MA: Harvard University Press.

Keller, M. (1984). Rechtfertigungen. Zur Entwicklung praktischer Erklärungen. In W. Edelstein and J. Habermas (Eds.), *Soziale Interaktion und soziales Verstehen*. Frankfurt: Suhrkamp.

Mead, G. H. (1934). *Mind, self, and society*. Chicago: University of Chicago Press.

Noam, G., and Kegan, R. (1982). Soziale Kognition und Psychodynamik: Auf dem Weg zu einer klinischen Entwicklungspsychologie. In W. Edelstein and M. Keller (Eds.), *Perspektivität und Interpretation*. Frankfurt: Suhrkamp.

Noam, G., Kohlberg, L., and Snarey, J. R. (1983). Steps toward a model of the self. In B. Lee and G. Noam (Eds.), *Developmental approaches to the self*. New York: Plenum Press.

Nozick, R. (1974). *Anarchy, state, and utopia*. New York: Basic Books.

Introduction to the German Edition

Nunner-Winkler, G. (1984). Two moralities? A critical discussion of an ethic of care and responsibility versus an ethic of rights and justice. In W. M. Kurtines and J. L. Gewirtz (Eds.), *Morality, moral behavior and moral development.* New York: Wiley Interscience.

Rawls, J. (1971). *A theory of justice.* Cambridge, MA: Harvard University Press.

Rest, J. R. (1983). Morality. In J. H. Flavell and E. Markman (Eds.), *Manual of child psychology* (4th ed.). *Vol. 3: Cognitive development.* New York: Wiley.

Rest, J. R. (1984). The major components of morality. In W. M. Kurtines and J. L. Gewirtz (Eds.), *Morality, moral behavior, and moral development.* New York: Wiley Interscience.

Turiel, E. (1980). The development of social conventional and moral concepts. In M. Windmiller, N. Lambert, and E. Turiel (Eds.), *Moral development and socialization.* Boston: Allyn and Bacon.

Turiel, E. (1983). *The development of social knowledge: Morality and convention.* New York: Cambridge University Press.

I

**Charting the Moral Domain:
The Relationship between
Philosophy and Psychology in
Research on Morality**

The Necessity for Cooperation between Philosophical and Empirical Research in the Clarification of the Meaning of the Moral "Ought"

Ernst Tugendhat

The primary task of philosophical research consists, to my mind, in the clarification of concepts or meanings. Now there are cases where it is not possible to clarify the meaning of a word without empirical research. The most famous example is Einstein's clarification of the concept of simultaneousness. Here the problem consisted in attaining a generalized explanation of what it means for two events to be simultaneous, an explanation that could cover events that are at a very much greater spatial distance than any that occur in our everyday life. But in some cases even our everyday use of a word can be so deeply embedded in experience that the philosopher may be unable to unearth its significance without the help of the empirical investigator. The latter, in turn, may not know where to dig without obtaining previous information from what the philosopher can tell him on the basis of his preliminary reflections about that word. Such is the case, in my opinion, with the word "ought" when we use it in moral contexts.

The late J. L. Mackie has suggested as a first approximation for a general explanation of "ought" in all contexts that when we say that *a* ought to *G* we mean something like: "There is a reason for *a*'s *G*-ing" (1977, pp. 73f.). Mackie also points out that we use the word not only in practical but also in epistemic contexts such as when we say, "It ought to have dissolved." In the epistemic case it is the speaker who has a reason to assume that *a* is *G*-ing. In the practical case it is the actor *a* who has a reason to *G*. In this case the reason consists in a rule. Mackie further points out that in both epistemic and practical contexts, the more normal word is "must" with its contrary "cannot." "Must" and "cannot" are the strong words in both modal contexts—the epistemic and the practical—and "ought" and "ought not" are their weak counterparts. It is an accident that in philosophical jargon we have come to use for the practical "must" primarily the word "ought"; in everyday life we more commonly use "must," especially when we use it in a moral context.

In what follows we can forget about the epistemic use of "ought" and "must." The practical use seems to be, in all cases, connected with following a rule. We say that *a* does what he ought to do or must do when he follows the rule that he wishes to follow or that we have in mind. In that case *a* acts *correctly* relatively to that rule. (No such talk of following a rule or of acting correctly would be possible in the epistemic use of these words.)

Now there are many kinds of rules. To understand what it means to follow a rule of the different kinds, it seems appropriate to ask what would be the case if one did not do what one ought to do. This way we can explain what it *means* that one ought to do so and so. It might be objected that this amounts to a naturalistic reduction of what is meant by "ought," but I can see nothing wrong with that, and the alternative would be to leave the meaning of "ought" in the dark.

I shall, without claiming to attain completeness, distinguish three kinds: rational rules, rules that define a practice, and social rules.

1. Rational rules

In many cases, we can substitute for "You must do *D*" the statement: "It is rational for you to *D*." In all such cases we can also substitute a value statement: "It is best for you to *D*." The best-known type of rational rule is what Kant called the hypothetical imperative, e.g., "If you want to lose weight, then you must eat less," or ". . . then you ought to follow the following diet." Here we can substitute ". . . then it is good to eat less," or ". . . then it is best to follow the following diet," and in both cases we can also substitute "then it is rational to . . ." Another important type of rational rule is a rule that relates the demanded action not to a given aim but to the well-being of the person; e.g., "You ought to work less" equals "It will do you good to work less" equals "It would be rational for you to work less." It is characteristic of all cases of rational rules that the rule (or one of its corresponding value statements) contains a claim about what is objectively preferable, in the sense that this is the course of action for which we can give reasons or the best reasons. Intimately connected with this characteristic is the fact that a sentence that states such a rule is, if in the second person, an expression of *advice*, and, if in the first person, the outcome of *deliberation* (since when we deliberate, we ask ourselves what we ought to do—what is rational for us to do—either relative to a certain end or relative to our well-being). Now I said that a criterion of what we mean by the use of "ought" in each case is what we would say is the case if somebody acts contrary to what he ought to do. In this first kind of rule we would obviously say that he acts contrary to what is reasonable, that he is being irrational.

2. Rules that define a practice
By a practice I mean such a thing as skiing or dancing a tango or playing a game of cards or speaking a language. A practice thus is a complex action that is defined by a set of rules. Such a practice is in most cases social (in the sense that we can only perform it together with others), but it need not be. In the case of this type of rules we would not speak of advice but of teaching. The teacher corrects the apprentice by saying: "You ought to do so and so." This is what is correct (from the point of view of this practice), but it would not make sense to say that this is good or rational. To make a different kind of step in dancing would not be irrational, it simply would not belong to this practice (though it might constitute another practice). All we can say here, then, is that when one acts contrary to what one ought to do, one does not perform this practice. (A so-called maxim—a self-imposed rule such as a person's maxim to get out of bed every morning at seven—might also be subsumed under this class of rules.)

3. Social rules

These can also be called norms: by some authors the word
"norm" is used for all rules, but this is a purely terminological
matter that has no importance. Social norms usually constitute
a system. As a prototype of a system of social norms, we can
consider a legal system. Of the rules of such a system, it is
characteristic that we can say that they are in force or not. That
a rule is in force in a society means that the persons belonging
to this society *must* act according to it in the sense that if they
do not, they incur a sanction. So the "ought" or "must" of this
kind of rule is defined in its meaning by the social sanction.

As I have said, I do not think that these three types of rules
(these three meanings of "ought") are exhaustive. Besides,
there are overlappings between them, but I don't think that
this fact matters very much for my purposes. For example,
games are primarily practices, but social games also contain
sanctions. More interesting for us is that following a social
norm could be considered as a case of following a hypothetical
imperative, with the evasion of the sanction being the end or
aim. In this respect one could say that when we follow a social
norm, the "must" has the sense that it would be irrational not
to act so. But this would be a one-sided view from the perspective of the person for whom a legal sanction is simply one
of the many factors of his situation to be taken into consideration. A legal sanction is not just one evil among others. Legal
norms are established by society, and they could not be established if a dominant kernel of the society did not consider them
legitimate, and this means: justified. Those members of the
society who consider the legal norms legitimate have an understanding that they are *legitimately obliged* to follow them, and
this characteristic of social norms is sufficient to set them apart
from hypothetical imperatives. Now this aspect of legitimacy
might appear to be what is constitutive of the meaning of the
"ought" of social norms rather than the sanction. But this
would be a complete misunderstanding of the matter. To follow
the rule because of the sanction and to follow it because it is
legitimate are not meaningful alternatives. The alternatives are
(1) to follow the rule *merely* to evade the sanction and (2) to
follow it because one considers the rule, *and that includes the*

sanction, to be legitimate. At least in the case of a legal norm, everybody should be willing to agree that without the sanction the rule would not exist. This is precisely what is meant by saying that the obligation (what we mean by "ought" in this case) is constituted by the sanction. What is justified or considered as legitimate is precisely the sanction; if the sanction were not there, there would be nothing to justify.

These last considerations bring us close to my original question: what is the meaning of "ought" or "must" when it is used morally? After what has been just said, the following explanation might appear plausible: a moral norm is simply a social norm—that is to say, a rule constituted by a social sanction—*when* it is considered to be justified. If this explanation were satisfactory, we would have right there a full explanation of the meaning of the moral "ought" (provided that we know what is meant by a social norm being "justified"), and the philosopher would have no need, at least at this point, of the cooperation of the empirical investigator. In fact I had thought that this explanation is correct (see Tugendhat, 1984, pp. 75f., 83), but I have since come to find it unsatisfactory (pp. 133ff.). It seems to me now to be wrong to take the concept of "customs and laws" defined by external sanctions as primary and to define the concept of morality in terms of it. I now believe that the concept of legitimacy of a legal system presupposes in turn an independently defined concept of morality. This has led me to look for the meaning of the moral "ought" in a special, internal sanction, and it is here where I need the help of the empirical investigator.

This presupposes, of course, that I continue to believe that some sort of sanction *is* constitutive for the moral "ought." Since I have found that nearly everybody who comes into contact with this theory finds it initially distasteful, let us first see whether there are any alternatives. Surely, so one could argue against me, a person who acts morally (and not only in accordance with morality) is not motivated by any sanctions but by morality itself. But, I ask, what does that mean?

I see three possible ways to answer this question. The first is to presuppose a special moral feeling, e.g., sympathy. I do not wish to minimize the importance of sympathy for morality, but a feeling is something we either do or do not have, not something we can *demand* of each other. In a feeling like sympathy there is no "ought," or if a feeling be postulated that is a feeling specifically of an "ought," of obligation, we would only turn in circles.

The second possibility would be to say that to act morally is to act rationally in some higher sense. This way out has been well known since Kant. Now in Kant *Vernunft* has, in this connection, indeed a special sense, but then the word "rational" is being misused, and besides, its exact sense cannot even be spelled out. In the normal sense of "rational" we say that one acts rationally in the sense that I explained under the first heading of the three meanings of "ought": if one does not act as one ought to act in this sense, one acts irrationally. But we would not say of people who do not act morally that they act irrationally. It might be objected that although people who act immorally do not act irrationally, they act against the better reasons. "What you are doing," one might tell them, "is indeed in your interest and to that extent rational, but can you justify acting in such a way?" This seems to me, however, to be an abridged way of speaking. What the one who asks such a question means is not that immoral persons cannot give reasons (and the best reasons) why they act as they do, but that they cannot justify a claim that they *may* act as they do. But then the moral "ought" is already contained in this "may"; the reasoning in question presupposes the moral dimension and the latter cannot be constituted by the question for reasons.

It should also be clear that the way Kant spoke of an obligation (*Pflicht*) that is simply an obligation "of Reason" cannot be spelled out. It remains dangling in the air as an obscure feeling, whereas the task of philosophy is to clarify what is meant by "obligation." Besides, if there really were a continuous line from rational questions at the lower levels to this higher rational question, how does it happen that all of a sudden the word "ought" acquires a sense of obligation at the higher level that it did not have at the lower level? I contend that "obligation" has an irreducibly intersubjective sense and that it cannot be understood without an intersubjective sanction.

The third possibility is to reduce morality, as Philippa Foot (1972, pp. 157ff.) has done, to a "system of hypothetical imperatives." This means: the word "ought" is divested of the sense of "obligation." That I "must" help others in distress, for example, has now the sense that this is a necessary means toward my own well-being. This may be a beautiful proposal for the future, but it certainly is no candidate to explain what in the past has been called morality. Even if the word "morality" be retained—and indeed, we ought not quibble about words— it is a proposal to abolish morality in the sense of a specific moral obligation. Somebody who acts "immorally" in Foot's sense cannot be an object of blame or contempt—the word "blame" is now meaningless—but only an object of compassion and advice.

Of the three possibilities mentioned, the first and the third are attempts to replace the moral "ought" by something else; as long as these attempts are understood as proposals for a new way of life and not as explanations, they are of course perfectly in order, whereas the second is a misguided attempt to explain the moral "ought." We can apply to this attempt my question: If people do not do what they "ought" to do in this sense, what happens? I am afraid the answer is: Nothing happens at all, except that we may say that they do not act Rationally with a capital "R." But why should this be disturbing to them? The only thing that would be disturbing would be that they would suffer somehow, and this suffering is, of course, the sanction.

So far so good. But now the trouble starts. In my opinion we must distinguish two kinds of sanctions. On the one hand are punishments and rewards, which are occurrences that have an independent positive or negative value for the agent. On the other hand are such things as blame and praise, contempt and respect, which seem to be sanctions that are somehow analytically connected with the morality of the action. If I blame you morally, this is an internal sanction in the sense that this blame is irrelevant to you if you don't already wish to be moral.

One reason why I believe that the sanction that constitutes the moral "ought" must be an internal one is that a norm that is in force only by external sanctions cannot be understood as a moral norm. Of people who follow norms only for external reasons we would say that they suffer from a "lack of moral sense"; they are not in a position to understand the word "moral." I am not entirely confident about this argument, and it may be circular. But in any case, it seems to be true as a matter of fact that the sanctions by which moral norms are backed are internal.

However, the concept of an internal sanction is difficult. For if the connection between the sanction and the standard is entirely analytical, the sanction cannot really be a sanction. To serve as a sanction there must at least be *some* difference between the sanction and the standard. Let me explain. To esteem or praise somebody means to value that person in relation to some kind of achievement. We can highly esteem somebody in his quality of cook or crook. Now if he doesn't aspire to be a cook or a crook, this high esteem will mean nothing to him. How then is it possible that there is a kind of esteem that may lead people to intend something that they do not already intend? How can blame, praise, etc., serve as a sanction? I believe that this is possible only in the case where what is esteemed concerns the person *as such*, one's "self" (or, if you prefer such jargon, one's "identity," in a very narrow sense of this ambiguous word).

At this point I find it necessary to propose two empirical hypotheses and a corollary. They are:

1. A necessary condition for self-affirmation (in the sense of self-love that is a condition for one's willing to live) is that one experiences oneself as a real or possible object of love and friendship.

2. A necessary condition for having a relationship of love or friendship to a person is that we esteem him or her as a person.

3. If hypotheses (1) and (2) are correct, it follows that a necessary condition for self-affirmation is one's self-esteem as a person.

What does it mean to esteem somebody as a person? It means to consider him or her good—not as a cook or crook or anything else, but as a person. "As a person" may sound rather metaphysical, since it seems to refer to a "nature" of a person.

But I think one can give it a simpler meaning. In every society there is the presumption that "we all"—the members of this society (only in modern times or since Christianity does this term extend to all humanity)—are essentially so-and-so's; one can more or less well instantiate this quality or function of being essentially a so-and-so, and for this one is to be esteemed (or despised) *as such.* I would, then, define the moral rules (of a society) as those rules that form the standards in relation to which a person is esteemed (or deprecated) as such.

I have elsewhere (Tugendhat, 1984, pp. 154ff.) suggested a theory of what it means to justify such rules. In the present context it must suffice that I merely hint at my conception. In every society individuals make the discovery that they are esteemed only if they restrict their freedom according to certain rules. Should one ask why (the question of justification), one would be answered: "It is because you are essentially a so-and-so, and to be a so-and-so is essentially connected with a scale of better-and-worse relative to these rules." For example: you are essentially a child of God; and these rules are the commands of God; therefore all of us esteem each other in relation to how we follow these rules. A special situation of course arises in modern times when no such religious or metaphysical essence of humanity is believed in. All that is then left is a morality of mutual (and universal) respect, and this seems to be a minimal condition for the possibility of mutual esteem. I consider this one of the weak points of my conception as worked out so far, but it is not central to the present purpose. One aspect of the justification of moral norms that does seem to be central to the present topic is that every justification in whatever society (and that is to say: under whatever conception of what "we all" essentially are) presupposes that the individual has an interest in being esteemed as a person. My thesis is that the question of justification always amounts to the question of why this fundamental esteem must depend on just these norms. If some individuals have—presumably on account of an unhappy socialization—no interest in intersubjective esteem, then there is no way of justifying to them any moral norms; the word "moral" has no sense for them, and all they understand are external rewards and punishments; they suffer from a "lack of moral sense."

These last remarks show that the two empirical hypotheses that I proposed above cannot be maintained as they stand. Empirical research is needed to show under what conditions self-affirmation is dependent on the need for esteem and what happens to self-affirmation if one makes oneself (or is forced to make oneself) independent of this need.

But these empirical questions are at the periphery of my problem. The central question was to clarify the meaning of the moral "ought." It should now be clear that this can only be achieved by an empirical investigation of (1) what the internal sanction consists in, and (2) how it is being established in the process of socialization. That is, one would have to give a more precise meaning to what I have only hinted at intuitively in the two propositions proposed above. One fundamental question is: How are love and moral esteem connected, both genetically in the child and structurally in the adult? On the answers to these questions depend the answers to the questions: Just what is it that we mean by moral blame and praise, and, more particularly, what do we mean by moral admiration and moral contempt? Very closely connected with these questions are, obviously, the questions: What is meant by guilt, resentment, and indignation? Strawson (1968, pp. 71ff.) has shown that these three moral emotions belong intimately together: resentment is the emotion that we have when we believe that somebody has treated us immorally, indignation is the correlative emotion that we have vis-à-vis an immoral act that does not affect ourselves, and guilt is the indignation that we have with ourselves when we believe we have acted immorally. This triad is precisely the internal sanction. But to use these words does not yet mean that we can explain what we mean with them. If we could, we would have explained what we mean by the word "ought" in the moral context.

In the literature that I know, I have found little help. Among philosophers, only in Rawls's three "psychological laws" have I found something similar to my two empirical hypotheses (see

Rawls, 1971, secs. 70–72). But for Rawls this is only a problem of moral motivation, not a matter of understanding the very sense of the moral "ought." Besides, he leaves the concepts of esteem, etc., relatively unclarified. Rawls refers in this section also to Kohlberg, but as Bertram (1980, p. 732) has correctly observed, if one wants to find within the cognitive approach in moral psychology anything similar to what Rawls is doing here, one has to go all the way back to Piaget (1932/1965), who was very deeply concerned with the problem of moral *respect* in his contrast between unilateral respect and mutual respect, which for him was fundamental for the distinction of the two stages of moral consciousness. In contrast to all of the later cognitivists, Piaget was very clearly aware of the fact that the moral rules are constituted as rules by what he called respect and what I call esteem. But then Piaget has not done very much to clarify this relationship of respect. In the case of the unilateral respect he speaks repeatedly, following Bovet, of a "combination of love and fear *sui generis*"; but (1) the qualification *sui generis* is clearly an admission of embarrassment, and (2) neither love nor fear nor a mixture of them can explain the specific aspect of esteem that contains a value judgment. Further, mutual respect is not explained by Piaget at all, and it seems clear that the explanation given for unilateral respect could not be applied to it. One would surely want to think that, in spite of the differentiations in the different stages of moral development, there must be something that remains constant in the concepts of respect and esteem and those of guilt, indignation, and resentment. (This is probably also the main reason why the bulk of psychoanalytic literature is of so little help.) Also the self-condemnation of which Kohlberg speaks at his sixth stage must be understood in an intersubjective sense: on the postconventional level one must be able to speak of self-esteem and of a corresponding self-contempt that are independent of the actual evaluations made by one's fellows—and hence of an autonomous conscience. But this self-esteem can only have the sense that one believes that one would be esteemed by everybody of right moral judgment—otherwise such words as "self-respect" and "self-condemnation" would have no sense, nor would the very term "morality."

Charting the Moral Domain

References

Bertram, H. (1980). Moralische Sozialisation. In K. Hurrelmann and D. Ulich (Eds.), *Sozialisationsforschung*. Weinheim: Beltz.

Foot, P. (1972). Morality as a system of hypothetical imperatives. *Philosophical Review*, 81:305–316. Reprinted in P. Foot, *Virtues and vices and other essays in moral philosophy*, Berkeley and Los Angeles: University of California Press, 1978.

Mackie, J. L. (1977). *Ethics: Inventing right and wrong*. London/Harmondsworth: Penguin.

Piaget, J. (1965). *The moral judgment of the child* (M. Gabain, Trans.). New York: Free Press. (Original work published 1932)

Rawls, J. (1971). *A theory of justice*. Cambridge, MA: Harvard University Press.

Strawson, P. F. (1968). Freedom and resentment. In P. F. Strawson (Ed.), *Philosophy of thought and action*. Oxford: Oxford University Press.

Tugendhat, E. (1984). *Probleme der Ethik*. Stuttgart: Reclam.

The Possibility of Convergence between Moral Psychology and Metaethics

Thomas E. Wren

From the logical and linguistic analyses concerning the relation between statements of fact and moral judgments, especially those carried out by English- and German-speaking philosophers in this century, there eventually emerged two more or less distinguishable conceptions of the linkages between moral cognition and motivation. In the philosophical literature they are referred to as the *internalist* and *externalist* perspectives. As we shall see, these two perspectives can also be discerned in the psychological literature on morality if one looks carefully. They are not themselves moralities, but rather two contrasting ways of conceiving moral motivation and, retrospectively, of grouping such conceptions. Regardless of whether the two perspectives take the form of formal ethical systems or informal moral notions, what is basic to the internalist-externalist distinction is the essentially *metaethical* idea that conceptions of morality can be differentiated according to whether or not they build a motivational component into the very meaning of a cognition's being a moral judgment.

A side note: The prefix "meta-" is decisive here. Whereas ethics is that branch of philosophy that examines what is right and wrong, good and bad, etc., metaethics examines the very enterprise of doing ethics. Metaethics is a highly abstract form of philosophy not only because its immediate object is another branch of philosophy rather than existing persons, situations, and norms, but also because it proceeds by close, often hair-splitting conceptual analysis (e.g., Moore, 1903/1959). The boundaries between ethics and metaethics are not always distinct, which is one reason that philosophers who write about metaethical theory do not always bother to call it by that name. But whether it is called metaethics, ethics, or just moral philosophy, it is an important line of inquiry because it asks important questions, addressing such logical, epistemological, and linguistic problems as the meaning of the word "good," the boundaries of morality, and the rules of justification for ethical judgments. As we shall see, it also addresses in its own abstract way the topic of the present chapter, namely, the problem of how—and whether—moral belief is related to moral motivation.)

Reflective Equilibrium

It would be misleading to say that all philosophers are internalists, but few would deny that internalism is the dominant view in today's philosophical community. The general consensus of most philosophers who discuss the matter is that externalist theories are "unacceptable on their surface, for they permit someone who has acknowledged that he should do something and has seen *why* it is the case that he should do it to ask whether he has any reason for doing it" (Nagel, 1970, p. 9). Space does not permit us to go much below this "surface" in exploring the philosophical and linguistic arguments underlying this consensus, though I shall discuss some of its logical features in the following section. For now, the plausibility of the internalist perspective can be shown anecdotally, in the retrospective testimony of Pvt. Michael Bernhardt, one of the few soldiers at My Lai who refused to participate in the killing of the villagers. His testimony is somewhat disjointed, but clearly represents an internalist metaethic: "If I recognize something is right . . . and you can get pretty close to it . . . this is the first step to actually doing right. And this is the thing. I can hardly do anything if I know it is wrong. If I think about it long enough, I am just positively compelled" (Hersh, 1975, p. 25; cited in Kohlberg and Candee, 1984, p. 570).

It should be clear even from this thumbnail sketch of internalism and externalism that they are genuinely contrasting viewpoints, such that an adequate philosophical account of moral experience involves an at least implicit choice between them. Furthermore, some such choice seems inevitable, albeit usually inadvertent, for social and behavioral scientists who try to provide an adequate psychological account of morality and, in particular, of its motivational structure. However, it is important to recognize that the simple fact that a psychological account of moral motivation proceeds from a given metaethical perspective is no guarantee of either the empirical or the theoretical worth of that account. At any time in the history of moral psychology it can be the case that the best metaethical perspectives are lacking a satisfying psychological correlate, and conversely, that the most plausible motivational theories embody the least plausible metaethics. Once noticed, such discrepancies provide philosophers and psychologists with the incentive to reconsider their respective views in tandem, going back and forth to arrive at what Rawls (1971, p. 20), in a related context, has called reflective equilibrium.[1] This admittedly ideal state of affairs would be an equilibrium because at last our metaethics and our psychological model of moral motivation would coincide, and it would be reflective because we would know the metaethical principles to which our psychological inquiry conforms and vice versa.

In other words, to be true to their shared metaphysical assumption that reality is one, philosophy and psychology need to work toward a reflective equilibrium between metaethical convictions and scientific models of motivation. The alternative would be intellectual schizophrenia. However, the present situation is one of considerable disequilibrium: on the philosophical scene the dominant metaethical view (which I share) is internalist, and on the psychological scene the dominant model of all motivation, including moral motivation, is that of reinforcement by anticipated sanctions. To be sure, this generalization is intolerably coarse, not only because some prominent philosophers step out of the mainstream at this point and identify themselves as externalists, but also (and for this chapter, most importantly) because there are prominent moral psychologists, working in the long shadow of Immanuel Kant, who have adopted an internalist perspective. Accordingly, I shall try to qualify my generalization, not by reviewing (or attempting to refute) the arguments some philosophers have made for externalism,[2] but rather by taking a closer look at how the whole internalist-externalist distinction maps onto contemporary psychology. My intention is not to catalogue all the psychological theories of moral motivation, but only to show in a general way what it means for a psychological theory to have a metaethical perspective and then, more specifically, to show that Kohlberg's cognitive developmental theory proceeds, in its better moments at least, from the internalist perspective. However, before doing any of this, we need to get the metaethical issue more clearly in focus.

The Philosophical Concepts

The "built-into" relationship

As we noted at the outset, the pivot point of the internalism-externalism contrast is the question of whether a motivational component is or is not built into moral cognition. But just what, we must now ask, does this alleged "built-into" relationship consist in? An early answer to this question is contained in the eighteenth-century moralists' distinction between justifying reasons and "exciting," i.e., motivating, reasons (e.g., Hutcheson's *Illustrations on the Moral Sense*, 1728/1897, pp. 403 ff.). Accordingly, internalist views of morality are those that hold that in the domain of practical and, a fortiori, *moral* thinking, justifying reasons are also exciting reasons, or at least are to be counted among the latter's rational grounds (as the necessary or perhaps sufficient conditions for their being truly motivating reasons as well as justifying ones). Externalist conceptions, in contrast, are those views in which justifying reasons are neither the same as exciting reasons nor presupposed by them: the motives underlying moral behavior are regarded as instances of what Kant called "heteronomy of the will" and contemporary social learning theorists call "extrinsic motivation." Thus Thomas Nagel (1970, p. 7) has explained that externalism holds "that the necessary motivation is not supplied by ethical principles and judgments themselves, and that an additional psychological sanction is required to motivate our compliance."

However, the most influential statement of the nature of the built-into relationship is William Frankena's formulation. In what is now the *locus classicus* of the discussion, he cast the issue in terms of logical possibility, writing that

Many moral philosophers have said or implied that it is in some sense logically possible for an agent to have or see that he has an obligation, even if he has no motivation, actual or dispositional, for doing the action in question; many others have said or implied that this is paradoxical and not logically possible. (Frankena, 1958, p. 40)

Frankena's way of putting the matter led many of the next generation of philosophers to conceive of moral motivation and its related concepts in terms of the jargon of logical entailment. This approach, which I shall later suggest needs to be reconsidered before a meaningful and productive equilibrium can be established with moral psychology, is likely to seem quite forbidding to readers unused to the formalisms of analytic philosophy. Perhaps it is primarily for this reason that the internalism-externalism issue has remained entirely undiscussed outside the ranks of professional philosophers. Not a single psychological study of morality has explicitly referred to it, which is unfortunate in view of the fact that the subject of the distinction is the relation between the motivational and cognitional dimensions of moral behavior—a relation that ought to be central in any moral psychology as well as in moral philosophy. Over the last few years the issue has been debated often enough in various philosophical contexts, with a vigor that might obscure the fact that most moral philosophers favor the internalist perspective, albeit for widely diverse reasons. Of course there is no doubt on their parts that motivational factors external to morality also play an important role in the moral lives of most people. However, it seems safe to say that for most philosophers, the dominance assigned to nonmoral motives in the theories of moral action developed by the majority of social psychologists (especially but not exclusively Americans) is—to put it mildly—philosophically problematic. The latter, themselves neobehaviorists and learning theorists, assume that morality (like all social behavior) is motivated solely by nonmoral sanctions and hence conceive their task to be that of finding out which ones are most effective. This manifestly externalist assumption is of course in full disequilibrium with the tacit or expressed internalism of most moral philosophers, who tend to adopt other, more self-directive conceptions of human action.

Logical entailment

The conceptual heart of internalism is its claim that moral motivation is built into moral cognition such that a moral judgment presents the reflecting agent with an intrinsically motivating reason for action. For philosophers influenced by Frankena's formulation of the issue as a debate over what is "in some sense logically possible," the most adequate—and most concise—formulation of this "built-into" relation typically employs the logical jargon of entailment. Internalist theories of moral cognition are defined as those that hold that a proposition like

P1: "Eve believes that abortion is wrong"

somehow logically necessitates assertions of the form

P2: "Eve is at least somewhat motivated to oppose abortion."

So viewed, internalism boils down to the thesis that

P1 entails P2.

Externalist theories, in turn, are those that implicitly or explicitly deny this entailment, no matter what positive accounts they otherwise offer concerning the motivational features of moral living.[3]

Since the entailment in question between P1 and P2 is a logical implication and not, except indirectly, an actual causal relationship, the basic thesis of internalism is completely formal: at this level of generality, internalism claims only that from the truth of the first assertion we may infer the truth of the second assertion, without claiming anything more specific about how this entailment is to be construed or what justifies it. However, the formal statement can and should be supplemented with one or more relatively specific accounts of just what sort of entailment is alleged by internalist theorists (and denied by externalists) to exist between normative propositions like P1 and motivational statements like P2. Two such accounts are available from the history of moral philosophy, each of which has its correlates in the literature of contemporary moral psychology. Both accounts regard moral judgments as intrinsically motivating, in that the subject's disposition to comply with a moral principle is thought to be a direct function of the meaning of the principle in itself, and at most only incidentally a function of whatever rewards or punishments happen to be attached to such compliance. However, since a principle's meaning can be thought of as a composite of its formal structure and its material reference or contents, within the internalist perspective there are two alternate ways of expanding the central claim that moral motivations are built into the meaning of moral judgments: (1) by arguing that one is motivated by the formal features of a moral judgment—its universalizability, reasonableness, etc.—or (2) by arguing that one is motivated by the judgment's contents—values or sentiments such as loyalty, benevolence, truthfulness, etc.

I shall call the first of these two accounts the "causal" version of internalism, since it fleshes out the bare bones of the formal entailment claim (viz., P1 entails P2) with the idea that the fact (F1) referred to in the first assertion necessarily *brings about* the fact (F2) referred to in the second, e.g., the fact that Eve is motivated to oppose abortion.[4] As we shall see shortly, this version can be attributed to Kant and, with some qualifications, to cognitive developmental psychologists who have more or less explicitly ascribed causal efficacy to the intellectual component of moral judgment. I shall call the second version of internalism the "expressive" version. It can be imputed to Hume as well as to other nonrationalist philosophers and psychologists who believe that moral reasoning as exemplified in P1 is in some nondistorting sense the verbal representation or articulation of the de facto motivational structure (F2) referred to by P2. In other words, whereas the causal version of internalism holds that

P1 entails P2

because

F1 causes F2,

the expressive version holds that

P1 entails P2

because

P1 represents F2.

The difference between these two versions of internalism is deep-seated, and goes back to the opposition between rationalist and empiricist philosophies, as well as to the rather more specific opposition between deontological (duty-oriented) and aretaic (virtue-oriented) ethics. How it is reflected in the psychological literature is the subject of the next sections.

Contemporary Moral Psychologies

Internalism (causal versions)

We begin our sampling of the metaethical perspectives of contemporary moral psychologies with Jean Piaget's cognitive developmental account of moral reasoning. More accurately, we begin with his account of "autonomous" moral reasoning, which for our purposes best illustrates the causal role of thought as an intellectual activity that shapes actual, practical exchanges between the subject and his or her environment. In his later period Piaget spoke of "ideological feelings" (Piaget, 1962, p. 137), such as respect for democratic ideals, but his use of the term "feeling" in such contexts refers not to a moralized form of affect but rather to cognitive, albeit subjective, states from which the experience of obligation is derived. For instance, in his better-known early work *The Moral Judgment of the Child* (1932/1965) Piaget spoke of "the higher and purely immanent feeling of obligation, which is the product of rational necessity" (p. 370). Moral cognition is a more or less adequate adaptive organization of one's experience, or, in Piaget's famous terminology, a successful balance of accommodation and assimilation. When cognitions, including moral judgments, are perceived as inadequate, the subject's relation to the environment and indeed to his or her own whole cognitive history is thrown into imbalance or (to use the term that sets Piaget's concept off from the present chapter's concept of reflective equilibrium) "disequilibration." As I understand Piaget, this disequilibration is purely cognitive, and has none of the affect associated with the so-called "cognitive dissonance" proposed by Leon Festinger and others as a quasi-physical drive state (see Festinger, 1957). Exactly how this disequilibration leads the subject to construct better judgments that replace those already in effect is a long and delicate story, which we need not review here; we need only note that the process is construed by Piaget as continuous with action in the world. Apparently disequilibration leads the subject to replace not only inferior judgments but also potential behaviors that correspond to or embody the inferior judgments. Since the behaviors in question are hypothetical at this point rather than actual, he claims that this replacement is carried out at the level of intention, which simply means that the subject is motivated in the one direction rather than the other—all as a result of the ongoing cognitive project of constructing maximally adequate moral judgments. This may have been what Kohlberg had in mind when he compared his own cognitive developmental moral psychology with Plato's theory of the Good, both of which understand moral motivation simply as a response to the intrinsic appeal of Goodness formally understood (Kohlberg, 1973), as well as when he described himself as "claiming that the moral force in personality is cognitive" (Kohlberg, 1976, p. 230). But as we shall see later, Kohlberg's subsequent notion of moral motivation as a matter of responsibility judgments turned out to be considerably more complex.

Internalism (expressive versions)

Piaget can be cited also as an example of expressive internalism, on the basis of his distinction between verbalized and "concrete" judgments—a distinction that reflects the pragmatic underpinnings of his epistemology. Piaget believed that, for morality as well as for all other content domains, before reflective, symbol-laden thinking can take place "within" the individual, there must have been *action* in the form of an exchange "between" the subject and the environment. So understood, moral judgment is the "adequate and progressive realization" of concrete actions or action schemes (1932/1965, p. 117), a view that looks very much like what I am here calling expressive internalism. But we must not forget that Piaget believed that genuinely moral action, especially that performed at the autonomous stage, was directed by as well as symbolized by cognitive processes and that these processes, even when preverbal, are nonetheless rational. In short, he did not regard evaluations, concrete or verbal, as cognitive housings for inherently irrational processes—except of course in "deviant cases" such as insincerity, akrasia, or more profoundly pathological modes of moral breakdown.

As for whether Piaget's moral psychology is best thought of as illustrating causal or expressive internalism, I am inclined to regard him as trying to theorize out of both these metaethical perspectives at once. There is a certain chicken-and-egg quality to the question of whether Piaget believed that moral judgments (that is, sincere, autonomous, propositional verbalizations) precede moral action or vice versa. Fortunately for the present task, which is that of finding exemplars of the expressive internalist perspective among psychologists of morality, there are other traditions besides that of cognitive developmental theory where we may look. Freud of course comes to mind as one who thought moral cognition was expressive rather than causal, but it is by no means clear to me whether the enunciations of the superego are properly thought of as moral judgments at all. A much less problematic illustration is provided by old-fashioned personality theorists such as William McDougall (1908), who regarded moral tendencies as inborn dispositional traits whose function is to generate moral verbalizations rather than to be generated by them. McDougall and other early theorists of social motivation proposed theories of autonomous, intrinsically motivating moral sentiments that were genetically based. In this respect these psychologists are reminiscent of the eighteenth-century moral sense philosophers mentioned above, who held that moral inclinations were innate and that moral judgments reflected this fact by being motivational or "exciting" as well as discriminatory. After Lewin's (1931/1962) rejection of what he styled the Aristotelian approach in favor of the Galilean one, social psychology gave up most of its talk of innate, species-wide moral tendencies in favor of analyses of the effects that social variables have on individual actions. But talk of personality traits, including those such as altruism and honesty that are typically identified with morality, survived the change of idiom. G. Allport (1937), Cattell (1950), Burton (1963), Eysenck (1970), and others have used statistical measures with varying success to validate dispositional constructs that are conceived as cross-situational givens, though not as innate in McDougall's sense. Furthermore, the surge of interest over the last decade in sociobiology is explicitly innatist, though its status as an internalist account of reflective moral behavior remains unclear notwithstanding the sociobiologists' use of moralistic terms like "altruism."

Other, less happy examples of the expressive internalist perspective are provided by a diverse group of attribution theorists, personologists, ego psychologists, and others who reduce moral reasoning to a verbal syndrome that rationalizes primary motives and preverbal meanings. For them every moral judgment is exclusively post hoc, an epiphenomenon of actions or action choices that are themselves motivated in ways totally unrelated to the contents of the subject's moral reasoning. Besides Freud, one thinks here of the later, fairly cynical view of Robert Hogan (Hogan, Johnson, and Emler, 1978) about the self-serving features of morality. (To be fair to psychology, I should note that philosophers can be just as cynical. For instance, Unamuno wrote in 1921 [cited in Blasi, 1983] that "our ethical and philosophical doctrines in general are merely the justification a posteriori of our conduct, of our actions. . . . What we believe to be the motives of our conduct are usually but the pretext for it.") In these instances, the notion of "expression" is distended to the point that the mode of expression involved is one of self-deception rather than veridical representation, which of course turns morality itself into a chimera. However, in the hands of authors like the Jungian self-disclosure theorist Sydney Jouard (1971) or the more philosophical personality theorists Herbert Fingarette (1969) and Richard Wollheim (1984), expression and veridical representation do somehow manage to come together, in the sense that morality is credited with manifesting the subject's "real motives" even though it does so more or less obliquely. The manifestation is oblique because the primary function of morality is still often regarded as "defensive" in the psychoanalytic sense of that term, it remaining unclear whether, or under what conditions, moral defenses can ever be considered by such theorists as fundamentally veridical. However, they usually agree that when morals mask the so-called primary processes they do so in varying degrees, and that the masks are not altogether impenetrable even though distortion might be the usual case rather than the exception. That is, they apparently agree that it is possible in principle to overcome moral defenses by means of certain discriminating techniques of interpretation. If this is the correct characterization of those personality psychologists and others who consider moral cognition as a set of ego defenses, then it seems reasonable though perhaps a bit strained to call them expressive internalists.

Externalism

Whereas cognitive developmentalists and personality psychologists tend to be internalists in the ways indicated above, the approaches to morality that have been taken by most social psychologists are unrelievedly externalist. As I have argued elsewhere (Wren, 1982), none of their standard learning theoretic ways of viewing the general psychological relation between cognition, motivation, and behavior demands or even suggests any intrinsic linkage between motivations and the truth of moral beliefs. The reason behind this lack of linkage in the work of social learning theorists such as Aronfreed (1968), Bandura (1977), and W. Mischel (1968) is their commitment to the reinforcement paradigm and, with it, to the hegemony of extrinsic motivation. As anyone who has taken an introductory course in psychology knows, in the reinforcement paradigm all human action—and therefore moral action—is regarded as a response to arbitrary contingencies, whose features as rewards or punishments are disconnected from the propositional content of the moral beliefs that are learned. This conception of human action, which marks many programs of moral psychology but is most clear in the case of social learning theory, is neobehaviorist in the general sense that it follows directly from the behaviorist paradigm of learning, which replaces the idea of cognitive growth with that of a measurable increase in the probability of certain kinds of (observable) responses to certain kinds of stimuli.

It is true that somebody who believes that a is wrong on the basis of having been conditioned in a certain way is going to be averse to doing a on the basis of those external sanctions.[5] But it is important to be clear why this conception does not build motivation into moral judgment, since if we are not clear on this point social learning theory will seem to be a paradigm case of expressive internalism. The stimulus-response relation postulated in reinforcement accounts of moral learning is fundamentally different from the expressive relation involved in the second version of internalism as well as from the rational causation involved in the first version, both of which relate the agent's moral motivation directly to the meaning structure of the moral belief rather than to the circumstances under which the belief was acquired. In other words, for all their differences, the two forms of internalism both hold that the subject's repertoire of moral principles is retained in what Tulving (1972) called semantic memory, as opposed to episodic memory which stores such contingent facts as where, when, and how a concept was acquired. This is in clear contrast to the neobehaviorist view of moral socialization, in which the techniques of norm transmission—modeling, punishment, classical and instrumental conditioning, etc.—work the same way regardless of the semantic content of the social norms involved.

These comments about externalist moral psychology lead to an additional point about the conditions for the possibility of any moral psychology. By divorcing moral motivation from moral meanings, social psychology transforms externalism from a metaethical perspective into a scientific one that, from the moral point of view, is rather ominous to say the least. When it functions as a principle of psychological inquiry, externalism undercuts the regard that moral agents typically have of themselves as autonomous actors. It is replaced by what might be called the principle of universal heteronomy: that all moral actions are molded by sanctions arising neither from an objective moral order nor from one's own self, but rather solely from an environment populated by objectified "socializers," be they individual persons or institutions and other sorts of collectives. At first glance this appears to be an astonishing thing to say, especially about oneself. But it is at least as astonishing that the principle of universal heteronomy has either gone unremarked or, when noticed, been accepted without demurral by so many theorists whose professional interest in morality is, presumably, not unrelated to their personal experiences of trying to do the right thing, being sincere, etc.—in short, their own experiences of being a moral agent.

Responsibility Judgments: A Motivational Turn

I spoke above of Piaget's reference in 1932 to the "higher and purely immanent feeling of obligation, which is the product of rational necessity"—a bold empirical generalization that nicely illustrated the causal version of metaethical internalism. I also cited Kohlberg's reiteration of this theme over four decades later. However, I neglected to mention that during the intervening years many neobehaviorist critics of Piaget's and Kohlberg's cognitive developmental approaches vigorously reiterated a countertheme of their own: that no correlations had been established, by the cognitive developmentalists or anyone else, between moral thought and moral behavior. Among cognitive developmentalists, the first reaction to this criticism was understandably defensive, since from the outset they had stated their concerns very explicitly as having to do with the *structures* of moral reasoning—itself an intrapsychic process whose direct public manifestation was the moral judgment interview, not the moral deed. By insisting against their neobehaviorist critics that one could have the competence to reason at a certain level of complexity without always putting one's reasons into action, cognitive developmentalists tended to take the externalist line of saying that the capacity to make moral judgments has nothing to do with any tendency to act on them, i.e., that moral beliefs have no motivational dimension. This way of defending their structuralist theory preserved the intellectual integrity of the judgment process, but it undid or at least called into question the reflective equilibrium that existed between their theory and the internalist philosophical consensus concerning moral motivation. And so, without saying it in so many words, they appeared to have abandoned their original causal internalist perspective and with it the chance of coming into reflective equilibrium with contemporary philosophy.

But what actually happened was quite different. Sometime during the last decade or so their structuralism took what might be called a motivational turn, as new data revealed that correlations do indeed exist between moral cognition and moral behavior. These correlations were found not only in Kohlberg's own data (Kohlberg and Candee, 1984) but also in a great many other studies, including some conducted by their critics (reviewed in Blasi, 1980). The correlations exhibit what Kohlberg calls a monotonic pattern whereby subjects who were able to reason about justice issues at relatively high stages were also more inclined to be personally accountable for their actions as well as to demand such accountability of others. For instance, in a survey following the My Lai massacre they found that while nearly everyone agreed that killing the villagers was wrong, they disagreed consistently regarding the degree to which Calley should be held responsible for his actions. At each higher stage of abstract reasoning the subjects were more likely to demand that, for instance, Calley be brought to trial. Similar findings concerning individual differences in what might be called the sense of accountability have been reported regarding the subjects of the notorious Milgram experiments, who were told to give seemingly enormous electric shocks to an apparently unwilling victim, all in the name of obedience to the authority of the white-coated psychologist running the experiment. Other studies originally designed to test other psychological processes have confirmed these findings in various degrees.

However, the motivational turn that cognitive developmental theory took in order to account for these findings only partially restores its equilibrium with moral philosophy, since to account for these de facto correlations between moral thought and action it was deemed necessary to adopt a problematic new construct, that of a "responsibility judgment," whose compatibility with the internalist perspective remains to be seen.

What Kohlberg and his colleagues have done is to expand the notion of moral cognition so that it includes two equally cognitive but otherwise quite distinct processes. In this new approach, we are offered a cognitive model of moral cognition containing "two intervening judgments," namely, the deontic judgment about moral rightness or justice, and the responsibility judgment about personal requiredness. Unfortunately, the very concept of responsibility is polymorphous. In the philosophical literature, "responsibility" is typically used interchangeably with "freedom" in the two complementary senses of self-determination and accountability. This is not the case in the psychological literature, where the referential range of "responsibility" is often stretched to include the simple mindfulness of consequences (see Schwartz, 1977). But among cognitive developmentalists who use the term, two somewhat more specific ideas predominate. One is that of a relatively vivid concern to preserve what Kohlberg calls "a consistency between what one says and what one should or would do and what one actually does," i.e., the so-called "follow-through function" of moral cognition (Kohlberg and Candee, 1984, p. 518). The second, somewhat different idea is that of personal necessity, in which, to cite Blasi (1983, p. 198), "an action evaluated as moral is also judged to be strictly necessary for the individual, though external constraints are absent." The semantic problems associated with the construct of personal responsibility are considerable (see Wren, 1986), but they are not relevant here. What is of present concern is rather its metaethical status, i.e., whether it is possible to buy into the notion of a "follow-through" function from an internalist perspective.

Kohlberg himself must have thought it possible, since he continued to ascribe motivational efficacy to moral judgments even after he introduced his supplemental construct of responsibility judgment. But he has not made it clear just what it is that a responsibility judgment is supposed to provide that would not already be provided in a well-made deontic judgment concerning the same subject matter. On the face of things, it would seem either that deontic judgments are inert (externalism) or else that responsibility judgments are otiose (which leaves the above-mentioned monotonicity between judgment and action unexplained).

There are probably several ways of addressing this problem, and I shall only sketch a few in hopes of showing how moral psychology and philosophical metaethics can support each other without actually doing each other's work. One rather promising empirical way to address it is to look for individual differences, especially those that display developmental patterns, in the readiness that moral agents have for invoking responsibility judgments in the course of translating their deontic judgments into moral actions. This is the way laid out by Blasi (1983), whose own psychological study of personal responsibility was very influential for Kohlberg. Another, less empirical way to address the problem under consideration is to conceptualize deontic and responsibility judgments as lying on a continuum, such that deontic judgments are relatively underdetermined action tendencies and responsibility judgments are relatively overdetermined ones. Thus a garden variety deontic judgment such as "Abortion is wrong" would be seen as lacking the detail needed to engage the many real-life persons for whom the act in question is not just an act of abortion, but also a set of other acts: preserving their own lives and histories, promoting the prospects of their other children, and so on (as if these latter action descriptions were not themselves open-ended in the extreme). On the other hand, it often happens that a moral judgment *does* have enough detail to engage the real-life reasoner even though the content of the deontic choice at issue is not fully specified: it is not usually necessary, for instance, that a woman considering abortion know the sex or hair color or (perhaps) general life prospects of the fetus she is carrying before she can decide whether it is right or wrong for her to abort. Nor is it always necessary to fill out a deontic judgment with indexical terms such as "I," "your," or "this" before it can have a motivational bite. When deontic and responsibility judgments are relativized toward each other in this way, the answer to the question "When are moral cognitions motivating?" is: When the moral reasoning begins to be about reality and not just about propositions describing reality.

Still another way to deal with the question is to look at the occasions on which moral judgments are made. Common sense suggests that, except in artificial situations such as interviews, people only go to the trouble of engaging in moral cognition (deontic or responsibility judgments) when they care (at least somewhat) about doing the right or good thing. But it follows from the very fact that they have such a care that they will be inclined (at least somewhat) to act on the results of their moral deliberation, ceteris paribus. Perhaps part of the notion of a responsibility judgment is just this, that in making it a person who has already asked "What to do?" remembers why he or she asked the question in the first place. This approach to the motivational dimension of morality is by way of the pragmatics of moral cognition, but there is no reason to think it is in disequilibrium with the other two approaches just proposed, i.e., by way of individual differences in cognitive style and by way of the specificity of the moral judgments.

Nor is there any reason to think that these are the only ways one can approach the question of moral motivation. But there is reason to think that expanding the notion of moral cognition to include judgments of personal responsibility shifts a certain amount of motivational weight from deontic propositions over to aretaic or "self-regarding" (in the nonpejorative sense of that term) considerations, and that the latter sort of deliberation is more intuitive than propositional in nature (and hence much less amenable to the entailment jargon typically used in the philosophical debate over internalism and externalism). If so, then we can expect to see theories of moral psychology in which the quality and degree of one's moral motivation are regarded primarily as a function of one's sense of self, rather than (primarily) as a function of one's conceptualization skills on the one hand or a matter of anticipations of externally induced bribes and rewards on the other.

It is for this reason that I also expect that the psychological construct of a responsibility judgment will provide a new avenue to the ultimate goal of reflective equilibrium between philosophy and psychology. This goal is probably more of what Kant called a regulative ideal than an empirical possibility, but that does not mean we should cease comparing psychology and philosophy to each other. Of course, cross-checking their respective metaethical perspectives is not, in itself, the equivalent of verification or falsification: as I said at the outset of this essay, there are no preestablished axioms to guarantee that an adequate moral philosophy will share the same metaethical perspectives found in the most adequate moral psychologies. Nevertheless, it would be schizoid of us not to hope that in the final analysis these two domains are metaethically congruent, and that progress in either domain can have considerable heuristic significance for the other.

Conclusion

The obvious conclusion is that theorists in both disciplines still have much to do by way of working toward reflective equilibrium. For instance, cognitive developmentalists have done well to turn their attention to the category of responsibility, but a still sharper focus is needed. The functions of deontic and responsibility judgments need to be related more clearly to each other: to say as Kohlberg did of the responsibility judgment that it answers the question "Why me?" only stimulates the reader's awareness that this judgment deals with something very personal without saying what that something is. Furthermore, the enormously important linkage of responsibility and personal consistency with the "self," only alluded to in the preceding pages, requires much more conceptual elaboration, especially if we are to see just why being a person includes the presumably intrinsic motivation to be personally consistent.

For their parts, moral philosophers need to go beyond their usual portrayal of the "built-into" relationship as one of logical entailment, since this view, which might be suitable in the case of third-party judgments such as "Eve believes abortion is wrong," fails to capture the hermeneutical (i.e., self-regarding and reconstructing) features of first-person moral judgments, especially those judgments that are made in response to the pressures of real life but also, I think, moral judgments collected in a well-conducted interview situation. Finally, I would add that our metaethical theory must recognize the psychological fact that for the concrete individual moral evaluation is not always the final word, that what one morally "ought" to do does not always coincide with what one "must" do. As Bernard Williams (1981, p. 125) has pointed out, *ought* is related to *must* as *best* is related to *only*. In the case of a moral ought, which is arrived at by way of a moral judgment, what is decided upon is regarded as defensible in the public forum, i.e., as "right" on some objectively defensible grounds (which are themselves keyed to the subject's level of cognitive development). But the case of what we might call the "ultimate must," which is arrived at by way of a responsibility judgment, has an indissoluble private dimension, which for lack of a better term might be called one's "character." Life goes best when the demands of one's character are continuous with the demands of the public forum, but it would be rationalistic in the worst sense of that term to suppose that this is always the case. Even when the demands are continuous, however, it remains the case that to arrive at the conclusion that one *must*—in the sense of personal responsibility—do something is to make a discovery about one's very self as well as about the world one acts within.[6]

Notes

1. As Rawls himself notes, such tacking back and forth is not peculiar to moral philosophy. Goodman (1955, pp. 65–68) offers a similar account of the justification of the principles of deductive and inductive inference.

2. Bentham is an especially clear example of the externalist point of view, since he proposed a positive alternative to internalism. That is, he not only denied that the motivation for compliance to moral principles is provided by morality itself but also undertook in a preliminary but positive way the task of explaining where that motivation does come from. Most externalist philosophers are not so forthcoming, especially those of our own time (e.g., Milo, 1981) who focus mainly or even exclusively on the formal claim that there is no logical warrant for inferring the presence of motivation from the semantical properties of moral judgments. This selectivity is, I believe, usually a by-product of an antecedent commitment on their parts to an objectivist epistemology in which moral judgments are capable of being "right" and "wrong" in the strongest, agent-independent sense of those terms.

3. It is sometimes said, by logicians as well as other sorts of philosophers, that "entailment" can be a real relationship between events or states of affairs as well as a logical relationship between propositions. However, it is more precise to speak in the narrower fashion preferred by most contemporary logicians, in which the two members of an entailment relation are propositions, i.e., semantic vehicles that refer to facts but that are not (except secondarily) actually facts themselves. Furthermore, the first of the two propositions just mentioned, P1, has another proposition embedded in it, viz., the moralizing proposition ("Abortion is wrong") that is the object of Eve's belief-attitude. In what follows we must not think of P1 as though it were itself a moral judgment: that is, we must not confuse the embedded moral proposition (Eve's own moral judgment about abortion) with the biographical proposition P1 (which is not a judgment about abortion but rather about Eve as a moral cognizer). Of course nothing prevents Eve from taking a metaethical perspective, internalist or externalist, on her own moral judgments, but P1 would not have a different meaning when stated by her than it has when stated about her by a moral psychologist or any other sort of theorist.

4. It is often claimed that the very idea of causation precludes logical entailment between propositions describing the cause and those describing the effect. Since I have no desire to enter that discussion, suffice it to say that in the present context the "entailment" relationship between P1 and P2 (in the causal version of internalism) is to be understood as expressing the sort of necessary condition that any nomological rule produces. For instance, if a law or lawlike proposition L (e.g., "When water is boiled it turns to steam") is acknowledged as true, then for the appropriate P1's and P2's (e.g., "The water is boiling," and "The water is turning to steam") it will be correct to say P1 entails P2. It might be possible for P2 but not P1 to be true, but as long as L is itself true it's not possible for things to be the other way around, i.e., for P1 but not P2 to be true. *That's* what I mean by entailment in the causal version of internalism.

5. I am grateful to Ernst Tugendhat for making this point clear to me in a commentary on this paper. See also Tugendhat (1984).

6. Research for this paper was made possible by grants from the Spencer Foundation and Loyola University of Chicago, which are here gratefully acknowledged.

References

Allport, G. (1937). *Personality: A psychological interpretation.* New York: Holt.

Aronfreed, J. (1968). *Conduct and conscience: The socialization of internalized control over behavior.* New York: Academic Press.

Bandura, A. (1977). *Social learning theory.* Englewood Cliffs, NJ: Prentice-Hall.

Blasi, A. (1980). Bridging moral cognition and moral action: A critical review of the literature. *Psychological Bulletin,* 88:1–45.

Blasi, A. (1983). Moral cognition and moral action: A theoretical perspective. *Developmental Review,* 3:178–210.

Burton, R. V. (1963). The generality of honesty reconsidered. *Psychological Review,* 70:481–499.

Cattell, R. B. (1950). *Personality: A systematic theoretical and factual study.* New York: McGraw-Hill.

Eysenck, H. J. (1970). A dimensional system of psychodiagnostics. In A. R. Mahrer (Ed.), *New approaches to personality classification and psychodiagnosis.* New York: Columbia University Press.

Festinger, L. (1957). *A theory of cognitive dissonance.* Stanford, CA: Stanford University Press.

Fingarette, H. (1969). *Self-deception.* London: Routledge.

Frankena, W. (1958). Obligation and motivation in recent moral philosophy. In A. I. Melden (Ed.), *Essays in moral philosophy.* Seattle: University of Washington Press.

Goodman, N. (1955). *Fact, fiction, and forecast.* Cambridge, MA: Harvard University Press.

Hersh, S. (1975). *My Lai 4.* New York: Vintage.

Hogan, R., Johnson, J. A., and Emler, N. P. (1978). A socioanalytic theory of moral development. In W. Damon (Ed.), *New directions for child development. Vol. 1: Social cognition.* San Francisco: Jossey-Bass.

Hutcheson, F. (1897). *Illustrations on the moral sense.* In L. A. Selby-Bigge (Ed.), *The British moralists.* Oxford: Oxford University Press. (Original work published 1728)

Jouard, S. (1971). *The transparent self: Self-disclosure and well-being.* New York: Van Nostrand Reinhold.

Kohlberg, L. (1973). The claim to moral adequacy of a highest stage of moral judgment. *Journal of Philosophy,* 40:630–646.

Kohlberg, L. (1976). Moral stages and moralization: The cognitive developmental approach. In T. Lickona (Ed.), *Moral development and behavior.* New York: Holt, Rinehart and Winston.

Kohlberg, L., and Candee, D. (1984). The relationship of moral judgment to moral action. In L. Kohlberg, *Essays on moral development. Vol. 2: The Psychology of Moral Development.* San Francisco: Harper and Row.

Lewin, K. (1962). The conflict between Aristotelian and Galilean modes of thought in contemporary psychology. In *A dynamic theory of personality.* New York: McGraw-Hill. (Original work published 1931)

McDougall, W. (1908). *An introduction to social psychology.* London: Methuen.

Milo, R. D. (1981). Moral indifference. *Monist,* 64:373–393.

Mischel, W. (1968). *Personality and assessment.* New York: Wiley.

Moore, G. E. (1959). *Principia ethica.* Cambridge: Cambridge University Press. (Original work published 1903)

Nagel, T. (1970). *The possibility of altruism.* Oxford: Oxford University Press.

Piaget, J. (1962). Affect and intelligence in mental development. *Bulletin of the Menninger Clinic*, 26:129–137.

Piaget, J. (1965). *The moral judgment of the child* (M. Gabain, Trans.). New York: The Free Press. (Original work published 1932)

Rawls, J. (1971). *A theory of justice*. Cambridge, MA: Harvard University Press.

Schwartz, S. H. (1977). Normative influences on altruism. In L. Berkowitz (Ed.), *Advances in experimental social psychology* (Vol. 10). New York: Academic Press.

Tugendhat, E. (1984). *Probleme der Ethik*. Stuttgart: Philipp Reclam.

Tulving, E. (1972). Episodic and semantic memory. In E. Tulving and W. Donaldson (Eds.), *Organization of memory*. New York: Academic Press.

Williams, B. (1981). Practical necessity. In *Moral luck*. Cambridge: Cambridge University Press.

Wollheim, R. (1984). *The thread of life*. Cambridge, MA: Harvard University Press.

Wren, T. (1982). Social learning theory, self-regulation, and morality. *Ethics*, 92:409–424.

Wren, T. (1986). Moral responsibility. Paper presented to the Society for Value Inquiry, Boston, December 28.

How Should Psychologists Define Morality? or, The Negative Side Effects of Philosophy's Influence on Psychology

Augusto Blasi

In 1958 Peter Winch's *The Idea of a Social Science and Its Relation to Philosophy* appeared, in which the author programmatically stated: "I shall argue . . . that many of the more important theoretical issues which have been raised in those studies [in the social sciences] belong to philosophy rather than to science and are, therefore, to be settled by *a priori* conceptual analysis rather than by empirical research" (p. 17). This idea was not entirely new but this book exercised an influence among social scientists that was probably unequaled by any other similar work of philosophical reflection.

In the same year that Winch's book was published, Kohlberg's dissertation on the development of moral reasoning also appeared. Though his research had probably not been influenced by the type of ideas that Winch and others had been formulating, it certainly was and remained a clear, concrete exemplification of the use of philosophy in empirical work. True, Kohlberg followed Piaget's structural approach and his study on the development of moral understanding; however, Piaget's attitude toward philosophy was ambivalent at best. Outside of Piaget, psychological work on morality was characterized by philosophical naiveté and theoretical reductionism. That is, it was assumed that morality presents no conceptual problem because everybody knows what is morally good and morally bad; at the same time, moral behavior, like other behaviors, was explained in terms of reinforcement or of internalized anxiety.

Kohlberg, instead, consciously split with this tradition by accepting a philosophical view of morality that contradicted the implicit and unquestioned relativism of psychology and by assuming the necessity of a cognitive phenomenological perspective: morality must be defined by the individual's beliefs; these are constructed by the individual himself in interaction with his social world. The impact of this position was strong and, from my perspective, liberating. It was as if psychology were finally attempting to deal with morality as people experience it.

For a number of years there was a harmonious group of cognitive developmental psychologists working on moral development, united by a strong consensus around Kohlberg's basic ideas. Only recently the unity within the cognitive developmental approach to morality began to break down; the early harmony gave way to a picture of increasing fragmentation. Now one must recognize, next to Kohlberg's, the significantly different views of Broughton, Damon, Gibbs, Gilligan, Haan, Rest, Shweder, Sullivan, Turiel, Youniss, and others. The differences concern not only the specific area of inquiry and the methods, but also the concept of structure and the very definition of morality. It is interesting that the various theorists seem to have their "philosopher(s)-in-residence" in support of a definition or a particular perspective: by way of contrast to Kohlberg's Kant, Frankena, and Rawls, Gilligan cites Blum and Murdoch; Shweder cites MacIntyre; Haan cites Habermas (Habermas is used both to defend and to criticize Kohlberg's theory); Youniss cites Macmurray; and Sullivan cites a host of Marxian philosophers.

In sum, a certain degree of confusion and a sense of discomfort begin to be felt among cognitive developmental psychologists working on morality. A recent article by Haan (1982) is at the same time a clear example of this confusion and a keen expression of the discomfort that is generated by it. In my view, this sense of uneasiness does not simply derive from disagreement, but from a more serious problem, namely, our attempt to answer the philosopher's questions with analytic tools—those that define psychology as a discipline and characterize our mode of communication—that are radically inadequate for the task.

In considering this situation as a negative side effect of the influence of philosophy on psychology, I am implicitly acknowledging that philosophy's main influence has been positive, indeed badly needed. This paper, however, will exclusively deal with its negative consequences; it will do so by discussing, in three successive sections, (1) the unnecessary narrowing of the domain of morality, (2) the improper use of philosophical considerations in psychological arguments, and (3) the reduction of the subjective perspective.

The Narrowing of Inquiry

A definition by necessity has the double effect of unifying and differentiating: as it brings certain objects or events together, it separates them from other objects or events. The psychological study of morality is no exception: whether it starts from explicit definitions or from implicit, unarticulated understanding of its domain, it must exclude certain phenomena as being irrelevant to moral functioning. Definitions, however, are not arbitrary and can be more or less useful, more or less adequate to the aims of one's research. A definition may be too restrictive and exclude phenomena that should be included; in addition, a definition may be dictated by concerns that are not those of the discipline by which one's inquiry is framed.

To be more specific, I am suggesting that a definition of morality is too restrictive when it excludes phenomena that, according to common understanding and ordinary language, many would consider to be moral or morally relevant.

Theorists, including psychologists, do depart from common understanding and language. Examples of such departures can be found in Skinner's (e.g., 1953, 1974) and Freud's (e.g., 1923/ 1961, 1928/1961) writings. Within psychoanalysis, for instance, moral reasoning is frequently placed with other, morally irrelevant processes under the category of rationalization. Of course, these interpretations of ordinary language are, or should be, the conclusion and not the starting point of empirical theoretical investigations. Moreover, they need to be justified by demonstrating the correctness of the theory as a whole and by showing that those phenomena that ordinary language identifies as a special category of behavior, assigning to them the label "moral," are indeed misinterpreted and miscategorized by common understanding; that is, when one looks at their real psychological nature, they appear not to require a special category and a special label.

Psychologists, however, may adopt as the starting point of their investigation theoretical (as opposed to descriptive) definitions of the moral phenomenon, which are inspired less by the specific aims and methods of their discipline than by the aims and methods of another discipline, in this case philosophy. The criteria followed by ethical theories concern such issues as logical coherence, justifiability, and validity; by contrast, the criteria followed by psychological theories stress psychological processes, their functional articulations, and the conditions under which these processes originate and change. In Winch's (1958) language, in deciding which events should be considered as "the same," the philosophical and the psychological communities rely on different rules. Of course, psychologists may and do follow philosophical definitions for heuristic purposes, to explore how far these definitions can lead them toward the understanding of moral phenomena in psychological terms. In doing so, however, they do not abandon their typical perspective, goals, and criteria.

How have structural developmental psychologists been defining morality? If one focuses, as I wish to do in this paper, on moral action, one must acknowledge that we have been less than explicit in determining which actions should be considered morally relevant. Perhaps most will agree that an action is morally relevant when it is informed by moral judgment, at least if one does not try to determine the precise levels of awareness and articulateness that are required in order for moral judgment to give a moral meaning to action. This definition is admittedly vague and takes the question one step back, from the level of action to the level of judgment. Within the cognitive developmental tradition, a judgment is moral if it is guided by moral criteria; moral criteria, then, are frequently believed to form a structural whole or to be logical parts of a system of moral ideas. But here agreement ends even among cognitive developmentalists.

By contrast with action, this tradition has been more explicit in defining the nature of moral criteria and, therefore, of moral judgment. According to the two most influential views, Piaget's and Kohlberg's, moral criteria concern mostly or exclusively justice, namely, the resolution of conflicting interests and the balancing of rights and duties. Piaget did not worry about the definition of morality; however, in his moral psychological theory, he relies so heavily on cooperation and on equilibrated social interaction that, theoretically, he had no choice but to view all of morality, at least in its mature and rational forms, from the perspective of justice. Kohlberg, by contrast, is more explicit and more articulate in his choice. Even though he recognizes four "primary moral orientations" (1976, p. 40) and a number of aspects and values (p. 43), he is convinced that underlying the various strategies that people use to arrive at moral decisions there always is a concern for justice. In fact, his coding system has undergone a series of revisions, precisely in order to bring out and differentiate the deeper, structural aspect of justice.

The influence of this theoretical choice has been enormous, both in practically guiding research and in articulating theory (see e.g., Damon, 1977, p. 170; Rest, 1979, pp. 20, 159; Shweder, Turiel, and Much, 1981, p. 290; Turiel, 1983, p. 3). For example, Rest (1979) writes: "The word 'moral' as used here involves social interaction and does not concern individual values that do not affect other people. . . . Contrary to some philosophers who use 'moral' to include concepts of the good or worthwhile life, the use of 'moral' in this account is restricted to concepts of justice and fairness" (p. 20). This definition, I believe, reflects quite well the general cognitive developmental view.

It is not difficult to recognize that the justice approach is far from being restrictive. And yet, frequently though not always, four broad categories of action are excluded, which many would consider morally relevant: (1) those that proceed from benevolence and affiliative concerns (what Gilligan, 1982, refers to as ethics of care and responsibility); (2) those concerning obedience and one's relations to authority; (3) what Grice (1967) calls "ultra obligations"; and (4) what I will call "personal obligations."

I will only make two brief comments concerning the first category: first, I think that the benevolence approach is rapidly becoming part of the mainstream, particularly once this issue is differentiated from the sex differences controversy. One reason is that there is a strong and long-standing tradition in philosophy recognizing and even stressing the obligation of beneficence. Second, this approach may be less opposed to the justice approach than some believe. This is not to say, however, that the theoretical integration between the two perspectives will be automatic or easily accomplished. There seem to be aspects in the work of Gilligan and others (e.g., Haan, 1978; Holstein, 1976; Eisenberg-Berg, 1979) that may resist assimilation to a vision of morality based on rules and rights.

In discussing the second category (obedience- and authority-related behaviors), I will focus on the work of Turiel and his colleagues (see particularly Turiel, 1983). The importance of this issue lies in the central role that obedience, respect for authority, and social conventions seem to have in the moral life of many people, and not only children.

It should be noted that there is no real difference between Kohlberg or Piaget, on the one hand, and Turiel, on the other, in the belief that morality is different from sensitivity to conventions. For Kohlberg, people only slowly develop their ability to differentiate morality from conventionality; in their early stages, they confuse the two domains and give moral significance to respect for authority, social customs, and conventions. Turiel, instead, embedded this distinction in his definition of morality. Essentially he claims three converging contrasts: the abstract a priori definitions of the moral and the conventional domains differ from each other; from a relatively early age people are able to distinguish these two domains; ultimately, people give different kinds of reasons for why social conventions should be respected and moral prescriptions should be followed. Theoretically, Turiel explains this set of discriminations using Piagetian principles: understanding develops in interaction with one's social reality; since the conventional domain and the moral domain represent radically different social realities, even young children develop two cognitively distinct structures in interacting with these realities.

Turiel's empirical evidence is of the following order: when children are presented with a set of situations corresponding respectively to the conventional and the moral domains (namely, either representing infractions to such rules and conventions as table manners or dress code, or involving harm to others as in stealing or physically hurting others), they are able to differentiate them systematically. Specifically, they tend to (1) rate moral infractions as more serious; (2) say that the wrongness of conventional infractions depends on the existence of relevant rules, whereas the second type of misbehavior would always be wrong; (3) justify their classification with reasons that are appropriate to each of the two categories of action: in the moral case, fairness, others' welfare, or, in sum, what Turiel calls the "natural" or "intrinsic" consequences of the action; and in the case of conventional rules, the existence of rules or traditions, approval from authority, sanctions, and social coordination.

Much more could be said about the method and the findings of Turiel's group. From my present perspective, it is important to stress that, while Turiel gives the impression that his definition of morality is in fact so universally used as to constitute genuine common understanding, in reality it is the result of an a priori philosophical choice that he and his colleagues have made. In fact, we may accept Turiel's findings that children and adults do indeed reliably distinguish the two categories of action. But there is no evidence that they do so on moral grounds. From the subjects' perspective (though not from Turiel's external perspective), the two classes of action may be differentiated and yet be seen as equally moral, in the same way that adults differentiate altruism and honesty within the domain of morality. An important element of Turiel's empirical argument is that children acknowledge the prescriptiveness of social convention only when relevant rules exist. This would demonstrate that the prescriptive value of rules is not seen to be general and universal and, therefore, from the perspective of his definitions, to be moral. Of course, the prescriptiveness of obedience is contingent on authority, as mother's love is contingent on there being children and altruism is contingent on the presence of other people. Behind the superficial lack of generality in the prescriptiveness of rules there may be the understanding that obedience is a universal and nonarbitrary virtue.

In fact, Damon (1977), in an attempt to replicate and extend Turiel's results, found that children scoring at his levels 2 and 3 (corresponding approximately to 6–7 and 8–9-year-old groups) frequently do not differentiate between conventional and moral demands. This lack of differentiation occurs under different circumstances for the two groups of children: for the younger group, when the consequences are made equivalent; for the older, when conventions are regulated by formal rules. "In such cases conventions too are viewed as mandatory, since at level 3 it is considered socially necessary for everyone to respect rules" (p. 248). In my interpretation, these children view obedience as prescriptive, universal, and not based on pragmatic considerations, but they understand the value of obedience differently at different ages and in a way that is consonant with their moral understanding. Damon, however, does not consider this attitude as moral, because, in his definition, morality only concerns justice and "beyond enlightened self-interest, there is no social or moral basis for subservience to another" (1980, p. 44).

Again, the issue is not whether these definitions are correct from the perspective of philosophical theory or whether I agree with them, but whether those people, whose moral life we try to understand, agree with them also. The psychologist's task is not to decide which philosophical definition of morality is adequate, but to describe the different ways in which people understand moral obligations. I believe that for many children and a good number of adults obedience has a genuine moral value; psychologists may risk missing a large portion of these people's moral life when they are rigidly guided by definitions constructed within specific philosophical theories.

The last two categories of behavior that tend to be left out by the prevalent definitions of morality in psychological work are ultra obligations (Grice, 1967) and personal obligations.

Neither one of these categories has been received with much favor by philosophers for the simple reason that neither seems to meet widely accepted criteria of morality, in particular generalizability and universalizability.

In the case of ultra obligations, there is the experience of obligation but also the realization that one's obligation is not a response to others' rights. For instance, in giving his ration of food to a cellmate, a prisoner may explain: "I didn't really have to do it, but I felt I had to," which is awkwardly translated into: He did not have a right to my doing it, and yet I had to . . . simply because I had to. In these instances, objective observers may deny that there is any obligation at all and may not understand why the person in question should feel obligated. In sum, there is subjective obligation without objective rights, obligation without duty.

Sometimes, rarely, this type of action takes the form of heroic self-sacrifice; in its more ordinary form, however, these actions are frequent, an almost daily component of people's moral life. MacIntyre (1971), generalizing these observations, concluded that the moral experience of most people in most instances does not involve at all the consciousness of universalizability; in some instances, there seems to be the opposite kind of awareness, that what is obligatory for me is not obligatory for others.

As controversial as they may be as a category of moral action, ultra obligations still retain one important characteristic of morality as many philosophers define it, namely, that of being interpersonal and oriented to others' welfare. However, the last category, what I called "personal obligations," not only does not fit the definition of justice, but is not even interpersonal in its main thrust. I am referring to those actions that are perceived by the agent to have intrinsic moral value and to be obligatory, irrespective of any external consequences that may follow and independent of interpersonal actions and relationships. Even though what counts is the agent's perception, possible candidates for this category are sometimes mentioned: betraying one's ideals; destroying one's intellectual capacity and one's dignity; tampering with one's freedom of judgment; deceiving oneself in important matters. Some (e.g., Taylor, 1976) seem to think that all morality is at bottom personal, insofar as it necessarily implies the choice of a basic mode of life for oneself. But it is possible to hold a more limited position and simply believe that one genuinely moral dimension concerns the agent and only the agent in his personhood.

Frequently the moral character of these concerns is defined away by the distinction between morality and the "good life." As usual, morality is defined in terms of justice; the good life, instead, is referred to such issues as the pursuit of one's interests, the fulfillment of one's personality, the choice of a life style, and is thought to determine a domain of preference, not of obligation. But this distinction, important as it is, does not acknowledge the possibility that at least some people may judge these and similar issues as establishing obligations for themselves. Existential and other kinds of literature have sensitized us to the plausibility of this type of obligation.

In this context something should be said about a recent attempt to extend Turiel's division of social competencies into objectively separable domains and to exclude from the domain of morality, on empirical grounds, what is labeled the "personal domain" (Nucci, 1981; Smetana, 1981, 1983; Smetana, Bridgeman, and Turiel, 1983). As was previously clarified, morality is here defined as concerning fairness and others' welfare. The "personal domain," instead, combines two aspects: negatively, it does not involve moral prescriptions or social regulations; positively, "personal" actions are those that primarily affect the agent alone, define the private aspects of one's life, and are discretionary, that is, a matter of preference rather than obligation.

The empirical basis for the belief that the personal domain differs from morality consists of the following: when individuals of various ages are presented with situations such as watching TV on a sunny day, eating peanut butter on baloney, refusing to join a recreation group, or masturbating, they overwhelmingly rank these actions as being the least wrong in comparison with moral and rule-governed actions; moreover, they frequently explain such rankings by saying that these actions only affect the agent and are the agent's own business.

In my view, the conclusion that was derived from findings of this sort is unconvincing, for both conceptual and empirical reasons. Conceptually, this group of researchers seems to have confused the "morally irrelevant" or permissible with the personal. On the basis of their definitions, what is neither relevant to justice nor related to social rules must be "personal," that is, not rule-determined, therefore a matter of preference, therefore neither right nor wrong. But their tripartite division may not be adequate and there may be a fourth category, namely, the "personally obligatory." Having started with a definition of morality based on interpersonal consequences, the possibility of a genuinely moral obligation based on personal concerns could not have been taken seriously.

Empirically, Nucci and his colleagues did not try to test whether personal obligations exist, but whether people can differentiate justice concerns from what is morally irrelevant, a question that perhaps did not need to be investigated. Had they been serious about studying the possibility of personal obligations, they would have chosen some of those personal issues that are most likely to elicit a sense of obligation and would have selected a sample that might have developed a moral sensitivity around personal issues (Blasi and Oresick, 1986).

Of course, one may acknowledge the fact that some people experience obligation around issues of obedience, around purely personal issues, or when there are no objectively defined rights and duties, but then insist that the very ideas of obligation without rights and of obligation to oneself are absurd. Therefore—they would explain—these people are simply mistaken in their judgment and should not feel as they do. Whatever its validity, this argument supports precisely the point that I am trying to make: this is a philosophical, not a psychological concern. A psychologist is not interested in what people should think or feel, but in what they do think or feel. If, in observing John Smith, a psychologist finds that he believes helping others to be morally good and feels obliged to help and also believes that destroying one's intelligence is morally bad and feels obliged not to do so, he, the psychologist (but not perhaps a philosopher) will conclude that John Smith's morality involves at least two areas, altruism and personal dignity; this fact, then, will be the starting point of his theorizing.

To summarize this section, I tried to show that (1) psychologists within the cognitive developmental approach have relied on definitions of morality that were consciously inspired by philosophical theories; (2) these definitions emphasize the content of psychological processes rather than the psychological processes themselves (by content, here, I mean the type of judgments that people make, the issues about which they make them, and also the general criteria and cognitive structures guiding these judgments); (3) at least in part as a result of these definitions, broad behavioral areas have been neglected in empirical research and theory, even though these areas are frequently considered to be morally relevant in ordinary language and common understanding.

How serious are the consequences of narrowing the psychological inquiry of moral functioning in the way just described? Probably they are not serious in descriptive and quantitative terms. For one thing, the definitions of morality did not tightly control the choice of moral situations to be studied or, even less, people's responses to those situations. Thus concerns with altruism, care, and obedience have surfaced even when the investigator was looking for justice. Moreover, ultra obligations and personal obligations are not so frequent that their neglect has led to a significant distortion of what most people do and think morally in most instances.

However, the consequences may be significant from the perspective of theory construction. I will simply mention three theoretical issues for which new data may bring some light. The first concerns the structural hypothesis: if morality is not as logically united as the justice approach implies, one needs to investigate whether people do in fact construct global, logically coherent moral philosophies, when they do so, and how they go about it. The other two issues concern the processes and the determinants of development. For instance, the morality of obedience and rules seems to challenge the hypothesis of radical constructivism in moral development; at the other end, ultra obligations and personal obligations seem to challenge the complacent acceptance of role-taking, cooperation, and the construction of balanced social structures as the only natural foundation of morality in general.

The Use of Philosophical Considerations in Psychological Arguments

One could have predicted what actually happened. The explicit and public formulation of philosophical assumptions as the starting point of, and the logical basis for, empirical inquiry on the part of some psychologists eventually invited the same kind of reply in others. As a result, there was a significant shift of the ground on which the controversy concerning the explanation of moral functioning and moral development would be played among psychologists. We psychologists frequently resort to philosophical considerations to attack each other's theoretical positions, invoking philosophical theories and traditions to discount each other's data, interpretations, and conclusions.

I do not wish to deny that this kind of strategy can have positive, even liberating, effects; nor that the person who is a psychologist may, and should, also think as a philosopher about his subject matter and the nature of his or her investigation. Disciplines can be clearly separated only at the level of abstract logic, but they merge and interweave in the mind of the individual investigator trying to answer concrete questions. And yet I believe that there can be negative consequences in the use of what I will call the mixed argument, in which philosophical considerations are not simply used to generate hypotheses, but become an intrinsic part of the empirical argument.

The mixed argument has been used in different styles and with different degrees of sophistication. In its crudest and most unpleasant instances, it seems to follow this format: method and empirical data are almost completely ignored; for instance, neither the samples nor the coding schemes are analyzed in order to bring out biases and inadequacies; instead, the theorist's explicit, implicit, or assumed philosophical positions are zeroed in on; to these, other philosophical positions are opposed; both philosophical stands are presented in their simplest version, namely, stripped of their logical and evidential bases, as well as of any qualificatory statements.

Since Kohlberg has been the most frequent victim of this kind of treatment, I will give one or two examples in which his theory was the target of criticism by psychologists. In one article the author (Baumrind, 1978) declared: "My rejection of cultural universalism arises from a dialectical materialist social philosophy" (p. 62); "Marxists affirm . . . that different human environments necessarily produce different forms of human consciousness and self-realization and therefore different developmental progressions" (p. 64); "The definition of the 'common good' is not universalizable but dependent entirely on the concrete attributes of a given social order" (p. 67); "Thus, Rawls' two substantive moral premises—persons are of unconditional value and persons have the right to equal justice in all situations—are highly controversial. . . . To view any specific substantive set of values as supreme and universal is to defend cultural centration on a principled basis" (p. 68).

The author of a second article (Sullivan, 1977) states that "the 'model of man' adopted [by Kohlberg] is to some extent parochial rather than universal in character and wedded historically to the liberal conceptions of natural law at the time of the French Revolution and developed to maturity in the writings of Kant" (p. 360); "instead of seeing the Kantian categories as disinterested rationality, Marx and Engels (and subsequently Lukacs) argued that abstract formalism was the organizing principle structuring social relations of production within Western capitalism" (ibid.). And, later, "[Kohlberg] is thoroughly Cartesian in his rationality since he sees moral maturity as a deeper integration of 'clear and distinct ideas.' Most of us have at least a vague suspicion that this type of rationality is lacking in certain respects" (pp. 371–372).

These examples are rather extreme, but the basic problem remains also when the mixed argument is used in more thoughtful and balanced critiques, fortunately the more numerous ones. The problem is that it is not clear how philosophical considerations should be handled in psychological controversies. What can a psychologist reply to the characterization, or the accusation, of being a Kantian (or a Cartesian, a Rawlsian, a liberal, etc.)? One could apologize, as one may apologize for being Jewish, Italian, or for coming from a working-class background. Alternatively, one could reply in kind and characterize the critic as a Marxist, an existentialist, or a romanticist. A simpler and more appropriate answer would be: so what? This type of mixed argumentation, in fact, operates under the assumption, tacit and unsupported, that since Kohlberg's theory and data necessarily depend on the truth of Kant's (or Rawls's, or Descartes's) theory, and since Kant's (or Rawls's, etc.) theory is obviously absurd or has been conclusively shown to be incorrect, therefore . . .; or, vice versa, that since Kohlberg's (or anybody else's) theory and data contradict the very core of Marxist (or any other) theory, and since this theory has been proven to be the only correct one, therefore . . .

The actual replies that one finds to this kind of criticism tend to distinguish the empirical and the philosophical aspects of the criticism; for what concerns the latter, the validity of the critic's philosophical position is simply denied and the validity of one's own position is reaffirmed. This is typical also of the way Kohlberg answers his critics (see, e.g., Kohlberg, Levine, and Hewer, 1983). The answers end up being as simple as the criticisms; i.e., they do not deal with the deeper philosophical assumptions from which the criticism derives and, therefore, tend to slightly misunderstand the criticism itself.

My point is that even under the best of circumstances, when the debaters manifest good will and respect for each other, a psychological controversy based on philosophical considerations does not contribute to either philosophical or psychological understanding and is essentially sterile.

There is a way in which philosophical assumptions and theories can offer a genuine contribution to psychological controversies. The philosophical orientation of Psychologist A may sensitize him or her to the different philosophical orientation of Psychologist B and to the way this orientation led Psychologist B to specific biases in selecting the sample, constructing the method, and interpreting the data. Psychologist A may then be in a position to suggest which samples, methods, and interpretations will correct the bias and may even be able to compare the data obtained from the two different sets of assumptions.

This type of critique does not resort to mixed arguments and is rarely, if ever, done.

Kohlberg himself rarely engages in criticism of rival views within the cognitive developmental approach. However, he too occasionally uses philosophical or quasi-philosophical assumptions to evaluate the adequacy of theories that differ from his own. Kohlberg began his study of morality with a series of ten metaethical assumptions (Kohlberg, Levine, and Hewer, 1983, pp. 65–103): some of these are definitional in character (e.g., that morality implies judgment, that moral judgments are prescriptive); others, such as formalism and universalism, derive from specific ethical theories. Some of his assumptions are strictly philosophical, others are quasi-philosophical: that is, even though they could be stated in empirically testable terms and supported by empirical data, they are chosen for philosophical reasons and are used less as hypotheses to be tested than as a priori standards by which procedures and theories are selected and criticized. Kohlberg, in fact, explains: "There are . . . certain metaethical assumptions *necessary* to begin the study of morality, which psychologists using the stage concept and measure *must* at least partially endorse" (ibid., p. 65; my italics).

Two of these assumptions are related and will be used as examples for my discussion. The first (value-relevant stance) claims that a conception of morality cannot be value-neutral and that a psychologist, needing a conception of morality as his starting point, must begin with a stand concerning moral values. The second (formalism) claims that the core of moral judgment lies in the moral perspective or moral point of view, that is, in the form of one's understanding rather than in specific values and decisions.

From the assumptive necessity of distinguishing between the form of morality and specific moral values and principles follows the singular appropriateness of the structural method in the study of morality. The necessity of a structuralist position can also be supported by other philosophical considerations: the cognitive, rational, coherent nature of moral judgment seems to require, as a psychological counterpart, a coherent, reversible system of moral ideas, which is precisely how a structure is defined.

From the first assumption, the necessity of having a clear stand about moral values, it follows that, at the beginning of his or her inquiry, a psychologist should know what is the ideal terminus of moral development, namely, the most adequate moral structure; he should be able to evaluate this moral structure as more adequate than others and to order the various moral structures according to a hierarchy of moral adequacy.

In sum, according to Kohlberg, not only is the cognitive developmental approach the most appropriate for the study of morality, but a special version is needed, namely, one that yields what Kohlberg calls "*hard* structural stages." *Hard* stages are differentiated from *soft* stages in that they are defined by rigorously logical reversible properties of the system and allow, therefore, the articulation of the precise logical relations—of implication, differentiation, and organization—that exist among the various systems or stages. A theory that is based on *hard* stages perfectly corresponds to the metaethical assumptions of a value-relevant stand and of formalism, whereas *soft* stages do not. *Soft* stages may seem philosophically richer, as they may include conceptions of "human nature, of society, and of the nature of ultimate reality" (Kohlberg, Levine, and Hewer, 1983, p. 30). However, "what hard structural stages gain . . . is precision in their articulation of a structural logic of stages that will survive the everchanging growth of psychological knowledge about the self, its functions, and its development" (ibid.).

Consistently with this position, Kohlberg uses the ability to yield *hard* structural stages as a criterion to evaluate and criticize other cognitive developmental theories, such as Loevinger's, Kegan's, Gilligan's, Perry's, and Fowler's. He writes, for instance: "The ambiguity of the inner logic of Loevinger's and others' soft structural stage sequences reduces the plausibility of formulating a *normative* model of development. . . . Loevinger (1982) herself explicitly denies a normative model and makes no claim that a higher ego stage is a more adequate stage" (Kohlberg, Levine, and Hewer, 1983, p. 38; my italics). As for Gilligan, Kohlberg argues, her focus on moral content or moral style may prevent her finding hierarchically ordered structures; there are no data yet, "but we believe it unlikely that such research will find divergent moral 'hard' stage sequences for justice and care" (ibid., p. 141).

Briefly, Kohlberg also resorts to mixed arguments, but of a subtle kind, in which the philosophical assumption is hidden behind the empirical observation. Regardless of whether Loevinger's or Gilligan's descriptions fit the data, their theories cannot be adequate if, or because, they do not offer a sequence of *hard* stages. The basis for this empirical standard lies in a specific metaethical theory, in which formalism is considered a necessary characteristic of moral judgment.

I would argue, instead, that cognitive developmental psychologists, engaged in the study of morality, only need to accept some of Kohlberg's assumptions, those, namely, that aim at defining the moral phenomenon or the moral experience, but that they should not use, at least as starting assumptions, considerations that are derived from specific philosophical theories. This conclusion follows if the assumptive use of this latter kind of consideration (1) leads to negative consequences, and (2) is not necessary. Starting with the first point, the negative consequences I wish to emphasize lie in the inability of psychologists to follow the accepted rules of their discipline and the tendency to confuse the goals and questions of psychology with those of philosophy.

The main reason that psychologists should not use philosophical considerations in mixed arguments is not that they lack the background and the competence to do so, which is also true in most cases; it is, rather, that they cannot resolve philosophical controversies with the tools of their discipline and following the rules of evidence and adequacy that define psychology as a scientific community. When philosophical considerations become an integral part of the empirical argument, issues of methodology, data collection, and data interpretation cannot be isolated for scrutiny and criticism. In sum, communication becomes impossible and, as a result, the very existence of the discipline is threatened.

Moreover, the nature of psychological questions may become distorted and the purpose of psychological inquiry may become subordinated to answering the philosopher's questions. For instance, both a psychologist and a philosopher may begin by observing that moral experience involves an important cognitive component, particularly judgments concerning personal and interpersonal reality. In attempting to build a metaethical theory, the philosopher may conclude that *ideally* moral judgments *should* derive from broad systems of ideas, that these systems *should* be logically coherent, and *should* be such that they can be evaluated according to universal standards of adequacy and truth. The philosopher, therefore, will arrive at a theory in which morality is postulated to be cognitive, objective, formal, and universal.

This does not imply, however, that in all or most instances moral experience and moral judgments *actually* derive from and are based on logically coherent systems of ideas or that the agent, *in fact*, experiences his judgments as general, universal, or universalizable. There is no contradiction in believing that ideally morality *should* be x and in observing that, in many instances, it is in fact y. What *in fact* are the various forms of moral experience; under what conditions, if ever, these forms correspond to the philosopher's ideal expectation; which psychological processes account for the observed differences, etc.—these are the psychologist's questions.

If a psychologist is committed to cognitive developmentalism and understands structuralism in the rigorous Piagetian mode, as Kohlberg seems to do, then he may want to stress the formal properties of cognitive systems and perhaps emphasize the central role of justice; he will resort to precise logical analyses and will attempt to construct hard structural stages. However, these are choices that depend on specific hypotheses rather than on necessary assumptions. If he succeeds, he will be able to describe a series of stages that define not only a chronological sequence, but also a logical hierarchy. From these *facts*, however, he will be unable to answer the philosopher's questions of which dimension *should* be the core of morality and which set of ideas *should* constitute morality. In accepting the philosopher's conclusions as assumptions rather than as possible guidelines to construct his or her own hypotheses, the psychologist ends up looking for what should be rather than for what is, in the service of a specific philosophical theory.

The key question, then, is whether it is really necessary for psychologists to begin with assumptions derived from philosophical theory: if so, the negative consequences that have just been described may have to be tolerated for the sake of a more faithful psychological understanding of morality. I will come back to this issue in a later section.

Turning Away from the Subject's Point of View

I mentioned already the liberating effect that the cognitive developmental approach to morality and moral development had by taking what Kohlberg, Levine, and Hewer (1983) call the "assumption of phenomenalism," namely, by considering the individual's judgment and intention as necessary to define the moral phenomenon. As a result, psychologists focused on the dramatically different ways in which people understand concepts such as good and bad, right and wrong, fair and unfair, and on the different strategies by which they morally justify their behavior.

It is my impression that this programmatic emphasis on the subject's perspective is at times compromised, even within cognitive developmental research and theory. One example is the orientation that Turiel (e.g., 1983), Nucci (e.g., 1981), and their colleagues have taken in their work. These investigators, in fact, seem to define morality in terms of the intrinsic properties of actions rather than in terms of the subject's perspective; for instance, the moral domain is defined as comprising actions having *intrinsic* effects on others' rights and well-being. Even when it is acknowledged that concrete behaviors can be looked at under different aspects and in terms of different issues, certain issues are thought to concern morality objectively and others to be morally irrelevant. For example, in abortion one may either stress the life of the fetus or one's personal decision, but only the first consideration is assumed to be morally relevant (Smetana, 1981).

Sometimes the more general context within which a person views morality is disregarded and the meaning of moral judgment is interpreted from the perspective of the investigator. For example, in one study (reported in Rest, 1983, p. 592), a group of ultraconservative seminarians obtained unexpectedly low scores on a measure of moral judgment (DIT). The investigator interviewed them, trying to discover how they went about making moral judgments, and found that, for certain items, the seminarians would set aside their own notions of fairness and instead would react according to the items' congruence with their religious beliefs. "Some stated that value judgments should not be based on earth-bound, human rationality but on divine revelation" (p. 592). Rest uses this example to illustrate how people, under certain circumstances, may not follow their moral understanding. The implication seems to be that in this instance, and whenever there is "preempting by dogma" of moral thinking, the subjects were inconsistent with their moral beliefs. But this is true only if one cuts morality the way Rest does and separates it from one's general philosophy about life, a portion of which may be occupied by religion. It is not unreasonable to hypothesize that for these seminarians morality acquires real meaning only within the broader context of religion.

A similar dilution of the phenomenological assumption may be present in the interpretive reconstruction of an individual's system of moral ideas as including the position that this system is given in a stage hierarchy. In dialogue with the interviewer a subject may recognize as his own and appropriate the interviewer's interpretation of the moral principles that he, the subject, follows; however, he has no awareness that his moral understanding is inadequate and developmentally tends to a mode of moral thinking that, at present, he or she finds not only alien but objectionable. This lack of awareness and the fact that morality is thought to be subjective may explain the negative response that many express in finding that the moral system that they understand and on which they rely is judged to be inadequate on the basis of external criteria.

There is a sense in which the evaluative stance is an intrinsic component of the cognitive developmental project: i.e., its attempt to determine the, possibly universal, end state of a specific competence and to order the various forms that this competence takes on the basis of chronological sequence and logical hierarchy. Ordinarily, however, cognitive developmental psychologists deal with limited competencies (language, logic, mathematics, social perspective taking) and define adequacy according to limited empirical criteria. Thus, they do not mean to imply that human beings should, in an absolute sense, arrive at the ideal end state of development and acquire the most mature form of the skill in question. Moreover, the external evaluation of a skill, namely, the judgment of its adequacy from the perspective of its developmental terminus, does not distort the nature of the skill itself. That is, how competent a grammarian or a mathematician I am can be determined in an objective way and does not depend on what I think of my competence.

But the situation seems to be quite different in the area of morality: one reason is that morality, unlike specific skills, bears on the person as a person; thus, evaluating one's morality as inadequate implies that one *should* change it, in an absolute sense. A more radical reason is that morality essentially, that is, by definition, depends on the agent's subjective perspective, which is precisely what the "assumption of phenomenalism" is trying to convey.

One could argue that this limited reduction of subjectivity is necessary for empirical research. Habermas (1983) seems to think that it is impossible to interpret another person's moral system without criticizing it from the perspective of rationality. This idea is basic to his concept of "rational reconstruction." Habermas, in fact, writes that "the interpreters understand the meaning of the text only to the extent that they see why the author felt entitled to put forward (as true) certain assertions, to recognize (as right) certain values and norms, and to express (as sincere) certain experiences." And, he continues,

because it is not the same thing for reasons to be sound as for them to be taken to be sound . . . the interpreters cannot present reasons to themselves without judging them. . . . It may be that the interpreters leave certain validity claims undecided. . . . But interpreters can elucidate the meaning of an opaque expression only by explaining how this opacity arises, that is, why the reasons the author might have given in the original context are no longer acceptable to us. (Habermas, 1983, p. 259)

In this passage Habermas speaks directly of texts and authors, but intends his view to also apply to interviews and interviewees.

But there are different kinds of understanding, and interpreting a person's subjective meanings is only one kind. I would agree that a psychologist knows more about a person's moral thinking if, besides understanding why the person "felt entitled . . . to recognize (as right) certain values and norms," he could also explain how "opacity" arises in the person's ideas and why these ideas are not acceptable from the perspective of ideal morality. It does not follow, however, that the psychologist could not do the former if he could not do the latter. I would argue that it is possible to genuinely though incompletely interpret a person's moral understanding (why that person takes his reasons as sound) in its own terms, without relating this understanding to other people's understanding in terms of a hierarchy of moral adequacy. In fact, this is done all the time (e.g., in literary criticism or in psychoanalysis). I would also argue that this limited interpretation is the only one that a cognitive developmental psychologist needs, because the subject's reasons and why these reasons seem sound to him are what define his or her moral experience. Deciding *whether* people's moral reasons are more or less sound, more or less moral, is indeed a valid and important task, but one that belongs to philosophy and requires philosophical tools.

It is possible to evaluate objectively a person's moral *thinking* while acknowledging that the moral evaluation of the *action* can only be done by taking the agent's perspective, that is, by considering whether or not the action conforms to the agent's understanding of the situation. The recent attempt by Kohlberg and Candee (1984a, 1984b) to extend the theory to moral action goes a long way in completely retreating from the assumption of phenomenalism.

The argument is that the moral structure that characterizes Stage 5 in Kohlberg's scheme involves the ability to assume the most adequate moral point of view, namely, the one that is

singularly suited to discover that specific resolution of conflicting claims with which all could agree. Therefore, the argument
continues, if people at Stage 5 tend to agree on a specific
solution to a concrete dilemma as being the most moral, that
solution must be objectively and universally right; consequently, the moral choices that lower-stage people make can
be evaluated for their maturity according to objective and universal standards, namely, the choices on which the judgments
of Stage 5 people converge.

One serious consequence of this position is obvious: it is
possible to imagine a Stage 3 person who decides to follow the
judgment of people at Stage 5, even though he or she is convinced that it is morally wrong. In Kohlberg and Candee's view,
however, this person's action would be morally correct, because
it corresponds to objectively valid criteria.

In all these instances, the assumption of phenomenalism is
compromised because of preoccupations that are typically
philosophical, specifically, the desire to determine which dimensions of thinking are most genuinely moral and which
stage is morally most adequate.

Toward a Psychological Definition of Morality

In this last section, a number of ideas that were used in the
previous pages are brought together in a more systematic, even
though schematic, fashion. I will start with a triple distinction;
then I will attempt a definition of morality that reflects common
understanding and is oriented to a psychological perspective;
finally, I will draw some implications concerning the relations
between philosophy and psychology.

Common understanding and philosophical theory

Three concepts should be clearly differentiated, the concepts, namely, of common understanding or ordinary language, of philosophical theory, and of psychological theory.

Common understanding refers to the set of meanings—concerning people, society, and action—that are embedded in ordinary language and in social interaction, make communication

possible, and ground the existence of social norms and expectations. Even though these meanings need not be, and frequently are not, articulated, they are experiential, at least in the sense that the agent can recognize (1) when the conditions for a certain meaning have or have not been fulfilled and (2) when an interpretation corresponds to his experience.

Even though the meanings of common understanding are interrelated and loosely organized, they do not constitute a theory in the strict sense. And yet it is possible to provide a rational reconstruction or a theoretical account of common understanding; typically, this reconstruction (e.g., Piaget's structural reconstruction of concrete operations) is not a component of common understanding and can be evaluated only in terms of its capacity to represent the meanings implicit in common understanding.

Finally, in common understanding and ordinary language, meanings can be ordered hierarchically along a dimension of specificity and generality. Thus, people from different communities may be able to discuss their different views of friendship or of morality, because they share a more basic and more general concept of friendship or morality.

Under *philosophical theory* one can place systematic, logically coherent attempts to account for the basic nature of different domains of reality as well as for the sorts of knowledge appropriate to those domains. Even though philosophers have recently appropriated for themselves the level of common understanding, they have no special competence to determine what is or is not included in common understanding or ordinary language. Instead, common understanding is found by philosophers as already constituted, is used by them as a starting point for theory construction and as criterion for theory criticism.

In the domain of moral reality, philosophical theories have dealt with three main sets of questions: How can one logically and systematically unify knowledge that is already implicit in common understanding and thereby show its ultimate rationale? How should one construct a true normative theory of morality: what should be its first principles, their objective foundations, and the grounds by which the principles can be rationally justified? What are the logical status of moral claims, the nature of moral argument, the presuppositions by which common understanding of morality can have any rational meaning?

As a result, philosophical controversies typically concern the logical coherence of theories; the validity of the grounds for justifying first principles; and the ability of theories to represent morality at the level of common understanding (e.g., whether or not theoretical principles lack generality or distort ordinary language). Moral philosophical theory, then, tends to be critical and normative by its very nature: theories, concepts, and actions are evaluated according to standards of logic, rationality, and moral adequacy.

By contrast, *psychological theory* is a systematic, logically coherent account of human behavior in terms of psychological processes and their articulations. Like philosophy, psychology must begin at the level of common understanding (that is, *if* the explanandum is social action as social). However, it is not concerned either with the presuppositions by which logical and rational sense can be made of common understanding or with the validity of morality (at the level of common understanding or at any other level).

Its focus, instead, is on those psychological processes that underlie common understanding and are required by it, the differences and changes in these processes, and the conditions under which differences and changes occur. In the area of morality, the psychological processes include: actual perceptions and interpretations of dilemmas; reasoning strategies and their cognitive foundations; perception of adequacy of one's judgment and interpretation of the differences among people. Among the conditions possibly affecting change, one should include both the actual logical adequacy or inadequacy of a person's moral system and the perception of inadequacy and inconsistency. Thus, while philosophy tends to be evaluative and selective on the basis of rational norms (what is or is not genuinely, truly, adequately moral), psychology thrives on, and looks for, differences. Its classification is not normative-rational, but psychological.

A definition of moral action

An interpretation of the most generic common understanding of moral action should include three elements: (1) the action is intentional; (2) its intentional aspect is to be a response to the experience of obligation; (3) obligation is subjectively perceived as deriving from the demands of an objective ideal for oneself.

The focus of this definition, then, is moral action and its basic structure: other aspects are considered from the perspective of action. The direct determinant of moral intentionality is taken to be the experience of obligation, a psychological phenomenon that has been neglected (e.g., by comparison with judgment) by both philosophers and psychologists.

Obligation is understood here to have a motivational structure that essentially differs from that of needs, wishes, desires, tastes, etc., on the one hand, and of prudential considerations, on the other. Its characteristics are as follows: There is an element of necessity or compulsion; necessity derives from the perception, perhaps dim and unarticulated, of an "ideal," namely, an aspect of the social or personal world that is understood to be in some way opposed to the agent, transcending the agent, and establishing the value of the agent's action; this "ideal" is also understood to establish an objective, nonarbitrary demand. The present definition contains, indirectly but experientially, a cognitive component. The cognitive aspect of moral action is present both in its intentionality as a response to obligation and in the perception of obligation as being objectively grounded. For the first, moral action requires a network of concepts concerning the good, the right, the obligatory, etc.; for the second, it involves the expectation of giving reasons for and justifying one's obligation.

The cognitive basis of moral action opens the psychological study of moral cognition, its various structures and development. However, from the perspective of moral action, the variety of cognitive moral structures and their different formal and content characteristics are relevant only to the extent that they affect its intentional aspects (by contrast with its predictability). It is open to empirical investigation whether, as well as to what extent and how, the cognitive aspect of morality exercises its influence on action.

The definition presented here is generic: namely, it does not differentiate among and is not affected by various moral dimensions and contents. In particular, it applies to the dimensions that were mentioned earlier: justice, beneficence, obedience, ultra obligations, and personal obligations.

It could be argued that it includes too much. Whether it does or not should be decided independently by philosophical and psychological theories, on the basis of their respective criteria. Psychological criteria include phenomenological data (perceptions and interpretations) as well as such objective information as synchrony in development, correlations among the dimensions, and similarity in the correlational network of the dimensions.

Relations between philosophy and psychology

Considering only one side of the relation, from philosophy to psychology, I would suggest that psychological research and theory about moral functioning is not necessarily dependent on philosophical theory. The philosophical contribution to psychology is indirect, influencing the researcher's choice of hypotheses. This suggestion recognizes the necessity for psychology to have its starting point at the level of common understanding and ordinary language, but assumes (1) the distinction between common understanding and philosophical theory and (2) basic differences in aims and methods between philosophical and psychological inquiry.

Within this framework, it is possible to disagree as to what is specifically involved in common understanding. For instance, Kohlberg seems to believe that such properties as formalism and universalizability are arrived at by simply explicating common-understanding meanings. In my opinion, these and other characteristics are not components of common understanding, but derive from a rational reconstruction of it and, even more, from an attempt to rationally validate its prescriptiveness.

Philosophy's contribution to psychology mainly consists of clarifying the meanings of ordinary language and of inspiring specific hypotheses. Formalist ethics provides the basis for structuralist hypotheses in moral development. However, starting from the generic definition of morality suggested earlier, it is possible to focus on such substantive, content-related aspects of moral thinking as people's beliefs about the nature of persons, society, and ultimate reality—namely, on aspects that are ruled out by Kohlberg's approach.

Psychological hypotheses, then, whether or not they are inspired by philosophy, need to be formulated in empirically testable terms. In my view, the statement that Stage 5 is morally more adequate than Stage 3 is not empirically testable. Empirically testable hypotheses, including those inspired by philosophical theory, can be evaluated according to the rules of the empirical method. Thus, Kohlberg writes: "The validity of my assumption . . . in describing the moral development of individuals can only be assessed by the extent to which it provides order to empirical data and by the intelligibility of the order it defines" (Kohlberg, Levine, and Hewer, 1983, p. 109). I subscribe to this statement, with two minor modifications: I would replace "assumption" with "hypothesis," and I would specify "intelligibility" to read "psychological intelligibility," namely, the meaning that the data acquire within broader psychological theories.

The need for psychologists to begin with a philosophical (as opposed to ordinary language) definition of morality has been argued on conceptual and on methodological grounds. Thus, Haan (1982), Habermas (1983), and perhaps Kohlberg (Kohlberg, Levine, and Hewer, 1983) seem to believe that moral common understanding can only be determined from the perspective of philosophical theory. In my opinion, these views tend to ignore (1) the role of common understanding in grounding philosophical theories and establishing the basis for communication among them; and (2) the role of common understanding as a criterion for the validity of philosophical theories. In order to accomplish this function, common understanding must be interpretable independently, at least in part, of philosophical theory.

Conclusion

As a conclusion, I would like to summarize what psychological work on morality can and cannot accomplish, within this delimited understanding of its method and scope.

1. Psychology *cannot* determine which approach, e.g., formalist-structuralist or content-oriented, gives a more faithful picture of what morality should be. However, it *can* compare the sets of data collected under both approaches and decide which approach best accounts for actual moral functioning, whether moral functioning is viewed phenomenologically or from the perspective of predicting thinking and action.

2. Psychology *cannot* determine whether morality should be universal or how important are the universal aspects according to moral criteria. But it *can* determine whether certain aspects, and which, are universal; which factors affect the universality of the various moral aspects; and whether there are specific historical and ontogenetic trends (increase or decrease) in universality.

3. Psychology *cannot* decide which of the various moral dimensions (e.g., justice, beneficence) is the most centrally and most genuinely moral. But it *can* determine whether one or another aspect is perceived to be most important at different ages or by different genders; it *can* also determine whether any of the dimensions best accounts for, i.e., structurally integrates, the various moral data, and whether this integrative power of each dimension shifts with age or other factors.

4. Psychology *cannot* determine which stage should be the end state of development or whether one stage is morally better than another. But it *can* determine whether one stage is logically more differentiated and more cohesive than another; whether one stage, relative to another, carries with it a stronger sense of obligation and tendency to be self-consistent in action.

5. Psychology *can* determine how people of different stages perceive the adequacy of various moral criteria and whether they perceive it on moral grounds. It *can* also determine whether these perceptions are empirically related to abandoning certain ways of thinking, resisting certain pressures, and searching for new moral ideas.

The view of psychology presented here is indeed more limited than the more ambitious conception of its tasks found in certain brands of cognitive developmentalism, but it also avoids a number of pitfalls. Psychology is indeed a limited enterprise and a source of frustration and dissatisfaction for many of us, for whom philosophy and literature constitute an ever-present seductive force. I feel, however, that the integrity of psychology and, even more so, that of philosophy is worth the price of constraining one's ambition.

References

Baumrind, D. (1978). A dialectical materialist's perspective on knowing social reality. In W. Damon (Ed.), *New directions for child development. Vol. 2: Moral Development*. San Francisco: Jossey-Bass.

Blasi, A., and Oresick, R. J. (1986). Emotions and cognitions in self-inconsistency. In D. Bearison and H. Zimiles (Eds.), *Thought and emotion: Developmental perspectives*. Hillsdale, NJ: Erlbaum.

Damon, W. (1977). *The social world of the child*. San Francisco: Jossey-Bass.

Damon, W. (1980). Structural-developmental theory and the study of moral development. In M. Windmiller, N. Lambert, and E. Turiel (Eds.), *Moral development and socialization*. Boston: Allyn and Bacon.

Eisenberg-Berg, N. (1979). Development of children's prosocial moral judgment. *Developmental Psychology*, 15:128–137.

Freud, S. (1961a). The ego and the id. In J. Strachey (Ed. and Trans.), *The standard edition of the complete psychological works of Sigmund Freud* (Vol. 19). London: Hogarth Press. (Original work published 1923)

Freud, S. (1961b). Dostoevsky and parricide. In J. Strachey (Ed. and Trans.), *The standard edition of the complete psychological works of Sigmund Freud* (Vol. 21). London: Hogarth Press. (Original work published 1928)

Gilligan, C. (1982). *In a different voice: Psychological theory and women's development*. Cambridge, MA: Harvard University Press.

Grice, G. R. (1967). *The grounds of moral judgement*. Cambridge: Cambridge University Press.

Haan, N. (1978). Two moralities in action contexts: Relationships to thought, ego-regulation and development. *Journal of Personality and Social Psychology*, 36:286–305.

Haan, N. (1982). Can research on morality be "scientific"? *American Psychologist*, 37:1096–1104.

Habermas, J. (1983). Interpretive social science vs. hermeneuticism. In N. Haan, R. N. Bellah, P. Rabinow, and W. M. Sullivan (Eds.), *Social science as moral inquiry*. New York: Columbia University Press.

Holstein, C. B. (1976). Development of moral judgment: A longitudinal study of males and females. *Child Development*, 47:41–61.

Kohlberg, L. (1976). Moral stages and moralization: The cognitive developmental approach. In T. Lickona (Ed.), *Moral development and behavior*. New York: Holt, Rinehart and Winston.

Kohlberg, L., and Candee, D. (1984a). The relationship of moral judgment to moral action. In W. M. Kurtines and J. L. Gewirtz (Eds.), *Morality, moral behavior, and moral development*. New York: Wiley Interscience.

Kohlberg, L., and Candee, D. (1984b). The relationship of moral judgment to moral action. In L. Kohlberg, *Essays on moral development. Vol. 2: The psychology of moral development*. San Francisco: Harper and Row.

Kohlberg, L., Levine, C., and Hewer, A. (1983). *Moral stages: A current formulation and a response to critics*. Basel: Karger.

MacIntyre, A. (1971). What morality is not. In A. MacIntyre, *Against the self-image of the age*. New York: Shocken Books.

Nucci, L. (1981). Conceptions of personal issues: A domain distinct from moral or societal concepts. *Child Development*, 52:114–121.

Rest, J. R. (1979) *Development in judging moral issues*. Minneapolis: University of Minnesota Press.

Rest, J. R. (1983). Morality. In J. H. Flavell and E. Markman (Eds.), *Manual of child psychology* (4th ed.). *Vol. 3: Cognitive development*. New York: Wiley.

Shweder, R. A., Turiel, E., and Much, N. C. (1981). The moral intuitions of the child. In J. H. Flavell and L. Ross (Eds.), *Social cognitive development*. New York: Cambridge University Press.

Skinner, B. F. (1953). *Science and human behavior*. New York: Macmillan.

Skinner, B. F. (1974). *About behaviorism*. New York: Random House.

Smetana, J. (1981). Concepts in the personal and moral domains: Adolescent and young adult women's reasoning about abortion. *Journal of Applied Developmental Psychology*, 2:211–226.

Smetana, J. (1983). Social-cognitive development: Domain distinctions and coordinations. *Developmental Review*, 3:131–147.

Smetana, J., Bridgeman, D., and Turiel, E. (1983). Differentiations of domains and prosocial reasoning. In D. Bridgeman (Ed.), *The nature of prosocial development: Interdisciplinary theories and strategies*. New York: Academic Press.

Sullivan, E. V. (1977). A study of Kohlberg's structural theory of moral development: A critique of liberal social science ideology. *Human Development*, 20:352–376.

Taylor, C. (1976). Responsibility for self. In A. O. Rorty (Ed.), *The identities of persons*. Berkeley and Los Angeles: University of California Press.

Turiel, E. (1983). *The development of social knowledge: Morality and convention*. New York: Cambridge University Press.

Winch, P. (1958). *The idea of a social science and its relation to philosophy*. London: Routledge and Kegan Paul.

Against the Neglect of "Content" in the Moral Theories of Kohlberg and Habermas: Implications for the Relativism-Universalism Controversy

Rainer Döbert

This essay does not claim to be a systematic or exhaustive treatment of the philosophical and empirical-scientific problems raised in the course of the controversy between the universalist and relativist positions within ethical theory. Rather, my goal is simply to demonstrate that, contrary to what Kohlberg and Habermas believe, it is problematic whether the findings of moral psychology can be claimed as support for an unqualified or strict universalism. To demonstrate this will require an examination of the problem of structure and content within cognitive developmental psychology. Such an examination is needed because—and this is my fundamental thesis—in the moral theories of Kohlberg and Habermas, systematic misevaluations of the significance of content have had at least three unfortunate consequences: (1) They attempt to eliminate from the theories aspects of content that no ethical theory or moral psychology can do without. (2) They falsely assume that moral psychologists were studying structures of justice—which are difficult to universalize—whereas in fact they were studying development within a core domain of morality—that of the morally "right." In this area, to be demarcated by content, universalist claims are more easily "justified." (3) They subsume decisions of moral dilemmas under the concept of content, with the result that they vacillate between an unnoticed relativism and an unjustified universalism.

These misunderstandings have arisen because theory formation in moral psychology has been too strongly oriented toward extraneous philosophical schemes. As a result, what has actually been done in moral psychology by way of measurement has slipped out of sight. If one brings the measurement procedures back into view, the resulting outlook is not the universalism asserted by Kohlberg and Habermas but rather a distinctly differentiated picture. If moral psychology has any hope of making a contribution to the philosophical controversy between relativists and universalists, it may well lie in its power to make such a differentiation, i.e., in its ability to draw a precise line of demarcation between those action conflicts that should be dealt with universalistically and those that should be viewed relativistically.

General Remarks on the Theme of Form and Content

Cognitive developmental psychology is concerned with the reconstruction of the stagewise development of our capacity for knowledge and of our action competencies. Accordingly, it proceeds in good "Kantian" fashion from the premise that the views and ideas guiding our actions at any particular time can be analyzed into the two components of content and form or structure. In our dealings with social and nonsocial reality, we perceive certain phenomena and have certain experiences; and these must, as the *contents* of our thought, be dealt with in accordance with certain rules, which is to say that they must be subjected to structures or systems of operations. The totality of these structures or operations makes up the *form* of our thought. It is in the interaction of form and content that concrete knowledge and specific action decisions come about. Since the latter bear no visible marks of the processes that produced them (e.g., we cannot know whether someone has guessed a correct answer or really thought it through), Kohlberg has, in a somewhat unfortunate choice of terms, also called the results of thought (the action decisions) "mere content." As we shall see, this ambiguity in the concept of content has not been without consequences.

Although both form and content are necessarily present and dynamically interrelated in our thinking (only pure logic is concerned with content-free structures), the relationship between structure and content could still vary considerably, depending on how one construes development. Basically, there are three possibilities:

1. *Only contents develop, in which case development would be conceived as a sequential journey through an experiential space or as a step-by-step working through of a group of action problems or "functions" institutionalized in social roles.* The biographical theories used in sociology, Freud's psychosexual stage theory, and Erikson's reconstruction of the life cycle all correspond to this model. But we also find its traces in theories that are more heavily oriented toward structure. For instance, the dimension of "conscious preoccupations" in Loevinger's theory of ego development (Loevinger, 1966) includes action problems that are defined in content terms, such as control, reputation, achievement, and self-realization. As Kohlberg has argued, these theories depart from the concept of a "logical" hierarchy of stages, and thus they are marginal to a *strict* structuralism (Kohlberg, 1973).

2. *Only structures or systems of operations develop; contents, i.e., perceptions and experiences, can be taken as merely "given" and as such remain for the most part constant.* This is the position of structuralist developmental psychology in the Piaget-Kohlberg tradition. But it would be a mistake to conclude from the fact that Piaget's theory focused on structural development that a developmental theory should completely neglect the dimension of content. It is easy to see why things cannot be so simple. First of all, as I have already indicated, structures do not occur in "pure" form any more than contents do. It so happens that most developmental psychological research is concerned exclusively with structured content, where the content is of course determined by the experimental task. The child pours water into a glass (+), and he pours water back out (−); he does a wrong (+), and he makes amends for it (−). In doing so, the child is completely involved with content-specific actions: (+) and (−) are our abstractions of the operations. Furthermore, the construction of the test determines the complexity of the set of operations that are to be employed sequentially in order to complete the task, that is, to coordinate the given segment of reality consistently. And finally, the development of struc-

tures is always determined by given action problems or "functions," and these cannot be classified as "structures" either. The significance of functions cannot be overestimated within the framework of Piaget's dynamic structuralism, since without functions no understanding of the direction that development takes or the pressure to develop at all is possible. For this reason Piaget did not shrink from making a pointed critique of Foucault's "functionless" or "static" structuralism, calling it a "structuralism without structures" that ends in irrationalism (Piaget, 1970, pp. 134ff.). As I understand the present state of the discussion, none of this is at all controversial. Moreover, it is also completely in accordance with the position that it is only structures that develop. One could summarize the above by saying that operations work as coordinating mechanisms "behind" or "beneath" concrete, content-determined actions or thoughts, and that the pressure of a constant function compels these operations to reorganize themselves in such a way that they are better able to fulfill their task—in short, they are compelled to develop.

Now, this position is compatible with a wide variety of views about how, and how far, operations extend across action domains. On the one hand, one could assume that a given repertoire of structures applies in all domains of action. Accordingly, no matter whether physical or social reality was being dealt with, one would always find manifestations of, say, the INRC group of operations "behind" the various concrete actions of an adult, and these operations would constitute the structural core of the actions.[1] On the other hand, one could assume that, to construct an adequate definition of the structure of action, general cognitive structures such as the INRC group must be supplemented by other, domain-specific operations.

The last-mentioned strategy is the one implicitly adopted by Kohlberg, for whom cognitive development is a necessary but not sufficient condition for sociocognitive development, and the latter is in turn a necessary but not sufficient condition for moral development. Consequently, he believes that one of the principal, yet much-neglected, tasks of moral psychology is that of identifying the operations specific to the moral domain. In his recent publications, Kohlberg has tried to fill this need. His list of moral operations is as follows:

Each moral stage is reviewed by discussing stage-specific sociomoral perspectives on norms in general and upon the justice operations of equality, equity, reciprocity, prescriptive role-taking, and universalizability. (Kohlberg, 1984, p. 624)

In the work of Habermas, Kohlberg's list is reduced to three operations, namely, "reversibility of perspectives," "universality in the sense of the inclusion of all concerned," and "reciprocity of equal acknowledgment of the claims of every participant" (Habermas, 1983, p. 133). Space does not permit me to examine the validity of these proposals in detail. However, I cannot resist making one observation, based on Piaget's critique of Foucault.

Piaget points out that "what Foucault forgets is that the whole of cognitive life is linked to structures which are just as unconscious as the Freudian Id, but which reconnect knowledge with life in general" (Piaget, 1970, p. 131). Now it is difficult to see how the operations listed by Kohlberg and Habermas could be as unconscious as the Freudian Id. These "operations" seem to concern surface phenomena of moral consciousness, phenomena that could be explained as the result of more fundamental, "genuine" operations. To appreciate this point, let us consider the following questions. Reversibility of perspectives manifests itself in a satisfactory adjustment, but how are we to achieve that adjustment? Habermas himself treats universality as a criterion that is "analogous to truth," but is truth in the cognitive domain properly conceived of as an operation? And finally: Kohlberg's justice operations are conscious criteria for decisions; the principle of equality, the principle of desert, and considerations of equity are manifest distributive principles familiar to everyone. But what of the equally manifest fact that when these principles are applied they often lead to incompatible courses of action? Since they cannot simply all be followed simultaneously, they must be coordinated—at another level than the one they themselves occupy. I conclude, therefore, that the quest for "operations" should be more promising on this second level.

3. *Finally, there is the possibility that both structures and contents change in the course of the developmental process.* Given the present state of research on the development of moral consciousness, this seems to me to be the most plausible assumption to use in interpreting the empirical findings we have and integrating current theoretical models of moral development. This is so especially because at each stage of moral consciousness new contents (elements) are subjected to new functions and to new forms of coordination (structures). To give a few examples: In Stage 2, morality has the function of maximizing interests; in Stage 3, that of maintaining interpersonal trust and social approval; in Stage 4, that of maintaining the existing social order, and in Stage 5, finally, that of protecting the fundamental rights of individuals (cf. Kohlberg, 1984, Appendix A). It is obvious, I think, that new types of motives are connected with the emergence of new functions. When new types of motives appear, new elements enter into the moral deliberation. Whether and to what extent these elements are susceptible of reconstruction as condensed precipitates of structures (new object constancies) must remain for the moment an open question.[2] In the absence of a convincing reconstruction we seem to have no alternative to treating them in the same way that we have treated the functions, namely, as contents. (Similar problems come up in the reconstruction of ego development; cf. Döbert and Nunner-Winkler, 1982; Eckensberger, 1984.)

What, then, can we actually say about moral operations and their interaction with moral contents? To answer this question, I shall proceed from the idea that the very fruitlessness of the search for distinct, specifically moral operations suggests that no structures are to be found in the interpersonal domain that are different in principle from the structures found in our dealings with nature. In short, there are *no specifically moral operations.* To be sure, this assertion presupposes a certain level of abstraction. I could, of course, simply stipulate that, say, justifications and excuses are moral operations, from which it would logically follow that there are no comparable operations in the nonsocial domain that correspond to these so-called moral operations. But I can also address the problem more abstractly, by considering how justifications and excuses are related to the more general notion of interpersonal equilibrium (Döbert and Nunner-Winkler, 1978; Keller, 1984). Let us consider an instance of justification. Suppose that I have been reproached for having harmed someone, and redress is demanded from me. I can justify myself by pointing out that without my intervention still greater harm would have occurred. If so, then the scales tip in my favor, since the harm done is compensated for by the harm prevented. If I understand the matter correctly, this involves the operation of reciprocity (or, as Piaget later called it, the reciprocal). Or let us consider an instance of excuse-giving. Suppose I plead, "I was forced to do it." If so, then the action in question disappears from the ensemble of actions ascribed to me; and that will involve the operation of negation. I do not know what additional, specifically moral operation would be needed to determine the effect of justifications and excuses on the social equilibrium. But what we would have shown here is nothing more nor less than that excuses and justifications are instances of the N and R in the INRC group.

One could, of course, say with Kohlberg that a concept like compensation obviously belongs to the justice complex. I would not argue with such a claim. But in this case justice is a product, generated by reciprocity. The product level, however, is not the level on which operations, as rules for production, are to be located.

Even though it does not seem very plausible to me that there should be specifically moral operations, there does exist a specific form of perception, namely, role-taking, that makes possible knowledge of the moral problems at hand.[3] Once perceived, these problems can then be dealt with through the general operative intelligence. For role-taking to "click," the ego development of the interacting persons must be synchronized to some extent, since otherwise they would confront each other with motives that simply could not be mutually apprehended. And of course compassion for the fate of one's fellow man, and thus motivation, must be present.

This denial of any "moral operations" distinct from the INRC group is, of course, a controversial interpretation. But it has the advantage of being parsimonious. Furthermore, it maintains contact with other fields of research (e.g., the development of law, as Weber has shown, amounts to systematizing it and rendering it logical) and orients research toward "deeper" issues.

This interpretation also directly relates to familiar research findings concerning the relationship among cognition, social cognition, and morality. (Social) cognition is a necessary but not sufficient condition of morality because a specific motivation is required for morality. Even those who attempt to deceive must proceed with intelligence if they are to achieve their aims; however, they lack interpersonal engagement, and thus cognition is shown to be a merely necessary but not sufficient condition of morality. Whatever cannot be reduced to this trivial insight is, I believe, nothing but a research artifact produced at the operational level rather than the result of "real" relationships. Cognitive development is measured through experimental tasks that can be solved. However, it is quite otherwise for social-cognitive and moral judgment. These capacities are put to the test in interpersonal conflicts that are not only difficult but at times irresolvable even at the postconventional level. (Weak self-control on the part of research subjects who are faced with strong temptations may also play a role in the performance of research tasks, especially in the case of younger subjects.) The existing research findings could, I suspect, easily be turned around: If in the purely cognitive domain we gave as experimental tasks problems from mathematical catastrophe theory, while in the interpersonal domain we required only the conflict-free application of a moral rule, we would find that interpersonal reasoning can precede nonsocial reasoning.

To summarize, one could say that the interplay of structure and contents in moral development runs roughly as follows: ego development produces motives and needs, which are grasped through role-taking (whereby contents are perceived). If interpersonal engagement is also present (motivation), the given contents are dealt with through the structures of general operative intelligence in such a way that the person acts morally and the functions of morality are fulfilled.

Three Reasons for the Neglect of the Dimension of Content

We have seen that even the "strong" structuralist position according to which only structures or systems of operations develop could not entirely dispense with contents. Structures can be grasped only in ideas or actions that are content-specific; and functions, on which the directions that development takes and the pressure to develop depend, cannot be subsumed under the concept of structure. Even if one could assume that this strong structuralist position is valid—something about which one can certainly have one's doubts, as we have seen—one would expect to pay a certain price for the complete exclusion of the dimension of content from theory formation. This has largely occurred, and, as we shall see, the anticipated damage is certainly in evidence. As far as I can see, there are three reasons for this development. If in fact only structure develops and content, as "merely given," remains constant, then the latter is theoretically uninteresting and automatically ends up as ground rather than figure. Apparently it is not necessary to pay attention to it. In fact, in view of the circumstance that contents are manifest and structures are latent, may there not even be a danger that the content components will prevent us from proceeding to the level of structural learning? Neglecting the dimension of content then seems to follow logically.

A further reason derives from the circumstance that moral arguments and formulas by no means have to be produced out of nothing by the individual but rather are already at hand in social intercourse. They can simply be taken up by the individual and used formulaically, that is, without the individual's own structuring activity, as the coin of social intercourse. If one tried to reconstruct their full meaning, it would become apparent that they often represent in condensed form a relatively high structural level. One is thus tempted to take them as indicators of this structural level. But in fact this rating would often be erroneous, since they can be "parroted" without thought. In such a case we speak of "mere content learning," and it is of prime importance in the operationalization of the construct of moral consciousness to be able to identify and

eliminate this type of "mere content." This, of course, inten-
sifies the "content antagonism" on the theoretical level.

The last reason relevant here is connected with the history
of research on moral consciousness, specifically, with the substantial failure of characterological moral research, which did
not succeed in demonstrating correlations between moral behavior in varying situations. In his critique of Hartshorne and
May, Kohlberg points out that this failure is related, among
other things, to the fact that Hartshorne and May take into
account only their subjects' action decisions and neglect the
subjects' definition of the situation (Kohlberg, 1984, p. 263).
Of course Kohlberg's critique of the behavioristic framework
of this line of research is justified, but it is also dangerously
misleading because of its subsumption of action decisions under the concept of content. This is not only terminologically
inappropriate, since, as Lind has noted (Lind, 1978, pp. 181f.),
the concept of content thereby becomes ambiguous (content as
input and as output). It is also dangerous, because it is all too
easy to infer that, because mere contents do not develop, action
decisions have nothing at all to do with development. Kohlberg
himself did not fully succumb to this temptation, but as the
reception of his theory shows, others certainly did.

Given all three of these reasons, it is not surprising that
cognitivist moral psychology's lack of interest in content has
become a kind of "content phobia"—for which it has paid in
the end.

The False Identification of Morality and Justice

Kohlberg and, following him, Habermas, never tire[4] of repeating that in reconstructing the development of moral consciousness we are concerned with the development of
"principles of justice." The basis for this thesis lies not in the
matter itself but in the fact that during a certain phase of his
development Kohlberg was very strongly influenced by Rawls's
Theory of Justice (1971). Its reconstructive character, its openness
to learning processes, and its rationalist fundamental assumptions unquestionably make Rawls's theory an attractive model
for the social sciences. But there are competing rational ethics

that are much closer to what has actually been done on the
level of measurement operations and in the research actually
carried out in the Kohlberg tradition. This holds mainly because those ethics deal with the precise content that enters into
the dilemmas used in the studies inspired by Kohlberg. And
this content cannot be subsumed under the concept of justice.
That this could be overlooked is naturally connected with the
assumption that it is not necessary to pay attention to the
dimension of content. But neither morality nor the moral sub-
problem of justice can be defined independently of content. It
will be useful, then, to provide a brief sketch of the essential
content moments of morality and justice.

Justice problems

Since Kohlberg has recently cited Aristotle's theory of justice
as well, and since it seems to be best suited to justify his choice
of terms (Kohlberg, 1984, p. 226), it makes sense to begin with
Aristotle. The *Nicomachean Ethics* distinguishes two main forms
of justice:

Let us take as a starting point, then, the various meanings of "an
unjust man." Both the lawless man and the grasping and unfair man
are thought to be unjust, so that evidently both the law-abiding and
the fair man will be just. The just, then, is the lawful and the fair,
the unjust the unlawful and the unfair. (Aristotle, 1941, p. 1003)

Of justice in the sense of what is lawful, Aristotle further
says that it is "not part of virtue, but virtue entire" (ibid.,
p. 1004), whereas justice in the sense of the fair represents
only a part of virtue. Of this "part" he then writes:

Of particular justice and that which is just in the corresponding sense,
(A) one kind is that which is manifested in distributions of honor or
money or the other things that fall to be divided among those who
have a share in the constitution (for in these it is possible for one
man to have a share either unequal or equal to that of another), and
(B) one is that which plays a rectifying part in transactions between
man and man. (Ibid., p. 1005)

Now, when Kohlberg speaks of justice, is he referring to the
whole virtue or to Aristotle's particular virtue? Doubtless to the

particular virtue, for as forms of justice he lists the distributive, the corrective, and the commutative (the "procedural," which he also mentions, has a special status and does not belong in this listing of "material" principles; cf. Kohlberg, 1984, pp. 621f.). Precisely these forms of justice are designated by Aristotle as constituting "justice" in the narrower sense. And Kohlberg's list of "justice operations" hardly admits of any other interpretation: equality, equity, and reciprocity are distributive perspectives characteristic of justice in the narrower sense (Kohlberg, 1984, pp. 622f.).

At this point we must ask whether the Aristotelian distinction is reflected in our everyday-language intuitions and whether contemporary philosophy possesses an analogous distinction. Ordinary language allows for the Aristotelian distinction to some extent in reserving the concept of "justice" for Aristotle's "particular justice." We say, for example, that it is "wrong" to lie but "unjust" to treat someone unfairly. This ordinary-language usage of the concept of justice is completely in accordance with contemporary moral philosophy. Most important, Rawls himself, on whom Kohlberg relies, does not identify justice with morality at all. Principles of justice are provisions through which the advantages and the burdens of a form of social organization are distributed among various individuals: "They provide a way of assigning rights and duties in the basic institutions of society and they define the appropriate distribution of the benefits and burdens of social cooperation" (Rawls, 1971, p. 4).

But the problem of distribution is only one of the basic functional imperatives of societies, and Rawls points out that "there are other fundamental social problems, in particular those of coordination, efficiency, and stability" (ibid., p. 6). At the very least, the fulfillment of the imperatives of coordination and stability rests on a moral basis that has nothing to do with "justice." And the diagram of the whole realm of practical argument that Rawls provides on p. 109 of his book should convince everyone, even if only purely visually, that "justice" covers only a narrow segment of the whole field of ethical theory. Just as Hart distinguishes principles that refer to classes of individuals from those that are valid for individuals, Rawls also argues that "it is clear, however, that principles of another kind must also be chosen, since a complete theory of right includes principles for individuals as well" (ibid., p. 108). Among such principles are obligations (keeping promises, fairness, and loyalty) and natural duties (mutual aid, mutual respect, and refraining from actions that injure others or harm the innocent). In spite of certain differences in classification, this list of obligations and natural duties is very similar to the list of moral rules and ideals that Gert (1973) presents as the indispensable core of morality.

For the present, let us summarize as follows: Even though ordinary language and contemporary philosophy divide up the moral domain differently from Aristotle (commutative justice does not appear under that name), they are nevertheless in agreement with Aristotle's mode of proceeding insofar as they recognize the necessity of distinguishing functionally differentiated subdomains of morality from one another and from morality as a whole. And since in doing this one must have recourse to different functions, we are dealing with a content problematic. We have seen that Kohlberg's use of the justice concept refers to Aristotle's "particular justice." In Kohlberg's earlier publications, however—and in view of the theory's antagonism to content, this is not especially surprising—there is little indication that he recognized the possible relevance of the distinction between justice on the one hand and morality, as the more comprehensive domain of action, on the other.

The most general content of morality

If justice in the narrower sense has to do with the distribution of the benefits and burdens of social cooperation, how are we to characterize the content of the "whole virtue," that is, morality as such?

Among the contents that no viable ethical theory can do without are, first of all, some purely descriptive trivialities. Hart comments on these:

We are committed to survival as something presupposed by the terms of the discussion; for our concern is with the social arrangements for continued existence, not with those of a suicide club. . . . From this point the argument is a simple one. Reflection on some very obvious generalizations—indeed truisms—concerning human nature and the world in which men live, shows that as long as these hold good, there are certain rules of conduct which any social organization must contain if it is to be viable. (Hart, 1961, p. 188)

Among these truisms are human vulnerability, approximate equality among human beings (even the strong have to sleep sometimes), limitedness of altruistic motives, and limitedness of the necessary means for securing physical existence. Such statements, "the truth of which is contingent on human beings and the world they live in retaining the salient characteristics which they have" (ibid., p. 195), are included, however implicitly, in every moral theory. They prohibit us from defining morality in a purely formal way and relying completely on the universalizability of norms, as Habermas does.

Thus Gert writes, for example, on the criterion of universalization, "Morality does provide a guide to conduct acceptable to all rational men, but not every guide to conduct acceptable to all rational men is a moral one" (Gert, 1973, p. 4). Later he says, "All linguistic analyses of moral judgments fail because moral judgments are not distinguished from other judgments by their form, or by their function, but by their content" (ibid., p. 13). And this content has to do with furthering human interests and refraining from injurious actions. The moral rules and ideals that Gert examined are only specifications of this general content that is characteristic of morality. Thus they represent a de facto demarcation of the core domain of morality that does not require recourse to abstract definitions. One may safely assume that the individual normally enters the moral domain through the mediation of his acceptance of these concrete norms, and finally "appropriates" them in structural learning processes, that is, learns to handle them in a "meaningful" way.

We promote the interests of others and refrain from injurious actions when we respect our fellow men, encounter them with benevolence, and take an interest in their welfare. These are formulations that have been used again and again since Aristotle to define the content of morality. With them we have not named all the contents required for a comprehensive ethical theory, but rather only the highest maxims that must be acknowledged—however implicitly—if one is to do justice to the mundane fundamental conditions of our existence named by Hart.

It should also be emphasized that the welfare criterion can claim priority over the justice criterion. This is already true for Aristotle, for whom "if a man harms another by choice, he acts unjustly" (Aristotle, 1941, p. 1016). This priority results on purely formal grounds from the fact that justice is a subdomain of morality and must therefore bear the defining characteristics of morality (but not vice-versa). It is easy to demonstrate this in simple everyday terms: if the well-being of another is a matter of complete indifference to me, I will also not grant him what is his "just" share but rather will keep everything for myself.

Thus in analyzing justice problems it would be reasonable to expect to find the characteristic features of morality as such, but conversely it would not make sense to look for what is specific to justice in other areas of morality. As we shall see, however, Kohlberg chooses this second strategy.

To summarize: Contrary to what Kohlberg implies in his earlier writings, morality and justice are by no means identical. Morality is defined by mutual benevolence, which in dealing with problems of distribution or equalization manifests itself as distributive or retributive justice. This whole discussion would be purely terminological if Kohlberg had in fact made justice problems the theme of his research instruments.

Surprisingly, however, this is not what he did: scarcely any of the research dilemmas used by Kohlberg focus directly on the theme of justice. Instead, they deal primarily with moral conflicts in which moral rules and moral ideals (Gert) or natural duties and obligations (Rawls) come into conflict.

The Heinz dilemma deals with the question whether one may break the prohibition against stealing in order to save a human life; in the euthanasia dilemma there is a conflict between the duty to protect human life and the duty to relieve human suffering. In the Joe dilemma respect for legitimate authority stands in conflict with the duty to keep one's promise;

in the Judy dilemma sibling loyalty, the breaking of a promise, the duty to be truthful, and parental authority are in conflict. In the Korean dilemma the rights and duties of an officer, the soldiers' duty to obey, and the value of human life are in conflict (justice problems do appear here, at least in the selection of the "victim"); in the case of the brothers Bob and Karl it must be decided whether breaking and entering is a worse crime than deceiving a good-natured old man. Only the Valjean dilemma focuses directly on justice, and in fact on retributive justice (cf. Kohlberg, 1984, pp. 640ff.).

Thus not only are moral domains that should be distinguished from one another in terms of content collapsed into each other; most important, the distributive justice that Rawls is concerned with scarcely appears at all. In view of the fact that Rawls was a kind of philosophical archangel in the formation of Kohlbergian theory, this finding may well surprise us.

Procedural Justice and the Universal Core Domain of Morality

There appears to be a convincing justification for the neglect of the distinction between morality and justice: recourse to procedural justice. Procedures are classified as "just" or "unjust," "fair" or "unfair," and if one generates the whole domain of morality as a procedural theory, one judges every individual moral rule from a meta-level on which considerations of justice play the decisive role. Rawls's "choice" in the initial situation and Habermas's discourse are examples of this kind of procedure. If one proceeds in this way, the conclusion seems almost inevitable that in ethical theory everything does ultimately depend on justice and that the distinction between morality and justice is not so important, since in the final analysis both are produced through "justice." I do not consider this argument convincing, since I do not believe that we should make ourselves completely dependent upon "procedure," as, for example, that of consensus formation.

Further, we must not forget that philosophical procedural ethics are technical designs for the construction of moral norms. They cannot directly claim to grasp the actual mode of functioning of our everyday-language intuitions. Whether and to what extent we actually make use of procedural means in the resolution of moral conflicts is a completely empirical question. As far as I can see, research has provided little evidence that our moral intuitions are shaped in any significant way by procedural components. As a rule, in the research inspired by Kohlberg procedural suggestions actually appear only in the Korean dilemma, where an officer must select a soldier for a suicide mission. Here as a rule a lottery procedure is suggested by older subjects, since—and this is the decisive point—there are no legitimate criteria for selection. Where such criteria exist, on the other hand, procedural suggestions seem to be counterintuitive.

Another point to be considered is that we must submit to just procedures and support just institutions, and this "must" belongs to our natural duties in Rawls's sense of that term. In this respect the meta-level of procedural justice is again dependent on the "whole virtue" of morality.

Above all, however, we must select the right procedure. To substantiate this thesis we will have to return in more detail to the subject of the content of morality. Not all moral norms are equally binding: it may be morally praiseworthy to share my last dollar with a beggar; I am not, however, obligated to do so in the same way that I am obligated not to rob the beggar so as to have at least two dollars. Gert (1973) has made a detailed examination of such relationships and has identified a set of basic moral norms that represent the universal core of all morality. There is no functional equivalent for any of these norms; none of them has to assert itself against competitors, as do the justice principles. They occupy—even in Rawls's work, with all its emphasis on procedure—a special position in ethical theories, insofar as in them we have a secure and relatively undisputed center. Naturally, this center is then also generated by the procedures suggested. But that is secondary: because one knows what the result has to be in any case, one knows how the procedures have to be constructed. Without this certainty in the core domain, one could not design the procedures properly.

For there are various types of procedure: pure procedural justice, imperfect procedural justice, and perfect procedural justice. In pure procedural justice, a just result comes about simply in virtue of a correct execution of the procedure. There is no independent criterion in terms of which the result could be assessed (for example: the (re-)distribution to players of money bet in roulette). In imperfect procedural justice, in contrast, a desired (just) result is known, but no procedure is known through which it can be produced with absolute certainty (trial procedure). In perfect procedural justice one knows both the just outcome and also a procedure certain to produce it (division of a cake) (cf. Rawls, 1971, section 14).

Since there are various procedures, one can also construct a pure procedural theory without grounding it in a pure procedure. In the reception of Rawls's work this has been largely overlooked (for instance, by Habermas). Further, the existence of the moral core domain makes it extremely implausible to assume that all of ethical theory can be conceived as the embodiment of pure procedural justice. What would we think of a universalistic or procedural ethics that reformulated the fundamental moral rules and gave recommendations like "kill if you feel like it," "lie if it helps," or "steal what you need"? We wouldn't even ask what pseudo-arguments had produced this nonsense; we would simply reject the whole ethical theory. In the area of fundamental moral rules our moral intuitions are so sure that we cannot alter them. Different ethical theories take account of this fundamental characteristic of the core of our moral consciousness in different ways, but in this respect they are in complete agreement. Hart speaks of the "importance" of moral standards of conduct and their "immunity from deliberate change" (Hart, 1961, p. 164). Gert will be quoted somewhat more fully in this connection because he has produced the most refined attempt at reconstruction and he makes the point at hand in the way least likely to be misunderstood. He writes:

A moral rule is unchanging or unchangeable; discovered rather than invented. A moral rule is not dependent on the will or decision of any man or group of men. . . . Thus moral rules have a status similar to the laws of logic, or of mathematics. No one invents the laws of logic. (Gert, 1973, p. 67)

Of Rawls, too, one is justified in saying that in his philosophy the core domain of morality, which for him comprises the concepts of obligation and natural duty, has a special status. Although as a social contract theorist Rawls has to generate natural duties and obligations from within his "original position," it is clear that there is no set of possible alternatives from which these duties and obligations are ultimately selected. This "choice" could not have any other outcome. Here, then, the desired outcome of the procedure is unambiguously clear prior to its execution, since there are no functional equivalents to the moral rules. This is a crucial difference between this choice and the choice among justice principles. In the choice of moral rules and ideals we are dealing not with pure procedural justice but rather with perfect procedural justice. Here knowledge of the outcome is independent of the execution of the procedure; in fact, the choice of procedure depends on it. One could enter into a computer the totality of the rules ever followed by human beings and make a random selection from them. In this way we would have produced pure procedural justice in the realm of morality. The result could be characterized not as unjust so much as inappropriate to the matter at hand. No one would submit to a procedure of this kind!

And where does the procedural theorist derive his prior knowledge of the result of the procedure? Presumably from the implicit presuppositions of the procedure actually chosen. Social contract, rational discourse, etc., presuppose competent subjects capable of judgment, and we cannot define their competence through the procedure itself. It is probably reasonable, then, to understand competence as the capacity to interpret at least elementary moral matters correctly. This in turn evidently presupposes that such a thing as an uncontroversial moral problem exists at all. The moral core domain with its rules and ideals, which are in fact universal, represents such an uncontroversial field; it can serve as a gauge in choosing between procedures: we would not accept any procedure that did not produce the moral rules and ideals with absolute certainty. This does not exclude the possibility that we can construct the moral core domain procedurally. If we do so, however, we are simply submitting our moral intuitions—for the sake of certainty, if you like—to an additional test of validity devoid of surprises. Among other things, this explains why in interviews subjects do not derive the rules of the moral core domain through procedural reasoning. One has recourse to procedure where there is uncertainty or where one suspects that because of the interests involved a moral norm will not be followed impartially (Tugendhat, 1984).

Nor would we want to make ourselves completely dependent upon procedures, for the proposed procedures always involve a social mechanism. In view of this it is difficult to see how we can avoid the blind alley of total conformism if we do not equip the individual with the capacity to say "no" in clear cases on the basis of trustworthy intuitions.

In summary we can say that even the recourse to procedural justice cannot render plausible the notion that morality is ultimately determined by considerations of justice. For procedural theories implicitly presuppose a person who judges competently, and such a person could not be found if there were no certainty in the moral core domain.

The Uncertainties of the Justice Complex

Competition among principles

Kohlberg's and Habermas's assertions that ontogenetic moral research is concerned with the development of justice structures are especially surprising in that there are uncertainties in the domain of justice that are hardly resolvable at the level of our everyday intuitions. In this area one rarely encounters anything resembling "closed" structures, discernible just by the rational reconstruction of latent meanings (Kohlberg, 1984, pp. 217ff.; Habermas, 1983, pp. 127ff.). This also implies that in the domain of theories of justice we must be prepared for relativistic complexities, so that it is precisely the justice problematic that is least suited to support universalistic claims against relativistic positions.

To substantiate: On the level of our ordinary-language intuitions we find competing notions of justice (desert, equality, need, utilitarian maximization of happiness) that are successively acquired and equilibrated in the course of ontogenetic development. In societies of our type we find the following sequence: equality principle; principle of desert; combination of equality, desert, and need. There are wide variations in the weightings assigned, especially where need is concerned, which indicates uncertainties on the part of the subjects (Damon, 1977; Döbert, 1979). The findings of developmental psychology in this regard are supported by traditional social psychology (Mikula, 1980). It can be demonstrated clearly that the different notions of justice correspond to different functions within social systems and thus take on different weights in different contexts of action. Here, then, there are difficult problems of compromise formation. Nor can the competing justice principles be reduced to one another (cf. Miller, 1976). For the moment, then, it is a completely open question whether one will ever succeed in bringing them into an unequivocal hierarchy.

Since the beginnings of bourgeois society a "discourse" has been going on between competing political philosophies constructed upon different conceptions of justice. And this dialogue has never led to an unequivocal result. This cannot be an accident. This much should be clear: whatever a possible solution of this problem might look like, it will certainly not be located on the level of ordinary-language theories of action. As Rawls's book shows, the deliberations required are too complex. As far as notions of justice are concerned, then, Habermas is completely mistaken in thinking that "everyday moral intuitions do not require illumination by philosophers" (Habermas, 1983, p. 108). For the "certainty" with which we supposedly "put our knowledge into practice" (ibid., p. 107) certainly does not exist in this area. Here, then, presumably, we find ourselves in a domain of legitimate relativistic thought that cannot, as Habermas believes, simply be reduced to "false interpretations" that will be proven wrong by "natural intuitions" (cf. Lempert, 1985, p. 263).

I think we can now formulate the implications of what has been said for the relativism controversy. Since contents are of secondary importance for moral psychology in the Piagetian tradition, it was not noticed that theory formation was oriented to a philosophical account whose thematic (content) is different from the one to which one's own research practice was devoted. Rawls's theory is concerned with justice in the narrower sense; Kohlberg's dilemmas focus primarily on the core domain of morality. Since one has to reckon with relativistic gray areas in questions of justice, a twofold danger arises when one confounds morality and justice. On the one hand, justice questions are burdened with demands for rational proof that they cannot satisfy. The extension of the quest for certainty in the moral core domain to the justice complex may thus lead to rigid dogmatism in the area of political philosophy. There could be nothing worse for German political culture!

On the other hand, there is the danger that the moral core domain will be infected with the ambivalences characteristic of the justice thematic. In this way it too would be drawn—completely unnecessarily—into the vortex of relativism. On the metatheoretical level too, then, it is important to state unambiguously what Kohlberg's research is actually concerned with: the universal core domain of morality.

An escape hatch?

Over the years Kohlberg has sensed more and more clearly the problems with the thesis that moral development is the development of justice structures, and he has made more and more room for the utilitarian principle (see Kohlberg, 1984, p. 227). Yet he has continued to believe in the primacy of justice structures. In its structural core his moral theory is concerned, as always, with justice, since it focuses on "hard" stages (ibid., pp. 224ff., 236ff.). If there are "hard" stages, there are also "soft" stages, and with this distinction Kohlberg tries to buttress his insistence on the justice thematic. Soft-stage theories are concerned more with contents and functions of the personality than with structures; they include only "the individual's reflections upon the self's psychology" (ibid.,

p. 243), thus only "systems of second-order or metamodes of thinking" (ibid., p. 244). The stages defined in these theories are not subject to any rigorously defined developmental logic based on genuine operations. We find examples of soft stages in the works of Loevinger (1976), Perry (1968), Fowler (1981), Kegan (1982), Broughton (1978), and Gilligan (1982).

The hard stages are, of course, the exact opposite; they are based on identifiable systems of operations that constitute their developmental logic.

I will not pursue here the question to what extent elements from "soft" stage models are integrated into Kohlberg's stage descriptions. But they certainly cannot be neglected. In Stage 1, for example, only external behavior counts; subjective perspectives are added only in Stage 2. In that stage, then, we are concerned with the appearance of new elements, not directly with new operations (which may of course also be found). And are we not very familiar from Loevinger's theory with the orientation to social relationships, roles, social approval, and interpersonal trust characteristic of Stage 3? What would be left of the stage descriptions if we removed all these "soft" elements from them?

Even more important, one would in any case expect "hard" structures to define narrower margins of "appropriateness" for thought and action. Kohlberg thinks no differently:

The focus of Piaget and myself on morality as deontological justice springs, in part, from a concern with moral and ethical universality in moral judgment. The search for moral universality implies the search for some minimal value conceptions on which all persons could agree, regardless of personal differences in detailed aims or goals. (Kohlberg, 1984, p. 248)

After all that has been said above about justice principles, it will hardly come as a surprise that hard structures are unlikely to be found in the domain of justice. If there are hard structures in the domain of morality, they are in the moral core domain.

Now, the Kohlberg dilemmas are in fact very much concerned with the moral core domain, and one might think that Kohlberg's predilection for justice terminology would be without consequences. But in my view this is not the case at all, for

essentially the following reasons: In "hard" stage theories it is
of central importance that the operations can be specified precisely, and, as we have seen, Kohlberg is oriented in his "choice"
of operations to justice in the strict sense. His assertion, then,
must read that only justice operations can comprise the structural core of morality as such. The question then arises how
justice operations can be linked to problems of moral content
that have nothing to do with justice. Kohlberg lists three such
problem domains: maintenance of the normative order (rights,
duties); utilitarian consequences (good or bad consequences
for individuals or groups); and finally consequences for the
maintenance of ideals and harmony (character, self-respect,
social ideals, dignity, autonomy) (ibid., p. 309). In these three
moral domains, justice operations are used implicitly, whereas
in the justice thematic they are used explicitly:

While the use of the major justice operations is explicit when elements
of the fairness orientation are used, we shall explain at some length
how the major operations of equality and reciprocity are also used,
implicitly, in the other three justice orientations. (Ibid., p. 308; cf.
also pp. 622ff.)

We should add that, in addition to the two operations named,
Kohlberg also lists equity, prescriptive role-taking, and universalization as justice operations. In evaluating Kohlberg's
strategy in terms of its chances of success, one must bear in
mind that the "justice operations" he names are in part also
constitutive for morality as such (and thus naturally for justice
as well). This is true of prescriptive role-taking, universalization, and equality, since equal respect for all moral subjects is
"pre-scribed." If one defines reciprocity, with Piaget, as "reciprocal substitution of scales (*échelles*) or reciprocal substitution
of means and ends" (Piaget, 1977, p. 124), one can hardly
reach any other conclusion. In view of this, then, when Kohlberg succeeds in demonstrating his "justice operations" in other
domains of morality as well, he has not accomplished much,
since he has only proved thereby that when one calls everything
"justice" one can find "justice operations" everywhere.

But it is not as simple as that. Kohlberg interprets the universal moral operations in such a way that they reflect justice

in the strict sense. Thus it is not simply a question of a terminological maneuver. Let us take the "operation" of reciprocity. As Piaget defined it, it is not stamped by justice theory. Kohlberg, in contrast, understands it as follows:

We define a third justice operation, reciprocity, as an operation of distribution by exchange. Of course, what is considered just reciprocity varies by stage. However, in general terms reciprocity is an operation which exchanges merit or "just deserts," reward, or punishment in return for effort, virtue, talent, or deviance. (Kohlberg, 1984, p. 623)

I will now try to demonstrate that as a consequence of this strategy the interpretation of empirically established developmental sequences is seriously impeded, and that much of the interviewees' arguments simply falls through the meshes of this distribution-theoretical sieve. As a starting point let us take Kohlberg's remark that "what is considered just reciprocity varies by stage" (see above). In Stage 1, reciprocity is "a notion of 'exchange' of goods or actions without regard for the psychological valuing of goods or actions by self or others" (ibid., p. 625). In Stage 2, "the operation of reciprocity . . . defines a notion of concrete exchange of equal values or goods in serving the needs of self and other" (ibid., p. 627). Thus reciprocity is now related to the satisfaction of needs, no longer simply to physical things. But this distinction cannot be grasped with the concept of reciprocity. Reciprocity is present in both cases; the contents of the "operation" have changed. Thus the stage-specific change is not caught in Kohlberg's theoretical frame. And in my view this is by no means the only stage transition for which this can be demonstrated.

It can also be shown, I believe, that Kohlberg's distribution-theoretical perspective leads to somewhat forced interpretations of interviews. For example, an operation of equality is supposed to be "hidden" in the concept of responsibility: Heinz should steal the drug because "the druggist in his exploitation has failed to show any responsibility to his fellow man; or because he should have used this discovery to benefit humanity or society" (ibid., p. 313). This element can also be explicit, as in the following:

The druggist doesn't have a right to charge that much because, first of all, a drug is a potential benefit to mankind and to withhold it from mankind for economic reasons, for his own personal gain, is being selfish, unfair. I think people have a certain responsibility to each other, and just because one person has the skill or luck to come into possession of a thing which gives him power over others doesn't mean he should take advantage of this power to the point of exploitation. (Ibid.)

I would certainly not want to dispute the contention that the concept of equality is "somehow" also relevant to the concept of responsibility. But an element of equality would also be present if someone took the druggist's side in referring to property rights (ibid., p. 311). The difference between this reasoning and that of the subjects just cited would be relevant and would potentially constitute a difference in stage.

But the most important question is this: If we followed Kohlberg's theoretical strategy, what would be omitted from our interpretations of subjects' responses as irrelevant to the assignment of stages? What proportion of the moral interview is really captured by the concept of justice operations? Do not the most important moral arguments evade us? Justice operations are supposed to grasp the hard structures of the stage models. Should we then not also expect them to grasp the definitive components of a moral argument? I cannot see that Kohlberg's "operations" actually accomplish this.

One last example: An operation of reciprocity is said to be used implicitly when someone says that Heinz should steal the drug "because his wife can contribute to society." Kohlberg explains: "In this response is an implicit notion of fairness as reciprocity; that is, if a person is a contributor to society then he or she deserves the drug. She is a contributor. Therefore she should get the drug" (ibid., p. 310).

It seems to me extremely questionable whether a statement like this can be subsumed under the principle of desert. For the principle of desert guarantees the rights of the individual precisely against the collective benefit. It is individualistic insofar as it makes the rights of the individual central. But this is certainly not the case in the statement of the subject cited above. There society has priority, and the sick woman can be

helped to the degree to which she is useful to society. Thus it
is not a question of guaranteed claims of desert but rather of
conditional, limited concessions on the basis of usefulness to
society. That is almost the opposite of individualistic rights!

Perhaps we can say in summary that the attempt to accord
a special status to the justice thematic within the total domain
of morality on the basis of the notion that justice operations
constitute the hard core of stage models is not convincing. The
justice thematic is itself too "soft," and the proposed "justice
operations" apparently capture only a fraction of the arguments used by the experimental subjects.

Peculiarities of the Habermasian Concept of Value

In Kohlberg's work, contents are dealt with quite cursorily. As
we have seen, this has led to the identification of morality with
justice and to some theoretical misconceptions that need to be
resolved. In Kohlberg, however, "aversion" to content has not
led to the elimination of essential content aspects. With Habermas it is a completely different matter: In the attempt to
"liberate" structural moral theory from "mere content," Habermas excludes even those contents without which the universal core domain of morality cannot be constructed. This will
be demonstrated through a discussion of Habermas's concept
of value.

Diverging from, and in fact in almost diametrical opposition
to the conceptualization that has been dominant in sociology
since Weber and Parsons, Habermas defines values in such a
way that they are logically connected with particularity (Habermas, 1983, p. 118; Habermas, 1984, pp. 250ff.) Value postulates are not subject to any universal validity claims and thus
ultimately we can choose them as we choose among makes of
automobiles (cf. Habermas, 1983, p. 141). As he conceives it,
"the pluralism of value contents has nothing to do with the
differences among the aspects of validity under which questions of truth, justice, and taste can be differentiated out and
rationally dealt with as such" (Habermas, 1984, p. 250). According to Habermas, only their "rational treatment" results in
structural learning, not, however, our activities in the domain

of "particular values" such as "wealth, power, health, and the like" (ibid.). Fortunately Habermas has applied his conception in at least one case, so that we are not left simply to infer its implications. Habermas comments as follows on a critical remark of Weber's on the problem of euthanasia in medical treatment: Medical care, "as the practice of healing, is directed to a specific value content—the health of patients. . . . Empirically this value is almost universally accepted; nevertheless, it is a matter of a particular pattern of values that is by no means internally connected with one of the universal validity claims" (ibid., pp. 252–253).

In reading statements like this, the moral researcher schooled in Kohlberg is immediately taken aback, because the problem of euthanasia is a focal theme of one of Kohlberg's dilemmas, one that is taken very seriously by research subjects, especially postconventional ones. Certainly we cannot demand of ethical theories that they have a ready-made solution to every moral conflict, but we may expect them to permit adequate recognition and reconstruction of the seriousness of the conflict. It is just that which Habermas's theory, with its remarkable concept of value, cannot do. If health is merely a particular pattern of values not connected with validity claims in which structures are embodied, then in the euthanasia dilemma we are dealing only with a pseudo-conflict that is historically and culturally determined. It is precisely the respondents on the postconventional level who would, under this supposition, be in the best position to see that here one can—as Habermas puts it—choose as one chooses among makes of automobiles. But such a view would be unacceptable on both moral and empirical grounds: as ethical reasoning it is grossly inadequate, and it is thoroughly incompatible with the research experience of those who have collected and analyzed moral judgment interviews and other such data.

I cannot deal with the background assumptions of Habermas's conception of value in detail here. A few indications must suffice. Habermas constructs his ethical theory as formally as possible, since on the one hand relativistic positions can be most readily justified through appeal to the range of variation of cultural historical "value contents," and since on the other hand he wants to adduce Kohlbergian moral psychology as empirical confirmation of his ethical theory. Kohlberg's work offers the possibility "of deriving the empirical multiplicity of moral conceptions found from a variance of contents as opposed to the universal forms of moral judgment" (Habermas, 1983, p. 128). An ethical theory is "formal" when it can delimit its own object domain through purely formal means of construction. This is precisely what Habermas is trying to achieve with the principle of universalization (Habermas, 1983, chs. 3–4): moral norms are those that can be universalized. If one proceeds in this way—despite sharp warnings from Hart, Gert, and others (see above)—then one has to conceive nonmoral values as particular, since otherwise they would belong to the domain of morality.

Furthermore, if one holds, as Habermas does, the view that universalization is a genuine operation, one must also conceptualize particular values as structure-free "material." For the structuring of this material would lead directly to its universalization. This line of argument, then, makes obligatory the conception of cultural values as merely particular value contents.

On the face of it, this argumentation even finds support in Piaget, whose terminology is adopted by Habermas: "Values do not, of themselves, have 'structure,' except precisely to the extent that certain forms of value, such as moral values, are based on norms" (Piaget, 1970, p. 103; see also Piaget, 1972, pp. 241ff.; 1977, pp. 100ff.). Isn't this exactly what Habermas means? To be sure, in order to understand this sentence by Piaget one has to include the one that follows it: "Value seems, then, to point up a distinct dimension, the dimension of function." In other words, for Piaget values are subjective representations of functions, mere needs, the quintessence of desire. He uses the term "value" to designate the economic concept "utility," which has nothing to do with "validity claims" characteristic of the "cultural values" Habermas speaks of. The latter are called by Piaget "normative values," and are distinguished from the former (i.e., utility values) by means of a normative stabilization. Unfortunately, Habermas does not recognize that Piaget's "simple" values are not his "cultural values," and goes on to devote hundreds of pages to apply to the latter sort of values what Piaget has said about utility.

The result of this very German contribution to ethical theory is simply disastrous. The trivial fundamental conditions of our existence that Hart named require that in addition to moral values (human dignity, the value of the individual), pragmatic values (health, property) also be morally normed. Without them the human form of life would not be thinkable, and for this reason no morality can do without them. That one should not torture others, should not do violence to them, cannot be made comprehensible without recourse to a "particular" value like health. "Do not steal" refers to a material value like wealth. If one were to follow Habermas's conception of value, fundamental moral rules would have to be eliminated from the moral core domain. But to say this is to reject it! If anywhere, it is here that "natural intuitions" are corrupted through "false interpretations." Clearly this is not Habermas's intention, but that is not the point. Theoretical definitions have something of the machinelike functioning that Weber so often evoked: their implications unfold independently of intentions.

Content as Output: Moral Decisions

To this point we have been concerned with the contents that enter into our moral deliberations as inputs; they determine what kind of moral conflict is to be resolved. When we apply the structures of our moral consciousness to these contents, we come eventually to a decision that we then translate into action. This action decision is also covered by the concept of content, because in itself it permits no statement about what stage the subjects belong to. One can do the right thing accidentally or for the wrong reasons.

Nor can we be sure that the structures of a given level of development are "strong" enough to make all moral conflicts unequivocally resolvable: different decisions could be compatible with a single structural level. Not only could this be so, it is so! Consequently, scoring manuals and standardized measuring instruments had to be organized in such a way that stage-specific structures were always embodied in two action decisions (pro or con). Since this was done for all stages, including the postconventional, the impression grew stronger that structural development and decisions in dilemmas had nothing to do with one another—"mere content"!

Kohlberg himself does not adhere to this view—although on the basis of the way his work is operationalized it is a compelling one. The reception of his work, however, has often resulted in action decisions being declared irrelevant (the author confesses himself guilty in this regard). This view, however, cannot stand, as it has devastating theoretical implications. Perhaps these can best be made clear through an analogy: If one transferred into the realm of theoretical knowledge the postulate that the direction (pro or con) of the action decision is irrelevant, the result would be a theory of cognitive development in which it was a matter of indifference whether or not higher stages lead to true statements about reality. No one would be interested in cognitive development if we could not take it for granted that only formal operations can guarantee true knowledge with some degree of certainty.

But it is just this fundamental assumption that is called into question when one qualifies moral decisions as "mere contents" that can take one form or the other, even on the postconventional level. This position is untenable in terms of developmental theory, because it implicitly amounts to a separation of structures from functions. Whether my interests and needs are adequately taken into consideration in a situation of moral conflict is ultimately a question of the result of argument, that is, of a decision. If one decides against mercy killing in the euthanasia dilemma, for example, the interests of the sick woman who is suffering are not taken into consideration in the same way as the interests of those who must be protected against malpractice (and vice-versa). And it does not matter what degree of formal elegance characterizes the arguments with which the decision for or against the parties concerned is reached. Interests and needs diverge and come into conflict because they lead to incompatible results on the level of action, the level of concrete decisions, and for this reason whether a successful coordination of interests has been achieved in the concrete case depends primarily on the content of the decision.

If we may not proceed on the basis that postconventional structures lead to consensus-enabling decisions in a greater number of cases, it is difficult to understand why we should be interested in the structural development of moral consciousness at all. We would not be treated any better or any worse if development stagnated than if it progressed. In that case, however, we would no longer be able to explain how moral development could contribute to a better, more certain fulfillment of the function of morality. Moral development would be theoretically "functionless"; one could do without it altogether. But structures without functions are "meaningless."

The practical implications of this view are completely unacceptable as well. This much should be evident: If developing structures were generally so indifferent with respect to moral decisions, cognitivist developmental psychology would finally have provided the scientific basis for ethical relativism. Higher-level arguments would, of course, be distinguished by their stage level, but we would be able to do whatever we wanted, since a corresponding argument could always be marshaled. Of course this result was not intended by moral researchers, but it would follow inevitably if it proved true that the pro/con direction of moral decisions could be eliminated from developmental theory as "mere content."

Neither Kohlberg nor Habermas has fallen into this trap of an unintended relativism, and as best I can see, both have held steadfastly to their universalistic claims, even with regard to the action decisions themselves. Kohlberg even incorporates the possibility of making unequivocally correct moral decisions into his definition of moral action. A moral action must be subjectively motivated by reasons that are formally acceptable and at the same time "consistent in content with the objectively right choice" (Kohlberg and Candee, 1984, p. 36).

These are strong claims. How can they be reconciled with the apparently completely different logic used to operationalize the construct of moral development (pro and con)? By asserting that only postconventional structures are differentiated enough to make the morally correct decision reliably and on the proper basis. Accordingly, one would expect that postconventional subjects would no longer be distributed equally over the two action options but rather they would select the "correct" alternative in an overwhelming majority. This is the position of Habermas, as well as of Kohlberg and Candee.

What evidence do they have to support this position? Candee conducted a study using dilemmas that concerned Watergate and the trial of Lieutenant Calley (My Lai) (Candee, 1976). He presented his items to "experts" and had them judge which decision or assessment corresponded to philosophically uncontroversial moral norms and hierarchies. This gave him an "objective" standard, and he could then investigate how subjects whose moral consciousness was in different stages of development distributed themselves between correct and incorrect decisions. His results seem to confirm the universalist position: in contrast to the preconventional and conventional subjects, postconventional subjects almost always made the "right" decision. Kohlberg (Kohlberg and Candee, 1984; Kohlberg, 1984, p. 253) reports similar results with the Heinz dilemma and the Joe dilemma.

But he does not report similar results from the other dilemmas. And as impressive as Candee's results are, they do contain divergent data as well: only 54% of the postconventional subjects, for example, considered it right for Ellsberg to have stolen the Pentagon papers. Everyone who has followed the public discussion knows that there are respectable arguments pro and con in the abortion problem. Perhaps the euthanasia dilemma will attain the semblance of unequivocal decidability as the experiences of the Nazi period are forgotten. One can accept or refuse military service on grounds of principle. In these cases the universalistic findings to which Kohlberg and Habermas—very selectively—appeal can certainly not be reproduced; and if they could, one would search for an explanation in currents of public opinion rather than in the nature of structural learning.

Thus the state of the data is completely mixed, and that is the decisive point. There is a third position lying between universalism and relativism: the position of a qualified universalism advanced here. It assumes that there are clearly decidable moral questions, but also moral gray areas in which more than one decision possibility must be admitted. The operationalization of Kohlberg's theory has led to the center, or at least into the neighborhood, of such gray areas, and this is why the opinions even of postconventional subjects are divided in the corresponding dilemmas. To conclude from this that the direction of a decision, the so-called "mere content," has little relevance for structuralist theory, is just as much of an overgeneralization as the assumption that structures unequivocally determine the decision, at least on the postconventional level.

The universalistic and relativistic exaggerations that have crept in are due to the circumstance that the logic of the theory's operationalizations was inadequately integrated into theory formation. The dilemmas touch on, or are located in the middle of, moral gray areas because they are so constructed that undisputed moral norms come into conflict with one another. Where no unequivocal hierarchies (Heinz dilemma: life has priority over property) are in evidence, or where subjects do not yet possess the structures to construct them, they are in the position of Buridan's ass: they can vote for this haystack or that one. It would be extremely surprising if such cases did not appear, since otherwise one would have to presuppose that norms of equivalent status could in principle not come into conflict. Why should we be able to count on that kind of preestablished harmony?

In fact, the brilliance and fruitfulness of the Kohlbergian operationalizations derive precisely from the fact that gray areas (varying from stage to stage) are touched upon. Only in this way can the experimental subjects be stimulated to use their argumentation potential to the fullest. Refusal of military service, the cremation of widows, euthanasia, and abortion are themes that prove effective in interviews with postconventional subjects precisely because in these dilemmas it is not completely certain, even for those subjects, whether it is really possible to select one of the decision possibilities rather than the other on convincing grounds.

Difficult decisions are thus definitely advantageous. If one simply had a norm from the moral core domain conflict with a nonmoral interest, not enough variance would result, since arguments on lower moral levels are already sufficient to reconstruct the meaning of the elementary universal rules.

Breaking a promise leads to the loss of trust, and that is sufficient reason to keep promises. Where is the need for a post-conventional argument?

Kohlberg's dilemmas are "difficult" because truly indisputable norms from the moral core domain conflict in them. In practice it does not happen that a subject feels obliged to reflect on whether "you should not kill, lie, or steal" are moral norms that should be respected. Rather, subjects always find themselves occupied with a pure problem of application: should I maintain Norm A if I have to sacrifice Norm B for it; or should I maintain Norm B if in doing so Norm A is violated? Application problems of this kind can be open—the findings accumulated in the Kohlberg tradition attest to this—but they do not have to be so (indisputable formation of hierarchies, as in "Heinz"). Kohlberg's reluctance to moderate his strict universalistic claims is probably related to the fact that he has had to put himself into a paradoxical position to defend universalism. In order to reach the universal structures without which universalizable decisions cannot even be conceived, he had to design his measuring instrument in such a way that it included moral gray areas. This was certainly not intentional, for now results appear that the relativists can use for their own purposes, since they assiduously overlook the fact that we can also construct moral measurement operations in such a way that most people agree.

Habermas is able to hold to his unqualified universalism without problems because he ignores, and has to ignore, the strategy through which Kohlbergian moral research is operationalized. He is trying to create backing for moral psychology through discourse ethics and vice-versa. Discourse ethics, however, certainly is unsuited of itself to contribute anything substantial to the analysis of the logic of Kohlberg's dilemmas. As Habermas says,

With the principle of discourse ethics it is the same as with other principles: the principle cannot settle the problems of its own application. The application of rules requires a practical wisdom that is prior to the practical reason expounded in discourse ethics. (Habermas, 1983, p. 114)

If this is accurate, however, we can be sure that discourse ethics can be of only very limited usefulness in the theoretical interpretation of the data produced by the Kohlberg research. To assert anything else indicates just a superficial grasp of the research practice. For application problems, almost exclusively, are the object of research in the psychology of moral development, and perhaps that should be noted unequivocally.

In closing, let me add only this. In this section we have seen that the credo of cognitivist developmental psychology, whereby only structures develop, has led to some confusion in interpreting moral decisions. Conceived as mere content, the decision itself had to fall into the vortex of relativism. Kohlberg and Habermas have resisted this, although at the price of a blanket universalism. This was able to creep in only because the dilemma content was largely neglected in theorizing. If we consider this analysis in conjunction with our analysis of input contents, do we not have reason enough to pay more attention to the apparently so peripheral contents?[5]

Notes

1. According to Piaget, in formal-operational thought the mental actions present at earlier stages of thought become combined into a single system. This system comprises a set of transformations that, because of their initial letters, are known collectively as the INRC group: the Identity transformation, Negation (or inversion), Reciprocity, and Correlativity. Piaget calls these transformations "propositional operations," and explains them through reference to the logic of algebra. [Translator's note: cf. *Logic and Psychology* (Piaget, 1957, pp. 23–37, esp. p. 33).] The best account of Piaget's theory of the INRC group, whose transformations can have different concrete realizations, is still that found in Flavell (1963, pp. 215ff.). Flavell summarizes Piaget's analysis of a *physical* realization of the group, from which the reader may infer what type of analysis would fit the *moral* INRC group.

2. As the terminology suggests, what I have in mind here is systems theoretic research, especially that done within a Piagetian framework (see n. 1). The reconstruction of object constancies seems to me to be an important research frontier, albeit one neglected by Piaget himself. Cf. Flavell (1963).

3. For the sake of simplicity I am abstracting here from the fact that one's role-taking ability also develops and thus involves operational learning.

4. I conclude from their contributions to this volume that they have at least begun to tire. Fine!

5. I am indebted to W. Edelstein, G. Nunner-Winkler, W. Lempert, A. Blasi, and E. Tugendhat for their critical comments on this essay; I bear the sole responsibility for its faults. I have also to thank the translator of this article, Shierry Weber Nicholsen, for her sensibility in turning my terrible teutonic scientific language into readable English. Finally, Tom Wren has to be celebrated for the editorial energy which he expended on the formidable task of bringing this essay into its present form.

References

Aristotle. (1941). *Nicomachean ethics.* In R. McKeon (Ed.), *The basic works of Aristotle* (W. D. Ross, Trans.). New York: Random House.

Broughton, J. M. (1978). The development of concepts of self, mind, reality, and knowledge. In W. Damon (Ed.), *New directions for child development. Vol. 1: Social cognition.* San Francisco: Jossey-Bass.

Candee, D. (1976). Structure and choice in moral reasoning. *Journal of Personality and Social Psychology*, 34:1293–1301.

Damon, W. (1977). *The social world of the child.* San Francisco: Jossey-Bass.

Döbert, R. (1979). Zur Rolle unterschiedlicher Gerechtigkeitstrukturen in der Entwicklung des moralischen Bewußtseins. In L. Eckensberger (Ed.), *Bericht über den 31. Kongreß der Deutschen Gesellschaft für Psychologie.* Göttingen: Hogrefe.

Döbert, R., and Nunner Winkler, G. (1978). Performanzbestimmende Aspekte des moralischen Bewußtseins. In G. Portele (Ed.), *Sozialisation und Moral.* Weinheim and Basel: Beltz.

Döbert, R., and Nunner-Winkler, G. (1982). Formale und materiale Rollenübernahme. In W. Edelstein and M. Keller (Eds.), *Perspektivität und Interpretation.* Frankfurt: Suhrkamp.

Eckensberger, L. H. (1984). On structure and content in moral development. Unpublished manuscript, University of Saarland, Germany.

Flavell, J. H. (1963). *The developmental psychology of Jean Piaget.* Princeton, NJ: Van Nostrand.

Fowler, J. W. (1981). *Stages of faith: The psychology of human development and the quest for meaning.* San Francisco: Harper and Row.

Gert, B. (1973). *The moral rules: A new rational foundation for morality.* New York: Harper and Row.

Gilligan, C. (1982). *In a different voice: Psychological theory and women's development.* Cambridge, MA: Harvard University Press.

Habermas, J. (1983). *Moralbewußtsein und kommunikatives Handeln.* Frankfurt: Suhrkamp.

Habermas, J. (1984). *The theory of communicative action. Vol. 1: Reason and the rationalization of society* (T. McCarthy, Trans.). Boston: Beacon Press.

Hart, H. L. A. (1961). *The concept of law.* Oxford: Clarendon Press.

Kegan, R. (1982). *The evolving self: Problem and process in human development.* Cambridge, MA: Harvard University Press.

Keller, M. (1984). Rechtfertigungen. Zur Entwicklung praktischer Erklärungen. In W. Edelstein and J. Habermas (Eds.), *Soziale Interaktion und soziales Verstehen.* Frankfurt: Suhrkamp.

Kohlberg, L. (1973). Continuities in childhood and adult moral development revisited. In P. B. Baltes and K. W. Schaie (Eds.), *Life-span developmental psychology: Personality and socialization.* New York: Academic Press.

Kohlberg, L. (1984). *Essays on moral development. Vol. 2: The psychology of moral development.* San Francisco: Harper and Row.

Kohlberg, L., and Candee, D. (1984). The relationship of moral judgment to moral action. In W. M. Kurtines and J. L. Gewirtz (Eds.), *Morality, moral behavior, and moral development.* New York: Wiley Interscience.

Lempert, W. (1985). Forderungen, Fortschritt und Schrittmacher der praktischen Vernunft. *Zeitschrift für Pädagogik,* 31:255–274.

Lind, G. (1978). Wie mißt man moralisches Urteil? Probleme und Möglichkeiten der Messung eines komplexen Konstrukts. In G. Portele (Ed.), *Sozialisation und Moral.* Weinheim and Basel: Beltz.

Loevinger, J. (1966). The meaning and measurement of ego development. *American Psychologist,* 21:195–206.

Loevinger, J. (1976). *Ego development.* San Francisco: Jossey-Bass.

Mikula, G. (Ed.) (1980). *Gerechtigkeit und soziale Interaktion.* Bern: Huber.

Miller, D. L. (1976). *Social justice.* Oxford: Clarendon Press.

Perry, W. G. (1968). *Forms of intellectual and ethical development in the college years.* New York: Holt, Rinehart and Winston.

Piaget, J. (1957). *Logic and psychology.* New York: Basic Books.

Piaget, J. (1970). *Structuralism* (C. Maschler, Ed. and Trans.). New York: Basic Books.

Piaget, J. (1972). *Erkenntnistheorie der Wissenschaften vom Menschen.* Ullstein. (Includes chs. 3–4 of *Tendances principales de la recherche dans les sciences sociales et humaines,* UNESCO [Mouton], 1970.)

Piaget, J. (1977). *Etudes sociologiques.* Geneva: Librairie Droz.

Rawls, J. (1971). *A theory of justice.* Cambridge, MA: Harvard University Press.

Tugendhat, E. (1984). *Probleme der Ethik.* Stuttgart: Reclam.

Moral Relativism and Strict Universalism

Gertrud Nunner-Winkler

This paper does not claim to give any systematic analysis of all philosophical and empirical problems raised by the universalism-relativism controversy. Rather I intend to make use of this opportunity to discuss a few different positions on the continuum between absolute relativism and strict universalism. I will proceed as follows. First, the relativism-universalism continuum will be briefly sketched by denoting a couple of different positions. Then the positions held by Gilligan, Kohlberg, and Habermas will be criticized from the position of a "qualified universalism." Finally, I will add some speculative hypotheses concerning a possible reconstruction of the ontogenetic development of the concept of relativism.

The Relativism-Universalism Continuum

Neither "moral relativism" nor "moral universalism" denotes a clearly defined position. Rather, both labels are used for quite different sets of assumptions. In the following a few of these will be briefly outlined.

Relativistic positions

Moral nihilism
This position denies that there is such a thing as an independent realm of morality. As Skinner puts it: "Nobody acts because he knows or feels his behavior right; he acts because of

the contingencies which have shaped his behavior" (1974, p. 193) or: "A person 'wills' to follow a rule because of the consequences" (ibid., p. 192). In his ideology critique Geiger also identifies norm-following behavior with mere avoidance of sanctions: "'Good' and 'bad' are absolutely imaginary concepts," and "Contradictions between demanded ways of behaving make it difficult for the individual to move about risklessly. But such contradictions are merely factual, they contain no moral value problem. It is only a question of maneuvering in the social milieu" (1962, p. 411). Both authors thus reduce human behavior to one type of action, strategic action, i.e., action guided by a monologic strategy of minimizing risks and costs. Their theories leave no room for actions guided by values that cannot be reduced to interests and factual action consequences.

Moral relativism
In contrast to this complete reduction of all types of human behavior to strategic action, Max Weber explicitly insists on distinguishing regularities of behavior resulting from an orientation to common interests (market behavior) or from an orientation to shared norms or values (norm-oriented behavior). Within the realm of values Weber further differentiates between moral and nonmoral values; however, any contradictions among these are in principle irreconcilable: "Ethics is not the only sphere that counts in this world; besides it, there are other value spheres, whose values only he can realize who takes ethical 'guilt' upon himself" (Weber, 1956, p. 269). There is no rational way to decide whether moral or nonmoral values, or within morality what ethical principles, should have priority: "Even such simple questions as 'Does the end justify the means,' or 'Should nonintended consequences be put up with,' or, lastly, 'How are conflicts between contradictory desirable or binding goals to be solved,' are wholly questions of choice or compromise. There is no (rational or empirical) procedure whatsoever that might generate a decision" (ibid., p. 273). Thus, each individual will have to make his own decision: "Each soul . . . chooses his own fate" (ibid., p. 272).

Two moralities

Gilligan holds an interesting transitional position between relativism and universalism. She accepts neither the cultural relativist's assumption of "endless variation," nor the
universalist's assumption of "unitary moral growth" (1984,
p. 1); instead she advocates an "alternative formulation,"
namely the existence of two primary moral orientations, associated with the male and female sex respectively. Her position
is relativistic insofar as she does "relinquish the comfort of a
single right answer and the clarity of a single road in life"
(ibid., p. 22); it is universalistic insofar as she does accord
justifiable validity to the considerations forwarded by each of
the "two moral voices." Neither of the two moralities present
the full story, both need to be taken together to "provide a
mapping of human experience" (ibid., p. 32).

Each of these three positions is increasingly less relativistic.
In moral nihilism the existence of any moral value is denied.
Moral relativism assumes the coexistence of many different
values, yet denies that there may be a rational procedure of
hierarchically ordering them. The two-moralities approach implies the universalistic assumption of rational justifiability of
moral considerations; however, it denies that morality is a unity,
on the grounds that there are two moral views that cannot be
integrated and that are accorded equal validity, although the
standpoint from which this equal validity is posited remains
unexplicated.

Universalistic positions

Universalistic positions also differ in the range of their claims.
Rational justifiability can be claimed for the procedure used to
generate or examine moral norms, for the moral norms deduced from this procedure, or even for the concrete solutions
produced for specific moral dilemmas.

Kant

Kant proposes the categorical imperative as the moral procedure. This procedure generates two types of structurally different moral duties: perfect duties and imperfect duties.

Perfect duties are negative duties, i.e., duties of omission, such as "Do not kill, steal, lie," whereas imperfect duties are positive duties, i.e., duties of commission that do not prescribe specific acts but only formulate a general maxim to guide action, such as "Practice charity." Negative duties are "perfect" in the sense that they hold at all times and places and with respect to everyone, since they only involve refraining from specific acts; the application of the maxim guiding positive duties, however, needs a specification with respect to time, place, and type of persons toward whom the duty is to be performed. These two types of duties are hierarchically ordered: negative duties enjoy absolute priority over positive duties. Kant also maintains that negative duties have to be followed without exception. Thus, for example, he explicitly states that even if lying to a murderer might have saved a friend's life this is not justifiable, for "truthfulness is a perfect duty valid under all circumstances" (Kant, 1793/1959, p. 205). It thus follows that all moral conflicts have one and only one justifiable solution: negative duties by their very definition (demanding nonaction only) cannot collide since they can simultaneously be fulfilled at all times and places. Therefore a moral conflict can only arise by a collision between a negative and a positive duty. Negative duties, however, enjoy priority and allow for no exceptions. "Two mutually opposing rules cannot be necessary at the same time. . . . It follows, therefore, that a conflict of duties and obligations is inconceivable (*obligationes non colliduntur*)" (Kant, 1797/1965, p. 25). The categorical imperative thus represents a rationally justifiable procedure that allows us not only to generate or examine moral norms but furthermore to specify an unequivocally right solution for all moral conflicts.

Kohlberg

Kohlberg proposes hypothetical reciprocal role-taking as the universally valid procedure for deciding in moral conflicts. This procedure ("moral musical chairs," as he calls it) is analogous to Rawls's idea of moral decision-making in the original position under the veil of ignorance. It is to ensure the universalizability and impartiality of judgment that Kant had aimed for in his categorical imperative, while at the same time transcending the essentially monologic structure of Kant's moral deliberation process by demanding reciprocal role-taking.

In addition to this formal procedure, Kohlberg postulates a universal hierarchy of values according to content. Contrary to his former assumption of the analytic independence of content and structure of moral decision-making, Kohlberg now maintains "a linkage between stage structure and content choice." Thus more than 75% of the Stage 5 subjects select what he calls the "autonomous choice" in the Heinz dilemma, i.e., to steal the drug or to show lenience toward Heinz from the position of the judge, and, in the Joe dilemma, to refuse to give the money to the father (Kohlberg, Levine, and Hewer, 1983, p. 44). These action choices "empirically agreed upon by subjects of Stage 5 represent the more 'just' course of action or solution to the dilemma" (ibid., 1983, p. 46). This idea of a hierarchy of values also appeared in the preliminary edition of Kohlberg's revised scoring manual: "There is a hierarchy of rights and values. Stealing is justified as serving a universal right to or value of life which is prior to laws. This hierarchy is not just one recognized by society or religion, but a judgment of hierarchy rational individuals would make based on logic (i.e., property values presuppose the value of life)" (Colby, Gibbs, and Kohlberg, 1979, p. 80).[1]

Thus for Kohlberg, universal justifiability refers not only to a moral procedure but also to specific content values, and thus to specifiable solutions of moral dilemmas.

Habermas

Attempting to present the truly intersubjective nature of morality, Habermas substitutes the real ethical discourse procedure for Rawls's and Kohlberg's hypothetical role-taking. Constitutive for morality, according to Habermas, is a universalizing principle: "Every valid norm has to satisfy the condition that the consequences and side effects that its universal observance will in all probability entail for the satisfaction of the interests of each individual are freely acceptable to all involved" (Habermas, 1983b, p. 131). As reformulated within discourse ethics, this principle reads as follows: "Every valid norm would find the consent of all concerned if they could only participate in the practical discourse" (ibid., p. 132). As a mere formal procedure this rule "prejudges no substantial regulation. All contents, whatever fundamental action norms they may refer to, have to be made dependent upon real discourses. . . . The ethical discourse principle forbids specifying normative contents . . . and stipulating them as ethically valid once and forever" (ibid., p. 133). Despite this utter "relativism" with respect to specific contents (values, norms, principles), the procedure can be expected to result in norms or moral conflict solutions that are universally valid, since in contrast to aesthetic or therapeutic discourses, in the moral discourse "a rationally motivated consensus [is] always reachable in principle (i.e., as long as argumentations are openly exchanged without any time restrictions)" (Habermas, 1983a, p. 115). The procedure "allows [us] in principle to bring about consensus in moral argumentations" (ibid., p. 76). In fact, it is this criterion of "being in principle rationally decidable, that allows us to separate moral from evaluative questions (questions of the good life, or of self-realization)" (ibid., p. 118).

All three positions share the assumption that rationally motivated consent is achievable with respect to the moral procedure, the moral norms generated by this procedure, and even the solutions produced to settle concrete moral conflicts. However, the last assumption—consent concerning concrete solutions—rests on quite different premises in the three positions just presented. In Kant it follows from a clear hierarchical ordering of structurally defined types of duties and from the premise that exceptions to strict duties are not permissible. In Kohlberg it follows from a hierarchy of values specified by content that is assumed though not proven to be implied by the moral procedure; in Habermas specific moral norms and choices cannot be deduced a priori, but (by the very definition of morality) can be expected always to result from moral discourses. Thus all three positions are nonrelativistic in a strict sense: rational decidability is claimed not only for moral procedures and moral norms but even for concrete solutions to moral conflicts.

Criticism of the Positions Presented

Criticism of Gilligan's two-moralities relativism

Gilligan's position can be criticized on the conceptual and on the empirical level. On the conceptual level it is a question of there either being one or no morality: if validity is to be claimed for two different types of morality, this can only be done from a "meta-" point of view specifying a criterion to judge the adequacy of both moralities. I will not pursue this criticism any further but turn to the empirical validity of Gilligan's claims. Basically Gilligan postulates three aspects of female morality that are neglected in the male "justice approach" as exemplified by Kohlberg's theory of moral development (cf. Nunner-Winkler, 1984):

1. Females are more likely to take concrete situational contingencies into account when making moral judgments while males tend to rigidly follow abstract principles defining rights and duties without giving due consideration to specific circumstances or costs incurred.

2. Females do not feel an "obligation to fulfill an abstract duty but an injunction to respond with care and avoid hurt" (Gilligan, 1984, p. 4). In the classic dichotomies between "reason and compassion, fairness and forgiveness, justice and mercy, . . . thought and feeling" (ibid., p. 12), females always opt for the latter pole.

3. The "female" ethic of care and responsibility corresponds to the experience of the self as "connected," i.e., as part of relationships; the "male" justice orientation on the other hand, is an expression of an autonomous, "individuated" self.

In the following I want to present empirical evidence to counter the first two of these assumptions. The data are taken from a research project conducted by R. Döbert and myself. We made extended in-depth interviews (on adolescent crisis, moral judgment, coping and defense, value orientations, etc.) with 112 male and female subjects between the ages of 14 and 22 years, of different socioeconomic backgrounds. In order to discuss the first claim, namely, that females show more consideration of situational particularities, I want to summarize an argumentation that Döbert and I have elaborated in a different context (Döbert and Nunner-Winkler, 1986). We compared the reactions of males and females to two dilemmas presented: the legitimacy of abortion and the justifiability of draft resistance. In the abortion dilemma twice as many girls as boys (48% vs. 24%) pointed out the costs arising for the woman in case of an unwanted pregnancy (e.g., the mother is too young, she cannot complete her education, her life is in danger); also, the costs or negative consequences ensuing for the unwanted child are much more frequently mentioned by the girls (38% vs. 22%). In the case of draft resistance, however, the results are exactly reversed: Here it is mainly the girls who exclusively focus on abstract moral considerations (e.g., one should not kill, or wars are evil: 63% of the girls vs. 23% of the boys). Most of the boys, on the other hand, in justifying their moral judgment explicitly refer to concrete costs and consequences of both action choices (e.g., military service requires unthinking compliance to an authoritarian hierarchy, alternative service in hospitals or homes for the elderly is strenuous but more meaningful: 59% of the boys vs. 12% of the girls).

Thus our data do confirm Gilligan's claim that females take concrete costs and situational details into account—in the abortion dilemma. However, the fact that the sex-specific ratio of abstract principled arguments to situation-specific considerations is reversed in the case of draft resistance suggests that focusing on concrete details is not a question of sex membership but rather a question of personal involvement (or else moral maturity [cf. Nunner-Winkler, 1984]). Gilligan based her interpretation on a dilemma that women are much more vitally concerned about. Now it could be argued that the consideration of consequences is often a sheerly instrumental sort of cost-benefit calculation. This, however, is not the case in argumentations that combine facts and moral considerations. Also, there is further (albeit indirect) evidence that being an interested party in a conflict need not increase the likelihood that one will use solely instrumental reasoning. Thus in a representative study on attitudes toward abortion (BMJFG, 1981),

it was found that females of childbearing age express significantly more liberal attitudes toward abortion than the average.
This again might be taken just to reflect the nonmoral interests
of those more concerned. That this need not be the case can
be shown by the finding that, on the whole, reactions tended
to be the more liberal the more details of concrete abortion
cases were given. Those subgroups of subjects, however, whose
personal life circumstances are depicted in the case illustrations
do not propose a more lenient solution but react with greater
uncertainty. Thus, for example, divorced females or mothers
of many children would hold back their judgment in case
stories depicting the problematic situation of a divorced woman
or a woman with several children who is pondering an abortion. This result—noted as surprising but left unexplicated by
the authors—might be taken to reflect awareness of the fact
that those concerned always run the risk of being too generous
when it comes to granting themselves excuses. In order to avoid
doing just this they react with uncertainty in situations where
they would otherwise tend to grant an exception to someone
else. In other words, one who is personally concerned more
sensitively perceives the costs involved, costs that an uncon-
cerned, impartial spectator would more readily recognize as
legitimately justifying exceptions.

Now to Gilligan's proposition that females primarily want to
avoid hurting others. We presented the following dilemma to
our subjects: "In India it was traditional to burn the widow
when the husband had died. When the British came to the
country they forbade this tradition. Did the British have the
right to interfere or does each people have the right to live
according to its own traditions?" This dilemma confronts the
duty to respect the integrity of another culture, an abstract
entity, with the responsibility to avoid horrible harm done to
concrete persons. From Gilligan's assumptions one would expect females to speak up clearly for intervention. This expectation, however, is not borne out by the data: 48% of the male
subjects but only 33% of the females advocated British intervention. Females more often than males presented arguments
such as: "One should not change a culture by force; the Indians

must be given time to change by themselves; in the Indian culture death has another meaning; we would not want to have anybody else interfere with our traditions." In contrast the following argument was forwarded quite often by males, but never by a female: "The British had to civilize this underdeveloped country." Females thus seem to focus more on the integrity of the culture than on the integrity of the individual. Now this might be held to agree with Gilligan's third assumption, that females experience themselves as connected selves rather than isolated individuals. Yet in this dilemma perceiving the widow solely as part of a set of social relationships implies accepting horrible harm inflicted on concrete human beings. If in fact the experience of connectedness were the reason for the female plea for nonintervention, it would be obvious that avoiding harm is not the overriding goal. Döbert (1980) has proposed another explanation: females seem to shy away from actively interfering with other people's business. This might be a correlate of sex-specific socialization: while males are more accustomed to imposing their will or what they feel as right on others, females are more trained to refrain from voicing their own opinions so as to be more flexible in adjusting to others.

All in all, these results seem to cast considerable doubt on the empirical validity of Gilligan's claim to two moralities.

Criticism of strict universalism

Strict universalism can be criticized from a position of "qualified universalism" that is based on the following assumption: there is a universal moral procedure—such as Rawls's conception of impartial judgment under the veil of ignorance or Gert's public advocacy—yet consensus cannot be reached on the "right" solution to all moral conflicts.

A very trivial empirical fact lends a first plausibility to this position: the fact, namely, that some dilemmas have remained dilemmas over the ages without ever having found a final solution (e.g., the problem of tyrant assassination). In what follows I will argue that strict universalism is untenable and that "qualified universalism" is as far as one can go in fulfilling universalistic claims. In support of this position I will draw heavily on Gert's explication of morality (see Gert, 1973).

First, the structure of a moral dilemma needs to be explicated. A dilemma arises whenever duties collide. Since negative duties can never collide (omission of actions are possible at all times, all places, and with respect to everybody) it must be a question of a negative duty conflicting with a positive duty. Gert, starting from Kant's original distinction between negative and positive duties, introduces a further differentiation among positive duties: moral ideals (to prevent evil) and utilitarian ideals (to do good). Now true moral dilemmas arise whenever a strict duty conflicts with a moral ideal, so that following a moral rule might be seen to produce more harm than breaking it. Such conflicts are seen as "dilemmas" (rather than as tragic situations) only on the assumption that exceptions to rules are justifiable. This assumption, which Kant denied, is widely accepted today, as is evidenced by Ross's distinction between prima facie and actual duties, by Gert's "except" clause, and by Hare's differentiation between universalizability and generalizability; it will be taken for granted in the following.

If the decision in such dilemmas hinges upon the weighting of differential consequences, universal agreement on the right solution is not to be expected for two reasons: (1) the calculation of costs rests upon uncertain empirical presuppositions; (2) there is no universal hierarchical ordering of the value dimensions used for weighting costs incurred.

1. The estimation of costs of different courses of action involves all the well-known uncertainties and liabilities of social science prognoses. These arise from such practical difficulties as the lack of relevant data or the need to rely completely on purely statistical relationships. But it is also the case that social science forecasting is uncertain in principle, due to the hermeneutic structure of scientific research. As Habermas and others have argued, theories do not simply mirror reality but are themselves socially constituted: what is conceived as "data" depends on the theory pursued, and what is considered a theory worth pursuing depends largely on the paradigm accepted in the scientific community. For the social sciences the

situation is even more complex due to their "double hermeneutic" structure, i.e., the fact that the object of research is
itself symbolically structured and what is believed to be a sci-
entifically validated proposition about reality itself becomes
part of social reality (a self-fulfilling prophecy). Insofar as the
choice of theoretical paradigms is not completely determined
by falsificationism but also reflects preferences of interested
parties, and insofar as social science propositions influence the
very reality they are about, it is plausible to assume that not
even on the level of empirical statements will there necessarily
be unequivocal agreement as to what can be said to hold true.
Thus individuals may not be able to come to a consensus as to
what constitutes the "right" solution to a moral dilemma, simply
because they cannot even agree on the empirical assumptions
presupposed in the conflict. There are many cases of such
empirically based disagreements. To give but one example:
disarmament debates are controversial not because of disagreements concerning the goal (the stabilization of peace) but because of disagreements concerning the means, which are due
to conflicting interpretations of social reality (e.g., does disarmament increase or reduce the risk of war?).

2. Assuming for the sake of the argument that agreement
could be reached on the costs implied by the choice of alternative action courses in a moral dilemma, agreement need not
necessarily be achievable on the weighting of those costs. In
discussing rationality Gert points out that though all rational
men agree on what is evil (what all rational men must desire
to avoid: death, pain, disability, loss of freedom or opportunity,
and loss of pleasure) and what is good (that which no rational
man will avoid without a reason: freedom, opportunity, pleasure, voluntary abilities, health, wealth) (Gert, 1973, p. 47),
rational men need not agree which of two evils is worse or
which of two goods is better. "Rational men, when confronted
with choosing between increasing wealth and increasing knowledge, will not always agree, especially since both wealth and
knowledge have degrees. Thus it is pointless to talk of knowledge being better than wealth, or vice versa. Similarly there
will not be complete agreement among all rational men about

which is worse, pain or loss of freedom. Obviously there are degrees of pain, to escape from which all rational men will choose some loss of freedom. But we cannot expect complete agreement where different kinds of evils are involved. Death is usually the worst evil, for all rational men are prepared to suffer some degree of the other evils in order to avoid death. However, there are degrees of the other evils which result in reason allowing one to choose death" (ibid., p. 50). If this is accepted then it follows "that two people, both rational and both agreeing about all the facts, may advocate different courses of action. This can happen because they may place a different weight on the goods and evils involved. One man may regard a certain amount of loss of freedom as worse than a certain amount of pain, while another man may regard the pain as worse. Reason allows choosing either way. Thus there is not always a best decision" (ibid., p. 51).

Now to apply these considerations to Kohlberg's and Habermas's "strict universalism." As has been pointed out, Kohlberg originally assumed that choice of action and stage of moral development varied independently. A problem arises, however, when he postulates a universal hierarchy of values next to and besides an elaborate definition of a formal procedure for moral decision-making. If the procedure would in fact result in universal agreement on the hierarchical ordering of values, extra identification of specific values would be superfluous. If, on the other hand, the procedure does not result in agreement, there is a contradiction between the two ways of finding the moral solution: going by the procedure or orienting to the value hierarchy. Now, in the Heinz dilemma stealing might well seem the more preferable course of action. As a general rule, however, it is not undisputed that life is and should be accorded unquestioned priority over laws. If it were, Robin Hood's strategy of unlawfully taking from the rich and giving to the starving (or to the poor leading lives of lower quality) should unequivocally be held by all to be the most "just" solution to the problem of social inequality.

Habermas shows how the procedure of moral discourse will lead to consensual justification of moral norms. The problem discussed here, namely whether consensus can be reached not only on norms but on specific solutions for concrete moral conflicts as well, i.e., the problem of the application of norms, is one to which Habermas—unjustifiably—accords only minor importance. Even though he acknowledges that the ethical discourse principle cannot control problems of its own application (Habermas, 1983a, p. 114), he does assume—at least in the long run—that no such problems will arise; he assumes that consensual solution is possible for all cases of moral conflicts: "The history of human rights in modern constitutional democracies by many examples proves that the applications of principles, once those are acknowledged, do not vacillate, but take a directed course. . . . In the dimension of judicious application of norms . . . learning processes are possible" (ibid., p. 115). So he claims that "moral questions can in principle be rationally decided upon" (ibid., p. 118), or else that truly moral issues are only those that can be discussed "rationally and with a prospect of consensual solution" (ibid., p. 114). Thus Habermas seems to deny the existence of a realm of moral dispute where consensus may not be reachable.

With this assumption, Habermas—I would maintain—gets caught in a self-contradiction. Despite consensus on the moral procedure and despite consensus on the moral norms, it is possible that consensus may not be reached on the right application of norms in moral dilemmas because of the inability of the participants to agree on the evaluation of the specific consequences of different moral choices—or even on whether the consequences in question do in fact occur. Such evaluations necessarily touch questions of the "good life" that, according to Habermas (1983a, p. 115), do not necessarily lead to consensual solutions since "they can be rationally discussed only within the unproblematic horizon of a historically concrete way of life or individual biography" (ibid., p. 118).

Now if moral conflicts involve the weighting of consequences and such weighting takes place according to the contingencies of individual biographies or social commitments, then it follows that although consensus can be expected for a moral procedure, there may be moral issues where procedure is all that consensus can be expected for; i.e., there may be conflicts whose solutions contain an irreducible residuum of "decisionism."

Appendix: Interview Material Illustrating the Positions Presented

In this paper I have tried briefly to sketch some metaethical positions on the relativism-universalism continuum with respect to moral norms and conflict solutions. These positions are exemplified by the following quotations taken from our interview data on the widow-burning dilemma. As mentioned above, the question posed was: Did the British have the right to interfere (i.e., ban the burning of widows), or should one let each country follow its own customs?

Moral Nihilism:

The British had no right. The Indians can do as they please. (Subject 87)

Moral Relativism:

One should let each country follow its own customs. Civilizing other countries does not guarantee that all aspects introduced are necessarily good. One might well maintain that this ban on widow-burning is inhumane. That widow-burning has a deeper meaning for the people concerned than a European might presuppose, that for the woman it is even dreadful not to be burnt with her husband. (Subject 109)

Two Moralities:

On the one hand from the perspective of our social structure the Indians had no right to just burn the women, since these women might well live on without their husbands, especially since in India extended families could well provide for these women. On the other hand, if this is their tradition, the British don't have any right to interfere. (Subject 4)

Moral Universalism, à la Kohlberg:

The British were right to rely on the highest command in our society: Life holds first place. In fact, it was right to protect life, regardless of whether this is the highest command in our society. (Subject 103)

Moral Universalism, à la Habermas:

The British were not right. For the Indians this was no crime; the women perceived this as a kind of divine service. They wanted to live together with the man beyond death. . . . This is a case where people act according to their own rules in common assent . . . what matters is that the victim does participate in the decision and belongs to the group and adheres to the same rules. (Subject 57)

Looking at the stage levels of the subjects quoted, a kind of hierarchical ordering of positions suggests itself. The moral nihilism position is represented by a subject at Stage 2 and it is clearly based on the Stage 2 assumption: "that everybody has his own interests to pursue and that these conflict, so that right is relative (in the concrete individualistic sense)" (Kohlberg, 1976, p. 34). The moral relativism position is expressed by a conventional subject and it is indeed a result of "putting oneself in the other guy's shoes," taking the point of view of the system without taking a point of view outside the specific society from which to judge (ibid.).

While the cultural relativist maintains a conventional stance that each society has its own rules that are likewise "conventionally" justified, that is by the mere fact of their actual institutionalization, the two-moralities approach represents the transition to the postconventional stage: while there already is the intuition that there are valid moral judgments, contradictions cannot yet be integrated into a consistent judgmental structure; the two moral considerations are assigned universally valid truth value and treated as rightfully requiring equal respect, as two equivalent ways of looking at the issue at stake.

Both "universalistic" answers were given by postconventional subjects. They argue for contradictory solutions: one, appealing to life as the highest value, is demanding British interference; the other, appealing to the right of self-determination of those concerned, who may very well not accord highest priority to physical survival, is demanding noninterference. Insofar as both argumentations do claim rationality, their contradictoriness might be seen as further support of the position of "qualified universalism."

Note

1. The final edition of Kohlberg's revised scoring manual (Colby, Kohlberg, and collaborators, 1987) presents a more differentiated discussion of the issue of life, one that does away with the inconsistency, criticized here, that can be found in Kohlberg's earlier writings. Thus Stage 6 reasoning is described there as follows: "Joan is non-relativist but not an absolutist; for instance she does not define the preservation of human life as an absolute in all situations. Rather she has a sense of the features of a moral point of view that she thinks everybody should take to resolve moral dilemmas" (ibid. p. 35). This description seems to be quite similar to the position of a "qualified universalism" that I have proposed here.

References

Bundesministerium für Jugend, Familie und Gesundheit [BMJFG] (1981). *Materialen zum Bericht der Komission zur Auswertung der Erfahrungen mit dem reformierten Art. 218 StGB*. Stuttgart: Kohlhammer.

Colby, A., Gibbs, J., and Kohlberg, L. (1979). *The assessment of moral judgment: Standard form moral judgment scoring. Part 3, Form A*. Harvard University: Center for Moral Education.

Colby, A., Kohlberg, L., and collaborators. (1987). *The measurement of moral judgment. Vol. 1: Theoretical foundations and research validation*. New York: Cambridge University Press.

Döbert, R. (1980). "Was mir am wenigsten weh tut, dafür entscheid ich mich dann auch." Normen, Einsichten und Handeln. *Kursbuch 60*. Berlin: Rotbuch.

Döbert, R., and Nunner-Winkler, G. (1986). Wertwandel und Moral. In H. Bertram (Ed.), *Gesellschaftlicher Zwang und moralische Autonomie*. Frankfurt: Suhrkamp.

Geiger, T. (1962). *Arbeiten zur Soziologie*. Neuwied: Luchterhand.

Gert, B. (1973). *The moral rules: A new rational foundation for morality*. New York: Harper and Row.

Gilligan, C. (1984). New maps of development: New visions of maturity. In *Annual progress in child psychiatry and child development*. New York: Brunner/Mazel.

Habermas, J. (1983a). Diskursethik: Notizen zu einem Begründungsprogramm. *Moralbewußtsein und kommunikatives Handeln*. Frankfurt: Suhrkamp.

Habermas, J. (1983b). Moralbewußtsein und kommunikatives Handeln. In J. Habermas, *Moralbewußtsein und kommunikatives Handeln*. Frankfurt: Suhrkamp.

Kant, I. (1959). Über den Gemeinspruch: Das mag in der Theorie richtig sein, taugt aber nicht für die Praxis. *Kleinere Schriften zur Geschichtsphilosophie, Ethik und Politik*. Hamburg: Felix Meiner Verlag. (Original work published 1793)

Kant, I. (1965). *The metaphysics of morals*. (J. Ladd, Trans.). Indianapolis: Bobbs-Merrill. (Original work published 1797)

Kohlberg, L. (1976). Moral stages and moralization: The cognitive-developmental approach. In T. Lickona (Ed.), *Moral development and behavior: Theory, research, and social issues*. New York: Holt, Rinehart and Winston.

Kohlberg, L., Levine, C., and Hewer, A. (1983). *Moral stages: A current formulation and a response to critics*. Basel: Karger.

Nunner-Winkler, G. (1984). Two moralities? A critical discussion of an ethic of care and responsibility versus an ethic of rights and justice. In W. M. Kurtines and J. L. Gewirtz (Eds.), *Morality, moral behavior and moral development*. New York: Wiley Interscience.

Skinner, B. F. (1974). *About behaviorism*. New York: Random House.

Weber, M. (1956). Der Sinn der "Wertfreiheit" der Sozialwissenschaften. In *Soziologie— Weltgeschichtliche Analysen—Politik*. Stuttgart: Alfred Kröner.

II

Morality and Cognitive Development: Principled Thinking as a Developmental End State

The Study of Moral Development: A Bridge over the "Is-Ought" Gap

Dwight R. Boyd

The study of morality presents a unique problem for interdisciplinary work. It is clear that both psychology and philosophy provide useful perspectives for such an area of study, and it seems clear to me at least that to neglect either is to run the risk of seriously impoverishing (indeed, perhaps invalidating) one's understanding of this aspect of human experience. However, as Blasi (1980) has noted, this need for interdisciplinary work is apparently ignored by the "prevalent view" within (at least) North American psychology. Similarly, I am often astounded at how little inclined philosophers are to acknowledge, let alone test, their often substantial but implicit psychological claims.[1] Perhaps part of the reason for each side's neglect of the other is that acknowledging the necessity of the other says nothing about how the two can be integrated. And *this* is a very difficult question. It is, in short, to raise one variation of the "is-ought" question; any positive claim of integration thus bucks the tide of a strong tradition that would have the activities of either side clearly separated by an impenetrable conceptual border. A developmental view of human morality must, I believe, challenge this tradition, and my paper will explore how a developmental integration of psychology and philosophy can be articulated.[2]

In a previous paper (Boyd, 1986), I approached this problem through an analysis of different ways in which Lawrence Kohlberg's work straddles the border between psychology and philosophy. Kohlberg himself said quite a bit about this issue, and thus his theory and claims offer a convenient entry point. However, my intentions here are less exegetical in nature and more problem-oriented and interpretive. That is, the Ringberg discussions (including the response to my earlier paper) confirmed my belief that we need to face head-on the question of how philosophy and psychology are related to each other in the context of the study of moral development. This stance requires both a clear appreciation of what makes that relationship problematic and an openness to reconceiving what we need to explore in trying to deal with that problem. The generally accepted view of the "is-ought" distinction, I believe, does have something to say for it; i.e., there *is* an essential difference between psychology and philosophy that reflects this conceptual distinction. However, that is not all that can be said. What I am exploring here (through Kohlberg) is what else we can say. That is, I am aiming at an articulation of how psychology and philosophy can be (indeed, must be) seen as *positively* related to each other *given* a certain characterization of a fundamental distinction between "is" and "ought" that I think we need to maintain. The study of morality from the point of view of developmental psychology, I will argue, necessitates a means for moving back and forth across this "is-ought" gap.

The "Is-Ought" Gap—A Statement of the Problem

In order to focus the problem of the relationship between psychology and philosophy, the description of the two can be taken down to the level of basic conceptual orientations. At this level one can then delineate the boundaries of attention and claims that characterize the two theoretical perspectives as normally construed. Thus, psychology is claimed to be (only) descriptive, to deal only with "is" statements about certain aspects of contingent reality; its function is only to describe and explain certain facts, not to prescribe or assess the worth of those facts. By contrast, philosophy (in the context of this paper, *moral* philosophy) is claimed to be (only) concerned with judgments about what ought to be; its function is to clarify and justify normative, prescriptive claims. The relationship between statements of fact and moral judgments, between description and prescription, between describing and evaluating, between explanation and justification—in short (and as a loose way of referring to all of these), between "is" and "ought"—is commonly thought of as a gap across which it is impossible to travel. In philosophy this gap is most often described in logical terms, such as "you cannot derive an 'ought' from an 'is,'" or "no set of factual premises alone can yield a moral (ought) conclusion," with the logical work implied by "derive" and "yield" being interpreted in deductive terms. Since I think that this way of putting it may actually contribute to making the problem unsolvable, I want to avoid such expressions. On the other hand, I also think some sort of "gap" is real and that it is important not to lose sight of this fact. How one expresses this legitimate sense of gap between "is" and "ought" is very important, however, because what one will look for in addressing the problem of how to integrate psychology and philosophy in the study of moral development—indeed, how one even conceives the problem—will ultimately depend on how one conceptualizes the distinction between "is" and "ought." Thus what I want to aim at is an expression of the "is-ought" gap that is as neutral as possible (i.e., one that does not demand a particular kind of logical solution) but also captures what lies behind our intuitive sense that there is indeed a crucial difference between making "ought" claims and making "is" statements.

So what is it that lies behind this intuitive sense? What is it that conceptually motivates our wanting to keep "is" and "ought" separated? Since a "gap" is a metaphor in this context anyway, perhaps it would help to explore the meaning of the metaphor by inflating it. Then one might say that we sense the distinction between "is" and "ought" as the moat that protects the castle of our moral claims from being overrun by the multitude of changeable contingencies. What I am after with this metaphor is not only the notion that our "ought" claims do some kind of work for us that is different from that done in "is" statements, but also that this work is somehow more crucial to our functioning as human persons. The "work" that our "ought" claims do for us is to provide some sort of superior perspective for us both to criticize whatever description of existing conditions is thought to hold true (whatever set of "is" statements one believes) and to apply prescriptive "leverage" to change those conditions in some direction. For the purposes of this paper, the kind of conditions I have in mind are the ways in which human subjects inter*act*, i.e., how people treat each other in their actions, interpreting "acting" here broadly to include the attitude(s) with which one approaches others, as well as what one actually does to or with them. The metaphor of the moat around the castle is then meant to express our sense that this kind of important work that our moral judgments perform for us needs to be set off from what happens to be the case. There are a multitude (perhaps an infinite number?) of possible contingent descriptions of human relations; any number of "is" statements could be true. But what we want from "ought" claims is some guidance on the question of which one(s) we should *strive toward making true*. And in order to do this kind of work for us, "ought" claims cannot be just one of the bunch, indistinguishable from any one of the other multitude of "is" statements; they have to be set apart in some way for them to do their required prescriptive work. This is what is meant by what I take to be a looser but more viable expression of the "is-ought" distinction: namely, "ought" claims are not reducible to "is" statements.

Assuming that all this is not too far off the mark, then what I want to consider is how a developmental theory of moral judgment, such as Kohlberg's, deals with the "is-ought" distinction. A developmental theory is after all a *psychological* theory, and would thus seem to consist of some set of "is" statements. Yet the phenomenon under study is our capacity for making and evaluating "ought" claims, and Kohlberg's theory does not make the common error of trying to study moral judgment as if it were something else. Thus the problem: can a developmental theory both respect the moat *and* bridge it? If so, how? What is the nature of the developmental bridgework that supports some integration of "is" and "ought," of psychology and philosophy, without vitiating the function of the moat?

Some Rejectable Kohlbergian Answers

Since Kohlberg's theory is one of the strongest examples of a developmental account of moral judgment currently existing, and since Kohlberg (1981) expressed challenging intentions with regard to the issue under concern,[3] for heuristic reasons I will explore the above questions initially through an interpretation of the nature of his theoretical position and his claims about it. Some of what Kohlberg said about the "is-ought" problem is rather opaque. As a result, many critics have taken him to task for positions that, I believe, he never really held.[4] In later responses to some criticisms and suggestions from Jürgen Habermas, Kohlberg attempted to clarify his stance, a clarification that involved both emphasizing some earlier claims while rejecting others (or misinterpretations of them) and agreeing with Habermas as to the proper characterization of how he understood the relationship between psychology and philosophy. It is the latter thrust that will be the focus of my attention. However, in order that it not be simplistically misunderstood or reduced to partially correct but incomplete claims, the more positive characterization must be prefaced by a clear account of what Kohlberg was *not* claiming.

The first preliminary point that needs explicit recognition is that, whatever else he may have wanted to say, Kohlberg was not advocating some logically naive move from the fact ("is" statement) that people do change their moral judgment patterns in the order laid out by his stage sequence, to the moral ("ought" claim) conclusion that the identified end point of the sequence, Stage 6, is for this reason alone morally correct or justified. One *might* reach this conclusion from looking at the title of his central paper on this topic: "From Is to Ought: How to Commit the Naturalistic Fallacy and Get Away with It in the Study of Moral Development." However, any coherent and cogent interpretation of that paper must come to grips with the fact that he clearly repudiates just such naive moves:

There are two forms of the naturalistic fallacy I am not committing. The first is that of deriving moral judgments from psychological, cognitive-predictive judgments or pleasure-pain statements, as is done by naturalistic notions of moral judgment. My analysis of moral judgment does not assume that moral judgments are really something else, but insists that they are prescriptive and *sui generis*. The second naturalistic fallacy I am not committing is that of assuming that morality or moral maturity is part of biological human nature or that the biological order is the better. . . .

Science . . . can test whether a philosopher's conception of morality phenomenologically fits the psychological facts. Science cannot go on to justify that conception of morality as what morality ought to be. . . . Moral autonomy is king, and values are different from facts for moral discourse. Science cannot prove or justify a morality, because the rules of scientific discourse are not the rules of moral discourse. (Kohlberg, 1981, pp. 177–178)

When Kohlberg asserts that "moral autonomy is king, and values are different from facts for moral discourse," I take him to be affirming the description of the "is-ought" distinction in much the same way as my description above. There is then, on his view, clearly something across which a bridge needs to be constructed.

On the other hand, the second preliminary point that needs acknowledgment is that Kohlberg did clearly recognize that his theory, *qua developmental theory*, does not give a purely factual account of some phenomenon:

Not only are the moral judgments we score normative judgments, but our theory, upon which our scoring system is based, is itself normative in nature. While we have argued against classifying persons into evaluative "boxes," our scoring procedure does not specify a value-neutral attitude toward the moral judgments of subjects. On the contrary, our method and our theory presuppose a stance toward the greater or lesser moral rationality of the moral judgments being interpreted. Thus, our stage interpretations are not value-neutral, they do imply some normative reference. In this sense our stage theory is basically what Habermas calls a "rational reconstruction" of developmental progress. Our theory is a rational reconstruction because (a) it describes the developmental logic inherent in the development of justice reasoning with the aid of (b) the normative criterion of Stage 6 which is held to be the most adequate (i.e., most reversible) stage of justice reasoning. (Kohlberg, Levine, and Hewer, 1983, pp. 13–14)

The relevant point here for my purposes is that Stage 6 is clearly seen as the "normative" criterion (or "ought" claim) that "aids" or organizes the empirical methodology that aims at explaining moral development.

However, it is also clear that Kohlberg intended to say something about his view of the "is-ought" connection that is more controversial than either of the first two points. This subsequent point he often put in terms of a claimed "isomorphism" between the *theoretical* perspectives of developmental psychology and moral philosophy (Kohlberg, 1981, p. 180). My third preliminary point here is that Kohlberg explicitly rejected any interpretation of this "isomorphism" that reduces it to a claim of "identity":

The isomorphism claim we now renounce states that the normative theory as to the greater adequacy of each stage *is the same thing* as an explanatory theory of why one stage leads to another. (Kohlberg, Levine, and Hewer, 1983, p. 16)

What this move still leaves unclarified is what other interpretation of the "isomorphism" claim Kohlberg still wanted to hold to. This question is the focus of the remainder of the paper.

A Complementary Analysis

In addition to criticizing Kohlberg for sometimes blurring the distinction between psychological accounts of the "is" of moral development and philosophical or "natural" moral reasoning about "ought," Habermas has also offered a more positive interpretation of Kohlberg's intentions. Habermas calls this interpretation the "complementarity thesis," claiming that Kohlberg "rightly insists" on this relationship of psychological and philosophical theories:

This "complementarity thesis" states the case more adequately than the identity thesis does. The success of an empirical theory which can only be true or false may function as a check on the normative validity of hypothetically reconstructed moral intuitions. "The fact that our conception of the moral 'works' empirically is important for its philosophic adequacy." It is in this way that rational reconstructions can be put on trial or "tested," if "test" means an attempt to check whether pieces complementarily fit into the same pattern. In Kohlberg [1981, pp. 177–178], the following is the clearest formulation: "Science, then, can test whether a philosopher's conception of morality phenomenologically fits the psychological facts. Science cannot go on to justify that conception of morality as what morality ought to be." (Habermas, 1983, 266–267)

As Kohlberg subsequently accepted the distinction between the two theses, "identity" vs. "complementarity," and clearly affirmed the complementarity interpretation (Kohlberg, Levine, and Hewer, 1983, p. 16), it is important to try to elaborate more fully the nature of the connection being asserted.

In order to clarify how, within a developmental theory such as Kohlberg's, psychology and philosophy might be "complementary" (or how a psychological account of the "is" of moral development might "complement" a philosophical account of the "ought" of moral judgment, and *vice versa*), it is necessary first to get a clearer picture of the nature of Kohlberg's empirical methodology—why, in short, he refers to his theory (following Habermas) as a "rational reconstruction of developmental progress" (Kohlberg, Levine, and Hewer, 1983, pp. 13–14). Although there are some substantive problems that I cannot go into here, the essential point is that within Kohlberg's approach, empirical data are generated by one person (the interviewer) assuming an "interpretative" or "hermeneutical" stance vis-à-vis another person (the subject)—or at least this is the paradigmatic case underlying the approach. What this means is that the theoretical orientation of the interviewer's task is likened to that of interpretation, which "rests on trying to come to agreement *with* another member of a speech-community who is *expressing his or her belief about something* in the world" (ibid., p. 11). In outlining how this orientation is manifested in his cognitive-structural approach, Kohlberg makes the following points:

The first meaning of cognitive for us is that observations of others are made phenomenologically; i.e., by attempting to take the role of the other, to see things from his or her conscious viewpoint. Second, we mean by cognitive the fact that interviewing and scoring are acts of "interpreting a text" around some shared philosophic categories of meaning. Insofar as each of us has been through the moral stages and has held the viewpoint of each stage, we should be able to put ourselves in the internal framework of a given stage. To understand others, to put oneself in the framework of others, is to be able to generate from their statements other statements that they can or do make from this framework, not because we are imposing upon them a framework to predict future speech acts but rather because we can organize the world as they do; i.e., for the moment we can share their meanings. (Ibid., pp. 11–12)

In order to understand this fully, we need first to uncover an assumption that is left implicit here, but without which Kohlberg's methodology does not get off the ground. This assumption is that the "other" (the respondent in a Kohlbergian interview situation) perceives a problem of "rightness" in one of the dilemma stories—indeed, the *same* problem that is intended by the interviewer—and in his or her response is intending to say something about the solution to that problem. Another way of putting this that I think proves helpful is to utilize Habermas's distinction between the objectivating and performative attitudes. One of the clearest expressions of this distinction that I know of is the following:

Those who observe or believe or intend to bring about "p" take an *objectivating* attitude toward something in the objective world.[5] Those who participate in processes of communication, saying something and understanding what is said—whether this is a perception, belief, or intention stated; a promise, order or declaration made; or a wish, feeling, or mood expressed—have to take a *performative* attitude. This attitude allows for changes between the third person, or objectivating, the second person, or conformative, and the first person, or expressive, attitudes. The performative attitude allows for a *mutual* orientation toward validity claims (such as truth, normative rightness, and sincerity), which are raised with the expectation of a "yes" or "no" reaction (or a quest for further reasons) on the part of the hearer. These claims are designed for critical assessment so that an intersubjective recognition of a particular claim can serve as the basis for a rationally motivated consensus. (Habermas, 1983, p. 255)

In asking such questions as "Should Heinz have stolen the drug?" or "What do you think Heinz should do if it is not his wife dying but a stranger?," the interviewer invites the respondent to adopt a performative attitude toward the problem—to make a validity claim of rightness with regard to Heinz's actions and (more importantly for the purpose of structural assessment) to "redeem" that validity claim by offering the best reasons for it that the respondent can bring to bear.

Assuming the correctness of this analysis, we can see that the point Kohlberg is making in the next to last passage quoted is really about the stance of the interviewer (and scorer) in response to the other's performative response. That is, to some extent the interviewer must also assume the performative attitude. Only by doing so can the interviewer hear and understand what is being offered as a reason by the respondent, and then go on to ask the right "probing questions" constituting a "quest for further reasons" that are understandable and meaningful to the respondent.[6] The interview setting, however, is not completely mutual. No "yes" or "no" response, together with justifying reasons, is expected of the interviewer in response to that of the interviewee; it is only the interviewee who must utter and redeem validity claims of rightness. Indeed, I suspect that an interview transcript revealing that the interviewer was making claims and arguing his or her case with regard to the dilemmas would be thought seriously compromised on psychometric grounds. One cannot help but wonder what would be the outcome of a more completely mutual "interview" methodology, if this is possible. However, that the general claims for the current conception of the stages and their sequence are not vitiated by this problem is suggested very strongly, I believe, by studies of peer dialogue, such as that of Berkowitz, Gibbs, and Broughton (1980). Moreover, it does seem that the interviewer must assume a performative attitude vis-à-vis the respondents sufficiently to "organize the world as they do," to "share their meanings." The stages that result from an analysis of the data so generated are then structural descriptions of the "pattern of connections within the subjects' meaning," or the "set of relations and transformations" (Colby, Kohlberg, and collaborators, 1987, pp. 2–3) of the "shared philosophic categories of meaning" identified as relevant by the end point of the stage sequence, which is itself performatively claimed by the interviewer.

One further point needs to be made about this matter before returning to the central question of how this bears on the "is-ought" question. And that is that the above points do not just apply to the interviewer, but also to one who attempts to "score" the interview. Thus there is something other than an evasion

behind Kohlberg's frequent insistence that an adequate understanding of the stages and the claimed sequence requires the
critic to learn and use his scoring system on some real data.
That is, many unsympathetic critics apparently read only short
stage descriptions and then "reduce" the stages to simple propositions, e.g., something like "Stage 3 is the belief that what
significant others think of you is more important than getting
what you want immediately." Then the sequence claim is reduced to a claim about the logical relationships among these
propositions.[7] But the stages are, rather, ways of looking at the
social world and resolving its perceived conflicts; they are different patterns of reasoning that result from assuming the
performative attitude on certain kinds of questions; they are
postures of knowledge-in-use. To reduce them to differing sets
of propositions is to lose this essential dynamic aspect. It is,
perhaps, to objectify them. Only by engaging the meaning of
subjects' interview responses through the interpretative framework reconstructed by the stages, as operationalized by the
scoring method, does one have an accurate understanding of
Kohlberg's theory. (What one does with the results from the
interviews, subsequently scored, is another matter, however.
The danger, or one of the dangers, at this point can be expressed as taking an objectivating attitude toward the other
"through" the theory, failing to keep in mind that the whole
theory, qua developmental theory, is performatively loaded.)

So how does all this bear on the "is-ought" gap? In what way
does this analysis of the nature of the interview context from
which developmental data are generated help clarify how
psychology and philosophy might be "complementary" in
this context? Actually, in explaining what he means by
"complementarity," Kohlberg first refers back to two earlier
points:

The complementarity thesis to which we still subscribe makes the . . .
claim that an adequate psychological theory of stages and stage movement presupposes a normative theory of justice; first, to define the
domain of justice reasoning and second, to function as one part of
an explanation of stage development. For instance, the normative
theoretical claim that a higher stage is philosophically a better stage

is one necessary part of a psychological explanation of sequential stage movement. (Kohlberg, Levine, and Hewer, 1983, p. 16)

The first point here is a reiteration of the general acknowledgment that any developmental theory does presuppose a normative guiding framework. The second point, I believe, is a more careful statement of what Kohlberg intended to convey in a previous claim about the relationship between a "scientific theory as to why people do move upward from stage to stage" and "a moral theory as to why people should prefer a higher stage to a lower." Previously he had overstated this claim, suggesting that the different theoretical perspectives were "broadly the same" (Kohlberg, 1981, p. 179), which in turn led to Habermas's criticism that Kohlberg was blurring an important distinction (Habermas, 1983, p. 266). The point is, rather, that because the phenomena under study are the patterns of making and redeeming rational validity claims of rightness, part of the psychological account of change from one pattern to the next will involve the subject's construction of the very reasons that convince a philosopher that one pattern is better than another. Both of these points are significant and should not be lost sight of. However, neither by itself, nor both together, gives a full account of the notion of complementarity.

Indeed, in accepting Habermas's characterization of the developmentalist's view of the "is-ought" relationship as one of complementarity, Kohlberg acknowledged more clearly that, in order to give a full psychological explanation of the developmental progress through the stage sequence, the psychologist must adopt a perspective and utilize concepts and truthfulness checks that are "external" to the interpretative stance that facilitates the reconstruction of qualitative changes in how the performative attitude in justice reasoning is manifested. Habermas points out that the psychologist must at this point assume and be restricted to an "objectivating" or "third-person" attitude, one that seeks to explain the data in a way that meets the relevant standards of propositional truth claims (Habermas, 1983, p. 266). In Kohlberg's words,

the psychological theory adds explanatory concepts in its explanation of ontogenesis, such as mechanisms of cognitive conflict, which are not reducible to the concepts of the normative philosophic theory. Thus, the empirical verification of the psychological stage theory does not directly confirm the normative validity of theories of justice. (Kohlberg, Levine, and Hewer, 1983, p. 16)

In short, what this appears to leave room for is exactly the sort of difference between "is" and "ought" that preserves the critical leverage of normative moral judgment. Though an essential move, this in effect makes any further sense of complementarity more difficult to articulate.

So what, then, does the complementarity thesis come down to? There seem to be at least two ways in which it might be given further explanation. One of them, primarily negative, is the interpretation that both Kohlberg and Habermas seem to adopt. Although this way has some plausibility, I believe it also could be interpreted as vitiating the difference between "is" and "ought" that we have just seen reaffirmed in Kohlberg. I will first examine this interpretation, and then briefly suggest a more positive interpretation that looks promising and avoids this problem.

First of all, as we have seen above at the beginning of this section, Habermas states the strength of the complementarity thesis in a negative mode: "The success of an empirical theory which can only be true or false may function as a check on the normative validity of hypothetically reconstructed moral intuitions"; i.e., "rational reconstructions can be put on trial or 'tested.'" This claim is the interpretation that Kohlberg subsequently clearly reaffirmed:

Falsification of the empirical hypotheses of our psychological theory would, we believe, *cast doubt on* the validity of our normative theory of justice. In this sense, psychological findings can provide indirect support or evidence justification for the normative theory, although that theory also still requires philosophic or normative grounding (Kohlberg, Levine, and Hewer, 1983, p. 16, italics added)

The problem here is that neither Kohlberg nor Habermas explains what is meant by phrases such as "function as a check," "put on trial or 'tested,'" or "cast doubt on." There are some senses that would perhaps yield a relatively unproblematic claim. Thus, to put it in Kohlberg's terms, if the "doubt" that is "cast on" one's sense of the rightness of a normative theory of justice is read as just *some* doubt," rather than "*sufficient* doubt to reject," then the relationship suggested seems credible.[8] That is, it would mean simply that one might be reasonably motivated to rethink one's normative position, to examine its justification even more carefully, if empirical data indicated that human subjects showed no indication of developing in that direction, but instead offered at a mature level a form of judgment fundamentally at odds with one's own position. But this would then seem to me to amount to a much weaker relationship between psychological fact and normative "ought" claims than is suggested by "complementarity."

On the other hand, for "sufficient" doubt, the danger is that this negative formation of complementarity runs the risk of cutting the ground out from under the critical leverage that our concept of "ought" supplies. If negative empirical results relevant to some aspect of the psychological theory (such as the failure of a predicted developmental change within specified natural or experimental conditions) were seen as fundamentally threatening to the normative validity of the moral theory, then "ought" claims would lose their unique power. On the sense of the "is-ought" distinction with which I have been working, "ought" claims function to "cast doubt on" the legitimacy or acceptability of the facts of the case, not the other way around. Moreover, although this is a complex question going beyond what I can deal with here, it seems to me that Kohlberg showed little evidence of having his faith shaken in the normative validity of Stage 6, even though the empirical evidence has yet failed to verify its existence, and indeed the upper end of the sequence seems lacking in some cultures (Snarey, 1985). Rather than rejecting the normative position identified as Stage 6, he was more inclined to discuss why certain cultures might be lacking in sufficient social interaction and what might be changed in our educational efforts so that people *would in fact* evidence the approved normative position. But this is not a criticism. Rather, the observation is meant to suggest that Kohlberg did indeed affirm the legitimate function of the normative "ought" and thus that the negative interpretation of the complementarity thesis, if I have understood it correctly, is difficult to maintain.

How might the complementarity thesis be given a more positive interpretation that avoids this problem? What is required, I believe, is that we go back to the interpretative stance of the developmental psychologist outlined above. It seems to me that this stance is not entirely restricted to the attempt to understand from inside the way the other (subject) is determining moral meaning and rightness. Rather, there is a sense in which it must also be extended in the different direction of explanation. That is, as we saw above, in order to generate the data that facilitate the reconstruction of the ontogenesis of justice reasoning, the Kohlbergian interviewer must provisionally adopt the performative attitude along with the subject, to understand from the inside the subject's way of making and justifying "ought" claims of normative rightness in the context of certain kinds of moral problems. However, a simple description of the different patterns of reasoning so determined does not fully constitute a developmental theory such as Kohlberg's; rather, what is also required is an account of how the patterns are hierarchically ordered and why people change from one to the next. Part of this task will involve making predictions about what will happen in a variety of conditions and then utilizing the appropriate scientific methodology to test those predictions for truth, procedures which, as we have already noted above, require restricting one's stance to an "objectivating" or "third-person" stance. However, it does not seem to me that all of this task can be so described; and thus Habermas may have overstated the case when he implies that the psychologist's orientation in this task of explanation is limited to *only* an objectivating attitude concerned with propositional truth alone (Habermas, 1983, p. 266).

The point is this: the developmental psychologist is required not only to "interpret" how a person *is* making and evaluating "ought" claims, but also to "interpret" why persons would *change* their way of making and redeeming "ought" claims and why this change is systematic in a particular direction. Why is there change from *X* to *Y*, say from Stage 3 to Stage 4, and not vice versa? Explaining this kind of change cannot be done solely from an objectivating attitude; to do so would be to give up the unique strength that this theory starts with, namely, the view of the subject as a rational constructive moral agent. A developmental theory such as Kohlberg's is grounded in the assumptions that human beings are potential agents that construct meaningful interpretations of situations, that they make judgments about those interpretations, that these judgments are (at least in part) rationally based, and that action is (in some way) related intimately to this capacity for rational judgment. To assume that developmental change can be explained entirely from within the objectivating attitude would be to repudiate, to step outside of, these central assumptions. It would mean, among other things, that one would have to assume that the reasons why one stage is better than another could not function as part of the explanation for the unidirectionality of change, that the developmental "action" of changing one's way of making and redeeming rightness validity claims is fundamentally different from all other action in that it is totally arational. As this seems an untenable implication, an attempt to articulate some alternative account of developmental explanation seems warranted.

In order to suggest a more positive direction here, I need to back up and call attention to one way I have "fudged" the working description of the "is-ought" gap. That is, I put it in terms of the distinction between, and irreducibility of, "ought" *claims* and "is" *statements*. And in the course of the discussion I found it useful to utilize Habermas's distinction between the performative and objectivating attitudes in order to describe how a developmental theory such as Kohlberg's examines the capacity for "ought" claims of subjects. Since "is" statements are made from within the objectivating attitude, whereas "ought" claims are clearly performative, an implication might seem to be that all psychological consideration of "is" must end up on the objectivating side—and thus any attempt to make psychology and philosophy more complementary stops at this barrier. However, the picture is more complicated than this. One can assume a performative attitude on matters of truth as well as on matters of rightness—on "is" as well as on "ought"—and thus make "is" claims as well as "ought" claims. In the case of most systematic psychological accounts (i.e., theoretical explanations), this is done only on a kind of meta-level, that is, after one has determined what one regards as the psychological "facts" of the matter; then one offers one's account in performative competition with other theoretical accounts (e.g., in published journal articles and interchanges, or in conference discussions such as at Ringberg). Although this is as true for developmental accounts as for any other sort, I want to suggest that it is not the whole picture, that it does not exhaust the performative attitude with regard to truth that must characterize developmental psychology. And it is the rest of the picture, I believe, that opens up a plausible view of how, within developmental psychology, "is" and "ought" must be more complementary.

If it is legitimate to try to capture in question form the developmental concern from within the objectivating attitude, then it might be expressed in something like, "Why does/did *one* change from *X* to *Y*?" What I want to suggest then is that, given the assumptions central to developmental theory noted above, the developmental psychologist must assume mutuality with other subjects as place holder in this question, thus also at the same time asking "Why do/did *I* change from *X* to *Y*?" Thus part of a developmental explanation of change itself requires the psychologist to adopt the performative attitude vis-à-vis the subject-as-other, though now with regard to truth claims rather than rightness claims. What is being performatively offered is what one has "found out" by previous engagements of the objectivating attitude with regard to the change under consideration—including especially the observations one has made on one's own development. But, in addition, we must remember that *X* and *Y* in this truth question of change are not simple states of affairs that can be captured in propositional form; rather, they are coherent patterns of making and redeeming "ought" claims of rightness, themselves generated through an interpretative stance, performatively guided. In other words, the change from *X* to *Y* is also one about which it is appropriate and necessary to make "ought" claims and seek to redeem them. Thus the developmental psychologist must also ask, along with the subject, "Why ought I change from X to Y?" In order to make sense to humans as moral agents, the psychological explanation of moral development must include the performative examination of this question; that is, the truth claim about change cannot be redeemed independently of the "ought" claim about change. Conversely (and this is much more difficult to say), part of the "grounding" of a justified "ought" claim—that is, part of the ongoing task of redeeming an "ought" claim such as the Stage 6 conception of adequate moral judgment—is that it be congruent with a performative examination of the "is" questions of change that account for how such a normative position can be manifested in the moral judgment of humans. Without this part, the "ought" claim ultimately has no grip on us by which it can provide the prescriptive leverage that is its central, distinguishing function.

I am trying to suggest how developmental psychology is in a unique position to effect at least some bridging of the "is-ought" gap. Other forms of the psychological treatment of morality must remain entirely within the domain of the objectivating attitude on propositional truth. Compared to this, the performative attitude on rightness (whether in the ordinary moral judgment of anyone, or in the philosophical reconstruction of such) appears separated more by a chasm than just a gap. What seems to me to characterize developmental psychology is an intermediate step that comprises an unavoidable linking or bridging of "is" claims and "ought" claims through the assumption of the performative attitude with regard to the different kinds of questions that must be asked of the human subject experiencing moral development. "Ought" claims and "is" statements are not reducible to each other, but they may in this way be seen to complement each other.

Concluding Remarks

It seems to me that further exploration of the ideas outlined above, in particular how the performative attitude is necessitated in different ways in the methodology of developmental psychology and how this attitude is integrated with that of the objectivating attitude, is warranted as one approach to understanding the relationship between psychology and philosophy in a way that is positive but also respects the legitimate function of the "is-ought" gap. However, even if this approach runs into problems (or until it is more fully worked out), what comes out of this attempt is a general point that we must not lose sight of. This general point is that the intellectual stance of the developmental psychologist requires a kind of balance that is different from that usually exemplified in disciplines that encounter the "is-ought" issue. That is, this stance requires a simultaneous orientation to two logically distinguishable directions of thought and an acceptance of the need to struggle with how the different perspectives on the human subject achieved by those directions can be made coherent. The tension expressed here is simply a restatement of the problematic of this paper: one direction starts from the assumption that humans are just another part of the contingent world, and extends toward making more comprehensive, systematic, and truthful accounts of and explanations for that embeddedness; the other direction starts from the assumption that humans are different from the rest of the world in their capacity to intentionally change the world (including themselves) for better or worse, and extends toward making more coherent, integrative, and morally convincing visions of what should be done in that transcendence. The problem is that both of these perspectives are applicable to the same entity; yet they are clearly irreducible and both necessary.

As I noted in the introduction to this paper, the common response to this problem is to adopt one of the two perspectives and maintain a blindness to what might be required from the other. Thus we have whole "schools" of psychological theory that ignore the conscious intentionality of human thought and experience; similarly, most philosophical accounts of good moral argument ignore the psychological dimensions of a preferred conception of moral correctness. This tendency to go in one direction at the expense of the other was also, I believe, evidenced in some of our discussions at Ringberg. Perhaps the best example occurred in our more freewheeling "summary discussion" at the end of the formal papers. With the support of the rest of the participants, this discussion was shaped initially by Tugendhat's question, "What is developmental research important for?," i.e., "What questions do we have as adults that it might be important for?" Very shortly into the discussion, this question was focused even more to what Tugendhat apparently thought to be the real issue here, namely, how developmental research that yields facts of psychological development can be relevant to moral argumentation, to our claims of what is morally right. Most of the ensuing discussion was then limited by this way of posing the issue: the onus was clearly on the side of trying to show how any kind of psychological fact could possibly be relevant to—in the sense of contribute to—our judgment of what ought to be. The gap was thus firmly established from the philosophical direction, and most attempts to leap it were quite easily defeated.

Now I certainly do not want to imply here that this formulation of the issue is completely wrong. On the contrary, as I acknowledge at the beginning of this paper, it represents a clear statement of what constitutes an important distinction between "is" and "ought." However, what I do want to claim is that one cannot ask only this question and expect to get a balanced appraisal of how psychology and philosophy can be integrated in the study of morality. Rather, in addition to this question, one must also ask questions across the gap from the psychological side. Philosophically articulated conceptions of moral justification do not just fall out of the sky, given and convincing in their complete form to anyone who thinks a little about the matter. Instead, they are offered for our rational consideration by real persons who not only have their own personal history of development, but who also cannot avoid making empirical assumptions about what humans are like and what it is possible for them to be like, in their very conceptions of justification. Thus, surely we also have to ask some question like "What is the relevance of the (or this particular) philosophical conception of good moral argument for how we do in fact decide what is right? and for how we learn how to decide what is right in more adequate ways?" Indeed, not only must we ask both kinds of questions, but we must also aim at asking both in such a way that their answers start making sense together. Developmental psychology is, I believe, in a unique position to do this. It has so far been fairly successful in opening up our consideration of the philosophical dimension of developing moral agents, captured quite nicely, I would suggest, in Kohlberg's phrase, "the child as moral philosopher." What is needed now, as evidenced in the Ringberg discussions, is more consideration of what balances this orientation in the developmental stance: we need also to think of "the moral philosopher as developed and reconstructed child." Placing the real human moral subject at the center of our attention in this dual way necessitates that psychology and philosophy complement each other across the experienced "is-ought" gap.

Notes

1. A good example of this might be John Wilson's claims about how our moral capacity can be divided up into conceptually discrete parts *and* that this facilitates moral learning. As he put it to me once: moral education is really very simple—just teach the kid the concept of a person and why they should care for him, and that's all there is to it! For an introduction to his work see Wilson (1973).

2. Since its original presentation at the Ringberg conference (see Introduction), the main ideas and some portions of this paper have appeared in more exegetical form in Boyd (1986, pp. 43–63).

3. As Jürgen Habermas (1983, p. 262) has expressed it, "Kohlberg's declared intentions are at the same time risky and relevant—they challenge anybody who does not mutilate the social scientist or the moral and political philosopher in themselves."

4. See Boyd (1986) for a detailed exegesis of these various claims. For examples of critics who have mistaken positions attributed to Kohlberg, see Aron (1977), Craig (1978), and Benhabib (1982).

5. Actually, this seems a little misleading, since Habermas (1984, p. 238) has clearly acknowledged that one can also take an objectivating attitude toward what he calls, in contrast to the "objective world," the "social world." Also, McCarthy (1985) has raised questions about filling in some of the remaining boxes in this matrix.

6. Note that if I am right about this last point, then one implication (which I have suspected for some time) may be that a rigid "standardizing" of the allowable probing questions in the approved interview is to run a real danger of vitiating the very stance that makes this theory unique. To what extent the nature of the probes and the scoring response to them has avoided this is a problem worthy of more discussion.

7. Robert Halstead (1980) has made a similar point in more general terms, arguing that "propositionalism"—the reduction of knowledge to propositions or systems of propositions—is at the heart of the rigid distinction between psychology and epistemology, or discovery and justification.

8. I am indebted to Andrew Blair for bringing this point to my attention.

References

Aron, I. E. (1977). Moral philosophy and moral education: A critique of Kohlberg's theory. *School Review*, 85:197–217.

Benhabib, S. (1982). The methodological illusions of modern political theory: The case of Rawls and Habermas. *Neue Hefte für Philosophie*, 21:47–74.

Berkowitz, M. W., Gibbs, J. C., and Broughton, J. M. (1980). The relation of moral judgment stage disparity to developmental effects of peer dialogues. *Merrill-Palmer Quarterly*, 24:341–357.

Blasi, A. (1980). Bridging moral cognition and moral action: A critical review of the literature. *Psychological Bulletin*, 88:1–45.

Boyd, D. (1986). The oughts of is: Kohlberg at the interface between moral philosophy and developmental psychology. In S. Modgil and C. Modgil (Eds.), *Lawrence Kohlberg— Consensus and controversy*. London: Falmer Press.

Colby, A., Kohlberg, L., and collaborators. (1987). *The measurement of moral judgment. Vol. 1: Theoretical foundations and research validation*. New York: Cambridge University Press.

Craig, R. P. (1978). Some thoughts on moral growth. *Journal of Thought*, 13:21–27.

Habermas, J. (1983). Interpretive social science vs. hermeneuticism. In N. Haan, R. N. Bellah, P. Rabinow, and W. M. Sullivan (Eds.), *Social science as moral inquiry*. New York: Columbia University Press.

Habermas, J. (1984). *The theory of communicative action. Vol. 1: Reason and the rationalization of society* (T. McCarthy, Trans.). Boston: Beacon Press.

Halstead, R. (1980). The relevance of psychology to educational epistemology. In J. R. Coombs (Ed.), *Philosophy of education: 1979*. Normal, IL: Philosophy of Education Society.

Kohlberg, L. (1981). From Is to Ought: How to commit the naturalistic fallacy and get away with it in the study of moral development. In L. Kohlberg, *Essays on moral development. Vol. 1: The philosophy of moral development*. San Francisco: Harper and Row. (Originally published 1971)

Kohlberg, L., Levine, C., and Hewer, A. (1983). *Moral stages: A current formulation and a response to critics*. Basel: Karger.

McCarthy, T. (1985). Complexity and democracy, or the seducements of systems theory. *New German Critique*, 35:27–54.

Snarey, J. R. (1985). Cross-cultural universality of social-moral development: A critical review of Kohlbergian research. *Psychological Bulletin*, 97:202–232.

Wilson, J. (1973). *A teacher's guide to moral education*. London: Geoffrey Chapman.

The Return of Stage 6: Its Principle and Moral Point of View

Lawrence Kohlberg, Dwight R. Boyd, and Charles Levine

Since 1958, Kohlberg has been struggling to delineate and analyze the structure of a sixth stage of moral reasoning and judgment. His method in this task has been to seek a mutually supportive correspondence between empirical examples of reasoning in response to hypothetical dilemmas and the normative theories of moral philosophers. Examples of the earliest theoretical formulation of Stage 6 were found in the interviews of adolescents. These examples of moral judgment were characterized by a number of interrelated notions: decisions of conscience that seemed to embody a "Kantian" sense of categorical oughtness; a sense of the universality of basic duties; a sense of the intrinsic moral value of certain norms such as the saving of human life and the keeping of promises; and finally, a sense of the "moral law" as higher than the "legal law" when the two are perceived to be in conflict. Further longitudinal study indicated that some of these Stage 6 adolescents developed an awareness that one could view decisions of conscience, even those expressing categorical moral obligations, as subjective and relative, an awareness that was sometimes expressed as a thoroughgoing skepticism. For reasons discussed at some length elsewhere (Kohlberg, 1984, ch. 6) these cases of skepticism were interpreted as problematic phases in the transition from conventional to postconventional forms of moral judgment. The fact, then, that some instances of this early conception of Stage 6 disequilibrated and were vulnerable to extreme relativistic questioning was to Kohlberg an indicator that the original way of formulating Stage 6 needed further philosophical refinement and psychological clarification. The task of this refinement and clarification has been first of all to show how the core idea of the notions used to identify these early examples of Stage 6 was not adequately manifested in existing Stage 5 cases. At the same time the task has also been to reconceptualize the Stage 6 core idea in a way that resolves the problem of consensus seeking in moral deliberation more adequately than the Stage 5 notion of social contract.

As we have implied above and will more fully articulate later, there are deficiencies with Stage 5 reasoning. Hence we are faced with the task of defining Stage 6 as the developmental end point of Kohlberg's stage hierarchy. We see two reasons why this continued effort is logically necessary. First, one requires a clearly articulated conception of a developmental end point in order to identify the data that are to be counted as falling within the domain of morality and moral judgment. Second, the conception of this developmental end point determines the criterion in terms of which one argues that the stage sequence represents an order of increasing adequacy in moral reasoning. We should note that what we are attempting to achieve in this paper is not a philosophically complete argument for our conception of the "best" form of moral reasoning. We are, however, attempting to articulate the psychological basis and the outline of a normative-ethical rationale for a form of reasoning we call Stage 6. Our aim is not to provide a traditional philosophical argument for the Stage 6 position as much as it is to describe this position in such a way as to make its greater adequacy plausible. We believe that the plausibility of a complete and successful argument for this greater adequacy is enhanced by showing how the Stage 6 form of moral judgment utilizes some of the central ideas found within that tradition of contemporary moral philosophy that attempts to explicate the necessary ingredients of what has been called "the moral point of view." As we will seek to show, this notion of the moral point of view operationalizes the principle of respect for persons that, properly interpreted, grounds both the earlier and our current conception of Stage 6.

Our description of Stage 6 begins with a general discussion of morality as a mode of regulating human interaction with the aim of maintaining respect for persons, an attitude that seeks to integrate the concerns for both justice and benevolence. This attitude of respect for persons is then shown to take a principled form at Stage 6, one that entails the seeking of consensus through dialogue and is constituted by a set of cognitive operations. We identify these operations as "sympathy," "ideal reciprocal role-taking," and "universalizability," and we explicate these operations in the order listed to show how they are coordinated in the form of Stage 6 principled thinking. Throughout our discussion we illustrate points with material drawn from recent moral judgment interviews with two persons, neither of whom are part of Kohlberg's original longitudinal sample. This material does however exemplify some of the essential aspects of the form of thought we identify as Stage 6. Then with the use of some examples that *are* drawn from Kohlberg's longitudinal data, the paper concludes with a brief discussion of some of the ways we understand Stage 5 to be inadequate compared to Stage 6.

Respect for Persons as Both Justice and Benevolence

The core idea that has always been the integrating factor in Kohlberg's conception of Stage 6 is that of respect for persons. In the past, discussions of the idea of respect for persons have focused primarily on a conception of justice as an essential part of this idea. Thus these discussions have emphasized the components of Stage 6 that are appropriately articulated in terms of such notions as rights, reciprocity, and equality. As Boyd (1980) has pointed out, however, an equally essential part of the idea of respect for persons is oriented toward some notion of benevolence, or "active sympathy" for others. Thus we begin our discussion of Stage 6 with our understanding of respect for persons as necessitating the awareness that justice and benevolence concerns are both necessary dimensions of moral relationships and that a coordination of these concerns must be sought in resolving moral problems.

There are problems of language here and throughout the remainder of the paper, problems that interact with our substantive concerns. One problem is that "respect for persons" can be interpreted as both an attitude, a dispositional intention to *regard* others in a certain way, or as a principle, the purpose of which is to actualize the intention, i.e., to make this intention *work* through a flexible set of actions and operations of thought. Another problem is that both of the components of respect for persons—benevolence and justice—can themselves be interpreted as either attitudes or principles. And this is further complicated by the linguistic imbalance of the fact that we have two words to use for the former; i.e., "benevolence" is normally used to refer to the attitude (or disposition, trait, virtue, etc.), whereas "beneficence" is used for the *principle* of doing good for others (see Frankena, 1973, p. 64). But in the case of justice we have only one word to serve both functions (though "fairness" *might* be offered as the attitudinal expression of the principle of justice). In this paper we are concerned to show how Stage 6 is anchored in the attitude of respect for persons and then how it takes a principled form utilizing dialogue and the moral point of view in seeking to maintain and operationalize this basic attitude. Thus we choose to use the term "benevolence" (as opposed to "beneficence"), together with the unusual expression of an "attitude of justice," in order to focus initial attention on the attitudinal foundation of respect for persons, while also seeking to show how these two are coordinated in the Stage 6 principle of respect for persons.

This dual concern for both benevolence and justice within the notion of respect for persons can be seen in the understanding of moral problems exemplified in the interviews of two respondents that we are using as illustrations of Stage 6 reasoning. For example, when asked "What is the problem in the Heinz Dilemma?" (which asks whether a husband should steal an expensive drug to save his wife), "Judge D." says:

There is more than a single conflict. There is the obvious one for Heinz: the conflict between doing something to help his wife versus whether he should break the law. There must be a conflict on the part of the druggist as well: between his compassion for Heinz and his wife and his own selfish desire to make money. There is also a conflict on the part of the lenders: between their awareness of the problem of Heinz and his wife and their unwillingness to lend Heinz the $1,000 (all the money) he needs.

Judge D. sees more than a single kind of conflict. The first kind of conflict he sees is what we would call a justice conflict, i.e., Heinz's conflict between helping by saving his wife's life, and breaking the law. The respondent considers the conflict that each actor in the dilemma faces or experiences as moral, not just Heinz's conflict. In addition, Judge D. says that for the druggist there is a conflict between compassion for the needs of Heinz and his wife and his own desire to make money. There is a similar conflict for Judge D. in his perception of the dilemma faced by the money lenders. In these two statements Judge D. identifies the actors' realization that persons feel an urge to help others, a disposition we are calling benevolence, which Judge D. sees as implied by the notion of respect for the dignity of human beings. He states that Heinz should steal the drug because:

She's desperately ill and others won't give it to her. . . . She's a human being and I'd do everything I could to help her. Since she's my wife it's doubly my duty and obligation. . . . Her life can be saved and she could be restored to the dignity of a human being and that justifies doing whatever I can to do that.

"Should Heinz steal the drug for a stranger?"

If it were a stranger, I would give the same response because I have the conviction that people ought to save others' lives if they can, because of the dignity of human beings . . . without life you don't have dignity to save or respect.

Another respondent, "Joan," whose reasoning we have identified as an example of Stage 6, sees the problem in the Heinz dilemma in a very similar way. She states:

The problem for Heinz seems to be that his wife is dying and that he's caught between obeying societal law of not stealing and committing a crime that would result in saving his wife's life. I would like to think that there's a conflict for the druggist as well in that the druggist has a desire to make a profit, and assuming it's a capitalistic society, doing all those things that are a part of that. But at the same time, I would like to think there is a conflict for him too—of the fact that his desire to make money and fulfill his own desires are done at the expense of another person.

Just like Judge D., Joan sees each person in the dilemma as having conflicts. For example, the conflict for the druggist, as she articulates it, is a conflict in which the considerations of justice and benevolence are fused, i.e., he wants to fulfill his own desires at the expense of another person. In addition, like Judge D., she resolves Heinz's conflict with an appeal to the idea of respect for persons. She states:

I think, just by virtue of being a member of the human race, Heinz has an obligation, a duty to protect other people (I guess that's a way to put it). I think that the protection of human life is more important.

"Why is life important?"

I think just basically because we're alive. That there are certain responsibilities implied just by the act of being a living, autonomous creature.

"If Heinz doesn't love his wife, should he steal the drug for her?"

I don't think that he should steal it out of a sense of love. I think that Heinz should steal the drug, if it comes down to that far-reaching point, out of a sense of responsibility to preserve life.

"And what does responsibility mean to you?"

I think responsibility, as I'm using it here, means a recognition of dignity, integrity on the part of every, well, I would say every living being, but I could narrow it down, if you like, to persons. And responsibility, I think, is really something that's entailed by that recognition. If I respect you, then I respect you as a creature with dignity and integrity and your own unique, I don't know, special being.

The idea of respect, for Joan, not only includes avoidance of violating the rights of another person in a negative sense, but also includes a sense of positive responsibility for the needs and welfare of another person. In continuing to explain her idea of respect for persons, Joan states:

In recognizing that I won't intrude on you, I won't purposefully harm you—there's this whole series of negatives that go along with

being responsible and there's also some positives. And that's to recognize you as being unique, important and integral, in some sense,
and to do what I can to preserve all that.

From a Stage 6 standpoint the autonomous moral actor has
to consciously coordinate the two attitudes of justice and benevolence in dealing with real moral problems in order to
maintain respect for persons. The way of regarding the other
that we are calling benevolence views the other and human
interaction through the lens of intending to promote good and
prevent harm to the other. It is an attitude that presupposes
and expresses one's identification and empathic connection
with others, or as Joan says, "is part of the responsibility of
being a member of the human race." Thus, as a mode of
interaction between self and others that manifests a Stage 6
conception of respect for persons, benevolence is logically and
psychologically prior to what we are calling justice. On the
other hand, justice views the other and human interaction
through the lens of intending to adjudicate interests, that is,
of intending to resolve conflicts of differing and incompatible
claims among individuals. Given this adjudicatory lens, justice
presupposes a momentary separation of individual wills and
cognitively organizes this separation in the service of achieving
a fair adjudication through a recognition of equality and reciprocal role-taking. Thus, these two attitudes of benevolence and
justice may be experienced in potential tension with each other.
This tension is expressed by Judge D. in the framing of his
initial response to the Heinz dilemma. He states:

There is more than a single conflict. There is the obvious one for
Heinz: the conflict between doing something to help his wife versus
whether he should break the law.

We wish to emphasize that although these two attitudes are in
tension with each other, they are at the same time mutually
supportive and coordinated within a Stage 6 conception of
respect for persons. This coordination can be summarized
thus: benevolence constrains the momentary concern for justice to remain consistent with the promotion of good for all,
while justice constrains benevolence not to be inconsistent with
promoting respect for the rights of individuals conceived as

autonomous agents. In other words, the aim of the autonomous Stage 6 moral agent is to seek resolution of moral problems in such a way that promoting good for some does not fail to respect the rights of others, and respecting the rights of individuals does not fail to seek promotion of the best for all. As Baier (1965, p. 106) has succinctly put it, the moral point of view must evaluate "for the good of everyone alike." We think this coordination is what makes the golden rule so compelling and timeless. That is, in its positive interpretation, "Do unto others as you would have them do unto you," it expresses the attitude of benevolence, as elaborated in the Christian maxim of "Love your neighbor as yourself." On the other hand, in its proscriptive interpretation, "Do not do unto others as you would not wish others to do unto you," it expresses the attitude of justice as respecting and not interfering with the rights and autonomy of others.

The Role of Principles and Dialogue at Stage 6

Although respect for persons is an idea that can be and is expressed in moral judgments at earlier stages, its expression takes a principled form at Stage 6. As we have utilized this notion in previous discussions (Kohlberg, 1981, ch. 5; Boyd, 1978, 1984), a principle is a generalized prescriptive proposition that guides individuals in making moral judgments about situations in which there are conflicts between otherwise acceptable rules or norms. The two cases we have just quoted exemplify this understanding by articulating respect for persons as a principle of equal consideration of the dignity or worth of all persons, which, as we can see, they use to guide their specific moral decisions and generalize from one dilemma to another.

We noted above how Joan used the principle of equal respect for the dignity of persons to choose between the rules of preserving life and obeying law in her response to the Heinz dilemma. Below, we can see her employing the same principle in response to the euthanasia dilemma. Although, in this dilemma, the principle leads Joan to a different choice (i.e., in the Heinz dilemma she chooses preserving life whereas in the euthanasia dilemma she favors upholding the right to choose life or death), her response nevertheless indicates her generalized and consistent application of the principle of equal respect for the dignity and integrity of persons.

"Is it important to do everything they can to save *another's* life?"

I think that depends a lot. If I'm walking down the street, yes, I would do anything I could to save somebody else's life. I mean if I saw somebody walking in front of the car, I would jerk that person out of the way of the car. That would be the way I would react automatically. But, in other situations it depends. If you are terminally ill and you have decided that you would prefer rational suicide, or would prefer not to go through any more chemotherapy, any number of those things, I don't feel that I have the right to intrude on that position of yours, to say that you must take this chemotherapy, it's going to extend your life for a week longer, or a month longer or something. I don't see myself doing that, no.

Here Joan differentiates the principle of equal respect for human dignity from the rule of preserving life and generalizes this principle. Thus she concludes that "I'm not saying that preserving life is the essential or ultimate thing. I think that preserving a person's dignity and integrity are the important things."

Judge D. also differentiates the principle of equal respect for human dignity from a rule about preserving life and generalizes it to other dilemmas. This is shown by his response to the lifeboat dilemma. The lifeboat dilemma presents a situation in which there are three people in a boat with almost no chance for survival unless one person goes overboard. The three parties are the captain who best knows how to navigate, a young strong man, and a weak old man with a broken shoulder who cannot row the boat effectively. No one volunteers to go overboard. There appear to be three choices to this dilemma. The first is an extreme utilitarian solution aimed at the greatest chance of saving the most lives. This solution requires the captain to order the old man overboard. The second solution, which might be considered the fairness solution, would be to draw straws to see who goes overboard. The third solution is that no one go overboard, in which case there is a high probability that all will perish. In response to this dilemma, Judge D. says:

I think they actually should have drawn lots. That way, at least, would be consistent with my conviction of the equality of human beings. No life is better than any other and there is no reason in the world why two should take the life of the other. And the reason is just the same I've been referring to all along, that is, the respect for the dignity of human life.

Thus our notion of a principle is exemplified in our two interviews. Both Joan and Judge D. differentiate the principle of respect for human dignity from the rule to preserve life (or even the most lives), generalize this principle across dilemmas, and use it to generate specific choices for resolving dilemmas.

So far we have discussed Stage 6 respect for persons as integrating justice and benevolence and as being articulated in the form of a principle. At Stage 6 there is an additional aspect of respect for persons that consists of a concern for the way in which people with differing views and principles discuss with each other their disagreements. This is the attitude of recognizing the necessity of entering into dialogue in the face of disagreement about what is right. This disposition toward entering dialogue is recognized as necessary because it is only through dialogue that one can actualize the principle of equal respect for persons. That is, dialogue is necessitated as that mode of engaging others that aims at reaching mutually acceptable agreement. It functions then as an interactive expression of the principle of respect for persons, one that is a necessary initial step in assuming the moral point of view and is normatively congruent with the formal characteristics of the moral point of view. What we mean by dialogue is the process by which each person offers his/her best reasons for choices and listens to others' reasons in the mutual endeavor of solving the problem. As Thomas Perry (1976, p. 64) puts it, "in adopting, offering, accepting, and rejecting moral reasons and arguments, we [have] the following objectives: to reach agreement in our autonomous moral views and judgments, and to foster mutual respect even when we fail to reach agreement." In addition to recognizing the necessity of dialogue in this context, Frankena (1973, p. 112) more explicitly connects this necessity to what he and other philosophers call the "moral point of view," the components of which we will subsequently discuss:

Our judgment or principle is really justified if it holds up under sustained scrutiny of this sort from the moral point of view on the part of everyone. Suppose we encounter someone who claims to be doing this but comes to a different conclusion. Then we must do our best, through reconsideration and discussion, to see if one of us is failing to meet the conditions in some way. If we can detect no failing on either side and still disagree, we may and I think still must each claim to be correct, for the conditions never are perfectly fulfilled by both of us and one of us may turn out to be mistaken after all. If what was said about relativism is true, we cannot both be correct. But both of us must be open-minded and tolerant if we are to go on living within the moral institution of life and not resort to force or other immoral or non-moral devices.

This Stage 6 understanding of the principle of respect for persons as aiming at agreement-seeking through dialogue is expressed by Joan in the following way in response to the Heinz dilemma:

As soon as more than one person knows about a situation, O.K., that there's shared conflicts and the conflicts of each person sort of play off one another. And I think that the conflicts can be resolved to some extent by kind of "pooling" that, by (I'm not sure how to say this) . . . So when there's a situation involving more than one person, I think that as soon as more than one person becomes aware of the conflict that there are automatically problems to be resolved by each, things to be considered by each; and each person then has the power to affect what happens in the conflict . . . If I were Heinz I, you know, would keep trying to talk with the druggist . . . I have a hard time thinking of any decisions as being static and it seems to me that dialogue is very important—and a continuing dialogue in this kind of situation.

As we have seen, Judge D. solves the lifeboat dilemma with the principle of respect for persons manifested in the option to draw straws. He does not, however, interpret this principle as necessitating seeking agreement through dialogue. This omission on his part qualifies our identification of Judge D.'s responses as fully exemplifying Stage 6. In contrast, Joan's conception of respect for persons commits her to agreement-seeking through dialogue to the point of maintaining dialogue in the lifeboat situation even though the probability of survival of all under these conditions is severely jeopardized:

"What should the captain do?"

Well, I don't think that the captain should do anything on his own, of course. I think it's a decision that needs to be made by the three people involved.

"How would they go about making that decision—if no one would volunteer to go over—since that's part of the situation?"

Well, I certainly understand that at the moment no one is volunteering to go over. You know, it may be something that needs to be discussed over a long period of time, and thought about by each person individually and discussed more. So it's a cooperative decision. No one has the right to make that decision on his own. I understand all the figures about what would happen, you know, what the chances of survival, etc., are over a three-week period . . . There may be a lot of things that can happen. It could be by the time that one of the three decides to give himself up for the good of the others, that it's two weeks down the line, you know, and there's a chance of survival to some extent. But I don't think that any person has the right to take another person's life or to make that decision. I think that a person on his own has the right to make that decision. But in this kind of situation there has to be a discussion by the three of them.

"Then what should be done? If the decision isn't going to be made, all three will die."

Well, then the three of them are going to have to decide together.

"But they can't come to consensus."

Well, in that situation I guess I have a hard time believing that nobody would make the decision to go overboard and if not, then I guess they all die. I mean the three of them are in the situation together, and it has to be a cooperative decision or nothing.

While we do maintain that the disposition to enter dialogue is a necessary part of the moral point of view, we also would question whether Joan's commitment to agreement-seeking through continuing dialogue to the point of all perishing is the morally correct solution to this dilemma. As we noted earlier, Frankena clearly links the necessity of dialogue to the moral point of view. He is also, however, aware of the fact that dialogue can break down. In such an instance, Frankena argues that the mature moral thinker would not claim an actual consensus, but rather, an "ideal consensus." As he says (1973, pp. 112–113):

The fact that moral judgments claim a consensus on the part of others does not mean that the individual thinker must bow to the judgment of the majority in his society. He is not claiming an actual consensus, he is claiming that in the end—which never comes or comes only on the Day of Judgment—his position will be concurred in by those who freely and clear-headedly review the relevant facts from the moral point of view. In other words, he is claiming an *ideal* consensus that transcends majorities and actual societies. One's society and its code and institutions may be wrong. Here enters the autonomy of the moral agent—he must take the moral point of view and must claim an eventual consensus with others who do so, but he must judge himself. He may be mistaken, but, like Luther, he cannot do otherwise.

The Formal Characteristics of the Moral Point of View of Stage 6

Our discussion thus far indicates that the problems that Stage 6 has to resolve are (1) how to coordinate justice and benevolence in a single decision about what is right, and (2) how to seek an ideal consensus or agreement, when it is realized that agreement cannot be reached in actual dialogue.

To speak to these problems, modern moral philosophers have elaborated the notion of a set of imaginative procedures for choosing principles and interpreting them, ones that give equal consideration to everyone's interests by constructing perspectives from which the relevance of particular factors can be assessed. As James Fishkin (1984, p. 755) has put the matter:

Theories adopting this strategy start with the assumption that our common moral understandings are biased. They are irremediably contaminated by socialization, self-interest and perhaps self-deception. However, we can *imagine* a way of arriving at principles that escapes this contamination. While we do not live in a social world of objective moral notions, such notions may be available to us through thought experiments—hypothetical exercises that permit us to shed enough of our biases to provide a firmer basis for principles of justice.

John Rawls's (1971) conception of adopting the "original position" under the "veil of ignorance" for the purpose of choosing principles is an influential and excellent example of such a thought experiment. Rawls asks his reader to evaluate principles for the basic institutions of society under the condition that they do not know who they are to be; i.e., they do not know their relative position in society, whether they are rich or poor, black or white, male or female, Christian, Buddhist, or Jew. In ignorance of these particular identities one must choose independently of, and without favoring, a particular conception of the good life, i.e., a notion and plan of what makes life intrinsically worthwhile and worth pursuing. Rawls uses his thought experiment to derive two lexically ordered principles of justice for a society—roughly: (1) each person is to have the maximum liberty compatible with the like liberty of others, and (2) no inequalities of goods and respect are justified if they are not to the benefit of the least advantaged and attached to positions equally open to all. Rawls's thought experiment can be interpreted as a variation on, or elaboration of, the Golden Rule; i.e., by not knowing who we are to be we must take the role of, or imagine ourselves to be, any possible member of society, and especially someone in the least advantaged position. Kohlberg (1981, ch. 5) has elaborated an alternative "thought experiment" that requires full knowledge of each person's position and values and involves what he calls the process of ideal reciprocal role-taking, or more whimsically, "moral musical chairs." He then attempted to use his procedure to demonstrate that actual consensus could be reached on particular dilemmas like the lifeboat dilemma, through support of the choice of drawing straws against other alternatives. Such devices may be seen as active processes of thought that attempt to operationalize the intention of respecting persons. Such thought experiments help free the principle of respect for persons from any necessary metaphysical or religious presuppositions. They also help free the reasoner from the strictly deductive "top down" strategy of applying a principle to a case, somewhat characteristic of Judge D.'s reasoning, while at the same time providing a "monologic" interpretation of the principle when dialogue is impossible or has failed to produce agreement. These thought experiments are central to various philosophic writings on the moral point of view and make clearer the psychological "deep structure" or thought operations involved in Stage 6 in a way that is consistent with our notion of structures of reasoning at earlier stages.

We will now proceed to describe the necessary components of the thought experiment that actualizes respect for persons at Stage 6. These components can be understood as cognitive operations that enable the individual moral reasoner to construct solutions imaginatively to dilemmas, solutions that putatively express claim to an ideal consensus even under conditions in which dialogue does not lead to actual agreement. For instance, in the Heinz dilemma, dialogue between Heinz and the druggist does not lead to actual agreement. The problem then is how to maintain mutual respect in the face of this failure to reach consensus. It is at this point that the rational, autonomous moral agent must enter the thought experiment of the moral point of view.

For us, the actor enters into this thought experiment with certain operations of thought: sympathy, ideal reciprocal role-taking, and universalizability.

Sympathy

The operation of thought we are defining as sympathy is the cognitive organization of the attitude of identification and empathic connection with others. We must emphasize once again that this attitude of identification and empathic connection with others is the substantive grounding of the benevolence component of respect for persons. Sympathy is the active interpretation of this empathic connection through at least two interrelated dimensions of social understanding: (1) the understanding of *persons*, and (2) the understanding of general facts of the human condition within which persons exist and interact.

With the phrase "understanding of persons" we mean first that persons are understood as "self-determining agents who pursue objects of interest to themselves" (Downie and Telfer, 1970, pp. 28–29). Further, we mean that what these objects of interest are and how they are pursued by others are understood as derived from and supportive of a life plan actively constructed and reconstructed by persons over time. What characterizes the special quality of the transformation of empathy into sympathy at Stage 6 is first the awareness that what the others' interests are cannot be assumed. This is the case because an awareness of the self-determining nature of the other precludes assuming the validity of one's *own* conception of the actual interests of other persons *a priori*. With the idea of "general facts of the human condition within which persons exist and interact" we mean that sympathy at this stage understands that one's perception of persons and their construction of interests in terms of life plans are not independent of contingencies such as psychological, social, structural, historical, and cultural factors.

Ideal reciprocal role-taking

As our discussion of sympathy spelled out the benevolence dimension of regarding persons, the adjudicatory dimension of respect for persons is interpreted through a particular understanding of adjudication that is aimed ultimately at fairness. As the empathic connection is actively transformed into sympathy by certain knowledge constraints, so, too, is the adjudicatory way of regarding the other actively interpreted through the intention to balance interests. The intent to balance interests enters moral problems seeking a mutually acceptable resolution by attending to the interests of actual persons directly involved in the problematic situation or affected substantively by its resolution.

The intent to balance interests is facilitated through the mental operation of ideal reciprocal role-taking. This process involves *first* taking the perspectives of the other in the problematic situation in question. The perspective of others are taken in order to understand their interests, as expressed in their claims about their interests, and as perceived through a construction of their own autonomous views of the good. *Second*, the intent to balance interests through ideal reciprocal role-taking involves the assumption that relevant others are attempting to do the same thing. With the understanding of the mutuality of this endeavor, the *third* step involves temporarily separating the actual identities of persons from their claims and interests in order to assess what would be the relative merits of those claims and interests from the point of view of any person implicated in the dilemma. While not distinguishing them in the same way we have, Taylor (1978, p. 51) nevertheless recognizes these steps of balancing interests in his discussion of a verification test for what he calls "substantive impartiality," an idea that in his view is integral to the idea of respect for persons:

From these considerations we can derive a kind of verification test for substantive impartiality that, though difficult to carry out in practice, is a way to make clear the underlying idea. This test is applicable whether or not there is a conflict of basic interests among agents. A rule or standard is substantively impartial by this test if and only if it would be acceptable to each agent, were he or she to put him or herself in the place of every other (generally described) agent and judge the norm from *that* agent's standpoint. The judgment of the norm, however, must not be based on the question: If I had the value system of this agent, would my basic interests be furthered by the adoption of this norm? The judgment must, instead, be based on the question: Is the norm fair to others as well as to myself, when I take into account everyone's basic interests (generally described) and give them equal weight with my own? . . . To take the moral point of view is to transcend the particularity of every personal point of view and to look at the situation from a position that considers every individual value system in the same way, disregarding whose value system it happens to be. It is in this sense that the test of putting-oneself-in-the-role-of-another provides a method for deciding whether the condition of substantive impartiality has been met.

This intent to balance interests, carried through with the operation of ideal reciprocal role-taking, provisionally terminates when the self judges a particular claim derived as being reversible. When rational, autonomous moral agents derive what they think is a reversible claim, they have come as close as possible to expressing the orientation that an ideal consensus would take. In other words, by the reversibility of a solution or choice we mean the fact that it would be arrived at from the point of view of anyone in the same situation engaging in these cognitive activities we have been discussing. It is in this sense that reversibility produces the choice required by ideal consensus.

As we have indicated above, Kohlberg (1981) has described this operation of ideal reciprocal role-taking (or "moral musical chairs") as a procedure that aims at ideal consensus, in the context of the Heinz dilemma. In this procedure the person imaginatively takes the role of each other agent in the situation and considers the claims they would make from their own points of view. Thus, for example, such an individual would acknowledge the wife's claim to life and the druggist's claim to property. Then the individual would imagine the agents themselves trading places and considering the claims of each other in a similar way. Thus the wife considers the claims she would make were she the druggist, and the druggist considers the claims he would make were he the wife. Based on this ideally mutual or reciprocal role-taking, which could also be called "multilateral," each would agree that the druggist's claim to property would be relinquished since it was a claim that failed to recognize the wife's claim. When that claim is given full consideration, it is realized that the right to life takes precedence over the druggist's right to property. Thus this imaginative exercise leads to a decision to which even the druggist would agree. It follows, then, that this is a fully reversible moral judgement and that it is morally correct for Heinz to steal the drug.

Universalizability

From our perspective, universalizability is an operation that comes into play once a reversible choice has been constructed with the operations of sympathy and ideal reciprocal role-taking. It is an operation that imaginatively validates the reversible choice in the context of two interrelated dimensions. First, one's description of the situation being judged is projected into the array of an imagined universe of all situations that could be considered similar and of all persons who could be moral actors in these situations. Second, with this universe in mind one commits oneself to consistently accepting the choice in each instance of such circumstances. There are, then, two aspects of this check on consistency that characterize the result of the operation we are calling universalizability. The first is an awareness that in judging *this* to be *right* in *this* circumstance, one is committing oneself not just in this particular instance, but also in all other instances that can be judged to be relevantly similar in nature. This awareness is manifested in the recognition that when two situations calling for moral judgment appear similar, if one is inclined to solve the second differently from the first, then the onus is clearly on providing reasons as to how the two situations are qualitatively different, reasons that successfully emerge from the preceding operations of sympathy and ideal reciprocal role-taking as well as those that resulted in the solution to the first situation. In addition, there is a second aspect of this consistency check within the operation of universalizability that follows directly from how the two preceding operations function. That is, when one seeks to balance sympathetically determined interests through ideal reciprocal role-taking, part of the process, as we have indicated above, is a momentary separation of personal identities from particular interests. The aim is to find a solution that is ideally acceptable from the point of view of anyone. Thus, the operation of universalizability also aims at consistency in that one is willing to say that *others* should judge and act in a way according to the principle that grounds one's own solution to this particular moral problem.

Components of the Moral Point of View in Case Material

Up to this point we have used material from the interviews with Judge D. and Joan to illustrate solving the different moral dilemmas through the principle of respect for persons. In addition, we have shown how this principle includes the general attitudes of both benevolence and justice and seeks to coordinate these in service of resolving the dilemmas. In what follows we will continue to use this case material to examine to what extent the cognitive operations of Stage 6 we have identified above—sympathy, ideal reciprocal role-taking and universalizability—are exemplified in the actual thought processes of Joan.

First of all, as we have interpreted the operation of sympathy, it is not simply some vague empathic connection to others, but it is what Joan calls the "recognition of the dignity and integrity" of others as "unique special beings." Thus it entails an active understanding of the other in terms of his or her *own* interpretation of personal uniqueness.

Second, we have articulated the operation of ideal reciprocal role-taking as manifested in the disposition, in cases when actual dialogue is not successful, to engage in a "thought experiment" aimed at ideal consensus through completely reversible claims. As we have seen in earlier quotations from Joan's interview, her first orientation within each dilemma is to emphasize the necessity of discussion among all the parties involved. At the end of her discussion of the Heinz dilemma, Joan is asked "Is there any one consideration that stands in your mind above all others in making a decision of this sort?" In reply she says:

I would say that there are two things. The first thing is that no person has the right to make a decision that affects the dignity and integrity of another person without there being cooperative discussion among the people involved. Number one. The second thing is that, you know, in this very strange situation where it would come down to being, you know, the single person's decision (and I have trouble conceiving that as ever happening), then it comes down to preserving the dignity and integrity . . . and for the reason of life usually is involved in that, of another person. So I guess I'm saying that, well . . . I'm not saying that preserving life is *the* essential or ultimate thing. I think that preserving a person's dignity and integrity are the important things.

Our interpretation of what she identifies as the "first thing" that stands out in her mind includes two ideas. Part of this is her emphasis on *actual* dialogue. But more important for the point at hand is her notion of *"cooperative discussion"* among the people involved. As we quoted earlier, she states:

As soon as more than one person knows about the situation that there's shared conflicts and the conflicts of each person sort of play off against one another . . . the conflicts to some extent can play off against one another, can be resolved to some extent by a kind of pooling . . . there are problems to be resolved by each, things to be considered by each, and each person then has the power to affect what happens in the dilemma.

While she does not clearly articulate the thought experiment we have called ideal reciprocal role-taking, we believe this is the operation that is exemplified in her emphasis on *cooperative* discussion, in the context of her understanding of the dilemmas in terms of "shared" or "pooled" conflict. That is, discussion is "cooperative" only to the extent that each person genuinely takes the point of view of every other party to the dilemma. We have argued theoretically that ideal reciprocal role-taking must also involve a temporary masking of the identities of the parties. This is a logical implication of reciprocal role-taking that is not directly expressed by Joan. What she does say, which represents the moral point of view at Stage 6, is her assumption that if each person is seen as possessing liberty and the respect for one another required to consider each other's point of view, there will be a "pooled" or consensual resolution of the dilemma. In other words, if each took the "moral point of view" to the dilemma, there would be a consensual solution arrived at through dialogue. Since the druggist is stated by the interviewer as refusing to take this point of view or to continue the dialogue, she is forced to a "monologic" solution to steal the drug.

Returning to the quotation above in which Joan identifies two things as standing out in her mind in her response to the Heinz dilemma, we can see that the "second thing" she intends is the operation we have called universalizability. In discussing the components of the moral point of view at Stage 6, we have summarized this operation as a general, projective "check on consistency." Joan explicitly uses at least one of the two aspects of this operation in response to the question, "Is there really some correct solution to moral problems like 'Heinz,' or when people disagree, is everyone's opinion equally right?"

Well, of course there is some right answer. And the right answer comes out of the sense of recognition of other people in the ways that I've described and out of recognition of one's responsibility, well, to do a couple of things: to preserve all the integrity, dignity, etc., and to, in a general sense, act as if you would like to see others acting. I don't know really how to explain that except that when I do things, particularly things that I do not really want to do very much, you know, but what I really feel is the right thing to do, usually what sort of sets me over the edge and makes the motivation enough for me to do it has to do with, well, how would I like to see people in general act in this case. What do I think is right in general? That's what I do.

When Joan says one must "act as if you would like to see others acting," we interpret her to be appealing to the Golden Rule, or what we have formally called "ideal reciprocal role-taking," in her approach to solving moral problems. It is, then, the solution arrived at through this operation that she reconsiders with the further operation of universalizability. That is, she goes on to say she is also concerned about the question of how "people in general," or everybody, should act in this case. This concern for how *everyone* should act is what Kant expressed as one form of the Categorical Imperative, namely, to act only on the maxim that you can at the same time will to be a universal law. Indeed, in her earlier response to the question of what Heinz should do in this dilemma, she more explicitly identifies her concern for universalizability in Kantian terms:

Ultimately it comes down to a conflict of duties. Heinz has a duty to—uphold the law isn't quite the right way to put it—Heinz has a duty, I think, to—I hate to put it this way, but I really tend to think of things in a Kantian sense—I don't think that Heinz should be doing anything that he wouldn't be willing to say that everyone should do. And breaking into a store and stealing, etc., is not an action that can be prescribed for humanity, for our societal group as a whole. On the other hand, Heinz, I think as, just by virtue of being a member of the human race, has an obligation, a duty to protect other people (I guess that's a way to put it). And when it gets down to a conflict between those two, I think that the protection of human life is more important.

We would agree with Joan that both the obligation not to steal and the obligation to preserve life are *prima facie* universalizable norms. Like Joan, we would argue for the solution to this dilemma in terms of the moral imperative to preserve human life because it is more clearly grounded in the principle of equal respect for human dignity, which she reiterates throughout her interview. Her understanding of this principle combines the Kantian notion of universalizability with her paraphrasing of the Golden Rule, or what we have called ideal reciprocal role-taking. Thus her use of the operation of universalizability is more fundamentally directed at her maintenance of the ultimate principle of respect for persons. It is this insistence on grounding her judgment in the universalized principle of equal respect for personal dignity that we believe motivates Joan's repeated emphasis on the necessity of dialogue with others throughout moral decision-making. Thus, immediately after her claim in the above quotation that "I think that the protection of human life is more important [than not stealing]," she goes on to qualify this with:

But, again, I wouldn't want Heinz to make the decision on his own. I think that his wife has a lot to say about this.

With this qualification she is advocating that Heinz must still validate his decision to steal to save his wife's life as that which best respects human dignity by raising it through dialogue with the person whose life is at stake. In the lifeboat dilemma she goes even further with her maintenance of respect for persons through dialogue. That is, she would continue dialogue as that which alone can validate a decision when it is one life against another. In contrast, Judge D. felt that the lifeboat dilemma could be resolved by using the principle of equal respect for human dignity through the method of drawing straws, which treated everyone equally but did not involve their active participation. This difference between Judge D. and Joan, in terms of how integral dialogue is to moral problem solving at the level of validating individual or "monological" decisions in this dilemma, is to us now an open question. In Kohlberg (1981), Kohlberg took the strong position that the thought experiment of ideal reciprocal role-taking was sufficient to justify a solution like that of Judge D's, namely, the drawing of straws by the parties in the lifeboat. However, it seems to us now more uncertain what the limits of dialogue are when an autonomous

Stage 6 moral actor faces such an extreme moral problem that seems to call for monological decision.

An Examination of Stage 5 in Light of Our View of Stage 6

We turn finally to the sense in which some examples of Stage 5 reasoning seem to demonstrate deficiencies in comparison to the examples of Stage 6 reasoning we have quoted. In previous discussions of Stage 5, we have stressed that it has a "prior to society" postconventional perspective emphasizing human and civil rights, the public welfare, and a logical hierarchy of values or rights. This perspective is postconventional in the sense that it is cognitive action upon, rather than cognitive conformity to, the values and institutions of society. In order to solve dilemmas it operates on these values and institutions and stresses the importance of those that are fundamental to social life in general.

For some Stage 5 subjects, the emphasis is placed upon a notion of basic rights, civil or human. This is true for "Kim," one of our longitudinal subjects. With regard to the Heinz dilemma, he says:

I think he was justified in breaking in because there was a human life at stake. I think that transcends any right that the druggist had to the drug.

"Why does life transcend all other considerations?"

Well, supposedly man is the supreme being on this planet and we are the most valuable resource on the planet.

"What if it was to save a stranger?"

I think every individual has a right to live and if there is a way of saving an individual, I think any individual should be saved. It's not really different. I am looking at it from my point of view and I enjoy living and I'm sure the next person does too. I would know if my wife were enjoying living but I wouldn't know if a stranger were enjoying life and wanted to live.

Kim resolves the Heinz dilemma with reference to the general right to life, but does not articulate the idea of respect for life based on an underlying principle such as that of equal respect for human dignity or personhood. For this reason Kim's prioritizing of the value of life is difficult for him to justify on moral grounds. Instead, in justifying this right he turns to a utilitarian and hedonistic consideration of human life and says "we are the most valuable resource on the planet" and "I enjoy living and I'm sure the next person would too." In contrast, on this dilemma, our Stage 6 subjects argued for the imperative of saving life on the basis of what they considered morality to be all about, i.e., the principle of treating persons as beings of equal dignity. Stated in different terms, Stage 5 reasoners like Kim focus on fixed general rights, whereas Stage 6 reasoners orient first to the principle of respect for persons and their equal worth, a principle that fixed rights are designed to serve and from which they are derived.

In our discussion of Stage 6, we have stressed the tendency to search for an ideal consensus, either through the actual cooperative dialogue that Joan stresses, or through the use of imaginative devices such as ideal reciprocal role-taking, sympathy, and universalizability, devices through which each participant in a dilemma sheds the ego's particularities and considers the needs and claims of the others. This tendency we have called "taking the moral point of view." Kim uses an element of balancing perspectives in his reasoning, the operation of reciprocal role-taking, but not in the ideal manner of Stage 6 reasoners. In saying "I enjoy living and I'm sure the next person does too," he implicitly uses the Golden Rule in a self-projective form. His use of the Golden Rule is made explicit, however, when asked "What does the word morality mean to you?" He answers: "It is presumably recognizing the rights of other individuals, not interfering with those rights, acting as fairly as you would expect them to treat you."

Kim's use of the Golden Rule, or reciprocal role-taking, is more clearly defined and more general than is its usage at Stage 3, since it focuses on and justifies respect for the rights of others. His reasoning lacks an awareness of two dimensions, however, that Stage 6 reasoning must focus upon. The first is the need to make reciprocal role-taking ideal, or multilateral; i.e., to make sure that one's method of balancing perspectives is not used in an egocentric, self-projective manner. Kim takes the role of the wife and the druggist in the Heinz dilemma, but does not see the need for these two persons and Heinz to take the points of view of each other. The second omission in Kim's reasoning stems from his failure to be aware of the individuality of the values, needs, and attitudes of relevant others whose perspectives he is taking. He says that he would know whether his wife wanted to live but that he would not know whether a stranger would. Faced with this unknown, instead of engaging the others in dialogue as does a Stage 6 reasoner, he simply attributes his own values or desire for life to the stranger. Hence we can say that his use of sympathy is also projective.

Reciprocal role-taking, implicitly or explicitly used, does not deal sufficiently with the issue of fairness. With only reciprocal role-taking Kim takes the meaning of fairness for granted when he says "treat others as fairly as you want them to treat you." In his reasoning, fairness is not really recognized as an issue involving balancing perspectives but is reduced to pres-uming a few central rights. When he is asked "What does it mean to say something is morally right?" he answers, "Basically, to preserve the human being's right to existence. Second, the human being's right to do as he pleases, again, without inter-fering with someone else's rights." Kim's liberty principle is clearly reciprocal; i.e., for him liberties are limited by the like liberties of other individuals. His thinking is unclear, however, about where the good of others, conceived either as individuals or societies, can be integrated or recognized in this context of rights. In contrast, we claim that Stage 6 reasoning clearly coordinates or integrates the recognition of individual rights with considerations of benevolence. In this reasoning, respect for the equal dignity of persons requires an active sympathy for each unique individual and a coordination of this operation of sympathy with ideal reciprocal role-taking and universaliz-ability. Such a coordination is lacking in Kim's thinking. Kim was asked a variation of the lifeboat dilemma, the Korea di-lemma of whether an army captain who could best lead a retreat should order a man on a suicide mission to blow up a bridge so the others might be saved. His initial answer is:

If no one would volunteer and he is the only one who could lead the retreat, he'd have to order a man to stay back and blow up the bridge. It's kind of hard to get down to numbers, it is callous in a way. But he would be able to save the greatest amount of human lives by leading the retreat.

"Does the captain have the right to order a man?"

I'm not familiar with army rules but as far as having the right I don't think he has the right to order someone to his certain death. Each individual has a right to live and you are taking away an individual's rights. I don't think I can order anyone back.

For Kim, benevolence is constructed as a "callous" utilitarian solution of saving the most lives. In his thinking this orientation is then put into marked conflict and he changes his mind when the dilemma is framed in terms of justice and individual rights. In contrast, Judge D. finds a partial solution toward coordinating these choices by drawing straws, a method he says is compatible with equal respect for the dignity of each, while Joan seeks the solution through cooperative dialogue based on the principle of equal respect. We see these latter two solutions as more adequately coordinating justice and benevolence when compared to Kim's oscillation, ending with a justice solution. What is there about a utilitarian principle of maximizing the greatest happiness or welfare of all that leads to this unstable resolution? First, this general principle fails to give explicit due weight to fairness and rights, even if each is to count as one in the calculation of maximum welfare. Second, it does not "fit" as well with the moral point of view, interpreted as conditions for seeking a consensus through dialogue or the exchange of moral reasons in a communication based on equality and mutual respect. In short, psychologically, utilitarianism makes use of both sympathy and universalizability, but tends to omit any intervening operation of ideal reciprocal role-taking.

In fact, however, not all our Stage 5 subjects are as deontologically oriented to rights as is Kim. "Will," in his reasoning, is more consequentialist than is Kim. Will says, "Moral thinking can be done better if we sort out the consequences of behavior in a logical or scientific manner in terms of observations about behavior." He also has more sense of relational connection determining obligation, rather than the idea that obligation derives directly and simply from rights. When asked about stealing for the stranger, he goes on to say:

I can say he should because it's a human life and you should be willing to do it for anybody. On the other hand, he is risking his own future freedom for someone with whom he has not much of a relation or an obligation. But then, not feeling any obligation to someone you don't know doesn't make any sense. The value of human life is higher than the material values the druggist is after. What I am thinking now is the parable Jesus tells of the guy at the side of the road and the stranger that helped him. He felt human and that was enough of a bond.

For Will, then, obligation comes out of a sense of the relational bond, first felt toward family and those close, but ultimately for all human beings.

Will's solution to the Heinz dilemma is in terms of a hierarchy of values a society should hold, according to a "social contract":

Society depends on a set of common agreements among people on what is acceptable behavior. It's necessary for people to have some mutual understanding and predictions of the future. Everyone benefits from that. People benefit from each other's labor and ideas, and communication is facilitated. Material wealth has its place but it is in the service of the quality of life, of human relations, of higher ends for which mutual goods are means. I think that life is to be valued intrinsically.

"Saving life," Will says, "is a kind of implicit contract we have with everyone else; it is an extension of the contract we have for self-protection."

Like Kim, Will also sketches out the essentials for an acceptable society. He does this not in terms of rights, as did Kim, but in terms of socially agreed-upon values. However, he does not attempt to formulate the values society needs to agree upon in terms of a general principle, as would a Stage 6 reasoner. His only use of the term "principle" occurs in a legalistic sense when he compares Heinz's effort to protect his wife with "the well-accepted principle that murder is accepted if you kill someone only in self-defense."

Equality (or equality before the law) is also something Will sees as fundamental to society. He says:

That all people should be equal before the law is a premise upon which our whole society is founded. We all come into the world fairly equal, kicking and screaming and very dependent upon other people, and the law is an attempt to maintain that equality or restore it. We are all human and have human awareness and feeling. Each of us experiences the world with us as the center, but, we are all better off if we are all treated equal.

To this value of equality Will adds a concern for both coop-eration and liberty, though both are seen as constrained by equality. As he says, "Laws operate to enhance the quality of life for everyone, and it may require some minimal levels of cooperation—'my freedom ends where yours begins.'"

Will, in a clearer way than Kim, sees all the "fundamental moral values" (or what Kim calls rights) as foundational to our society or any reasonably good society, and as secured by actual or implicit social agreement and contract. In contrast to Kim and Will, however, our Stage 6 examples integrate these fun-damental moral values—i.e., life, liberty, equality, mutually beneficial social interaction—as the single moral principle "equal respect for human dignity." In integrating them into a principle, they are also adopting "the moral point of view." The "moral point of view" requires the moral judge to go beyond identifying the basic rights and values of our society that seem reasonable or appealing to the speaker and applying them to cases. It entails constructing the idea of rational moral agents involved in a conflict situation considering one another's points of view or reasons with the aim of seeking ideal consen-sus through dialogue or through thought experiments, or both. Unlike a Stage 5 reliance upon notions of prior social agree-ments to resolve dilemmas, the principle of equal respect and the moral point of view of Stage 6 construct anew each case or dilemma in an effort to reach ideal consensus.

We see the reasoning of exemplary moral leaders like Lin-coln, Gandhi, and Martin Luther King as cases of Stage 6. Each of these men felt very deeply that the core of morality, and what should be the core of society, was equal respect for human dignity. Each also was able to show the mutual respect presupposed by the "moral point of view" by recognizing the moral requirement of engaging in dialogue with those who profoundly disagreed with him. It was these characteristics that made them not only great moral visionaries, but also great moral educators. In this paper, we have used "ordinary," less charismatic cases whose leadership in changing society has been far less. We believe their moral reasoning structures, however, are similar to those of our "moral exemplars," both from the point of view of structural psychology and from the point of view of moral philosophy. Even though we believe our Stage 5 subjects to be correct in seeing the elements of what we have called Stage 6 morality as partly institutionalized in constitutional democracy, we also believe a morality addressed to changing society can be no less structurally complex and no less philosophically defensible than the Stage 6 thinking of our cases. Equal respect for persons is a principle governing the means of moral action as well as an end or ideal for action. While moral leaders need not be trained moral philosophers, their intuitions must be capable of "rational reconstruction" from both a psychological and a moral philosophic standpoint, the effort to which this paper has been directed.[1]

Note

1. The authors express their deep appreciation to Robert Ryncarz, who collected the interview material used in this paper and contributed substantially to conceptual background discussion for this paper. We would also like to acknowledge the comments of Bill Puka, whose own paper in this volume takes a somewhat different position on the issues raised here.

References

Baier, K. (1965). *The moral point of view: A rational basis of ethics.* New York: Random House.

Boyd, D. (1978). An interpretation of principled morality. *Journal of Moral Education,* 8:110–123.

Kohlberg, Boyd, and Levine: The Return of Stage 6

Boyd, D. (1980). The Rawls connection. In B. Munsey (Ed.), *Moral development, moral education, and Kohlberg: Basic issues in philosophy, psychology, religion, and education.* Birmingham, AL: Religious Education Press.

Boyd, D. (1984). The principle of principles. In J. L. Gewirtz and W. M. Kurtines (Eds.), *Morality, moral development, and moral behavior.* New York: John Wiley and Sons.

Downie, R. S., and Telfer, E. (1970). *Respect for persons.* New York: Schocken Books.

Fishkin, J. (1984). Defending equality: A view from the cave. *Michigan Law Review,* 82:755–760.

Frankena, W. K. (1973). *Ethics.* Englewood Cliffs, NJ: Prentice-Hall.

Kohlberg, L. (1981). *Essays on moral development. Vol. 1: The philosophy of moral development.* San Francisco: Harper and Row.

Kohlberg, L. (1984). *Essays on moral development. Vol. 2: The psychology of moral development.* San Francisco: Harper and Row.

Perry, T. D. (1976). *Moral reasoning and truth: An essay in philosophy and jurisprudence.* London: Oxford University Press.

Rawls, J. (1971). *A theory of justice.* Cambridge, MA: Harvard University Press.

Taylor, P. W. (1978). On taking the moral point of view. *Midwest Studies in Philosophy,* 3:35–61.

The Majesty and Mystery of Kohlberg's Stage 6

Bill Puka

The deepest secrets in Kohlberg's vision of moral development lie hidden at Stage 6, the highest stage of moral reasoning in his system. Here rest the great soul and Achilles heel of Kohlberg's overall approach. As Kohlberg sees it, the soul of the stage sequence is reciprocal justice, universal egalitarian justice. It threads each stage to the next and ties a firm knot at the top, but for many critics and supporters (including myself) Kohlberg's justice focus is a flaw in theoretic character. A more balanced combination of fair and kindly rationales in stage structure sustain development better. The very notion of tying a knot at the end of development, at Stage 6, seems arbitrary. Certainly there is no empirical basis for it in Kohlberg's system.

Unlike some critics, however, I believe that the more kindly and embracing spirit of respect in Kohlberg's stages can be saved while exorcising "demon" justice. Nevertheless, this salvaging process must begin at the roots of Stage 6 difficulties and move forward step by step. Stage 6 cannot adequately recant and reaffirm itself piecemeal, as had been Kohlberg's way most recently (Kohlberg, Levine, and Hewer, 1983).

I begin this process by recounting the extraordinary claims Kohlberg has made for Stage 6, and then take a somewhat lighthearted stroll through the "empirical caveats" of Stage 6, harkening to "the call of care" that depicts the deficits of justice relative to benevolence. These deficits are pictured at a deep logical level, underlying the largely symptomatic complaints made by critics such as Gilligan (1982). I contrast the moralities of individual respect and group concern along Kohlberg's stage sequence, observing that Stage 6 alone fails to integrate them fairly. In a subsequent section, I consider problems with Kohlberg's equilibration model, with its implication that Stage 6 justice can solve all moral problems in principle. Cases of individual merit and responsibility are posed that liberal-egalitarian principles at Stage 6 cannot accommodate. Finally, I challenge Kohlberg's claim that rights and duties are fully symmetrical at Stage 6 and that this symmetry accounts for problem-solving adequacy. (Some loose ends of Stage 6 are exposed.) Kohlberg's correlativity criterion of adequacy itself is linked to the improbabilities of Stage 6 decision-making. The essay ends with suggestions for overcoming the difficulties posed.

This panoply of problems, I believe, requires that we first prune Stage 6 greatly, then eventually weed it out of the stage sequence entirely. Stage 6 seems neither a natural nor most adequate stage of moral reasoning. Nor does it seem even a promising candidate for these positions. The need for Stage 6 even as a hypothetical end point in Kohlberg's system has never been demonstrated. In fact, it has never been argued. There is little reason to believe that the stage sequence cannot stand much as it does now when its Stage 6 supports are pulled away.

I believe that Kohlberg's empirical accomplishments can withstand the expulsion of almost all his controversial claims in ethics, metaethics, and structuralism. His stages would be much unburdened by banishing them. (See Puka, 1990.) Of course, there may be some reason to speculate about whether there are higher stages of development yet to be uncovered. There are surely good reasons to consider what forms of reasoning would improve on naturally developing ones by extrapolating current stages beyond Stage 5. However, such metatheoretic speculations should not be included directly in a social scientific theory of cognitive development. Neither should they be its guiding psychological or philosophical light.

Setting the Stage

Clearly, for Kohlberg, Stage 6 is not simply the stage after Stage 5. Neither is it merely the most elevated stage in his sequence, as regal as this position may be. Accounts of Stage 6 powers are far more extravagant.

On the psychological side, Stage 6 is portrayed as the most adequate moral stage possible. It is *maximally* integrated and differentiated, reversible and equilibrated. This means that every key moral concept is distinguished from its quasi-moral correlates. (Prudential or conventional "oughts" are distinguished from moral ones.) Each concept also bears a fully symmetrical relationship to its reciprocal—for each duty there is a right and all rights and duties are equal. Moreover, Stage 6 principles of justice are universal, covering the entire range of fundamental moral concepts and able to solve all morally relevant problems in principle. Any morally relevant stage structure that was more inclusive, equilibrated, integrated, or differentiated would transcend the moral domain. It would encompass cosmological and ethical questions about the meaning and ultimate value of life. Thus it could not oversee Stage 6 on its own turf.

Kohlberg maintains, moreover, that not a single stage can be defined or rated without using a prior definition of Stage 6. It is through Stage 6 structure that we identify the moral constituents and adequacy of any stage as opposed to its role-taking or pragmatic acuity. Since Stage 6 is defined by the concept of justice, all stages are forms of justice: moral stages are *justice* stages. One stage is judged higher than another insofar as it approaches the particular sort of justice Stage 6 prefers—general, abstract, formal, principled, egalitarian, and rights-oriented. Kohlberg even credits his use of Stage 6 presumptions in research design with his uncovering stage structures in reality (Kohlberg, 1984, p. 305).

On the philosophical side, the role of Stage 6 is even more grandiose. It is pictured as the logical core of the ultimately valid moral theory. By conceptual inspection, Kohlberg concludes that moral philosophic theories simply elaborate stage structures. They merely refine the inherent rationales of moral common sense. Since Stage 6 is as far as moral logic can go without waxing cosmic—without questioning the meaning of life—the best moral theories can only vary its theme.

In addition, since Stage 6 is structured by a certain brand of justice, its claim to ultimate validity decides many age-old philosophical disputes. Stage 6 validates moral views that focus on right and wield the logic of right/wrong; it undermines views that look to the good and direct us to approach it on a continuum of worse to better. Stage 6 favors universal principles over pragmatic rules, or situational habits, or particular intuitions. It even favors Kantian respect for persons—equal regard for individual autonomy—over utilitarian concern for group welfare. Kohlberg has gone so far as to claim that the most sophisticated forms of utilitarianism, chief rivals to justice for the moral philosophic crown, are not even on a cognitive par. (Their inner core and fundamental foundation are a whole stage lower, a whole stage less cognitively mature than egalitarian justice.)

Stage 6 in Instructive Caricature

As Kohlberg sees it, then, our natural evolution in moral awareness leads "inexorably" toward Stage 6, morality's crowning glory. Each ethic, spontaneously fashioned to face life's dilemmas, is but a closer approximation of the ultimate ethic Stage 6 affords. Each approximation of Stage 6 is more fit to reality itself, Stage 6 most of all. Looking over the invariant sequence of stages with their unitary end-in-view, it is as if nature itself had written Stage 6 into our hearts, into our first tacit promises and shared rituals.

Yet despite this royal mandate from nature and our steadfast progress along the stage sequence, one after another of us mysteriously fails to realize our ordained, Stage 6 destiny. So Kohlberg's data show. Even the most sensitive of us barely scale the summits of Stage 5. Most of us lie marooned in the moral conventionalism of Stage 4, despite generous servings of morally stimulating social life in highly complex democracies. This is the great mystery of Stage 6 universalism. It is a paradox born of the occasionally transcendent relation Stage 6 bears to social science. For while Stage 6 is the only stage of moral reasoning that is truly adequate and principled, that does justice to justice, it is also the only stage that really does not exist.

Kohlberg has been quite frank about this reality (or lack of it) recently (Kohlberg, 1984, p. 240). Stage 6 is not included in the Colby-Kohlberg scoring system (Colby, Kohlberg, and collaborators, 1987) because, admittedly, it does not have adequate data behind it to be termed an "empirical stage." (An empirical stage theory should contain only empirical stages.)

Yet as with most magical things, Stage 6 seems able to pop in and out of reality. Under the stage scheme presented by Kohlberg for over twenty years, Stage 6 was vividly present. Supporting data and samples of Stage 6 reasoning appeared in all classic Kohlberg essays. Then, as new and empirically improved stage descriptions appeared, transforming Stages 1–5, Stage 6 slipped off, disappeared altogether. All stages supposedly rest on Stage 6; yet when it vanished, none noticed. Still, even as Stage 6 became a nonissue for Kohlberg's new science, it reappeared again as a hypothetical stage. As such, it defined the sequence conceptually, awaiting empirical confirmation in future. Moreover, after Kohlberg reanalyzed the most evolved and structurally distinct portions of current Stage 5 reasoning, the dim profile of Stage 6 again became visible. At least Kohlberg claimed to see it. Thus the search has resumed for the rest of its noble features.

Given this envisioned place in nature, it is no wonder that Stage 6 has a majestic aura about it. Given its unpredictable reluctance to take its place, or to stay in its place, it is no wonder that Stage 6 mystifies. No doubt it is the combination of these qualities that makes Stage 6 so unbelievable for many.

Rumblings Offstage: Empirical Caveats

The empirical status of Stage 6 always should have been in question since the data for Stage 6 have always been thin and anomalous, even when they supposedly existed. Kohlberg has never offered readers more than a few anecdotal responses from a handful of Stage 6 cases to illustrate its existence (Kohlberg, 1981, pp. 160–166, 205–214, 217–218). None at all were cited from the longitudinal sample that gave birth to his other stages. Rather, citations came from the unprobed writings of moral exemplars and philosophers and from the ruminations of conscientious objectors. Often Stage 6 responses were credited explicitly to "Philosopher 3" in Kohlberg's writings. The views of these especially reflective or committed individuals are likely to be influenced by special training and insight. They are least likely to be naturally developing and generalizable, the stuff of universal Piagetian stages.

Kohlberg's latest sample of Stage 6—the case of Joan, cited in this volume—is at least as puzzling as past cases.[1] Joan's way of thinking about interpersonal problems suggests that she is extremely reflective and especially experienced in this area. She is *personally* mature and insightful in this sense. However, Kohlberg provides no grounds at all for evaluating the *structure* of her moral reasoning at the principled level, much less at Stage 6. This is very disconcerting given the thrust of Kohlberg's theoretical renaissance over the last decade. Here differentiating style and structure, personal maturity and cognitive adequacy, has been central to redefining Kohlberg's stages. The new rigor of his qualitative data has been achieved by moving away from an intuitive sense of maturity in reasoning to an explicitly structural analysis. In replying to critics, Kohlberg makes much of this distinction between his "hard" structural stages and "soft-stage" reasoning found by researchers such as Fowler, Perry, or Gilligan (Kohlberg, 1984, pp. 236–249). Moreover, when discussing the religious and cosmological thinking characteristic of development in later life, Kohlberg drives a sharp wedge between the obvious wisdom often shown in such thinking and the surprisingly low structure of its moral stage.

Why then is Kohlberg so impressed with what Joan has to say in her moral interview? Why should *we* be? In fact, it is precisely the degree of Joan's reflectiveness and experience that should give us pause in evaluating her natural stage. Whatever spontaneous form her moral reasoning once took, it now seems to have been reworked as she thought through issues in a concentrated, self-conscious way. The so-called dialogical approach Joan takes in conflict resolution bears a striking resemblance to the interpersonal styles of political and personal-growth movements popular among American college students in recent decades. Of course, only research would show whether this resemblance is coincidental—whether Joan is an interpersonal ideologue and expert in some sense. But without such research, and given Joan's response profile, Kohlberg cannot assume a naturally arising universal structure; in particular, he cannot assume a dialogical structure such as that posited by Habermas (see Kohlberg, 1984, ch. 4).

Indeed, Joan makes explicit reference to Immanuel Kant's philosophical ethics. She not only studied this ethical theory but appears to have integrated it into her style of moral reasoning. This can be seen by her use of commonsense terms like "dignity" or "integrity" in the technical sense formulated by Kant. Normally "dignity" is used to mean an elevated quality of demeanor or a quality of life sufficiently free of "animal needs." "Integrity" normally refers to a virtue akin to honesty, or to the intactness of one's physical or psychological systems. Joan uses these terms as near synonyms, however, to refer to the Kantian moral self as a self-determined or autonomous unity. She also makes explicit reference to "special obligations" and "moral claims" in this connection, using these terms in the technical sense current among philosophers. The same tendencies are found in "Philosopher 3."

Kohlberg's a priori definition of Stage 6 and its use in designing research and theory raises some question about how empirically based the stages are. This suspicion is exacerbated when Kohlberg clings to Stage 6 and its "big brother" role in defining stages even as the data desert. The structural approach to moral judgment is somewhat interpretive or reconstructive by nature, even as it is descriptive in intent. It does not merely recount and organize the general rationales we ourselves identify and consciously use in making moral judgments. Rather it makes explicit the implicit logic embodied in the way we coordinate our piecemeal reasons, beliefs, and rules of thumb. In so doing, structuralism aims to describe. That is, it aims to go below the surface to show the organization of our intellect, whereby our reasoning processes unfold as they do. Structuralists claim that stages are empirical phenomena, a claim based on the capacity of formalization to provide a more profoundly accurate description of what the data show.

At the same time, this "description" is a posit, a stab at the best explanations for what causes moral judgments to take certain shapes. To be credible, the structuralist must be vigilant in assuring that empirical findings are not predetermined by conceptual assumptions. Kohlberg's approach, however, reverses the role of form and fact here, explicitly using Stage 6 as a formal hypothesis in search of formal, structural data. Yet if form is to be read into the data as it is found, where is the protection here against the hypothesis itself providing it? Surely such a biasing outcome is likely, despite Kohlberg's socalled "bootstrapping" reconstruction of his method.[2]

Ideologically Speaking

Many observers are struck by the ideological tone of Kohlberg's claims for the centrality in moral development of justice and equal rights. They are bothered especially by the alleged crosscultural supremacy of liberal justice. This Stage 6 claim still haunts the stages even as Stage 6 disappears from Kohlberg's scoring system. So long as the structure of Stage 6 remains in the wings, helping to guide research and theory, it may be criticized. The announcement of its return, in the present volume, can only rekindle ideological criticism even though critics must now speak mysteriously (I shall) as if Stage 6 both existed and did not exist.

As just noted, Kohlberg explicitly designed his research dilemmas to pull for just resolutions. These dilemmas pose conflicting individual claims of rights and duty. Moreover, Kohlberg himself claims to interpret responses to these dilemmas via a particular intellectual tradition in the West: the liberal, social contract tradition in its peculiarly Kantian form. Notably, Kohlberg never has cited a putative case of Stage 6 reasoning that occurs outside of western industrialized nations or the direct influence of their educational curricula. (Mohandas Gandhi's alleged Stage 6 reasoning was preceded by rigorous training in British conceptions of justice and equality at law school in London.) These sorts of observations have spawned two main criticisms. In the first, Stage 6 justice is portrayed as the favored ideology of particular socioeconomic systems and social historical conditions. Its rights are the tools of western individualism (of capitalist entrepreneurialism perhaps) and the bane of more communal, joint-responsibility traditions found in eastern or "third world" cultures. (Obviously there are many more and less reasonable variations on this theme; see Simpson, 1974; Sullivan, 1977.) In the second criticism, Stage 6 reflects particular sorts of social perspectives, roles, and relations, certain types of needs and ego-developmental processes related to gender and status. It is the typical logic of the demanding, alienated male, primarily, in a contentious and sexist society (Gilligan, 1982).

The first sort of criticism has not caught on, perhaps because its dialectical approach to social science seems more ideologically bent than Kohlberg's liberalism. Such views normally have two major problems. The dramatic correlations they draw between certain practices or interests in a society and the logic of its favored moral concepts are highly selective and incomplete. Moreover, the road they travel from correlation to causal dependency is breathtakingly short. (For example, since rights appear to occur most in western culture and sometimes to dramatically serve individualism, therefore they are the tools of western individualism and cannot be otherwise grounded.)

Since Kohlberg (1984, ch. 4) has recounted and responded to prominent versions of this critique, I will forego further detail here. However, if we take this sort of critique in moderate doses, as a view that apportions burdens of proofs, its challenge to Kohlberg cannot be denied. A system of moral reasoning that supposedly is universal must explain its failures to appear. This is especially so when its schedule of appearances breaks down along cultural or socioeconomic lines. There are plausible excuses for cognitive underdevelopment in individual cases. However, they do not seem applicable on so vast a social scale. Consider two.

On Kohlberg's equilibration model, cognitive structure adapts progressively to universals of social structure. We can imagine historical circumstances in which the basic structure of society was still in evolution or had been broken down due to war or natural catastrophe. Here even full adaptation to actual structure would not be full adaptation to social structure in a universal sense. Many third-world and eastern cultures, however, have been evolving in their way far longer than western ones have. Their basic social form is surely in place. Thus this first sort of dodge will not do. At the same time, extreme political repression, authoritarian customs, and religious ideologies can stunt development. They can keep members of certain cultures from the role-taking and critical thinking opportunities they need to view society from "all" points of view. But surely in some nonwestern societies, many members of privileged classes are free to think flexibly and critically. Surely they do not spend most of their time being oppressed or oppressing others, even ideologically. Such comparable conditions from the East to the West are ripe for Stage 6 liberal justice as Kohlberg describes it. Why did it not seem to appear in the East when it seemed to appear in the West? The second dodge falters also.

Ideological charges become compelling here if only because it would be so difficult for Kohlberg to explain them away. Imagine the scrupulous comparisons that would have to be made between the structures of different societies, and between societies in different cultures, to show their fundamental similarities. Only in this way can we depict social universals. Imagine the scrupulous distinctions that would be needed between morally essential social structures and culturally contingent ones. These distinctions would be all the more difficult and dangerous to make if we tried a third dodge, that of assuming that cultural universals are still evolving and so happen to arise in the complex secondary institutions of "western-style" nation states. These are the institutions that only Stage 6, supposedly, can negotiate adequately.

An objective theoretical justification of Stage 6 would help in this process. However, it could not stand its own ground against ideological charges unless it could demonstrate its own independence from cultural bias. By contrast, most justice theorists such as Rawls base their conceptions on so-called intuitions or considered judgments. These consist of moral beliefs that are commonly agreed upon in a society and built into the logic or ordinary moral discourse there. What better way is there to play into ideological hands?

Note again, however, that mere correlations between cultural mores and liberal justice are not the key to Stage 6 troubles here. The burdens of proof become unbearable when we combine: (1) the ultimacy of Kohlberg's adequacy claims for Stage 6, (2) the "thinness" of cross-cultural data, (3) the lack of standard "arrested development" explanations for Stage 6 no-shows, and (4) Kohlberg's own explicit association of Stage 6 reasoning with highly specific intellectual traditions in western philosophy. Normally claims for the universal supremacy of any commonsense system of belief would need overwhelming cross-cultural evidence. Instead, Kohlberg seemingly offers us none whatsoever.

Even though the first type of ideological criticism failed to attract a crowd, the second has created a sensation under Gilligan's banner of response ethics and relational care. In some circles, Gilligan's observations are believed to spell the demise of Kohlberg's stage theory. (Again, I believe this general sort of response is understandable given Kohlberg's attempt to define the whole stage sequence as relative to Stage 6 justice.) A large audience in and out of psychology seems to feel, at least, that Gilligan's levels of care seriously challenge the ethic of justice and Kohlberg's ultimacy claims for Stage 6.

With other critics, Gilligan notes that in most interpersonal situations of daily life, judgments of justice seem judgmental (in the negative sense) and often out of place. They have a formality and abstractness about them, a legalistic adherence to general principle even in the face of individual pain or frustration. As such they are often unresponsive to the lively dynamics of situational conflict or opportunity, to the differing aspirations and vulnerabilities of particular individuals. Worse yet, they willingly leave us hurt and resentful once morality has spoken, so long as the calculus of rights and equality has been served. Once we get our fair share, any further complaints are our own personal problem. In deciding that these lingering burdens of justice are not "legitimate claims," just judgment can often seem hegemonic and downright punitive.

Justice tends to overlook special loyalties stemming from "special" ties. (In fact it calls our natural, most intimate ties "special," and the institutional ties of institutional rights "natural.") Rather than orienting to people in relation, and in need of each other, justice presumes and sanctions the autonomy of each individual above all. It then depicts the morally salient aspects of these relationships as expressions of autonomy, as implicit contracts or agreements. At the least, this orientation is one-sided.

Moreover, this sort of slant can be attributed to various biases that infect Kohlberg's research methodology and theoretical reconstruction of findings. Among these are male gender bias in Kohlberg's original research sample and the use of abstract, hypothetical issues in moral judgment interviews. These issues pose potentially violent conflicts between individual interests that pull for regularized and explicit principles of conflict resolution. Such an individualistic slant at the methodological level seemingly mirrors the western cultural bias seen by some critics in Kohlberg's approach. It is reflected further in Kohlberg's theoretical assumption that morality, by nature, is a form of conflict resolution among individuals; it is a form of "unnatural" cooperative relationship through contractual rules. This slant also seems to correlate with the characteristic male sense of identity and self-other relation (uncovered by Gilligan's "self-description" interview) that conceives society as relatively isolated individuals in potential conflict. In this respect, Kohlberg's emphasis at the higher stages on "rights to noninterference" also extends apparent gender bias to the theoretical level.

In discussing concrete (and nonconflictual) moral issues with respondents, Gilligan finds an alternative moral theme in common sense reasoning, a theme that overcomes these moral deficits of justice. This theme orients to persons in a highly caring, empathetic, and personalized way. It attends and responds to their particular needs in particular contexts. It recognizes that their networks of interpersonal relationships are the most morally salient features of these contexts. The care theme seeks to engage others in flexible and cooperative struggle with moral dilemmas. It seeks to nurture interpersonal bonds, avoid hurt, and pursue what is "best for all concerned." These moral aims stem from a female sense of society as webs of intimate relationship, rather than as sets of strangers in isolation and conflict. Developmentally, the "different voice" of care passes through a level of self-protection (self-absorption) and of conventional altruism (self-abnegation) on the way to a fair and responsible balancing of self-care with care for others.

A Voice Too Soon

Gilligan's approach holds great promise, if only because it stands within two venerable traditions. One is the tradition of critical theory, which exposes and excoriates the competitive and possessive egoism lurking behind individual rights (Marx, 1843/1972; MacPherson, 1962). The other is the even longer benevolence tradition, which extends from the virtue conceptions of Aristotle, the Confucians, and (Christian) agapeism, through utilitarianism and the "self-actualization" conceptions of Fromm and Maslow.

Yet to bring out the promise of Gilligan's critical and constructive positions requires a great deal more theoretical analysis than she provides. It also requires supporting empirical research of a seemingly different sort than has been offered so far (e.g., Langdale, 1983; Johnston, 1985; Attanucci, 1984). Gilligan (1977) originally offered her "different voice" conception as an "interpretive hypothesis" and has reiterated this characterization more recently (1986). After ten years of first being heard, the "different voice" remains a hypothesis as far as moral development is concerned. Virtually no theoretical work has been done on Gilligan's justice critique, nor on the alternative theme of care as a developmental track. For example, Gilligan has never extended her piecemeal criticisms of Kohlberg's hypothetical dilemmas or forced-choice interview format with a rigorous and thoroughgoing analysis of Kohlberg's research methodology. Nor has Gilligan offered a standard review of the literature substantiating bias claims in Kohlberg research. To the contrary, Gilligan (1986) has failed to offer any serious response to Walker's (1984) review of Kohlberg studies, challenging charges of gender bias. Gilligan's recent writings (e.g., Gilligan and Wiggans, 1987) speculate broadly on care and its developmental origins. Smatterings of data from various areas of research are cited in these narratives. Yet such writings do not engage in the standard data-based form of theory-building where theoretical claims are derived exclusively and parsimoniously from the empirical results of case studies. (Gilligan seems to be aiming at a different sort of account, one that has its own sorts of assets.)

While empirical research has gone forward on care "focus" or "orientation," virtually no research has been reported in support of care *levels*, i.e., care *development*. Yet only care levels have clear relevance to Kohlberg's developmental stage theory. (Kohlberg has explicated themes of justice, and of other moral concepts, that do not appear to develop. These are explicitly left out of his stage descriptions. Themes of "moral honor" that have been prominent in "macho" cultures are a notable example.) As yet, no standardized or reliable scoring system for care levels has been developed. Lyons's (1983) system for scoring care does not code for levels. Thus it is not surprising that virtually no developmental theory of care has arisen. Moreover, Walker (Walker, de Vries, and Trevethan, 1987) has been unable to replicate the sort of findings that allegedly support a theory of care focus or orientation.

The urgent need for a comparative, moral philosophic analysis of care and justice themes also remains unfulfilled. Only through such an account can one demonstrate the "equal credibility" or "adequacy" of care relative to justice. Only through such an account can Gilligan show that Kohlberg's emphasis on justice constitutes bias. After all, if justice is a highly adequate moral theme, or at least more adequate than care, then it should be emphasized along the stage sequence. It should be especially prominent at higher stages.

As matters now stand, Gilligan's original critique of justice might be said to observe certain symptoms without diagnosing the disease. Importantly, this critique does not offer any distinction between the uses and abuses of justice reasoning in moral judgment. Moreover, it does not correlate care and justice at any developmental level to evaluate their comparative pros and cons. Is justice reasoning, with its legalistic Stage 4 rules or its individualistic Stage 5 rights, clearly less adequate than the pervasive selfishness of care at Level 1, or the utterly demeaning and disempowering self-abnegation of care at Level 2? (See Gilligan, 1982, chs. 3 and 4.) How is it determined that care at its mature Level 3 is more helpful or benevolent overall than Stage 5 justice with its utilitarian orientation and "ideal or harmony serving" orientation? (See Kohlberg, 1984, pp. 406, 631–536.)

In addition, Gilligan's original account fails to draw a clear relation between the "justice focus" and "justice orientation" she observes and criticizes, and "justice reasoning" at any Kohlberg stage. Indeed, Gilligan basically ignores Kohlberg's fundamental distinction between holistic, structural systems of cognitive-moral reasoning and cognitive orientations, styles, and types. The latter phenomena are explicitly recognized and excluded from Kohlberg's developmental stage theory. (In Kohlberg's theory, justice does not occur as a global orientation that exists outside, and in addition to, the different justice structures of particular stages.)

This apparent omission compounds with a far more serious one in Gilligan's account. This is the failure to address Kohlberg's crucial distinction between a type morality and a general one (Kohlberg, 1981, ch. 4). A type morality or moral theme expresses the sensibilities and interests of certain (broad or narrow) types of people or groups. It supports certain favored values and serves circumscribed purposes. The theme Gilligan terms "justice focus" is characterized as a type morality that favors the characteristic outlooks and interests of males. As such it promotes the values of individualism, free competition, and the like. The theme Gilligan terms "care focus" is characterized as a type morality as well; it reflects the characteristic female sense of relatedness to others and promotes values of intimacy, security, and so on, as Gilligan notes.

A general morality, by contrast, is explicitly designed to recognize and accommodate the range of type moralities or circumscribed moral themes. It is designed to render them compatible where they diverge. Kohlberg's higher-stage notion of "egalitarian justice" or "unconditional respect" is a general morality in this sense, designed to foster general cooperation amid various forms of divergence. And it is perfectly possible for "justice focus" and "care focus" to function compatibly with "justice reasoning" in Kohlberg's sense. They can function at different levels, serving different ends. Gilligan's account does not consider this option.

According to Gilligan, Kohlberg's justice theme is biased because it favors the characteristic outlooks and values of males over those of females or relational types. This could mean: (1) Kohlberg's justice theme is a type morality that is biased only when it is represented as a general morality; (2) Kohlberg's justice theme not only represents an overgeneralized type morality but is a biased and inadequate morality per se, malfunctionally rigid, impersonal, and overly individualistic; (3) Kohlberg's justice theme is a general morality that places undue emphasis on certain outlooks and values that happen to correlate with a certain type morality. This emphasis causes justice to be limited and skewed in the performance of its functions. This correlation also makes justice partisan and unfair. It prevents justice from accommodating divergent type moralities evenhandedly.

By contrast, adequate and mature moral judgment, according to Gilligan, combines or balances the equally credible themes of care and justice (Gilligan, 1982, p. 100).

Yet if (1) is the problem, then it is unclear how adding care to justice would help. Two type moralities do not add up to a general morality. And this is so even if characteristic male types and female types exhausted human types (or moral types), which they do not. (There are uncharacteristic types, for instance gay and lesbian types, bisexual and androgenous types.) Typing also occurs in the values and functions and purposes of type moralities, as well as in the features of those who typically hold and pursue them. Indeed, type moralities are, by nature, primarily in-group moralities. The aim of fostering cooperation amid diversity often is secondary to them. Thorny issues of cooperation occur primarily in regard to a dissident fringe who are pressured, tolerated, or cast out. General moralities are melting-pot moralities by nature. Dealing with divergence is a central and ongoing task in which every type has a comparable say.

If (2) is the problem, then we must wonder why care would aspire to be "comparably credible" to justice. What does the "different voice" announce, after all: that justice is not the only highly problematic theme in morality? That there is an alternative, caring way to think poorly?

If (3) is the problem, then Gilligan must show why this is so by comparing option (3) with a further option that goes as follows: (4) Kohlberg's justice theme places proper emphasis on issues of equal respect, individual rights, principles of fairness, and the like. This is because these issues serve the purposes of a general morality best, given the existence and strength of divergent type moralities and human interests. While key features of this general theme correlate with some features of a particular type morality (justice focus), this does not render justice reasoning partisan or inadequate. The functions and purposes of this type morality may be more inherently like those of a proper general morality than existing alternatives. (Males may be well socialized to occupy positions of broad social authority.) Alternatively, these type features may be more inadvertently like general ones, since the social and conceptual mechanisms that serve individual egoism, self-protection, and competition may be serviceable also for broad and varied forms of social cooperation. After all, many forms of human cooperation occur indirectly, at a great distance. They occur among varied individuals and (ethnic) groups with little knowledge of each other and a history of mistrust and prejudice. Here self-concern and protection may make great sense. (We may not like this, and may want to change it, but it is a recalcitrant fact.)

It is easy to scoff at option (4) as a not-so-subtle expression of patriarchy, or as merely liberal (rather than radical) feminism. But "scoffing," like "claiming," is not theoretical analysis. It is notable also, in this context, that the gentle and highly personal ethic of caring has exerted powerful political force, historically, in the hands of social and religious reformers. In the same way, a certain economic system seemingly spawned by individual greed and ruling-class interest has typically fostered general economic efficiency, enhanced human productivity, and the spreading of literacy, opportunity, and even culture among the general populace. Justice may not be well-intentioned enough, but it may serve best. Only exhaustive theoretical analysis will tell. And only such analysis can dispel the mystery of how moral themes portrayed as conflicting with one another can simply be balanced or combined in one's mature judgment. How does one amiably combine the punitiveness and aloof judgmentalism of justice with the dialogical struggle and "not hurting" of care? (See Puka [in press-a; in press-b; in press-c] for detailed discussions of Gilligan's "different voice" hypothesis in relation to Kohlberg's theory.)

Given how much is missing from Gilligan's original account of moral development—as one would expect of a *hypothesis*—it is remarkable that the Kohlberg-Gilligan debate is still taken seriously. It is surprising that Kohlberg (in Kohlberg, Levine, and Hewer, 1983) replied to Gilligan's critical remarks in such detail, making concessions to care that might seem unwarranted. Perhaps this testifies to the obvious weakness of the Stage 6 ideal, as well as the obvious need for "something more" alongside "mere" justice. But it is a sad commentary on the field otherwise, as I think Gilligan would agree. For she has not even attempted to fill in the gaps I have cited here: she has not sought to create a theoretical alternative to Kohlberg's stage theory or to promote a Kohlberg-Gilligan debate.

Nevertheless, Gilligan's original account has merit and potential. To empower it, and to render it more clearly relevant to Kohlberg's, we must go deeper into the heart of justice and care. The critique of justice should address the core structure and defining logic of Kohlberg's moral stage reasoning. (Alternatively, it must present an elaborate theoretical account of why logic or a structural emphasis is inherently inadequate [i.e., less adequate than something else] in moral cognition.) Gilligan's alternative theme of care also should show its alternative structure or logic. (Alternatively, it must demonstrate equally credible "ways of knowing" at the levels of moral perception, dialogue, response, and the like. Again, this must be accomplished explicitly, in a thoroughgoing way, to transform hypothesis into theory.)

For example, the account of care might note that we (westerners?) tend to identify primarily with our individuality, with our unique personality features, talents, motivations, and friendships with others. By contrast, some of us (non-westerners?) tend to identify our selves with groups, with the family, tribe, or clan. Caring attends to both. Yet justice supposedly respects us as persons by respecting our essential personhood, our shared and equal personhood. This is the part of us that does not distinguish us from others as unique personalities, but does distinguish us from groups and relationships. (Essential moral personhood resides in psychological capacities primarily.) Moreover, justice advocates claim that to do otherwise would mean injustice, inequality, tyranny. Supporters of care may wonder, then, if justice truly can respect us as persons, either as the unique persons we now are or as those we will be when it respects us fairly and equally. Correlatively, can justice truly be fair when it respects us as us? Here justice may seem morally inadequate as a matter of principle, its own principle. It seems troubled not merely by being cold and callous, not caring enough, but by a basic contradiction in its own moral logic. In this context, *caring* seems the best way to *respect* persons.

These are the sorts of questions and problems that Kohlberg's theory cannot ignore. They not only attend and show responsiveness to Kohlberg's basic moral assumptions in their own terms, but they base their alternative suggestions on those very assumptions. I believe that this sort of account can be developed for benevolence. Let us consider how to begin.

The Call of Care

As with the previous ideological critique, we can pare back the extent of Gilligan's critical claims and focus on apportioning Kohlberg's burden of proof. Any strengths of care (or a like ethic) that justice overlooks or overrides can be used philosophically to question the ultimacy of Stage 6. Ironically, the empirical likelihood and moral theoretic adequacy of Stage 6 justice is challenged most strongly when we combine the best insights of caring critics with the caring components of Kohlberg's own (empirical) Stages 3–5.

Starting with Stage 3, each stage in Kohlberg's sequence has two main components. One deals with respect and toleration for individual life and liberty and the other with group stability and welfare. These concerns are most integrated at Stage 3, where rights are accorded relative to our loyalty to the group and our empathy toward others. By Stage 5, the orientations of individual respect and concern for group welfare are highly differentiated into two orientations, namely individual rights and social utilitarianism. Even here, the respect accorded individuals is based on their accepting the principle of mutually beneficial cooperation.

At Stage 6, however, a radical transformation occurs. The Stage 5 rights orientation is carried forward in refurbished components of new and more universal rights, but individual rights nonetheless. However, the social utilitarian orientation is recast in the logic of positive rights or rights of aid. This transformation signifies that our concern for the welfare of others and our valuing of relations or the group are now assimilated under the logic of respect—respect for people's free pursuit of welfare and cooperation. Group welfare is only to have moral impact (in defining obligations) where it is freely pursued by individuals who may form groups or relations, but need not do so. Group welfare counts only to the degree that individuals actually count it by choosing it, not in the sense that it morally *should* be chosen or pursued.

The problems caused by this Stage 6 anomaly are twofold. Cognitively, Stage 6 seemingly reverses structural trends preceding it in the stage sequence. It integrates respect and concern *at the expense of* higher-stage differentiation between them. This structural distortion engenders a second problem of moral reductionism. Stage 6 logic assumes that morally valid portions of concern for the *quality* of *experience* and for *relations* or *groups* can be captured by respect for individual autonomy. It assumes that the logic of promoting good on a continuum can be captured by the disjunctive, all-or-none logic of just/ unjust, permissible/intolerable. But it clearly cannot. (This is why the deontology-teleology debate between Kantians and utilitarians still rages, despite Kohlberg's claim to have resolved it.) Concern and respect are different moral attitudes. They are directed at very different features of persons and in very different ways. My concern for your welfare should cause me sometimes to enhance it, and sometimes to pursue your best interests over your actual desires. It also should lead me to weigh the value of relationships and the welfare of groups more heavily than the value of individuals; considerations of welfare and good are aggregative. Concern leads me to do what is *best* for *all* concerned. Empathy pulls toward the greatest amount of suffering. By contrast, my respect for your autonomy applies to you primarily as an individual. Our (free) wills are metaphysically individualized even if they can be influenced strongly by others or used cooperatively to create joint decisions. To respect your choice as an individual means not to infringe on it, or to help you fend off infringements (natural or otherwise). All additional aid toward you merely broadens your options—the scope and force of your will—or increases your welfare. It does not accord you autonomy as a person. I need not violate your rights to hurt you, nor do you have a right that I attend to you, befriend you, or cooperate in your pursuits.

Considerations of respect and concern, rights and utility may often accompany and complement each other. Yet they orient differently even when they overlap, and they must sometimes conflict. Indeed, if rights and utility did not conflict, we would not need rights, and Kohlberg would not set himself up as a deontologist. A major function of individual rights in deontological justice is to protect the individual against overwhelming social interest.

Gilligan's critique of justice actually focuses on negative features of this particular antisocial role that rights play. As noted, she couches them in attitudinal terms—callousness and unresponsiveness, formality and impersonality, legalism and punitiveness. Yet these deficiencies of an equal-rights orientation can be tied to the very logic of rights and hence to the central strengths of Stage 6 justice. Regardless of how compassionately or flexibly one attempts to apply rights or justice, basic features of care must be ruled out on principle. This is required by the tolerationist implications of respect and the all-or-none, liberty-versus-coercion logic of rights as conveyers of toleration. Thus in order to guarantee individual autonomy, rights must be indifferent to how autonomy is used, to what values our freedoms embody or pursue. In putting rights first (as Kantian deontologists do) we therefore provide a protected haven for any value pursuits or forms of life that do not violate others' rights. Through equal protection we place morality in the impossible position of being indifferent on principle to the selfish greed of one and the altruism of others. After all, you cannot grant me a (near-absolute) right of way *as a person* and then constrain me to go a certain way. At the least you cannot interfere with whatever way I choose to go—even by competing—so long as I do not tread on you or (at Stage 6) neglect your basic needs.

Worse yet, since rights are correlative to duties at Stage 6, my duties of justice themselves constrain you from intervening for good. They prohibit you from benefiting others by utilizing *some* of my *unneeded* goods or "pressing" (obliging) me into (some) service. In fact, the morality of equal rights requires you to stand by while I willfully or whimsically destroy resources—burn my property, blow my brains out—regardless of what good my life or resources could do others. It would give my claim to destroy goods the right of way over your claim to benefit others or society with them. Even highest-stage liberal justice prefers, as a matter of course, any activity that can be performed self-sufficiently (without violating rights) over any pursuit that requires cooperation but cannot attract it sufficiently. Moral quality cannot matter.

At this level of ultimate duties, we can see why the justice/care dichotomy is not one of obligation versus supererogation (i.e., going beyond). It is not one of rights and duties versus virtues and ideals. Morally misconceived duties of respect threaten and restrict our liberty and responsibility to care as surely as threats or wrongful coercion do—at least for the morally conscientious.

I do not mean to imply that we should force people to relate to each other or cooperate toward benevolent ends. (Still, in some instances where needed infringements are few and slight and the ends at stake are great and pervasive, such coercion may be preferable.) Rather I am claiming that basic moral differences between certain uses of autonomy should be accorded basic moral place. So should the good-enhancing rationales we should adopt toward them. The point is not to override rights and respect with care and welfare. Rather it is to formulate moral concepts, orientations, and obligations that build in the proper relation of respect and concern in the first place. Stage 6 individual rights do not. Utilitarian maximization rules may not either. But at least a rule-utilitarian, rights principle can give rights stronger standing (utility) when they are directed to good ends. It illustrates that equal respect need not imply liberty toward the good in a way rights cannot countervene.

In principle, Stage 6 justice is indifferent among these values. In effect, it favors selfish possibilities over joint ones and restricts our basic liberty in defense of perverse value priorities. Therefore, it is logically and morally deficient—deficient on principle and to the core. Stage 6 justice is also silent on our responsibilities to *increase* the good, and to nurture virtue in ourselves and others. (These are not matters of "*more* just" or "*un*just" behavior.) Thus it is morally negligent as well. Structurally, Stage 6 is distortive and reductionistic, ineptly differentiated and integrated.

Bad Prospects

Thus far we have considered four major problems with Stage 6.

1. Apparent data for Stage 6 always have been too thin and confounded to support a natural and highest moral stage.

2. New alleged cases of Stage 6 reasoning are not structurally defined by Kohlberg. The case of Joan, like previous cases, seems confounded by special training and reflection.

3. Kohlberg's use of such cases to support Stage 6, and the continued use of stage 6 in defining the stage sequence, raises suspicions that his stages are somewhat unempirical and biased.

4. Burdens of proof have not been borne regarding the empirical universality and scientific neutrality of Stage 6, that seem at odds with its apparent biases toward liberal ideology, patriarchy, individualism, and rights. Similar burdens of proof have not been borne in justifying the universalizability of justice and its capacity to practice what it preaches on respect for persons.

Such problems in Stage 6 not only impugn its reputed existence and adequacy at present, but also reduce its prospects of arising in the future. If the stage sequence were to proceed beyond Stage 5, it would not move toward Kohlberg's universal rights. At least such an outcome is unlikely if later stages properly integrate previous structural differentiations of respect and concern. Additional considerations not only strengthen this doubt, but increase the unlikelihood that any brand of Stage 6 would ever arise—just, caring, or otherwise.

The first consideration is that Stage 5, as a high-level, post-conventional structure, is extremely well equilibrated. It is well adapted to its environment and internally stable. Thus it is not likely to be unsettled by any new dilemmas that the basic universals of our social environment can devise. Stage 5 is especially unlikely to yield to a liberal-egalitarian form of Stage 6 justice since it already has an equal-rights orientation. Its rule-utilitarian orientation also has an egalitarian focus. (The rule for this orientation is to protect equal rights as preferred means to utilitarian social good.) Importantly, Kohlberg's own research methods seem based on these beliefs and doubts. He found it necessary to devise special, sophisticated dilemmas to uncover differences in higher-stage reasoning, differences between the egalitarianism of Stages 5 and 6. His lifeboat and Korea dilemmas pull for either Stage 6 egalitarian reasoning based on equal rights alone, or Stage 5 egalitarian reasoning that includes social utilities. (Stage 5 considers the value of our actions and abilities in calculating our equal claims; Stage 6 committedly ignores these values.)

For such differences in our egalitarian reasoning to develop naturally in the first place—for some of us to forsake Stage 5 equality for Stage 6—our basic social environment would have to exert even more refined and subtle pulls on our cognition than these special dilemmas do. And these pulls would have to take the same direction. Universals of our environment would have to grip our consciousness with vivid but subtle forms of inegalitarianism. Yet in this venture they would not have the luxury of morally focused hypotheticals. Nor could they use Kohlberg's unrelenting probe questions to keep our moral perception and deliberation to the point. Rather our social world would have to catch and hold our egalitarian attention with whatever real-life dilemmas it could muster and press forward amid the complexity and confusion that make up daily life. Its press would have to be so strong or prolonged—it would have to make so much trouble for Stage 5 egalitarianism—as to pull this preeminently integrated structure apart. Moreover, the damage would have to take a form that only Stage 6 might remedy.

Suppose this disintegration were to happen. Then the ultimately arduous process of constructing an even more evolved and reintegrated Stage 6 replacement would have to begin. Is there really enough social support among the bare universals of our complex and often unjust world to support this process? Consider that moral development through Stage 4 had a range of existing social conventions to adapt to, to help guide structural construction. Even Stage 5 had certain constitutional ideologies to help guide its evolution—Bills of Rights from many nations, always balanced with principles "providing for the common good." But where in the world can Stage 6 look for constructive help to carve out its fully universal rights and fully egalitarian principles? Where would it look for the even more balanced mix of universal benevolence and justice that it needs? There seems no model for Stage 6 to grapple with, no model to suggest the feasibility of such a seemingly utopian and speculative cognitive enterprise.

As things stand, not even the concerted (often hypothetical) reasoning of philosophers has been able to solve the problems that Stage 5 faces in trying to balance individual rights and social welfare. Moral theory has been locked in this controversy for a full century. Most important, its contestants see much of their task as theoretical: is a utilitarian reduction of rights to social welfare or a Kantian reduction of social utility to equal rights more theoretically elegant? Each of these reductionist "Stage 6" structures can *simulate* the workings and results of the other if it is rigged to do so, but not in a refined, tidy, or honest way. While either version may improve on Stage 5, as current Stage 6 logic may, it is not clear that these improvements are required by everyday problem-solving. Yet only in this way, according to Kohlberg's view, could any Stage 6 naturally arise.

Stage 6 as Moral Philosophy

Let us conclude our consideration of Stage 6 with a closer look at its moral philosophy. Kohlberg's case for the ultimate moral adequacy of Stage 6 combines structural with moral philosophic considerations. The ultimate structural adequacy of Stage 6 rests ultimately on two features of the equilibration model. The first is adaptivity, the capacity of Stage 6 to solve all moral problems in principle. The second is reciprocity or reversibility, the complete correlativity of individual rights and duties at Stage 6. Presumably it is the functional struggle to solve problems, to deal with society effectively, that leads to the complete internal symmetry of Stage 6. Likewise, this internal symmetry affords Stage 6 its functional effectiveness. Such an interrelation of functional and logical virtues affords the sort of stability and efficiency, as well as the consistency, completeness, and elegance that an adequate prescriptive theory requires.

Unfortunately, Kohlberg has never really shown how well Stage 6 solves the broad range of moral problems. Rather, he has offered alleged Stage 6 solutions to a dozen or so unusual problems, most involving life and death. Only one study reported by Kohlberg even purports to show that Stage 6 subjects agree on solutions to moral problems, a crucial feature of *ultimate* problem-solving adequacy. In this study (Erdynast, 1973) only two moral problems are confronted by only a handful of Stage 6 respondents. Moreover, it is now clear from Kohlberg's standard scoring manual that these respondents should have been scored at Stages 4 or 5.

Kohlberg derives the moral adequacy of Stage 6 from a philosophical evaluation of reputed Stage 6 problem-solving. Stage 6 judgments meet criteria of adequacy set by Kantian, formalistic, deontological justice theorists. Moreover, Kohlberg claims, these criteria are the best around. My previous criticisms of justice logic, framed from the perspective of benevolence, were meant to cast doubt on this claim. Even more primal doubt can be cast on Stage 6 by *using* this claim, by arguing from Kantian assumptions in just the way Kohlberg does against care, to fault liberal egalitarianism itself. Consider the following.

The recent Rawls-Nozick debate within Kantian justice theory revived perennial questions of whether individual merit or equality should determine just due or property rights (Rawls, 1971; Nozick, 1974). Which basis for rights truly respects our persons? Kohlberg tries to skirt this dispute by claiming that Stage 6 is neutral between such options. At the level of basic moral structure they are both egalitarian—equality by merit, equality by person. He views the dispute as a matter of theoretical detail rather than basic logical structure. This will not do, however, since, among other things, it is inconsistent with Kohlberg's own position. Meritocratic justice (just desert reasoning) is characteristic of Stage 4 reasoning. But it does not figure into the defining criteria of Stage 5 or 6 judgment at all. Moreover, tying merit considerations to the sorts of rights Kohlberg describes at Stages 5 and 6 consistently yields judgments that oppose those proposed by Kohlberg at Stage 6.

This is seen clearly in the central Heinz dilemma. According to Kohlberg, Stage 6 directs a husband (Heinz) to steal a drug that can save his wife's life (even a stranger's life) if its owner-inventor (the druggist) will not sell it at a feasible price. This is because life takes precedence over property as a universalizable principle of moral preference. Moreover, the need to respect rights overrides any bad consequences of doing so. (These consequences would include financial loss for the druggist, arrest, trial, and likely incarceration for Heinz, and judicial costs to the taxpaying community.) Put in ideal role-taking terms, anyone would be willing to suffer great costs or take great risks to save another's life assuming, ideally, that he or she would be willing to do likewise for me (or anyone).

However, once individual right claims become meritorious, the druggist's claims to withhold his drug *must* or *might* be put first. (Either alternative is unacceptable at Stage 6.) Here we might not be willing to slide back and forth between roles, playing "just anyone," playing simply "a person" in need or a person with property, regardless of how that need or property arose.

The first alternative might be posed by a libertarian version of meritocracy. As Nozick might argue, Heinz's wife is dying of a disease, of cancer, not of the druggist's greed. The druggist has not caused her disease nor stolen the remedy from her. He is not even withholding the remedy from her; this would imply that the drug is a free good (like air) or that she has stronger claims to it than he. Actually, however, her claim to the remedy is need, and need alone obviously does not produce remedies, goods, or *holdings*.

The druggist, by contrast, has a merit claim to the drug as an expression of his effort and choice. The drug is his autonomous self expressed or objectified, his free labor congealed in a product. It should be respected as such from the Kantian point of view. The moral conflict here is not between life and property. It is a question of whether we can violate a (meritorious) right claim in order to promote a good consequence or uphold a value. From Nozick's point of view, Kohlberg's Stage 6 solution is utilitarian (perhaps caring), not Kantian or just. It uses the druggist's choice and free activity (autonomy) as mere means to good ends—to prevent evil or loss, not to prevent wrong. (Dying of disease is not being murdered.)

Just as Heinz's wife could not have obliged the druggist to produce the drug in the first place, even to save her life, she cannot now oblige him to sell it at a price she and Heinz have "set." (You and I are not obliged to become biochemists or physicians just because people are gravely ill.) It is through his choices and efforts that the very possibility of her cure has come to exist at all. The druggist chose to research and produce this drug as a part of his occupation, as a product he might sell for a fee. A primary and legitimate aim in taking on this extra work was to increase his (family's) standard of living. Admittedly, his material costs of production were far lower than the price he set for the good, but undertaking this research meant foregoing other activities, experiences, and possible accomplishments that he may have found more gratifying. The druggist could not be sure his efforts would come to anything. His risky investment of labor and effort would not have been compensated by Heinz or other potential consumers had he failed to produce a cure.

In all these ways the druggist's pricing policy seems reasonable and fair. Indeed, it may reflect proper Kantian self-respect rather than selfishness. At the least it is within the druggist's rights to set prices based on a reasonable estimation of his sacrifices and the worth of his labor or self-investment. Moreover, pursuing even a high standard of living through special effort, free trade, and fair pricing certainly seems permissible if it harms no one else in itself. (Not lowering a fair price is not a harm in itself.) Even when motivated by greed, such a pursuit does not seem to violate or commit an injustice toward others.

This brand of justice, of respect for persons, will satisfy some of us but outrage most. While it captures our relations to products well enough, it all but ignores our relations and responsibilities to each other. (Holdings should be mere instruments for carrying on such relations.) Note, however, that we need not accept the libertarian line holistically or even substantially in order to question Stage 6 liberalism. If there is anything significant to this meritocratic rationale, even as a subsidiary component of justice, the ultimate adequacy of Stage 6 begins to crumble. It is important to note, also, that even Nozick as libertarian would find Heinz's druggist callous and cruel, unfeeling and inhumane. Faced directly with the desperate couple, the druggist should have acted with compassion, at least letting Heinz pay for the drug on time, perhaps simply giving it to him for nothing in this exceptional case. Even where there is no personal involvement, we should create charities or even government programs to handle such emergencies (so long as no one is forced to contribute). But, crucially, such aid would not be an individual's right (for the libertarian). It would either be an ideal, or a primarily social responsibility. It would express joint concern or care for our human "neighbors," but not mere respect or just treatment. As such, the need for aid could not override or violate rights; it could not be enforced.

The caring perspective may accommodate part of this argument, the part that distinguishes obligations of justice from those of concern. But it may balk at having rights override care as the libertarian prefers. Still, there are less libertarian versions of meritocratic justice that may satisfy care and justice perspectives outside of Stage 6. Their emphasis would fall more strongly on the relation between our responsibility for a situation and the duties others bear to us in that situation.

Suppose the drowning man (in Kohlberg's dilemma of the same name) were a daredevilish and vicious hoodlum. Suppose he jumped into dangerous water on a whim, or to avoid enemies, or to make new ones. Let us assume, by contrast, that you, a passerby and his potential savior, are an Oxfam (hunger-relief) fund raiser and a very safety-conscious individual. According to Stage 6, you would be obliged to assume a grave and near equal risk of drowning to rescue this villain. He would have a basic right that you do so that overrides your noble commitments. After all, a life is at stake. To neglect your duty here is either (1) to confuse an unconditional right to life with the quality of a person's character; (2) to advance the greater good at the illegitimate expense of that right; (3) to "punish" someone (cosmically?) for being careless or ill-intentioned; or (4) to allow your moral choice to be determined by the morally arbitrary accident that he, and not you, is in trouble. (Stage 6 reminds us that "there but for the grace of God go I.")

But actually the hoodlum is not at grave risk by accident. Rather it is largely his own choice and negligence that landed him in the soup. (He is not a hoodlum purely by accident either.) The same can be said, in part, for why you are safe and dry. Whether or not you desire that the bad "get theirs" or that "the greater good be served," it is unclear why you should take on the *full consequences* of the hoodlum's irresponsibility and viciousness (or even of those who helped make him so) out of mere respect for his person. The threat to his life is not merely there in his being. It did not simply happen to him. Rather, he put it there, and thereby imposed on you the duty to aid him. To "refuse" a daring rescue is not to neglect his rights or even to claim that his rights have been altered by his actions. It is merely to note that our duty to him and his claims on it have been lessened by his actions, by his voluntarily assuming the foreseeable burdens of them. (It is *Kohlberg's* task to show that rights and duties are correlative.) When we assume the other person's role as an equal person we can then discount these burdens, for the most part, as his own special affair. In the same way that toleration need only respect the choosing *person*, not the particular *values* chosen, so my duty to the hoodlum (or to anyone) need not put me equally in his *place*, especially the place he has made for himself. Kohlberg's roles and duties at Stage 6 cannot accommodate these distinctions.

Consider a more difficult and heart-rending case. Suppose a group of destitute villagers refuse to move out of an area perennially plagued by drought, flood, disease, and war. They have fervent, culturally defining beliefs about the importance of ancestral traditions and homelands. Need we who can aid them (or steal for them) do so, and do so often, out of mere respect for their persons? Would this not amount to subsidizing their traditions and beliefs, their cultural interests, at a significant threat to our own? Their choice to stay put, as important as it is, renders their destitution an unfair burden on us to a large extent. But Stage 6 cannot see this to any extent. (And if our villagers' problems were largely the doing of economic imperialists in our society, do we violate rights by not paying victims the compensation that these victimizers owe them?)

Of course we owe the destitute or endangered *something* just because they are people, no matter what they have done. And surely they can never be wholly responsible for their plight, far from it. Kohlberg trades on this by posing our most ultimate moral claims in his dilemmas. But Stage 6 must show that this is all there is to it, that (basic) duties cannot be altered in degree by changes and inequalities in responsibility. It must show that our ultimate regard for the irresponsible or vicious is not primarily compassion rather than respect.

Even when people's plight is beyond their control and is no one's fault but nature's, we need not take on the full burdens of their tragedies and misfortunes. At least it is not their right that we do so. The liberal-egalitarian prescription to so do at Stage 6 is more a form of cosmic (Stage 7?) justice than moral (stage) justice. This is because it attempts to compensate for, rather than merely ignore, nature's indifference to our moral systems. Stage 6 tries to right tragedies and misfortunes as if they were wrongs or injustices, by redistributing their burdens equally to each. This is what ideal role-taking requires of us. It has us *take on* others' problems as if they happened to us, as if they were our fair share of obligation. Here responsibility is thrust on us as if we assumed it.

Cosmic justice translates into supererogation when seen from the noncosmic justice perspective. Consider Stage 6 directives to attempt daring rescues and to steal for the poor or afflicted. Are these not the heroic and exemplary ideals of the very good Samaritan rather than the normal duties of the merely fair individual? While we may applaud Stage 6 for going beyond the call of justice, should its justice not own up to caring?

The life and death focus of many Kohlberg dilemmas obscures the power of responsibility and merit, as well as the tendency of Stage 6 egalitarianism to overstep individual rights. The need to preserve life seems to override every other moral consideration, including the ever-partial degree to which we are responsible for our plights. It seems to demand heroic effort. But consider other, wholly different ranges of cases that Stage 6 must solve, cases posing trade-offs among less ultimate interests. Suppose Heinz's wife is ill but not dying. Suppose she and Heinz are spendthrifts and well-known "party animals," facts that account in part for her ill health and Heinz's inability to buy medicines. (Of course we will assume, by contrast, that the druggist has always scrimped and saved except when charities came to call or friends were in need.) Must the druggist now sell a $2,000 drug for $1,500 if this is all Heinz can raise? Can Heinz steal the drug now?

Similar questions can be raised about other Kohlberg dilemmas. For instance, in Kohlberg's Stage 6 judgment we must transport someone to an appointment so long as the cost of doing so does not outweigh (or equal?) the cost of not showing up. (We would normally call this doing someone a favor. But not doing this "favor," for Kohlberg, constitutes a violation of rights.) Does it make a difference if the person needing the ride often makes appointments with no idea of how to keep them, perhaps assuming that some sucker will give him a ride? Does his irresponsibility in the matter not decrease one's own?

Again, if there is any strength to these "meritocratic" rationales, even as components of liberal justice, the ultimate adequacy of Stage 6 justice is in serious doubt. And this doubt merely compounds the doubts that care raised earlier. I believe the strengths of these rationales are clear.

Kohlberg has not appreciated the demands for adequacy taken on by touting Stage 6 as the ultimate structure of moral theory. It will take its shape only by dealing well with the sorts of everyday problems social universals can generate. How could this process generate the necessary logical finesse to handle the sorts of philosophic hypotheticals hurled at moral theories? The adequacy demonstrated by problem-solving, by equilibration to the environment at Stage 6 concerns only one feature of moral theoretic adequacy, namely, prescriptivity. At best, universal problem-solving adequacy would qualify Stage 6 justice as a champion applied ethic. Yet this still leaves open the question of how well Stage 6 structure can explain and justify moral judgments, as any adequate moral theory must. Most philosophical theories focus on a certain territory in the moral domain—rights, distributive justice, virtue. And they do so to a limited theoretic extent—justification, prescription, or application.[3] By contrast, Kohlberg touts Stage 6 structure and principles as the ultimately adequate basis for performing all these theoretical tasks—social, political, and interpersonal; justificatory, explanatory, and prescriptive. Running Stage 6 through this gauntlet is all the more amazing when one considers that its developmental training program is focused on solving problems, not on explaining solutions. While Kohlberg searches for stages, and characterizes them in the modes of explanation, or justification, their adaptive developmental logic is supposedly applied. If Stage 6 is to approach criteria of adequacy for moral philosophical theories, then it should address the differences between the theoretical tasks of justification, explanation, prescription, and application. From the research point of view, this might mean testing them more explicitly in the mode of choice or deliberation for choice than Kohlberg does. It might mean describing them in that mode as well in theory. At the least, differences between practical utility and logical or theoretical impeccability must be acknowledged.

Reversibility and Correlativity

The more specifically logical and theoretically relevant side of equilibration is reversibility. At Stage 6 every right in every role has a correlative duty to respect it, and vice-versa. There are no loose ends. Thus we can advance claims or judgments at Stage 6 consistently as we change or reverse points of view on a moral conflict. This operational balance accounts for the functional stability and efficiency of Stage 6, and for its decisiveness when making judgments. This full symmetry of conceptual relations also affords Stage 6 structure a logical unity and elegance that the more philosophically elaborated portions of moral theory can only envy. Conceptual elegance is key to *theoretical* adequacy in particular. Perhaps then when we view these internal virtues of Stage 6 *at their junction* with problem-solving acuity, Kohlberg's Stage 6 boasts will seem sensible.

Unfortunately, there are at least three critical problems with Kohlberg's reversibility criterion that he has not addressed. I can only touch on these here. The first concerns how we decide which moral concepts, rationales, and perspectives to correlate with each other in the first place, and which possible match-ups to ignore. How do we determine the correct correlations to draw, and know when they are complete? Starting at Stage 3, Kohlberg speaks of there being social roles and social perspectives, individual rights and duties, and general principles of justice. If at Stage 6 individual rights and duties match within individual roles, what happens to social perspectives and general principles? How are they related to these individual matches? Consider briefly the serious consequences of how we answer or fail to answer the question. As Stage 6 presently stands, each individual is bound to aid others, even to risk death (in the drowning man dilemma) or jail (in the Heinz dilemma) in order to fend off dire threats and deprivations. Clearly this leads to a seriously arbitrary and unfair distribution of the burdens and benefits of justice itself across society. The burdens fall unfairly on those who are close by, on those who happen by, and on the more morally conscious or kindly. The typical way a just society handles this problem is through institutional arrangements—fire departments and rescue squads to save those in danger, public health and welfare programs for the destitute and gravely ill. This assures justice from the "social perspective." Yet, crucially, a Stage 6 logic that simply matches individual rights and duties cannot prefer this "more just" alternative. It cannot handle these inequities caused by justice itself. (Nowhere in Kohlberg's Stage 6 solutions are provisions made to compensate the druggist *in any amount* for the illegal theft of his drug, or to compensate Heinz on any level for having to become a thief and risk jail.) Yet if we add a distributional principle of justice at the social level—to handle inequities, to complement Stage 6 rights and duties—how can we maintain full logical symmetry and correlativity?

One possibility is to maintain that for each individual right there is both an individual duty (to each other) and a single general duty at the social level. For each individual duty there are individual rights and a general social right. Likewise, individual perspectives correlate with each other and with "the social perspective." Though this does not preserve a one-to-one symmetry of rights and duties between roles and persons, it does yield a neat set of matched triangles. It relates each person to each other directly and indirectly through social principles of justice, leaving no rights or duties dangling. The problem is, however, that there can be no Stage 6 social rights per se (except explicitly delegated special rights to enforce individual rights). Society has no actual will of its own, it is not a person. And to sanctify the "social interest" through rights is to "outlaw" dissent and insure majority tyranny. Thus full symmetry breaks down and we must either drop the social perspective or correlate individual rights and duties to a general social duty of justice alone. Both of these options and the ambiguity between them violate Kohlberg's reversibility criterion. Moreover, the moral consequences of choosing the social duty option are implausibly onerous at Stage 6. Greater obligations would be placed on us through this correlativity of duties than the logic of mere fairness or respect toward persons should require.[4]

A second problem with the reversibility criterion concerns role-taking. Unlike philosophical theories of justice that use hypothetical models of decision making—Rawls's original position, utilitarianism's ideal observer—Kohlberg's stage structures evolve and function through *actual* role-taking. This is a *competence* that could only evolve from prolonged *performance*. Two questions arise in this context. First, is it *possible* in practice for us to fully differentiate and integrate all the roles needed to make the kind of large-scale, cross-cultural moral judgments that most distinguish Stage 6 from Stage 5? Second, are the moral and logical prerequisites in place at Stage 6 to determine what considerations we can claim legitimately from each reciprocal role? Kohlberg assumes that because we can take and reverse roles in some manageable cases we can therefore handle unmanageable cases *in principle* at Stage 6. Yet we would need *some* evidence of actual decision-making in unwieldy cases to know that Stage 6 solves all problems *adequately* in principle. Maximum adequacy is the key.

Of course, we can reduce the size of the role-taking problem in these large-scale cases by putting whole sets of roles in the same class. "They are all the same in position," we might say, "so they will all have the same legitimate claims." Our final resolution of the dilemma then merely involves taking the roles of these larger classes or "representative persons." The problem is, however, that this is precisely the maneuver to be justified. A crucial part of how we find out that claims are legitimate in each role is by seeing whether we can advance them from *all* roles. This is the key to Kohlberg's argument for the inadequacy of utilitarianism as a moral theory; it is why Stage 5 balancing of rights and utility cannot work. We could not advance these sorts of principles reversibly, Kohlberg maintains, if we *really* put ourselves in the place of people locked in moral dilemma. In some of these actual roles, supposedly, we would sense a strong cognitive conflict and imbalance rather than feeling conceptually equilibrated and content.

As things stand, Kohlberg has never been able to specify what counts as a Stage 6 claim that one could advance in any role, much less all roles. More important, his Stage 6 principle cannot specify relevant claims as a logical class or component of cognitive structure. Do we advance *interests* in each role, or *needs* only? Do we advance both, but only after deciding in advance which ones are legitimate or just claims? (And how do we decide this?) Before we can fully integrate roles, rights, and duties, we must know what sorts of claims we are to feel equilibrated about. These typical problems of ethical reasoning are damning to Stage 6 adequacy, as anyone who seriously uses Kohlberg's Stage 6 ideal role-taking procedure will find. (And the ideal role-taking procedure is the intellectually *refined* version of Stage 6 role-taking.)

Finally, when we relate the internal criterion of reversibility to the external criterion of adaptivity or problem-solving, we find that reversibility itself is largely responsible for the implausible solutions that Stage 6 generates. (Full correlativity of *liberal* rights and duties, at least, leads to inadequacies in Stage 6 judgment.) As noted, the logic of Stage 6 implies that we each must take on extreme risks or deprivation out of (mere) respect for any other individual. Supposedly, to allow someone to suffer destitution, illness, or death for lack of our aid is to do them an injustice. Previously I noted that these implications seem to violate crucial distinctions between cosmic and moral justice, between duties of justice and benevolence (or care), and between obligation and supererogation. The correlativity of rights and duties fosters these abuses in two ways. First, it does not allow us to adjust our degree of duty or responsibility to others so as to reflect the degrees of responsibility they have assumed themselves. Thus refusing to satisfy needs that others have irresponsibly created for themselves looks like a failure to fully respect rights of aid. To discount our duty to them is to reduce our correlative rights. Second, correlativity does not allow us to conceive certain needs and claims as primarily social problems that invoke primarily joint responsibilities. Correlative rights and duties can only portray any individual's full need or claim as any other individual's full or near-equal burden. This is so whether or not the individuals concerned choose to bear it cooperatively. In all sorts of cases such a logic seems blatantly implausible.

To sum up once more, the much-touted reversibility and correlativity criteria actually undermine Stage 6 rather than clinching the case for its adequacy. Fully correlated rights and duties seem to leave out, or even violate, general principles of justice. In addition, fully reversible role-taking seems infeasible

in those very cases that distinguish Stage 6 judgment. It may
be psychologically impossible to integrate all roles reversibly in
large-scale or cross-cultural decision-making. It seems conceptually problematic to determine what goes into the roles one
should take. Neither the criterion of reversibility nor the principles of Stage 6 justice can guide us sufficiently here. Moreover, correlating rights and duties makes it impossible to adjust
our degree of responsibility toward others without seeming to
deny their rights. Yet a failure to recognize that the responsibilities that others take on diminish our duties toward them
causes Stage 6 to push us too far.

What Is to Be Done?

When we add these structural and philosophical problems to
those noted previously, the magic of Stage 6 seems more mystery than allure. I believe that these challenges to Stage 6
recommend certain steps that researchers influenced by Kohlberg might take.

1. Drop Stage 6 justice completely from the stage sequence
as an emerging structure, as a hypothetical structure, or as a
formal end point for defining structural evolution.

2. Drop the notion of a most adequate structural end point
of moral development (above Stage 5 or elsewhere) as well as
the claim that it is needed to define a developmental sequence
of moral judgment or conduct a nonindoctrinative program of
moral education.

3. Search for solid data (from longitudinal samples especially) regarding the possible existence of higher *natural* stages.
Interpret these findings in their own terms as the *data* best
dictate.

4. If necessary, hypothesize a variety of possible Stage 6
structures for interpreting moral judgment data that seems to
transcend Stage 5. At least one of these hypothetical structures
should *extrapolate* from Stage 5. Another should extrapolate
from Stages 3 and 4, or from possible mixtures of the two.
(This would counter methodological biases in describing higher
stages.) Another hypothetical structure might form a mixture
of just and benevolent logics at higher stages and levels.

5. Redescribe all stages in their own terms, and relative to each other, rather than in relation to Stage 6. (Differences between moral rights, social justice, and legal justice should be observed.) Piecemeal comparative criteria of adequacy may be used for these purposes, rather than a presumed end point of development. (Most evaluations of adequacy are performed in this comparative way.) Alternatively, morally neutral or bipartisan end stages might be used, along with the various hypothetical structures posed above. Or both types of criteria might be used in combination.

6. While continuing the moral discussion and just-community approach to moral education, do not place special emphasis in discussion on reasoning that approaches the peculiarities of Stage 6. (I doubt that this kind of higher-stage stimulation currently occurs very often in Kohlbergian education.)

7. Analyze current data and extend research on the structure of value judgments. Include also those judgments of character, merit, and virtue that are most closely related to fulfilling principles of justice and benevolence. This might fill out the structure of these principles and of their structural relations to each other.

8. Drop all claims about the superiority of Kantian, formalist, deontological, Rawlsian, or Habermasian justice in ethics and the support moral psychology may seem to offer for these claims. Adopt a more nonpartisan view toward the logics of right, justice, benevolence, virtue, and value, and rethink their possible interrelations at the levels of strict, special, and imperfect obligation.

I believe that if these steps were followed, surprisingly few changes would be needed in Kohlberg's stage sequence (1–5), and that these changes would bring out and extend the logic of benevolence. In my opinion, Kohlberg's theory is much more morally and empirically adequate than the flawed structure of Stage 6 makes it seem. Most of the criticisms of Kohlberg's theory can be swept aside by merely eliminating Stage 6 in all its forms and reputed influences in the theory. The mystery is how legions of Kohlberg supporters and critics were taken in by the dubious magic of this dubious stage for so long.

Notes

1. Kohlberg's coauthored chapter in the present volume now contains two alleged cases of Stage 6 reasoning. My commentary on the case of Joan is based on a previous draft by Kohlberg that presented her case alone and in greater detail.

2. Kohlberg has offered a reconstruction of his method (Colby et al., 1983) that may seem to contradict my criticisms here. As I see it, however, Kohlberg's bootstrapping model is a post hoc remedy for the dangers I cite, and a partial one at that. When it works, it shows that some initial biases can later be justified with data.

3. Rawls's theory focuses on justice only, and on social justice in particular. In addition it primarily considers the role of social justice in specifying the principled basis for enacting a federal constitution within a large-scale nation state. This involves the problem of which moral precepts we can legitimately enforce, rather than merely that of which precepts are morally legitimate. To approach even this circumscribed problem, Rawls makes the ideal assumption that the citizenry will comply with the constitution once it is enacted. His principles are designed solely to specify and justify certain general obligations; they all but ignore the question of what rights we might have and whether they are correlative to our duties. In addition, Rawls explicitly distinguishes his constitutional principles from those that would prescribe or justify particular public policies. He also distinguishes his theory of social and political justice from a moral theory of right that would handle interpersonal problems. Yet even such a theory would concentrate on explanation and justification, to parallel Rawls's effort, not on decision-making as Kohlberg's does. In order to decide cases and render particular prescriptions, general principles would need specific rules of application. Explanatory principles are not decision strategies as they stand. The whole field of applied ethics testifies to the difficulty of trying to move from such general principles to cases. In fact, many philosophers have abandoned the attempt as misguided and hopeless. Instead they try to generate applied or prescriptive theories by generalizing from the circumscribed rules of thumb we use to solve particular cases.

4. At Stage 6 all rights and duties are universal, not merely social (societal). They apply to all persons as persons all over the world. Thus whatever general duties we have, they cannot be tailored to our particular society or nation state. They cannot presume a particular social grouping as their framework or target in the first instance. (In this regard, Kohlberg's Stage 6 solution to the Korea dilemma should not take the side of American soldiers first and ask which of them should blow up a bridge to "stop the enemy." On principle, both sides should have equal claims—including civilians and the military—and separate accounts should be given of special obligations to one's country.) Thus our reversible social duty of justice must be, first, to form social aid organizations when they do not exist (and support them when they do) and, second, to do so on a worldwide scale. Consider further what such correlativity means. Out of mere respect for each other as autonomous beings, each of us would be obliged to help establish and maintain international (or multinational) institutions to deal with deprivation, danger, illness, and so forth. You would have a duty to each other person to do such things, and if you did not fulfill it, you would have helped perpetuate injustice among us. You would have violated individual rights insofar as they are correlated with the general duty of social justice. I assume that many readers may find this consequence outlandish, believing that we have gotten moral correlations confused. Such altruism cannot be owed each other merely as persons, merely out of fairness. But how does *reversibility* help us allay this confusion or modify these consequences?

References

Attanucci, J. (1984). *Mothers in their own terms: A developmental perspective on self and role.* Doctoral dissertation, Harvard University Graduate School of Education, Cambridge, MA.

Colby, A., Kohlberg, L., Gibbs, J., and Lieberman, M. (1983). A longitudinal study of moral judgment. *Society for Research in Child Development: Monograph Series, 48.*

Colby, A., Kohlberg, L., and collaborators. (1987). *The measurement of moral judgment* (2 vols.). New York: Cambridge University Press.

Erdynast, A. (1973). *Improving the adequacy of moral reasoning.* Doctoral dissertation, Harvard University Graduate School of Education, Cambridge, MA.

Gilligan, C. (1977). In a different voice: Women's conceptions of the self and of morality. *Harvard Educational Review*, 47:481–517.

Gilligan, C. (1982). *In a different voice: Psychological theory and women's development.* Cambridge, MA: Harvard University Press.

Gilligan, C. (1986). Response to critics. *Signs*, 11:324–333.

Gilligan, C., and Wiggans, G. (1987). The origins of morality in early childhood relationships. In J. Kagan and S. Lamb (Eds.), *The emergence of morality in young children.* Chicago: University of Chicago Press.

Johnston, K. (1985). *Two moral orientations—Two problem-solving strategies: Adolescents' solutions to dilemmas in fables.* Doctoral dissertation, Harvard University Graduate School of Education, Cambridge, MA.

Kohlberg, L. (1981). *Essays on moral development. Vol 1: The philosophy of moral development.* San Francisco: Harper and Row.

Kohlberg, L. (1984). *Essays on moral development. Vol. 2: The psychology of moral development.* San Francisco: Harper and Row.

Kohlberg, L., Levine, C., and Hewer, A. (1983). *Moral stages: A current formulation and a response to critics.* Basel: Karger.

Langdale, S. (1983). *Moral observations and moral development: The analysis of care and justice reasoning across different dilemmas in females and males from childhood through adulthood.* Doctoral dissertation, Harvard University Graduate School of Education, Cambridge, MA.

Lyons, N. (1983). Two perspectives: On self, relationships, and morality. *Harvard Educational Review*. 53:125–145.

MacPherson, C. (1962). *Political theory of possessive individualism: Hobbes to Locke.* Oxford: Oxford University Press.

Marx, K. (1972). On the Jewish question. In R. Tucker (Ed.), *Marx-Engels Reader.* New York: Norton. (Original work published 1843)

Nozick, R. (1974). *Anarchy, state, and utopia.* New York: Basic Books.

Puka, B. (1990). Reconstructing Kohlberg's theory: Preserving essential structure, removing controversial content. In J. Gewirtz and W. Kurtines (Eds.), *Moral development: Advances in theory, research, and applications* (Vol. 1). Hillsdale, NJ: Earlbaum.

Puka, B. (in press-a). Care—in an interpretive voice. *New Ideas in Psychology.*

Puka, B. (in press-b). Interpretative experiments: Caring and justice, in many "different voices." *Human Development.*

Puka, B. (in press-c). The liberation of caring. *Hypatia: A Feminist Journal of Philosophy.*

Rawls, J. (1971). *A theory of justice.* Cambridge, MA: Harvard University Press.

Simpson, E. (1974). Moral development research: A case study of scientific cultural bias. *Human Development*, 17:81–106.

Sullivan, E. V. (1977). A study of Kohlberg's structural theory of moral development: A critique of liberal social science ideology. *Human Development*, 20:352–376.

Walker, L. (1984). Sex differences in the development of moral reasoning: A critical review. *Child Development*, 55:667–691.

Walker, L., de Vries, B., and Trevethan, S. (1987). Moral stages and moral orientations in real-life and hypothetical dilemmas. *Child Development*, 58:842–858.

Justice and Solidarity: On the Discussion Concerning Stage 6

Jürgen Habermas

Are There Natural Moral Stages on the Postconventional Level?

Kohlberg has returned, albeit tentatively, to his earlier, temporarily suspended view that at the postconventional level there are two natural stages of moral development. His reason seems plausible enough: the construction of any stage hierarchy requires a normatively designated point of reference from which the developmental process in question can be described retrospectively as a learning process. However, Stage 5 moral judgment is not a suitable candidate for this reference point, since it fails to satisfy the criterion of stable, noncriticizable solutions. With Kohlberg (and in contrast to Bill Puka), I hold the view that cognitivist approaches in the tradition of Piaget necessarily require such a normatively determined end state for learning processes; in contrast to Kohlberg, however, I do not see why the highest moral stage would have to be conceived as a *natural* stage—that is, conceived in the same sense as Stages 1 through 4.

There are intrapsychic structures that correspond to the structural descriptions of natural stages. The same theoretical postulate has to hold for the description of the postconventional level of judgment: we have to assume a psychic representation of the capacity for principled moral judgment. Empirical evidence indicates that this competence manifests itself in a variety of typical strategies for resolving conflicts.

These strategies bear a resemblance to familiar moral philosophies: roughly speaking, they resemble either utilitarian approaches, or counterfactual constructs of the Hobbesian type (based on rational egoism), or the deontological theories developed from Kant to Rawls. Do these differences, which are variations in content, imply the existence of structural differences, and if so, can the latter be interpreted as natural stages? Two considerations suggest otherwise.

1. Differences in moral philosophical orientation are not equivalent, prima facie or necessarily, to psychologically relevant differences in the level at which systematic explanations are formulated: specifically, to differences in the level of reflection of the moral justifications given by Kohlberg's subjects. Different stages of reflection can be demonstrated, for example, in the way concepts of rules are applied. To be sure, all those who judge on the postconventional level are characterized by taking a hypothetical attitude vis-à-vis institutions and maxims of action as well as by judging and, if necessary, criticizing existing norms that are actually accepted in the light of abstract norms. But not all those on the postconventional level are able to distinguish such fundamental norms from simple rules on the basis that the former are principles. Not all those who in fact keep the logical roles of principles and rules separate[1] can order the variety of principles employed in a system in such a way that it is possible rationally to weigh principles from a still more abstract point of view—the "moral point of view." Not all those who adopt a moral point of view can distinguish their principle of morality from simple principles on the basis of its purely procedural character. And not all those who advance a procedural ethics of this sort adequately distinguish between applying the procedural principle monologically, in a merely virtual way, and conducting an intersubjectively organized test. If one disregards this last step in reflection (to which I shall return later), these stages of reflection do not permit any discrimination between different orientations in moral theory. All autonomous moralities, that is, those that are independent of metaphysical or religious background assumptions, can be expressed in terms of moral principles, and some of them can be understood as procedural

ethics. On the other hand, there are also moral theories—such as the critiques of ethical formalism from Hegel to Scheler up to the neo-Aristotelianism of our time (cf. Sandel, 1983)—that dispute the notion that higher stages of reflection represent an advance in moral justifications. Bill Puka's objections (see his essay in this volume) also tend in this direction.

As far as this discussion is concerned, I certainly do not subscribe to the view that "anything goes." In principle, I hold that it must be possible to decide on firm grounds which moral theory is best able to reconstruct the universal core of our moral intuitions, that is, to reconstruct a "moral point of view" that claims universal validity. Otherwise one would fail from the outset to capture the cognitive meaning of the "ought" of normative propositions. But from the debate among the philosophers one can also learn that—at least up to this point—the competing approaches do not adequately discriminate between those forms of justification whose structural features might be of psychological relevance. The strategies through which interviewees and philosophers ground their statements may indeed be distinguishable in terms of stages of reflection, but the strategies used by philosophers do not have "hard" status: one could hardly claim for them the status of "natural," intrapsychically represented stages of development. The debate among the moral philosophers cannot be settled with the *psychological* assertion that Kantians have better, structurally privileged access to their moral intuitions than do rule-utilitarians or social-contract theorists in the Hobbesian tradition. It was possible to read Kohlberg's original description of the two postconventional stages to mean something of that sort. However, the debate among cognitivist moral philosophers is concerned with the questions of how and by what conceptual means the *same* intuition potential that becomes accessible to *everyone* with the transition to the postconventional level of autonomous morality can most adequately be explained. It is a question of a better explication of an intuitive knowing, which, at the postconventional level, has already taken on a reflective character and to that extent is from the beginning already oriented to rational reconstructions. This contest can be settled only on the field of philosophical argumentation, not on that of developmental psychology.[2]

2. From the perspective of cognitive developmental psychology as well, there are several reasons to drop the postulate of natural moral stages at the postconventional level (which is itself presented as "natural"). It follows from the theoretical assumptions themselves that the relationship of psychologist to interviewee in the interview situation has to change as soon as the subject reaches the formal operational or postconventional level of thought or moral judgment. For at this level the asymmetry that exists in preceding stages between the subject's pre-reflective efforts and the psychologist's attempt to grasp them reflectively disappears. And with this, the cognitive discrepancy that was originally built into the interview situation disappears. Principled moral judgments are described theoretically as no longer representing merely the prereflective expression or reproduction of an intuitively applied know-how; rather, they already represent the beginnings of an explication of this knowing, the rudiments, so to speak, of a moral theory. On the postconventional level, moral judgments are not possible without the first steps in the reconstruction of acquired moral intuitions, and thus they already have in essence the significance of moral *theoretical* statements. At this level, learning processes can proceed only if the reflective abstraction previously operative as a learning mechanism is sublimated, as it were, into the procedure of rational reconstruction, however ad hoc and unmethodically that procedure may be pursued. The psychologist who proceeds reconstructively, who himself moves within the open horizon of a research process whose results cannot be predicted, can thus treat research subjects who are at the highest level of competence only as participants whose status in the work of scientific reconstruction is (in principle) equal to their own. All those who make moral judgments at the postconventional level, whether they be psychologists, research subjects, or philosophers, are participants in the *joint venture* of finding the most appropriate possible explanation of a core domain of moral intuitions to which they have access under fundamentally equal social cognitive conditions. If that is so, however, the substantial variations in structure and con-

tent in postconventional responses to moral dilemmas and in the various moral philosophical approaches cannot be attributed to natural stages.[3]

The arguments given in (1) and (2) above do not in any way diminish the value of the new attempt by Kohlberg, Boyd, and Levine (this volume) to expand and revise the criterion description of Stage 6, although they do place this attempt in a different light. I see their explanation as a stimulating and extraordinarily instructive contribution to a moral philosophical discussion that, as Kohlberg also believes, will determine the choice of the correct moral theory and thereby decide on the correct description of the normatively designated end state of moral development.[4] I take the insights of Kohlberg the philosopher just as seriously as those of the psychological author of a theory of moral development that is accepted in its fundamentals.

I will now first compare Kohlberg's explanation of the moral point of view with three other contemporary proposals (those of Rawls, Scanlon, and Apel/Habermas), in order to begin by clarifying the strengths and weaknesses of ideal role-taking. Then I will discuss Bill Puka's (this volume) central objection to all the deontological approaches derived from Kant and trace it back to its basic (and correct) insight. What interests me most is Kohlberg's suggestion that one can meet this objection by including the two moral principles of justice and benevolence under the point of view of "equal respect for all." Finally, I will try to show that this approach can be carried out more consistently—and thus also defended against further objections along the lines of Puka's—using the means provided by discourse ethics.

Procedural Explanations of the "Moral Point of View"

Formalist ethics designate a rule or a procedure that establishes how a morally relevant action conflict can be judged impartially—that is, from a moral point of view. The prototype is Kant's categorical imperative, understood not as a maxim of action but as a principle of justification. The requirement that valid maxims of action must be able to serve as the basis for a "general legislation" brings to bear both the concept of autonomy (as the freedom to act in accordance with laws one gives oneself) and the correlative concept that the corresponding actions are capable of general consensus: the point of view of impartial judgment is assured through a universalization principle that designates as valid precisely those norms that *everyone* could *will*. The quantifier "every" refers to everyone who could possibly be affected (that is, restricted in the scope of his or her action) if the norm in question were generally followed. The predicate "will" is to be understood in accordance with the Kantian notion of the autonomous will; it means "accept as binding on myself on the basis of my own insight." The fundamental intuition is clear: under the moral point of view, one must be able to test whether a norm or a mode of action could be generally accepted by those affected by it, such that their acceptance would be rationally motivated and hence uncoerced. This intuition has been reformulated in various ways by contemporary philosophers, primarily in such a way, however, that the procedural character of the proposed testing emerges more clearly than it did in Kant. The most illuminating are the following four positions, which with varying accentuations are based on social-contract or role-taking models, that is, on models that construe the process of reaching agreement in counterfactual terms.

1. The first position makes use of the central thought-motif of social contract theories (as it is commonly found in modern, rational natural-law theory since Hobbes), namely, the motif, derived from civil law, of a contractual agreement between autonomous legal subjects. Both in terms of the history of philosophy and systematically, this represents a return to *pre*-Kantian concepts. In order to bring the contract motif up to the level of the Kantian intuition, certain conditions must be added. For this reason Rawls places his contracting partners—who are to enjoy equal freedom of choice, to make decisions in a purposively rational way, and to pursue only their own interests (that is, not to be interested in their *mutual* welfare) in an original position. This original position is defined such that rational egoists must make their agreements under certain restrictions. The conditions that establish this framework, es-

pecially the "veil of ignorance" (ignorance of one's own status within the future social intercourse that is to be institutionally regulated), require that enlightened self-interest be reoriented toward the perspective of the universalizability of normatively regarded interests. The orientation that Kant built into practical reason through the moral law, and thereby into the motives of autonomously acting subjects themselves, now comes about only as the result of the interplay of rational egoism with the substantive normative conditions of the original position under which that egoism operates. At first, this seems to relieve the "theory of justice" from the presupposition-laden premises of Kantian moral philosophy. The parties making the contract need only act reasonably, rather than out of duty. To be sure, the theorist still has to check whether his construction of the original position and the principles agreed to in it actually accord with our moral intuitions. His assumptions, which are regulated only by the criterion of "reflective equilibrium," establish "the appropriate initial status quo which insures that the fundamental agreements reached in it are fair" (Rawls, 1971, p. 17). Only the procedure proposed in the theory guarantees the correctness of the results, and does so in such a way that "the parties have no basis for bargaining in the usual sense" (ibid., p. 139). Everyone who puts himself in the role of one of the contracting parties in the original position should be able to reach the same conclusions deductively that Rawls (with some obvious additional assumptions concerning life plans, primary goods, and so forth) develops in his theory. Like the categorical imperative, each person must be able to apply Rawls's model for testing on his own, i.e., "in his imagination."

These advantages, however, have their reverse side. Rawls has by no means completely captured the fundamental intuition of Kantian ethics in his model of a contractual agreement supplemented by a framework of conditions. According to Kant, everyone can grasp the moral law by virtue of practical reason; the benefits derived from the moral law satisfy strictly *cognitive* demands. According to Rawls, however, in the role of a contracting party in the original position, only instrumental-rational decisions are required. Here the voluntarism of a con-

tract model tailored to the understanding of private-legal subjects is readily apparent; from the point of view of those
involved, the fictive agreement in the original position lacks
any moment of insight that would point beyond the calculation
of their own interests. Moral-practical knowledge is reserved
for the theorist, who has to give a plausible explanation of why
he constructed the original position in this way rather than
another. If, however, the rationality of the rationally motivated
acceptance of principles and rules is not guaranteed by the
rational decision of the partners to the contract, but rather
results only from an interplay, into which they have no subjective insight, with a framework of conditions that are established
a priori, then the further question (raised by Dworkin, 1975)
arises: how can Rawls motivate his audience to place themselves
in the original position at all?[5]

2. On these and similar grounds, T. M. Scanlon (1982) proposes a revision that brings the social contract model closer to
Kantian notions. He drops the construct of an original position
occupied by rational egoists shrouded with a veil of ignorance,
and instead equips each of the contracting parties from the
outset with the desire to justify their own practice to all who
might possibly be affected, and to justify it so convincingly that
the latter could not (whether or not they actually do so) refuse
their assent to the universalization of this practice. Scanlon
(ibid., p. 110) proposes the following test principle for the
impartial judgment of moral questions: a mode of action is
morally right if it is authorized by any system of universal rules
for action that everyone concerned can rationally represent as
being the result of an informed, uncoerced, and rational agreement of all concerned. This formulation shifts the meaning of
"agreement" from the decision in making a contract toward a
rationally motivated understanding (judgmental harmony).
With this emphasis on the element of insight or understanding
in a process of will formation that is rational from the perspective of the participants themselves, Scanlon also hopes to
resolve the question of moral motivation. The desire to justify
one's own modes of action to others on the basis of norms that
are acceptable or worthy of agreement already provides a mo-

tive for avoiding actions that are morally wrong because they cannot be justified.

Through his cognitivistic reinterpretation of the social contract model, Scanlon revokes the distinction that Rawls undertook to make between the preestablished transsubjective, justice-compelling perspective of the original position, on the one hand, and the perspective of the participants, limited to subjective rationality, on the other. The moral philosopher is thereby relieved of the task of justifying a priori the normative construction of the original position. At the same time, the parties themselves, with knowledge of all the circumstances, are required to determine what sort of action could not be rejected on good grounds as a general practice by anyone within the sphere of those concerned—given that all participants are interested in an uncoerced, rationally motivated agreement. This procedure can no longer be applied in a strictly monological manner, as could Rawls's. It is no longer enough for me, in the role of a party in the original position, to determine what admits of universal approval from the perspective of that role (thus, from my perspective); rather, the revised contract model requires me to examine what everyone would, from his own perspective, judge to be capable of universal approval if he were oriented to the goal of reaching an agreement. The additional burden on the subject making the moral judgment is shown by the fact that he must at least imagine, that is, perform virtually, the intersubjective execution of a procedure that cannot be applied monologically at all. According to Scanlon, principles and rules find *general* acceptance only when *all* can be convinced that *each* person could give his well-founded assent from his own perspective: "To believe that a principle is morally correct one must believe that it is one which all could reasonably agree to. . . . But my belief that this is the case may often be distorted by a tendency to take its advantage to me more seriously than its possible costs to others. For this reason, the idea of 'putting myself in another's place' is a useful corrective device" (ibid., p. 122).

3. It is no accident that at this point Scanlon has to borrow from another model. Mead's fundamental notion that one participant in a social interaction takes the perspective of the other

is not a "useful corrective" to the social contract model; it is rather the alternative that presents itself as soon as it becomes clear that a consistent attempt to reach the level of the fundamental intuition of Kantian ethics under post-Kantian premises (that is, having dispensed with the two-world doctrine) exceeds the capacity of the fundamental notions of the contract model. Thus Lawrence Kohlberg explains the moral point of view of impartially judging moral conflicts with the help of the concept of ideal role-taking, which Mead (1934) had already used as the correlate of *universal discourse* in reformulating the fundamental idea of Kantian ethics within the framework of his theory of action (see Habermas, 1987, pp. 92ff.). Kohlberg develops this concept through a series of steps, beginning with simple interactions between at least two persons engaged in communicative action.

Ego must first fulfill the condition of sympathetic identification with the situation of Alter; he must actually identify with him in order to be able to take the precise perspective from which Alter could bring his expectations, interests, value orientations, and so forth to bear in the case of a moral conflict. Then Ego must be able to assume that the project of perspective-taking is not one-sided but reciprocal. Alter is expected to take Ego's perspective in the same way, so that the contested mode of action can be perceived and thematized in mutual agreement, taking into consideration the interests affected on both sides. In more complex circumstances, this dyadic relationship must be extended to an interlocking of perspectives among members of a particular group. Only under this social cognitive presupposition can each person give equal weight to the interests of the others when it comes to judging whether a general practice could be accepted by each member on good grounds, in the same way that I have accepted it. Finally, Ego must satisfy the condition of universalizability of his reflections, which initially are internal to the group and refer to simple interactions: Ego must disregard the concrete circumstances of a particular interaction and examine abstractly whether a *general* practice could be accepted without constraint under comparable circumstances by each of those affected, from the perspective of his own interests. This requires a universal interchangeability of the perspectives of all concerned; Ego must be able to imagine how each person would put himself in the place of every other person.

What was sympathetic empathy and identification under the concrete initial conditions is sublimated at this level to accomplishments that are purely cognitive: on the one hand, *understanding* for the claims of others that result in each case from particular interest positions; on the other hand, *consciousness* of a prior solidarity of all concerned that is objectively grounded through socialization. At this level of abstraction, sensitivity to individual claims must be detached from contingent personal ties (and identities), just as the feeling of solidarity must be detached from contingent social ties (and collectivities).

All the same, the procedure of ideal role-taking retains a strong emotivistic tinge from its origins in social psychology. Rawls made a procedure taken from the social contract model the basis for judging the capacity of norms to achieve consensus; we have seen that the element of insight then became less significant in comparison to that of decision, specifically, that of calculated agreement among parties capable of deciding. If, instead, a procedure in accordance with the role-taking model is made the basis of this test, practical reason is relegated to a secondary position in a similar way—this time in comparison to empathy, that is, the intuitive understanding that parties capable of empathy bring to one another's situation. The discursive character of rational will formation, which can end in intersubjective recognition of criticizable validity claims only if attitudes are changed through arguments, is here neglected in favor of achievements of empathic understanding. The presentation in this volume by Kohlberg, Boyd, and Levine demonstrates a tendency (which is in any case suggested by the passages from the interview with Joan) to view "dialogue" not as a form of argumentation but as a method from group dynamics for sharpening the capacity for empathy and strengthening social ties. Where this tendency becomes dominant, however, it is to the detriment of the purely cognitive meaning of ideal role-taking as a procedure for the impartial judgment of moral states of affairs.

4. To counter this emotivistic bias, one can, as Apel and I have suggested, interpret the role-taking model from the outset as a discourse model. There is already adequate support for this interpretation in Mead, who introduces ideal role-taking as the quintessential social cognitive presupposition of a universal discourse that extends beyond all purely local states of affairs and traditional arrangements.[6] Mead begins with the idea that what the categorical imperative was supposed to achieve can be accomplished through the projection of a process of will formation under the idealized conditions of a universal discourse. The subject making a moral judgment cannot test for himself alone whether a contested mode of action as a general practice would lie within the common interest; he can do so only socially, with all the rest of those concerned. When one recognizes (with Scanlon) that the goal of this sort of inclusive process of reaching understanding, namely, unconstrained agreement, can be attained only through the vehicle of good reasons, the reflective character of that universal discourse emerges more sharply than in Mead: discourse must be thought of not only as a net of communicative action that takes in all those potentially affected, but as a reflective form of communicative action—in fact, as argumentation.

With this, Mead's construction loses the status of a mere projection: in every argumentation that is actually carried out, the participants themselves cannot avoid making such a projection. In argumentation, the participants have to make the pragmatic presupposition that in principle all those affected participate as free and equal members in a cooperative search for truth in which only the force of the better argument may hold sway (see Habermas, 1984, pp. 22f.). The principle of discourse ethics—that only those norms may claim validity that could find acceptance by all those concerned as participants in a practical discourse—is based on this universal pragmatic state of affairs. It is those idealizing presuppositions, which everyone who engages seriously in argumentation must in fact make, that enable discourse to play the role of a procedure that explains the moral point of view. Practical discourse can be understood as a process of reaching agreement that, through its form, that is, solely on the basis of unavoidable general presuppositions of argumentation, constrains all participants at the same time to ideal role-taking. It transforms ideal role-taking, which in Kohlberg was something to be anticipated privately and in isolation, into a public event, something practiced, ideally, by all together.

Of course, when it is a question of examining norms with a genuinely universal domain of validity, that is, moral norms in the strict sense, this idea is purely regulative. By the standard of this idea, discourses conducted as advocacy or internalized—set in the "inner life of the psyche"—can serve only as substitutes. Arguments played out in "the internal forum," however, are not equivalents for real discourses that have not been carried out; they are subject to the proviso of being merely virtual events that, in specific circumstances, can simulate a procedure that cannot be carried out. This reservation becomes more acceptable, however, given that discourses that are actually carried out also stand under limitations of time and space and social conditions that permit only an approximate fulfillment of the presuppositions, usually made counterfactually, of argumentation.[7]

Is There a Place for the Good in the Theory of the Just?

From the beginning, deontological approaches in ethics have aroused the suspicion that they are on the wrong track in taking as their point of departure the question of the conditions of impartial moral judgment—and the question of the meaning of the moral point of view that assures impartiality. In particular, they arouse the suspicion that under the compulsion to assimilate practical questions to scientific ones they narrow the concept of morality to questions of justice and distort it by seeing it from the specifically modern perspective of bourgeois commerce carried on by subjects under civil law. There are several aspects to this critique. In part it amounts to a defense of classical ethical theories that emphasize the primacy of questions of the good life, the successful conduct of one's individual life, and harmonious forms of social life—character and ethos. In part it is concerned with defending motifs of modern utilitarianism, which aims at the welfare of all and subsumes the rights of individuals under the notion of distributable goods.

In part it has as its goal a defense of ethics of compassion and love, which accord a privileged position to altruistic concern for the welfare of a fellow human being in need of help. It is always a question of welfare and concrete goods—whether of the community, the greatest number, or the weak individual; the appeal is to a dimension of happiness and suffering that does not seem to be touched at all by the deontological question of the intersubjectively accepted justification of norms and modes of action. Is it not the case that one simply passes over the question of morally right action and the good life when one focuses, as Kant did, on the phenomenon of the "ought," i.e., on the obligatory character of commands—and thus on a question that is detached from all concrete life circumstances, all interpersonal relationships and identities, namely, the question of the grounds for the validity of maxims of action?

This philosophers' debate is currently being repeated on the field of a theory of moral development that shows its architect, Lawrence Kohlberg, to be a student of Kant. The debate has been further dramatized by Carol Gilligan's proposal to oppose an ethics of care to the ethics of justice. Bill Puka has already reduced this proposal to its proper proportions, but his own modifications of the theory point in the same direction. In his contribution to the present volume, Kohlberg responds to this critique with an attempt to bring the two aspects of justice and concern for the welfare of the other together within the framework of his theory, which is set up deontologically as before. To evaluate the status of this interesting suggestion, which does in fact go beyond Kant, we will have to make clear which controversies Kohlberg does *not* get involved in—and does not need to get involved in.

1. At first sight, Kohlberg's bringing together of justice and benevolence is reminiscent of Hegel's critique of Kant and of all the attempts to mediate between classical and modern approaches in ethics. Hegel already saw that the unity of the fundamental moral phenomenon is missed when one opposes the principle of justice to the principle of the general welfare, or to a concern for the welfare of one's fellow man—that is, when one keeps these two aspects separate. He grounds his concept of *Sittlichkeit* (ethical life) with a critique of two-sided

conceptions that are mirror images of each other. On the one hand, he takes issue with the abstract universalism of justice as expressed in modern individualistic approaches, in rational natural law as well as in Kant's ethics of duty. On the other hand, he rejects just as firmly the particularism of concrete welfare, as expressed in Aristotle's ethics of the polis or in the Thomistic ethics of goods. Kohlberg takes up this fundamental intention of Hegel's. However, he does so on the basis of the strictly postmetaphysical premise that evaluative questions concerning the good life must remain separate from normative questions concerning a just communal life—because unlike the latter questions, the former are not capable of being formulated theoretically, that is, they are not accessible to rational discussion that claims to be universally binding. Kohlberg proposes to investigate whether limiting rationally decidable moral problems to questions of justice is too restrictive and might exclude elements that have nothing to do with the evaluation of concrete wholes, whether they be life histories and persons or forms of life and collectivities.

2. In another respect, Kohlberg's inclusion of benevolence is reminiscent of the debate between utilitarian and deontological approaches that is again current. Here too, however, Kohlberg does not take a mediating position. The procedure of ideal role-taking goes beyond the boundaries of an ethics of conviction that excludes all orientation to consequences as inadmissible in moral justifications. Ideal role-taking is intended, rather, to guarantee that a well-founded consensus is made dependent on consideration of the consequences that a contested general practice would have for the satisfaction of the interests of all concerned. This by no means signifies, however, a swing to a purely consequentialist view. As is evident in his treatment of the lifeboat dilemma, Kohlberg agrees with Dworkin and Rawls that the fundamental freedom and rights of individuals may not be restricted by considerations of overall utility. Thus what Kohlberg has in mind is not limiting the principle of justice for the sake of the principle of utility, but rather the question whether the justice principle can be interpreted in the sense of equal respect for the integrity of each person, such that aspects of caring and concrete welfare are

brought to light that only seem at first to be in competition with the aspect of justice.

3. Finally, it may seem as though Kohlberg wants to extend a moral theory that was initially limited to questions of the right in such a way that the right can be mediated or integrated with morality—understood now in a broader sense, whether it be Aristotelian or utilitarian or Christian. Bill Puka, in his contribution to this volume, seems to be proceeding on this basis. Most of the examples he uses concern conflicts of rights in the narrower sense. At one point Puka speaks of rights as capable of being enforced. Even if we disregard this obvious confusion of moral rights with enforceable positive rights, the choice of examples suggests the implicit presupposition that questions of justice are identical to questions of rights. Puka is concerned with the boundaries of a moral theory that concentrates on questions of harmonizing and equally distributing subjective rights: thus with the question of how the autonomous will of each person can coexist with each person's freedom under universal laws. But this is precisely how the supreme principle of Kant's theory of law (*Rechtslehre*) reads, not his moral principle. If I am correct, this view is based on at least three misconceptions.

First of all, just principles and rules, that is, those that can be grounded through procedural ethics, can, especially when it is a question of the institutional regulation of "external life circumstances" in modern societies, naturally assume the form of negative freedoms and subjective rights as well—prototypically in the domain of basic rights and property rights. But justifications through procedural ethics apply just as naturally to principles of distributive justice, for instance, which are completely different from one another, depending on the structure of the action domain in need of regulation (the household, etc.); or to principles of care and aid to those in need of help; to conventions of self-restraint, consideration, truthfulness, the duty to enlighten others, and so on.

Secondly, one must understand that deontological approaches separate questions of justification from questions of application. The abstraction from contexts of the lifeworld, from the concrete circumstances of the individual case, that

Puka complains about is in fact unavoidable in answering the question whether contested norms and modes of action are morally right and deserve the intersubjective approval of those concerned. In the impartial application of well-grounded principles and rules to the individual case, however, this abstraction must be reversed. It is in the light of concrete circumstances and particular constellations of interests that valid principles must be weighed against one another, and exceptions to accepted rules justified. There is no other way to satisfy the principle that like is to be treated in like manner and unlike in unlike manner.

Finally, however, moral commands can go beyond what is commanded by positive law; even, in fact, when legal relationships in turn are based on morally justified fundamental norms. This is due to the complementary relationship of positive law and morality, which I cannot discuss in more detail here. Cases such as Puka mentions, in which someone makes use of his subjective freedoms in a way that is legally incontrovertible but morally questionable (e.g., destroys his resources—burns his property, blows his brains out—without regard for what his resources could do for others), find a satisfactory resolution when one takes this complementary relationship into consideration, if resolution has not already been found from the perspective of equality of the rights involved.

There is one idea in the spectrum of objections raised by Bill Puka that Kohlberg certainly has to take seriously. In modern doctrines of natural law and in Kantian ethics (according to one interpretation), the autonomous morality of the modern period has been conceived individualistically and in a one-sided manner. In this respect, deontological approaches have not been carried out radically enough. They are still caught up in the context of their origin and thus in bourgeois ideology, insofar as they begin with isolated, private, autonomous, self-possessing subjects who treat themselves like property—and not with relationships of mutual recognition in which subjects acquire and assert their freedom intersubjectively.

The concept of ideal role-taking borrowed from Mead provides Kohlberg with a basis from which he can reach the level of Kant's fundamental intuition without possessive-individualistic abridgements. Mead himself already appropriated Kant in this way: "The universality of our judgments, upon which Kant places so much stress, is a universality that arises from the fact that we take the attitude of the entire community, of all rational beings." He then adds the characteristic thesis: "We are what we are through our relationship to others. Inevitably, then, our [morally justified] end must be a social end, both from the standpoint of its content and from the point of view of form. Sociality gives the universality of ethical judgments and lies back of the popular statement that the voice of all is the universal voice; that is, everyone who can rationally appreciate the situation agrees [to a morally justified end]" (Mead, 1934, pp. 379–380). Valid norms derive their obligatory character from the fact that they embody a universalizable interest, and the autonomy and welfare of individuals as well as the integration and welfare of the social collective are at stake in the maintenance of this interest. I gather that these thoughts lie behind Kohlberg's attempt to bring to bear the principle of concern for the welfare of the other in addition to the principle of justice. Viewed against the background of the contemporary discussion in moral philosophy, this program, which is not to be confused with the projects discussed under (1) to (3) above, is pioneering. However, I do not find the way the program is carried out to be as convincing as its intention.

Kohlberg sets forth essentially three trains of thought. First, he relativizes the idea of justice derived from the moral point of view of impartial judgment of conflicts; this idea is downgraded to the status of a principle and supplemented by a second principle, the principle of benevolence. That principle, of doing good and avoiding doing harm, refers equally to individual and general welfare. On the level of attitude, this principle corresponds to concern for the welfare of the other, compassion, love of one's fellow man, and willingness to help in the broadest sense, but also to community spirit. The two principles stand in a relationship of tension to one another, but are nevertheless thought to be derivable from a common higher principle.

In a second step, Kohlberg grounds justice and benevolence in a further principle, one that since Kant has been considered the equivalent of the principle of equal treatment and thus of the justice principle. This is the principle of equal respect for the integrity or dignity of each person, which corresponds to the formula of the categorical imperative whereby each person is to be treated as an end in himself. Kohlberg establishes the connection to the principle of benevolence by an equivocation in the concept of the person. Equal respect for each person *in general* as a subject capable of autonomous action means equal treatment; however, equal respect for each person *as an individual* subject individuated through a life history can mean something rather different from equal treatment: instead of protection of the person as a self-determining being, it can mean support for the person as a self-realizing being. In this second variant the meaning of "respect" is quietly altered; strictly speaking, it does not follow from *respect* (*Achtung*) for the integrity of a vulnerable person that one *cares* for his well-being. Thus Kohlberg cannot accommodate the principle of benevolence under the principle of equal respect for every person without an implicit shift in meaning. A further difficulty is more serious. The principle of equal respect, like the principle of equal treatment in general, refers only to individuals. A principle of benevolence "derived" from it might on that account be able to ground concern for the welfare of one's fellow man (or for one's own welfare), but it could not ground concern for the common welfare, and thus not the corresponding sense of community.

In a third step, Kohlberg has to show how both principles arise from the procedure of ideal role-taking. Up to this point, the concepts of "the moral point of view" and "justice" have had equivalent meanings. Thus it was the meaning of justice that was explained with the help of ideal role-taking. Now Kohlberg makes room for the meaning of benevolence by analyzing the concept of ideal role-taking into three moments, as previously indicated. Perspective-taking is linked to two further operations: on the one hand, to empathy or identification with the respective other, and, on the other hand, to universalization. Then sympathy can be brought into at least an associative connection with concern for the welfare of the other, and universalization into a similar connection with justice. This argument, too, which is only suggested, loses much of its power when one reflects that with the transition to universalized, completely reversible perspective-taking, not much more is left of a sympathy that is initially directed to concrete reference persons than a purely cognitive feat of understanding.[8]

The Discourse-Ethics Alternative

Kohlberg formulates a correct intuition with the wrong concepts when he ascribes to the principle of equal respect for every person an expanded meaning that includes both equal treatment and benevolence. His intuition can be explicated through Mead's central insight that persons, as subjects capable of speech and action, can be individuated only via the route of socialization. They are formed as individuals only by growing into a speech community and thus into an intersubjectively shared lifeworld. In these formative processes the identity of the individual and that of the collectivity to which he belongs arise and are maintained with equal primacy. The farther individuation progresses, the more the individual subject is caught up in an ever denser and at the same time ever more subtle network of reciprocal dependencies and explicit needs for protection. Thus the person forms an inner center only to the extent to which he simultaneously externalizes himself in communicatively produced interpersonal relationships. This explains the danger to, and the chronic susceptibility of, a vulnerable identity. Furthermore, moralities are designed to shelter this vulnerable identity. Because moralities are supposed to compensate for the vulnerability of living creatures who through socialization are individuated in such a way that they can never assert their identity for themselves alone, the integrity of individuals cannot be preserved without the integrity of the lifeworld that makes possible their shared interpersonal relationships and relations of mutual recognition. Kohlberg is trying to develop this *double* aspect when he emphasizes the intersubjective conditions for the maintenance of individual integrity. Moral provisions for the protection of individual identity cannot safeguard the integrity of individual persons without at the same time safeguarding the vitally necessary web of relationships of mutual recognition in which individuals can stabilize their fragile identities only mutually and simultaneously with the identity of their group.

Kohlberg cannot do justice to this fundamental pragmatist insight, however, by overextending the concept of equal respect for the dignity of each person and then stopping halfway, i.e., at a notion of benevolence toward one's fellow man (a direction in which Joan's partiality to the use of communicative means, with its overtones of group therapy, does point, albeit misleadingly). From the perspective of communication theory there emerges instead a close connection between concern for the welfare of one's fellow man and interest in the general welfare: the identity of the group is reproduced through intact relationships of mutual recognition. Thus the perspective complementing that of equal treatment of individuals is not benevolence but solidarity. This principle is rooted in the realization that each person must take responsibility for the other because as consociates all must have an interest in the integrity of their shared life context in the same way. Justice conceived deontologically requires solidarity as its reverse side. It is a question not so much of two moments that supplement each other as of two aspects of the same thing. Every autonomous morality has to serve two purposes at once: it brings to bear the inviolability of socialized individuals by requiring equal treatment and thereby equal respect for the dignity of each one; and it protects intersubjective relationships of mutual recognition requiring solidarity of individual members of a community, in which they have been socialized. Justice concerns the equal freedoms of unique and self-determining individuals, while solidarity concerns the welfare of consociates who are intimately linked in an intersubjectively shared form of life—and thus also to the maintenance of the integrity of this form of life itself. Moral norms cannot protect one without the other: they cannot protect the equal rights and freedoms of the individual without protecting the welfare of one's fellow man and of the community to which the individuals belong.

As a component of a universalistic morality, of course, solidarity loses its merely particular meaning, in which it is limited to the internal relationships of a collectivity that is ethnocentrically isolated from other groups—that character of forced willingness to sacrifice oneself for a collective system of self-assertion that is always present in premodern forms of solidarity. The formula "Command us, Führer, we will follow you" goes perfectly with the formula "All for one and one for all"— as we saw in the posters of Nazi Germany in my youth—because fellowship is entwined with followership in every traditionalist sense of solidarity. Justice conceived in postconventional terms can converge with solidarity as its reverse side only when solidarity has been transformed in the light of the idea of a general discursive will formation. To be sure, the fundamental notions of equal treatment, solidarity, and the general welfare, which are central to *all* moralities, are (even in premodern societies) built into the conditions of symmetry and the expectations of reciprocity characteristic of every ordinary communicative practice, and, indeed, are present in the form of universal and necessary pragmatic presuppositions of communicative action. Without these idealizing presuppositions, no one, no matter how repressive the social structures under which he lives, can act with an orientation to reaching understanding. The ideas of justice and solidarity are present above all in the mutual recognition of responsible subjects who orient their actions to validity claims. But *of themselves* these normative obligations do not extend beyond the boundaries of a concrete lifeworld of family, tribe, city, or nation. These limits can be broken through only in discourse, to the extent that the latter is institutionalized in modern societies. Arguments extend per se beyond particular lifeworlds, for in the pragmatic presuppositions of argumentation, the normative content of the presuppositions of communicative action is extended—in universalized, abstract form and without limitations—to an ideal communication community (as Apel, following Pierce, calls it) that includes all subjects capable of speech and action.

For this reason discourse ethics, which derives the contents of a universalistic morality from the general presuppositions of argumentation (see Habermas, 1983, pp. 53ff.; in press-a), can also do justice to the common root of morality. Because discourses are a reflective form of understanding-oriented action that, so to speak, sit on top of the latter, their central perspective on moral compensation for the deep-seated weakness of vulnerable individuals can be derived from the very medium of linguistically mediated interactions to which socialized individuals owe that vulnerability. The pragmatic features of discourse make possible a discerning will formation whereby the interests of each individual can be taken into account without destroying the social bonds that link each individual with all others. For as a participant in the practical discourses each person is on his or her own and yet joined in an association that is objectively universal. In this respect the role-taking model used in discourse is not equivalent to the social contract model. Procedural ethics is one-sided as long as the idea of an agreement between subjects who are originally isolated is not replaced by the idea of a rational will formation taking place within a lifeworld of socialized subjects. Both in its argumentative methods and its communicative presuppositions, the procedure of discourse has reference to an existential preunderstanding among participants regarding the most universal structures of a lifeworld that has been shared intersubjectively from the beginning. Even this procedure of discursive will formation can seduce us into the one-sided interpretation that the universalizability of contested interests guarantees only the equal treatment of all concerned. That interpretation overlooks the fact that every requirement of universalization must remain powerless unless there also arises, from membership in an ideal communication community, a consciousness of irrevocable solidarity, the certainty of intimate relatedness in a shared life context.

Justice is inconceivable without at least an element of reconciliation. Even in the cosmopolitan ideas of the close of the eighteenth century, the archaic bonding energies of kinship were not extinguished but only refined into solidarity with everything wearing a human face. "*All* men become brothers," Schiller could say in his "Ode to Joy." This double aspect also characterizes the communicative form of practical discourse: the bonds of social integration remain intact despite the fact that the agreement required of all transcends the bounds of every natural community. On the one hand, every single participant in argumentation remains with his "yes" and "no" a court of final appeal; no one can replace him in his role of one who pronounces on criticizable claims to validity. On the other hand, even those interpretations in which the individual identifies needs that are most peculiarly his own are open to a revision process in which *all* participate; the social nature of that which is most individual shows itself here and in the mutuality of a consensus that adds the reciprocity of mutual recognition to the sum of individual voices. Both are accurate: without unrestricted individual freedom to take a position on normative validity claims, the agreement that is actually reached could not be truly universal; but without the empathy of each person in the situation for everyone else, which is derived from solidarity, no resolution capable of consensus could be found. Because argumentation merely extends, using reflective means, action that is oriented to reaching understanding, the consciousness that the egocentric perspective is not something primary, but rather something socially produced, does not disappear. Thus the procedure of discursive will formation takes account of the inner connection of the two aspects: the autonomy of unique individuals and their prior embeddedness in intersubjectively shared forms of life.

This does not amount to a reconciliation of Kant with Aristotle. When it opposes one-sided individualistic conceptions and emphasizes solidarity as the reverse side of justice, discourse ethics draws only on the modern concept of justice. The structural aspects of the "good life," which from the perspective of communicative socialization in general are universally distinguishable from the concrete totalities of particular forms of life (and life histories), are included in its conception. Discourse ethics stands under the premises of postmetaphysical thought and cannot incorporate the full meaning of what classical ethical theories once conceived as cosmic justice or justice in terms of salvation. The solidarity on which discourse ethics builds remains within the bounds of earthly justice.

Kohlberg wants to dispense with metaphysics in this way— and yet, so it seems, he does not want to pay the full price for doing so. Joan's responses to the Korean dilemma (which has the same structure as the dilemma that arises in the lifeboat where only two of the three passengers have genuine chances of survival) provide Kohlberg with an opportunity to bring into play not only the principle of benevolence but also dialogue considered as a means whose end is concern for one's fellow man. It seems to me that this dilemma is better suited to clarifying the limits of discourse ethics. No one would deny that the leader of a commando group who had to send one of its men on a suicide mission in order to preserve some chance of survival for the rest finds himself in a moral dilemma. But the dilemma can be "resolved" only through a sacrifice that cannot be morally demanded of anyone—and thus could only be made voluntarily. Supererogatory actions—the term itself indicates as much—cannot be justified as moral obligations; and for this reason no discourse, insofar as it serves as a justification procedure, will be of any use. The only thing one can rationally justify is the refusal, on moral grounds, to admit a utilitarian resolution of the dilemma, which would adduce as its proof the sum total of utilities.

It becomes clear that supererogatory action alternatives that cannot be grounded morally are involved when one looks at the dilemma as a demand for principles and rules that could be applied in a case of this kind. In this regard there is no interest that could be universalized, and there is no corresponding norm to which everyone who could not exclude a priori the possibility of ever being in a comparable situation would have to assent.[9] Thus this dilemma allows us to clarify something else as well. It is possible for the supererogatory character of the dilemma to remain hidden at first only if one understands the dilemma in a different way, namely, not as a heuristic stimulus to the grounding of norms but as an application problem, so that, in other words, presumably valid principles or rules are to be applied to a given cause. The postconventional level of moral judgment is distinguished, among other things, by the fact that here the two kinds of problems are strictly separate. Procedural ethical theories, in particular, first set themselves the task of indicating a procedure through which norms and modes of action can be rationally grounded or criticized, as the case may be. Because they must deal with this task separately, the impartial *application* of valid principles and rules arises only as a subsequent problem (Apel, 1986; Habermas, in press-d).

On the conventional level, problems of justification and problems of application have not yet become separate, because here the substantive morality of a traditional milieu has not yet been called into question in a fundamental way; the conventional morality forms a horizon within which the various concrete duties and norms still refer to corresponding typical roles and situations. At this level, the case narrative of an action conflict that poses a dilemma is an appropriate instrument for data collection. Using the narrative of the individual case as a basis, the interviewee can feel his way forward in two directions: on the one side, to norms and duties; on the other, to typical situations of application, for the two still form an internal connection. This context of morality is disrupted by the postconventional shift in focus to a reflectively devalued social world that has been stripped of its naturalness. Interviewees who operate at the level of principled moral judgment have to analyze a dilemma like this from two different points of view: first, in the role of the legislator who examines impartially what mode of action, viewed as a general practice, deserves acceptance; second, in the role of the judge who must impartially apply valid principles and rules to a concrete case. In the requirement that the judgment be impartial, practical reason gets a hearing both times, but the moral point of view comes into play in a different way in each of the two functions—as, moreover, does solidarity. Solidarity with what is uniquely particular to the individual case is demanded of the judge, who must first find the criteria by which like things can be treated in like manner, and it is demanded of him to a higher degree than it is of the legislator, who may not ignore the "no" of suppressed needs.

Like the moral philosophers from whom he takes his orientation, Kohlberg's interest is directed primarily to problems of justification. For autonomous moralities, problems of application form a second, broader domain of questions for which developmental psychology might very well have to develop different instruments of data collection and analysis.[10]

Notes

1. Following Dworkin (1975, 1977), R. Alexy (1983, pp. 71–103) gives an illuminating analysis of the distinction between "principles" and "rules."

2. The debate between ethical cognitivists and value skeptics is a different matter; it too has to be carried out on the field of philosophical arguments. Using a double coding, these opposing positions can be interpreted in terms of developmental psychology as well as philosophy; from this point of view, the value skeptics are trying to rationalize a moral consciousness that Kohlberg would ascribe to Stage 4½. (See Habermas, 1983, pp. 195ff.; English translation in Habermas, in press-b, sec. 5.)

3. Following Gibbs (1977) and McCarthy (1982), I have developed this thesis more fully in Habermas, 1983, pp. 185ff.; in press-b, sec. 5).

4. From this point of view it must also seem unproblematic that the discussion of Stages 5 and 6 is based on only two interview protocols in each case. The question of empirical demonstration of a "higher stage of reflection" does not become completely irrelevant, but it does lose its importance.

5. This is one of the reasons for later revisions; in his Dewey lectures, Rawls (1980) finds himself forced to introduce a concept of the person that has normative content.

6. I have previously appropriated Kohlberg's theory on these premises; cf. Habermas (1983; in press-c).

7. For this reason discourse ethics must assert the fallibility in principle of moral insights; nor can it proceed on the basis of the notion that conflicts in the social domain that are in need of regulation can be resolved through consensus within a set period of time. On account of these cognitive differences, if for no other reason, positive law must supplement morality to fill the need for functionally necessary regulation in socially sensitive domains of action.

8. Kohlberg's argument becomes completely problematic when he detaches ideal role-taking from the communicative form of discourse to such an extent that he is able to assign "dialogue" to empathy with the other and the principle of concern for the other's welfare.

9. It may in fact be the case in an individual instance that those involved agree to a lottery procedure; but this procedure would be universalizable only on the condition that it were voluntary, something that would have to be determined ad hoc. I see no ground on which the requirement of a lottery procedure could be morally justified in a situation of this kind.

10. Translated by Shierry Weber Nicholsen.

References

Alexy, R. (1983). *Theorie der Grundrechte*. Baden-Baden: Nomos Verlagsgesellschaft.

Apel, K. O. (1986). Kann der postkantische Standpunkt der Moralität noch einmal in substantielle Sittlichkeit "aufgehoben" werden? In W. Kuhlmann (Ed.), *Moralität und Sittlichkeit: Das Problem Hegels und die Diskursethik*. Frankfurt: Suhrkamp.

Dworkin, R. M. (1975). The original position. In N. Daniels (Ed.), *Reading Rawls: Critical studies on Rawls' A Theory of Justice*. New York: Basic Books.

Dworkin, R. M. (1977). *Taking rights seriously*. Cambridge, MA: Harvard University Press.

Gibbs, J. C. (1977). Kohlberg's stages of moral judgment: A constructive critique. *Harvard Educational Review* 47:43–61.

Habermas, J. (1983). *Moralbewußtsein und kommunikatives Handeln*. Frankfurt: Suhrkamp.

Habermas, J. (1984). *The theory of communicative action. Vol. 1: Reason and the rationalization of society* (T. McCarthy, Trans.). Boston: Beacon Press.

Habermas, J. (1986). Moralität und Sittlichkeit—Treffen Hegels Einwände gegen Kant auch auf die Diskursethik zu? In W. Kuhlmann (Ed.), *Moralität und Sittlichkeit: Das Problem Hegels und die Diskursethik*. Frankfurt: Suhrkamp.

Habermas, J. (1987). *The theory of communicative action. Vol. 2: Lifeworld and system: A critique of functionalist reason* (T. McCarthy, Trans.). Boston: Beacon Press.

Habermas, J. (in press-a). Discourse ethics. In Habermas, in press-c. (Originally published in Habermas, 1983)

Habermas, J. (in press-b). Moral consciousness and communicative action. In Habermas, in press-c. (Originally published in Habermas, 1983)

Habermas, J. (in press-c). *Moral consciousness and communicative action* (S. Nicholsen and C. Lenhardt, Trans.). Cambridge, MA: MIT Press. (Originally published as Habermas, 1983)

Habermas, J. (in press-d). Morality and ethical life. Does Hegel's critique of Kant apply to discourse ethics? In Habermas, in press-c. (Originally published as Habermas 1986)

McCarthy, T. (1982). Rationality and relativism. In J. B. Thompson and D. Held (Eds.), *Habermas: Critical debates*. Cambridge, MA: MIT Press.

Mead, G. H. (1934). Fragments on ethics. In G. H. Mead, *Mind, self, and society*. Chicago: University of Chicago Press.

Rawls, J. (1971). *A theory of justice*. Cambridge, MA: Harvard University Press.

Rawls, J. (1980). Kantian constructivism in moral theory. *Journal of Philosophy* 87:515–572.

Sandel, M. (1983). *Liberalism and the limits of justice*. Cambridge: Cambridge University Press.

Scanlon, T. M. (1982). Contractualism and utilitarianism. In A. Sen and B. Williams (Eds.), *Utilitarianism and beyond*. Cambridge: Cambridge University Press.

III

**Morality and Personal
Development: Moral
Experience as Self-
Transformation**

The Emergence of Morality in Personal Relationships

Monika Keller and Wolfgang Edelstein

Friendship is a special type of relationship, one that is grounded in emotionally significant reciprocal orientations of two (or more) persons to each other. Informal and personal in nature, it is characterized by strong mutual expectations and structured by reciprocally binding norms. Friendship is universal and represented in all cultures, and it is pervasive in the experience of individuals throughout their lives. Thus, friendship represents a developmentally significant experience of interpersonal relations. Moreover, friendship is a developmental mechanism serving to produce increasingly more reflexive forms of mutual attachments and to provide increasingly structured opportunities for the acquisition of practices of cooperation within a relationship of equality. Contrary to yet another type of emotionally and developmentally significant relationships—that between children and parents—friendship represents a specific type of peer relationship. As an ideal type, friendship is based in equality and reciprocity, whereas parent-child relations are characterized by the exercise of authority and unilateral constraint (Piaget, 1932/1965; Youniss, 1980).

These descriptions suggest that friendship is also a moral institution of a special type. Friends engage in a relationship that entitles the incumbents to expect acts and judgments from each other beyond those to which anybody is morally entitled from others. Thus, a degree of supererogation is built into friendship that is absent from most other roles and relationships (except for parent-child relationships, which are characterized by very special rights and duties that often border on the supererogatory). As Blum puts it:

Acts of friendship are morally good insofar as they involve acting from regard for another person for his own sake. . . . The deeper and stronger the concern for the friend, the greater and more genuine the regard for the friend's good, the more it is a morally excellent relationship. (Blum, 1980, pp. 67–68)

The purpose of this study is to investigate the development of commitment and obligation in friendship. The friendship relation provides a special opportunity for studying the development of the sense of obligation and responsibility. While Kohlberg's (1976, 1984) theory of moral development is mainly concerned with what is just and fair, that is, with formal rights and duties in various role relationships, by investigating morally relevant acts in friendship we expect to illuminate a larger set of moral principles than justice operations, one that may reveal a psychologically broader motivational base for morality in development. This larger set would contain principles of solidarity and care.

According to Kohlberg (1976, 1984), justice reasoning at the early stage of moral reasoning is characterized by negative feelings, such as fear of sanctions. Positive feelings, such as love and attachment, which Piaget (1932/1965), in agreement with Bovet, already identified as a significant further source of morality, do not play a significant role at the level of preconventional moral reasoning. Yet, as friendship is predominantly characterized by strong positive sentiments, we can hypothesize that these feelings must play a central role in the development of a sense of commitment in friendship relations. This implies a growing awareness of the moral aspects of interactions, which are summarized in the question: How ought one to treat others in order to construct, develop, and maintain a close relationship?

We take research on the understanding of friendship to be located at the interface between two domains. One is the domain of so-called "descriptive" social cognition. It focuses on the person's developmentally changing social knowledge systems, comprising the understanding of persons, their inner psychological world, their actions and reactions, or, more generally, their understanding of social situations and of the rules and norms governing these situations (Keller and Reuss, 1984). The other is the domain of "prescriptive" social cognition that focuses on the developmentally changing structures of the evaluation of actions and events in terms of standards of moral rightness and moral goodness.

Research on friendship has been conceptualized mainly as an area of descriptive social cognition (see, e.g., Selman, 1980; Shantz, 1983) and thus as an area specifically distinct from moral development. Yet the understanding of friendship involves aspects of prescriptive cognition as well, especially if the definition of morality is broadened to include the following question: How should interests and claims be pursued in a world of social relationships (Emmet, 1966) among which friendship is particularly significant? In friendship relationships claims and interests are evaluated with regard to two sets of standards: standards of what is right and reasonable in terms of fairness, and what is good in terms of ideals of self and relationships.

Development of Friendship Understanding

Friendship reasoning as a domain of social cognition deals with children's and adolescents' understanding of developmentally changing conceptions of relationship. Damon (1977), Selman (1980), and Youniss (1980) have described levels or stages of friendship understanding that refer to various aspects of friendship: what it means to be friends or best friends; reasons and motives for becoming friends; the meaning of intimacy, trust, and jealousy as well as specific behaviors between friends, such as helping, sharing, or solving conflicts. From interviews with children Damon (1977) inferred three developmental levels of the conceptualization of friendship. At the first level (about 5 to 7 years) friends are seen as playmates and fun to be with. At this level there is no differentiation between types of friendship in terms of closeness. At the next level (from about 7 to 11 or 12 years) friends are seen as persons endowed with special psychological qualities, in particular such specific attitudes and dispositions as are relevant for the friendship. Helping and trusting each other become central concerns. At the third level (early adolescence) friendship is interpreted as a relationship of intimacy, in which persons share inner feelings and thoughts and assist each other in the solution of psychological conflicts. At this level, communication between friends begins to play a major role. Selman's (1980) research largely confirms Damon's descriptions and at the same time delineates a developmental sequence of five levels of friendship reasoning whose structural features correspond to Kohlberg's levels of moral judgment. The common "dimension" underlying both friendship conceptions and moral judgments is the social cognitive ability to differentiate and coordinate the perspectives of self and other. The specific content aspects or "issues" that Selman explores are the definition and motivation of friendship, its maintenance and termination, the meaning of trust and jealousy, and strategies of conflict resolution. Each of these issues is seen as undergoing structural change in individual development. The developmental levels are assumed to form a hierarchy in which each lower level represents a necessary but not sufficient condition for the next higher level.

At the earliest level, Level 0, which is that of object-oriented momentary interaction, friendship is not yet conceived as a lasting relationship with psychological qualities, as there is no understanding of the specific subjective world of other persons. The perspectives of self and other cannot yet be differentiated. At Level 1, with the differentiation of perspectives of self and other, an understanding of the specific subjective world of another person is achieved. As perspectives cannot yet be coordinated, one perspective—mostly the perspective of the self—remains dominant. This leads to a friendship conception that Selman characterizes as a relationship of "unilateral constraint," where the perspective of the self predominates: the friend is seen as someone who satisfies the needs and interests of the self. At the next developmental level, Level 2, a basic understanding of reciprocity in relationships begins to emerge. The social cognitive prerequisite for this type of understanding is the ability to coordinate perspectives, and with it the begin-

ning self-reflection that represents the capability to see the self
through the eyes of the other. The coordination of perspectives
in the sense described above becomes the basis for a relationship of context-bound reciprocity that is characterized by Selman as "fair-weather cooperation." The person begins to
understand that in cases of conflict the interests, feelings, and
intentions of both persons have to be taken into account. According to Selman's interpretation, the interests and needs of
the self remain motivationally dominant until, at Level 3, a
truly interpersonal understanding of relationships is achieved.
This understanding is based on the differentiation of a third-
person perspective (also termed the perspective of the relationship), which permits the transcendence of the particular
viewpoints of the interactants. At this level friendship is perceived as a stable and lasting intimate relationship characterized by reciprocal feelings, mutual concern, and trust. The
relationship becomes more exclusive, and its maintenance becomes a dominant motivational concern for both friends. Level
4, according to Selman, is based on a generalized social system
perspective where self and other are seen as parts of more
encompassing interaction systems in a broader societal space.
At the corresponding level of friendship understanding this
structure implies less exclusive relationships that take into account the changing needs and interests of friends in a flexible
manner.

Both Damon's and Selman's results show that understanding
of friendship develops from a conception of it as a set of
unilateral, concrete, and specific behavioral acts to a conception
of it as a system of mutual expectations about modalities of
behavior, intentions, and feelings. Even though both authors
focus on descriptive aspects, their research has implications for
those who want to consider friendship from a prescriptive, or
moral, point of view. Selman (1980) points out that, at Level 3
of friendship understanding, adolescents spontaneously take a
moral point of view and present prescriptive arguments about
how one ought to treat one's friend in the light of standards
of trustworthiness, loyalty, and solidarity. But in spite of the
fact that children at the lower levels do not appear to use the
language of "ought," their reflections nevertheless can be put

into a prescriptive framework to exemplify expectations about how friends ought to act and feel toward each other. Youniss and his coworkers (Youniss, 1980, 1982; Youniss and Volpe, 1978) provide examples of developmentally changing forms of expectations in peer interactions including close friendship. Their results show that "by continuing to practice friendship, children formulate norms which in turn ensure that their relation will endure" (1980, p. 233). Practices of reciprocity constitute the heart of peer interaction already in early development. What changes with development is the nature of reciprocity. Younger children (from 6 to 8 years) adhere to a pattern of "symmetrical reciprocity" that characterizes positive interactions and expectations about sharing and helping (e.g., I let her play with my toys, she lets me play with hers) as well as retaliative ways of behavior (if she hits me, I hit her back). Between the ages of 9 and 13 years symmetrical reciprocity yields to an emerging principle of reciprocity that regulates interactions by a rule of abstract equivalence rather than by concrete identity of exchange. Thus, it is now possible without harm to the relationship to suspend reciprocating a friend's positive action over time. Reciprocation can await a situation of need in which help or assistance in terms of communication can represent the expected balancing behavior. This developmental change again shows that conceptions about friendship change from concrete behavioral acts to mutual expectations about behavior, feelings, and intentions, all in an ongoing interaction. Failure to help each other, to take friends' needs into account, and to give psychological assistance means not to live up to a legitimate expectation or obligation. It represents a violation either of concrete expectations or of the principle of reciprocity. Such breaches bring forth specific strategies of retaliation and repair designed to reestablish moral balance, such as physical or psychological punishment of the offender, verbal apologies from the offender, and a promise of correct behavior in the future. In this connection communication serves above all to establish and maintain intimacy and to reestablish moral balance in the case of violation of legitimate claims.

The developmentally specific descriptions of how friendship is established, maintained, or, in the case of conflict, reestablished imply evaluations of behavior, feelings, and intentions as legitimate or illegitimate, adequate, or inadequate, in the light of moral standards about how one ought to treat a friend. Thus, "descriptive social cognition" is necessarily transcended to include elements of "prescriptive social cognition" as well. From a moral perspective, the research on friendship presented here clearly refers to the broader definition of morality given at the beginning of this paper: it is the attempt to answer the question of how interests and claims should be pursued in a world of social relationships.

Development of Stages of Moral Reasoning

Stages of moral reasoning as outlined by Kohlberg (1976) provide a general framework for analyzing the understanding of what people see as fair and responsible negotiations in cases of conflicting claims. Thornton and Thornton (1983) have recently interpreted the structures underlying moral judgment stages as conceptual frameworks for identifying people's collective interests. Even though this view is generally compatible with Kohlberg's approach, it changes the focus slightly, shifting from the question of how societal rules are dealt with to the question of how interests and expectations of potential equals are dealt with. For Kohlberg (1976, Table 1, pp. 34–35), the concept of interest takes on specific meanings according to the social perspective of a given stage. Underlying the preconventional level of morality is an egocentric point of view in which the person "doesn't consider the interests of others or recognizes that they differ from the actor's. Actions are considered physically rather than in terms of the psychological interests of others" (1976, pp. 34–35). Kohlberg uses the terms "consider" and "recognize" equivalently, while from a social cognitive perspective (Selman, 1976, Table 1) it is more plausible that these interests are differentiated cognitively even though they are not taken into account in the process of negotiating conflicting claims. According to Kohlberg, from the concrete individualistic perspective underlying Stage 2 moral judgment, the person is aware of individual interests. In cases of conflicting interests everybody is entitled to pursue his or her own interests. According to Thornton and Thornton (1983), a question of common interests already arises at this level. It is recognized that on some specific occasions people may have different interests and yet they may have common interests and goals to pursue. Conflicting interests can be coordinated in a context-specific form.

According to Kohlberg, it is only at the third level, the perspective of the individual in relationship underlying Stage 3, i.e., conventional morality, that shared feelings, agreements, and expectations have primacy over individual interests. With the social cognitive achievement of the third-person perspective, persons come to understand the collective interests represented by the maintenance of certain practices of interaction, which Gouldner (1960) has subsumed under the *norm of reciprocity*. Thus, Thornton and Thornton mention "reciprocating affection, maintaining interpersonal trust, considering the feelings of others, and so on" (Thornton and Thornton, 1983, p. 83). This is taken to follow from the general belief that it is unpleasant to be involved in interpersonal relations in which affection is unreciprocated, trust is betrayed, or feelings are disregarded. Actions that violate practices of reciprocity are judged as wrong from a generalized moral perspective. In his definitions of the stages, Kohlberg ceases to mention the aspect of interests when he describes the social perspective of moral judgment at Stage 4. However, Thornton and Thornton (1983) maintain that at this stage collective interests are integrated into an overall social system. "Living in a social system which is predictable and which does not treat us unfairly, disregarding our interests in favor of those of others, and so on" (p. 83) becomes particularly important. It is only at this level that conflicts of interest between the social system and interpersonal considerations can be perceived. Even though these authors have not analyzed the nature of collective interests at the post-conventional level of morality, it appears plausible that at this level they would have to be defined in terms of interests common to the species, or to all rational beings, independent of the boundaries of concrete social system membership.

Given this broader framework, we can ask what are the dominant stage-specific *reasons* or *motives* for adjudicating rights, that is, for justifying why others' interests and expectations and collective interests, when defined in terms of moral rules and principles, ought to be taken into account in situations of conflicting claims. Kohlberg has described these reasons in Table 1 of his 1976 article (pp. 34–35). At Stage 1, rules are respected because of the power of authorities and the desire to avoid punishment. We conclude that the interests of others are taken into account for the same reasons. At Stage 2, the awareness that others have interests that are different from one's own interests is complemented by the awareness that others can request that one take their interests into account just as the self can request that others take one's own interests into account. However, Kohlberg defines fairness in purely instrumental and prudential terms. Moral motivation results from the insight that following rules and taking others' interests into account serves one's own interests best in the long run. It is only at the third stage that a truly social motivation in the sense associated with being a good and responsible person becomes the dominant motive for right action. At this level, altruism, empathy, and genuine concern for the good of others become a motivational base for the judgment of how one ought to act in cases of conflicting claims. What is right is judged according to the Golden Rule and to generalized standards of fairness and rightness. At Stage 4, the motives for doing right stem from the more impersonal conception of duty and loyalty of a member of a social system who has an interest in generally upholding social practices. At this level, the basic motivation lies in the respect for social contract, taking into account the welfare of all and the sense of commitment to universal moral principles.

Selman's (1980) levels of friendship understanding exhibit substantive conceptual similarity to Kohlberg's stages up to Stage 3. At the first level, "unilateral constraint," the relationship is seen as serving the self's needs. At the next level, "fair-weather cooperation," interaction is still basically guided by self-interest. Only at the third level, "intimate relationships," does a genuine concern for the good of the friend appear to emerge. Corresponding to the moral judgment stages, the concept of trust plays a major role at this level.

Various authors have doubted the assumption that genuine concern for the good of others plays no role in moral development below Stage 3. Hoffman (1976, 1982) and Eisenberg (1982) have emphasized the role of empathy and altruism as powerful motives for moral action. Hoffman has demonstrated how already at the preoperational level empathy emerges as the basis of positive concern for others.

Hoffman's and Eisenberg's research represents a shift of interest from the morality of justice and from the so-called "perfect duties" to the less obligatory acts of beneficence or supererogation (Blum, 1980). Gilligan's (1982) work also represents an attempt to outline developmental transformations of a morality of care and responsibility as separate from, but analogous to, a morality of justice. However, as Broughton (1983) has pointed out, Gilligan's stage conception, which is based on adolescents and young adults, remains strikingly similar to Kohlberg's, inasmuch as her stages depict developmental transitions from egoism through social conformism to autonomy. Youniss (1980) has criticized Kohlberg's implicit reliance on a concept of an isolated self that only gradually, that is, through development, enters into social relationships. In agreement with Macmurray (1979), Youniss stresses that the person must be seen as a member of relationships right from the beginning of his or her development. In the perspectives of both Gilligan and Youniss, moral development is concerned with how people grow to consider the interests of others and to promote their welfare.

Further, Youniss claims that his research sheds light on important differences in the structure of moral development as it relates to authority-bound relations of constraint and to peer relations that are based on cooperation and mutuality. While peer relationships and interaction among friends are characterized by forms of symmetric reciprocity, relationships of authority are characterized by complementary reciprocity. In the latter type of relationship one person has the power, the other person is obliged to comply. From descriptions of kindly behavior toward parents such as those given by Youniss (1980), it is clear that interactions are grounded in obedience and rule conformity. Being nice to parents means following their com-

mands (e.g., cleaning the dishes or tidying up the room). Youniss's results raise the questions of whether the two forms of
relationship, unilateral constraint versus cooperation, are organized by different rules and whether they can be traced back
to different motives to take into account the interests, claims,
and expectations of authorities or peers. The question then
arises whether the same basic motivations that Kohlberg (1976)
claimed underlie the morality of authority relationships
(whether in the personal or in the societal domain) operate in
situations and relations of intimacy that are not structured in
terms of power. There are hints in the literature that adolescents prefer Stage 3 reasoning when solving moral dilemmas
in contexts of intimate relationship, while they tend to solve
more formal dilemmas in terms of Stage 4 reasoning (Moir,
1974). Thus, the type of relationship in which a person is
engaged appears to play a role in the type of moral reasoning
chosen to solve a dilemma. Identification with concrete persons
tends to give greater saliency to the more emotional aspects of
the situation, while these aspects tend to be less salient in social
conflicts at the system level. Conversely, there are also hints
that, even in reasoning about classical Kohlberg dilemmas, arguments at the preconventional level manifest genuine concern
for the welfare of others—a concern that does not originate in
the fear of physical sanctions or in notions of instrumental
exchange (Keller, Eckensberger, and von Rosen, 1989).

The research discussed above raises the question whether
moral reasoning is universal and generalized, or whether it
varies in function of context, such as type of relationship (e.g.,
peer or authority) and type of obligation (e.g., perfect or imperfect duties). In friendship the evaluation of actions in terms
of what is right with regard to standards of fairness or justice
appears too narrow a concept to account for both the nature
of interactions and their justification. Standards of what is
reasonable and good in terms of ideals of self and relationship
have to be attended to as well. Thus, we have to refer to a
morality of justice as well as to a morality of responsibility and
care when analyzing morally relevant interactions in friendship. It should be specifically emphasized at this point that we
do not share the position of authors such as Gilligan (1982)

and Haan (1978; Haan, Weiss, and Johnson, 1982). These authors postulate a split between, on the one hand, a more formal and impersonal morality that is oriented toward principles of justice, and, on the other, a more person- or relationship-oriented and "female" morality in which principles of care or responsibility play the dominant role. In contradistinction, we propose that formal moral rules, for which a claim of universal validity is made, emerge from—and achieve significance in—particular, concrete, and intimate relationships. Thus, the developmental analysis of the concept of fairness must be complemented by an analysis of how the perception of what is good for the other person and the maintenance of the relationship develops in childhood and adolescence.

Development of Moral Reasoning about a Friendship Conflict: An Empirical Study

The research that we have carried out, which is reported below, deals with the following questions: How do children come to understand expectations and norms in close friendship; and how does this knowledge become relevant when thinking about action choices and evaluating them morally?

As mentioned at the beginning of this chapter, we see our research located at the interface between "descriptive" and "prescriptive" social cognition. This characterization refers to the methodological approach that we have chosen: the person's understanding of the morally relevant dimensions of a conflict situation is assessed by reconstructing the way he or she differentiates and coordinates the perspectives of the actors involved in a conflict. We assess the person's sociomoral knowledge structures when he or she spontaneously locates the conflict, thinks about action decisions and their consequences, considers strategies for regulating possible consequences of choices, and evaluates decisions in terms of moral standards. Sociomoral knowledge structures can be described as different levels of interpretation and evaluation of social reality. Keller and Reuss (1984) have described such knowledge systems as characterized by a typical repertoire of "naive" action theoretical categories that give rise to typical strategies for the coordination of actions. These categories include the following: (1) representation of persons, relations, and situations (typical vs. specific circumstances); (2) representation of internal states, such as needs, interests, expectations, feelings, motives, goals, means, and consequences (intended vs. nonintended, short-term vs. long-term); (3) representation of social regularities; of rules and norms of reciprocity, evaluative standards and principles, and regulative strategies (excuses and justifications, compensations, discursive strategies). (See ibid., p. 215.)

The development of the categories of a naive theory of action takes place through processes of differentiation and coordination of perspectives. Conversely, the structure of perspective-taking can be seen as the result of differentiation and coordination of these categories (Keller, 1985). The differentiation of the categories of a naive theory of action implies "descriptive" social cognition, inasmuch as it represents the general understanding of situations and actions. It implies "prescriptive" social cognition inasmuch as it refers to processes of evaluation of what is (morally) adequate or inadequate. With increasing sociomoral maturity, i.e., with the differentiation of the naive theory of action, the person comes to anticipate the moral evaluation of actions and experiences an increasing need to justify his or her actions. This need to justify can take the form of a desire to negotiate mutual acceptance of intentions and expectations by constructing strategies of justification, or, when another person's expectations or (justified) claims have been violated, the desire to reestablish a moral balance through strategies of excuse and compensation. In sum, in our research we have attempted to reconstruct the person's understanding of the psychological content of a situation including the morally relevant "facts," the ways in which the person makes use of his or her understanding in the process of structuring action (i.e., in decision-making) and thinking about consequences, and finally the ways in which persons evaluate actions in terms of moral standards of what is "right" and "good."

Method

The data presented here are based on longitudinal interviews with 120 children at the age of 7, 9, 12, and 15 years. Subjects were interviewed about a conflict situation in a friendship dilemma portrayed in a story taken from Selman (1980). The protagonist of the story has promised his or her friend to meet on a special day. Later the protagonist is invited by a third child, who has only recently moved to the neighborhood, to go to a movie that happens to be playing at the same time that he or she had to meet the friend. A variety of additional psychological details are mentioned in the story that further complicate matters, for example, that the friend has problems to discuss and that the friend does not like the new child. Since the interpretation and solution of the dilemma must take account of clashes of interest as well as conflicts between norms, an adequate reconstruction of social cognitive competence involves both descriptive and prescriptive aspects.

During the interview the categories of the naive model of action become important for various phases or components of an action sequence. First, the subject has to *define the action problem* in a preliminary way. Second, the subject has to make a (hypothetical) decision or choice and give *reasons for the choice* in terms of certain preferences or preferabilities. Furthermore, in order to systematically understand the specific relations of preference and preferability that are in play, reasons for the unchosen, alternative option are assessed as well. Thinking about the decision in this way gives rise to reflection on intentions and goals that are either problematic or unproblematic, legitimate or illegitimate, as far as their moral rightness is concerned. Third, action choices involve the anticipation and evaluation of intended and unintended, short-term or long-term *consequences* of choices for those concerned, including oneself. Fourth, a more inclusive awareness of the problems resulting from that evaluation process may lead to *regulative strategies* of discourse and compensation. These strategies serve to avoid or compensate for unwanted consequences for self and other. Fifth, the moral meaning of the hypothetical choice has to be evaluated in terms of standards of *moral rightness* and/or *moral goodness*.

These various components can be organized into a sequence of a more or less complex action totality. Each level represents a reorganization of the system of categories that constitutes a

naive theory of action. The levels are taken to form a hierarchical sequence in terms of perspective differentiation and
coordination (see Keller, 1984; Keller and Reuss, 1984). Additionally, the concept of promise-keeping is assessed according
to Kohlberg's stage definitions of moral judgment (Colby, Kohlberg, and collaborators, 1987) and the concept of friendship is
assessed according to Selman's (1980) definitions of stages of
friendship reasoning.

In this paper four issues are selected to represent the levels
of sociomoral reasoning. The first two issues are as follows:

(1) *Practical decision-making*, in terms of reasons and motives
underlying a hypothetical choice. (Why does the protagonist
go to the friend? Why, if the action choice is going to a movie,
would he or she have liked to go to the friend?)

(2) *Moral evaluation of action choices.* (Is the decision right,
why/why not; is it the only right decision, why/why not?)

As mentioned earlier, only the latter questions relate directly
to moral development research, while the former have tradi-
tionally been taken to refer to descriptive social cognition concerned with the interpretation (attribution) of motives.
However, as Keller and Reuss (1984) have argued, it depends
on the person whether the question about an action decision
is interpreted in terms of "preference" relations or in the light
of "preferability," in which case decisions are justified with
regard to moral and relationship standards.

In the context of practical decision-making, the focus of this
analysis is on reasons (motives and justifications) given for the
choice to go to the friend as promised. In the context of moral
evaluation, however, both action choices are taken into account.

In addition to the reasons for decision and the evaluation of
the choices, two further central concepts are analyzed:

(3) The person's general understanding of *friendship* as expressed in the course of the interview.

(4) The person's general understanding of the concept of
promise-keeping. (What does it mean to promise and why should
a promise be kept?)

Developmental levels were determined for the arguments
given in the context specific to each of the four issues. Arguments vary over the levels, ranging from the lowest, Level 0,

to the empirically highest, Level 3, including transitional levels (e.g., Levels 0/1, 1/2). In the following discussion, the main developmental levels will be described for the four issues (friendship concept, promise concept, action choice, moral evaluation of action choice) on the basis of subjects' arguments in the sociomoral interview. Our descriptions represent ideal types; empirically, however, individuals may score at different levels in the different issues. The transitional levels will not be described here.

Level 0

At this level—which is barely represented in our data—*friendship* is seen as purely object-related; it is not yet understood as a relationship across time. There is no understanding of what it means to give a *promise* and what consequences result if a promise is not kept.

As the situation is defined in purely hedonistic terms, the material offers that the friend makes to the protagonist become the dominant reasons for *choice* (the protagonist forgoes the movie because he or she enjoys the friend's toys). Questions designed to elicit the moral evaluation of the choice are not yet understood by the subject.

Level 1

In terms of the *friendship* concept at this level, "being friends" is interpreted as liking to play with each other and playing with each other often. However, the two types of relationship involved (friend, new child) are not clearly differentiated. The *promise* concept is understood in terms of concrete acts. It is clear that a person is supposed to keep promises and that it is wrong to break promises. Reasons refer to global and evaluative criteria (I was told it is bad, it means fooling the other, it is just bad, etc.). Compared to Kohlberg's (1976) definition of Stage 1 of moral judgment, in our data physical sanctions are not mentioned as moral reasons. However, consequences of not keeping a promise may be perceived in physical terms (hitting), or in psychological terms (the other is angry, getting into trouble, the person who has broken a promise feels bad or unhappy). *Reasons* given at this level for the *choice* to meet the friend refer for the most part to the interpersonal aspects of the situation, such as empathic concern (not wanting the friend to be alone), to some unspecified feature of the relationship (going to meet the friend, because they are friends or even best friends), or to possible consequences (not wishing to stop being with the friend). Only in very few cases is the normative aspect of the situation picked up as a reason for choice (wanting to come because one has said so or promised). The decision to go to the movie is evaluated as not right. In many cases no reasons for moral evaluation can be given. The two types of reasons mentioned refer to consequences (the friend would be angry) or global evaluations (it is foolish, not nice to break a promise, a promise breaker is not a good boy or girl). Confusion between an intersubjective sense of "right" and a subjective-particular perspective may still occur (going to the movie can be evaluated as "right" because it is more fun than going to meet the friend).

Level 2

At this level *friendship* is interpreted as a relationship over time. This is especially true in the case of being best friends, which means having been friends for a long time and knowing each other well. Knowing each other also implies knowing how the other will react to a decision that does not take his or her concerns into account. The *promise concept* is interpreted by reference to its normative aspects. It is admitted that people "normally" have to keep promises. Not keeping a promise is interpreted as betrayal or as letting others down. A person who does not keep his or her promises is considered a liar and a trickster. Consequences refer to the fact that no one will believe the person and everybody will consider him or her unpleasant or not nice. Failure to keep a promise leads to the promisee's being unhappy or sad about it, he or she will not want to be the actor's friend any more, or even become an enemy, and so forth. Apologies (saying "forgive me") are taken to modify or prevent these negative consequences.

Reasons for the *choice* of going to meet the friend frequently refer to both aspects: to the normative aspect of having given a promise as well as to the relationship aspect that is frequently cited as an explanation of why the actor decides in agreement with the promise given or even perceives it as obligatory to take such a decision. The normative aspects constitute one type of reason for meeting the friend (having given a promise, not wanting to break the promise, not wanting to betray the promisee). The obligatory nature of such a decision is sometimes pointed out (if the actor has promised, he or she must go). Reasons referring to the interpersonal aspects can be classified into three types: (a) those that highlight the nature of the friendship (being old friends, best friends, or at least good friends, knowing each other well, or not wanting to betray or let down best friends); (b) those referring to empathic concerns (that the friend would feel unhappy, miserable, left out, if the actor didn't come), which in this context are related to the normative aspect that the friend would feel betrayed and let down if the promise is not kept; and (c) reasons that refer to the possible consequences of failing to keep the promise to the friend (it would be unpleasant to break off the relationship, there is no desire to stop being friends, fear that the other person will sever the friendship, desire to maintain friendship). Even general maxims can become reasons for choice (nobody wants you for a friend if you cheat).

Moral evaluation: The decision to go to the friend is evaluated as right. The decision not to go to the friend is evaluated as not right. Types of reasons given for evaluation refer to the normative aspect. It is "right" to go to the friend because of the obligatory nature of the promise (one had said so, had firmly intended to, or had not promised the new child because the friend had called first). Not keeping the promise is not right (it's wrong to betray, one mustn't betray). Interpersonal concerns are further types of reasons frequently given in connection with the normative reasons: empathic concerns are mentioned (it is right because the friend would feel better, not be unhappy, not be left out) as are moral evaluations of the actor (one wouldn't be a good friend) and consequences (it is not right because there would be disagreement between the friends, the actor would regret having lost a friend). The category mentioned most often is the relationship itself (one must play with the friend because they are best friends, are always together, or are old friends, it is not right to betray old friends one has known such a long time, etc.). Finally, still another interesting aspect mentioned occasionally is the violation of standards of discourse (it is not right to go to the movie because the actor did not talk to friend beforehand).

While children at this level generally tend to evaluate the decision to pass up the friend in order to go to the movie as "not right" from a moral point of view, some pointed out the ambiguity of any such evaluation. Given the interviewer's question of whether such a decision would be uniquely right, some children are able to take into account the implications of the choice for the new child. They tend to state that the decision to go to the friend is not right, because it leaves the new child out. However, these two evaluations remain unconnected, that is, no criteria can be stated that permit an evaluation of whether one choice is more right than the other.

Level 3

Within the *friendship* concept, at this level the enduring aspect of the relationship is highlighted. In contrast with the preceding level, here the relationship is characterized in terms of intimacy, implying special obligations to take into account the friend's needs and feelings. They may refer to the friend's feelings toward the new child, which are now interpreted in terms of jealousy or fear that the relationship might be destroyed; or they may refer to the friend's situation-specific needs (the friend wants to talk to the protagonist). In contrast with the preceding stage, talking is no longer understood in terms of telling something exciting, but rather as talk about problems that may even be related to the new child. Norms of trust, reliability, and dependability are perceived as constitutive for a close friendship.

The *promise concept* at this level is centered around the obligatory aspect of keeping one's promise. The focus is on generalized norms of reciprocity, for example trustworthiness,

dependability, and reliability. One has to keep a promise because "the other depends on you or relies on you," but also
because one is a "responsible person." Consequences of failing
to keep promises are perceived in terms of trust: persons who
do not keep their promises would not be trusted any more,
others would be disappointed and would not want to associate
with this person, and so on. It is seen that promises can be
negotiated among those concerned but the rights of the promisee are granted precedence over the rights of the promisor.
The order of events contributes to the obligatory character of
the choice. This may be formulated in terms of a more general
maxim in some cases (you have to do what you promised first).
It also relates to the conception of a moral self who has to live
up to his or her commitments (the person has to stand by his
or her word). As the moral self is seen in terms of the relationship, "standing by one's word" also signifies friendship,
dependability, and trustworthiness.

At this level reasons for the *decision* to go to the friend refer
to the obligatory character of the promise (one has to keep
one's promises, one has to do what was promised first, one has
to stand by one's word). On the other hand, the necessity of
keeping the promise is closely tied to the aspect of not hurting
a friend's feelings (not wanting to hurt an older friend; not
wanting to break off the friendship or affect the intimate relationship). Consequences tend to be interpreted in terms of
destroying harmony and intimacy. Again, the nature of the
relationship is given as a reason for the decision and as a
background explanation, why the promise has to be kept (because they know each other so well or confided in each other,
the friend has priority). The obligation not to betray one's best
friend results from the notion of friendship (being a trustworthy friend). Additionally, at this level another type of reason
begins to guide action choice. These reasons refer to a friend's
situation-specific needs (the friend needs to talk to the actor,
the friend has problems). Thus, being friends at this level
implies that the other's situation-specific needs constitute
"good" (and obligatory) reasons for action choices.

Reasons for the *moral evaluation* again refer to the normative
aspect: keeping the promise is taken to be obligatory from a

more general perspective than at the preceding level (if one has promised, has promised first, or has said "of course . . . ," then it is only fair to keep it, one should always keep one's promises, one has to stand by one's word). The obligatory nature of keeping the promise is deeply interconnected with the interpersonal aspects of friendship (it is not right to betray or lie to one's best friend; it is right to go to the friend because they have had a longstanding friendship, or because they have always been together and share many things). A more general evaluative perspective can be adopted from which the two types of relationship are compared (one always has a deeper or firmer relationship with a person one has known for a long time). Empathic concerns are embedded in this perspective of the relationship (the friend would be unhappy or hurt, because he or she has known the actor for so long and now feels disappointed about the relationship). Consequences (anger or disagreement) are not mentioned at this level as criteria for moral evaluation, although consequences in terms of "destroying trust" and "losing one's best friend" may play a supplementary role.

Compared to answers at the preceding level, in many cases children at this level are aware of the ambiguity of the decision when considering criteria of moral rightness. The decision to go to meet the friend is judged as neither right nor fair to the new child, who may be unhappy or hurt. It is considered unpleasant (less than nice) to leave the new child out, or to leave someone out who is new and has no friends. However, at this level the criteria for the comparison of decisions in terms of moral rightness begin to appear. They highlight the temporal order or priority of the commitments (having given the promise first) as well as the comparison of the relationships in terms of time and closeness (the friend would be more hurt; one is more obligated to a friend).

Standards of discourse are mentioned frequently. A possible decision to go to the movie can be morally right if the actor establishes consensus with the friend (if the actor talked to the friend before, if the friend agreed, if the friend would not mind). In such a situation "both would have to decide," but somehow it seems characteristic of this level that it is the friend's anticipated reaction that counts most, that is, the actor would not think it right to go to the movie if the friend had objections.

Discussion

The developmental analysis of interpersonal moral understanding shows that moral development must be understood as part of a more general understanding of persons, relations, and actions. The understanding of what it means morally to stand in a relationship develops in correspondence to the unfolding of the subject's naive theory of action. Only at the lowest level, Level 0, does a sense of what it means to stand in a relationship in terms of commitment and responsibility appear to be absent. Concerning action choice, children at this level consistently—and at the next level predominantly—decide that the protagonist chooses to go to the movie. At this premoral and prerelationship level persons are perceived solely in terms of their hedonistic value for the self's interests. It is apparent from the analysis of the categories of the naive theory of action that at this level the psychological meaning of action is not yet understood, in the sense of being able to reconstruct an action in terms of its motives and consequences. It follows that a moral perspective implying agency and attribution of responsibility is not yet established. Thus, actions cannot yet be evaluated in terms of criteria of moral rightness. In sum, Level 0 can be characterized as premoral in the sense of moral development stages.

Level 1 of sociomoral reasoning clearly corresponds to Kohlberg's and Selman's first levels, but also modifies their conception. At this level, a perspective of what is intersubjectively right emerges. Obligations and expectations are interpreted very concretely by reference to the protagonist's "declaration of intent," to a friend's concrete situation (waiting), and to regularities of interaction (frequent play). The types of reasons used for decision-making and moral evaluation in our opinion cannot be taken to fully support Selman's conception of Stage 1 as a "unilateral" conceptualization of friendship that implies an orientation to the self's interests only. Neither does it fully

support Kohlberg's description of Stage 1 of moral development. In contradistinction to the structure of arguments in his
examples (see Colby, Kohlberg, and collaborators, 1987) physical sanctions do *not* appear to play a dominant role, either in
moral evaluations of actions or in guiding action decisions,
whereas psychological consequences (especially anger) following the violation of an expectation or obligation already play a
role at this level. Nor is the category of unquestioned obedience
to rules (Piaget, 1932/1965) reducible to fear of physical sanctions. Yet we observe the phenomenon that children who cannot go beyond emphasizing that a promise should be kept, or
who justify promise-keeping by statements of global interpersonal evaluation (not nice, bad), may perceive physical sanctions as the consequence of an action that violates an
expectation or obligation. However, it is highly questionable to
infer from statements about consequences that the anticipated
sanctions are the reasons or motives for doing right, as Kohlberg (1976) has assumed.

Our account of the second level of sociomoral understanding
corresponds to Kohlberg's and Selman's definitions, but again
our results modify theirs. In the context of practical decision-
making, normative aspects of the situation are taken into account. They result from the understanding of moral obligations in the sense of concrete moral rules (a promise must be
kept); moreover, they result from the understanding of interpersonal responsibilities grounded in established action patterns that are generated in, and basic to, the relationship. Thus,
friendship at Level 2 has a quasi-normative character. Given
the distribution of action decisions at this level (twice as many
children decide that the protagonist should go to the friend)
and the reasons used to justify decisions as well as moral evaluations, the interpretation of Level 2 as "fair-weather cooperation" (Selman, 1980) or as "concrete reciprocity" (Kohlberg,
1976) with prudential reasons serving to maximize (long-term)
self-interest, appears doubtful. Rather, genuine concern with
the relationship in terms of obligations and commitment to a
friend appears to emerge at this level.

These obligations and commitments are interpreted as
rather specific behavioral requirements, such as having to keep

one's promises to the friend or keeping special dates (routines of interaction). The types of reasons given represent empathic concern with the other's feelings as well as genuine moral concern (not wanting to betray, letting the other down) that is anchored in the nature of the relationship (liking each other, having known each other for such a long time, and wanting to maintain the relationship). The concrete reciprocity types of reasons cited by Kohlberg as reasons for keeping a promise (keeping promises so that the other will keep them in the future) are virtually absent from our data. In sum, we find a kind of reasoning at Level 2 that, from a Kohlbergian perspective, one might tend to evaluate as Stage 3 moral reasoning, where the concern for the relationship is a predominant motive. We still claim that this is reasoning at Level 2, since in terms of perspective-taking these arguments resemble prototypical arguments at Kohlberg's Stage 2 of moral judgment. The structure of Level 3 arguments looks markedly different— very much in agreement with Kohlberg's and Selman's third-stage reasoning (Keller, Eckensberger, and von Rosen, 1989).

At Level 3 of interpersonal moral reasoning a far greater conceptual similarity to Kohlberg's and Selman's stages obtains than at the preceding levels. The predominant concern at this level is that of being a "good friend" in the sense of being loyal, trustworthy, and dependable. These concerns guide action choices as well as the evaluation of such choices in the light of what is fair and what is responsible behavior. Due to the interviewing technique adopted, which asks for both descriptive and prescriptive statements, we observe that at this level children in many cases spontaneously take a moral point of view. In answering the question "How will the protagonist decide?," they spontaneously focus on the question of how a good friend ought to act. Thus, preferences are spontaneously evaluated in terms of what is preferable from a moral point of view. The types of reasons given for the decision and for the moral evaluation are basically identical. These reasons emphasize a morally responsible self, a self defined in terms of relationships, in particular in terms of friendship relations. In contrast to the preceding level, the situational aspects of the relationship are taken into account: the friend's situation-specific needs (that he or she has problems to discuss) are judged as good reasons obliging the protagonist to a course of action and justifying the decision chosen by the interviewed subject. The distribution of action decisions at this level shows a close relationship between general interpersonal moral understanding and hypothetical action decision. Practically all children scoring higher than Level 2 decide that the protagonist should go to the friend. Thus we conclude that, at a certain point in development, interpersonal moral understanding predicts the hypothetical action choices: an understanding of intimate friendship as given at Level 3 obviously requires taking the friend's welfare into account when planning action.

Beginning at the previous level, children also construct the alternative (the new child who invites the protagonist to the movie) in terms of moral claims. They begin to understand that there are moral obligations and responsibilities that transcend the particular friendship (e.g., to help someone who is alone). Thus, at Level 2 some children already see the ambiguity of the decision to go to the friend from a moral point of view. At Level 3, criteria of precedence are established, which determine why it is "more right" to go to the friend than to accept the new child's invitation in spite of an acknowledged moral responsibility toward the new child as well. Interestingly, understanding moral obligations and responsibilities toward the third child is most salient at Level 3, a level characterized by friendship, intimacy, and exclusiveness and, in most cases, by feelings of jealousy toward the new child. What is interesting and new, compared to what we know from Kohlberg and Selman about Stage 3 reasoning, is that moral obligations as well as obligations toward relationships come to be seen as negotiable under standards of discourse (Keller and Reuss, 1984, 1988). But even though many children at Level 3 state that it would be right to go with the new child if the friend agreed to such a decision, practically all children at this level spontaneously opt for the friend and thus give the friend's concerns predominant weight.

From preliminary data we have cues that, at Level 4, the claims of the friend, the third child, and the self are weighed against each other in order to achieve an equitable decision.

Compared to Level 3, where the friend's possible objections acquire action-guiding force, we expect that at Level 4 it is perceived as obligatory for a friend to take into account the claims of others who are in a relationship with the self, as well as the self's own legitimate claims. In sum, at Level 4 we expect a more equal distribution of action decisions to emerge again—together with the elaboration of clear standards of discourse that regulate how morally relevant conflicts have to be resolved.

To summarize, our study shows the developmental transformations of a sense of commitment and responsibility in relationships. With regard to a morality of justice, as distinct from a morality of care and concern as discussed in the theoretical part of this paper, our data can be taken to show that justice may be too narrow a concept for fully understanding morality. However, with regard to Gilligan's claim against Kohlberg that persons can be classified in terms of the basically different moral orientations of justice or care, the developmental progression of arguments about the friendship dilemma rather emphasizes the interconnection of both. What is judged to be morally good and fair is deeply rooted in the understanding of relationships. Moral rules acquire significance in the context of particular, emotionally meaningful relationships in which care for the concerns of the other plays a predominant role. As Broughton, in his review of Gilligan's work (Broughton, 1983), has aptly observed, considerations of justice as well as considerations of care and concern for others are represented in most people's moral reasoning.

References

Blum, L. A. (1980). *Friendship, altruism, and morality*. London: Routledge and Kegan Paul.

Broughton, J. M. (1983). Women's rationality and men's virtues: A critique of gender dualism in Gilligan's theory of moral development. *Social Research*, 50:597–642.

Colby, A., Kohlberg, L., and collaborators. (1987). *The measurement of moral judgment* (2 vols.). New York: Cambridge University Press.

Damon, W. (1977). *The social world of the child*. San Francisco: Jossey-Bass.

Eisenberg, N. (1982). The development of reasoning regarding prosocial behavior. In N. Eisenberg (Ed.), *The development of prosocial behavior*. New York: Academic Press.

Emmet, D. (1966). *Rules, roles and relations*. Boston: Beacon Press.

Gilligan, C. (1982). *In a different voice: Psychological theory and women's development*. Cambridge, MA: Harvard University Press.

Gouldner, A. (1960). The norm of reciprocity: A preliminary statement. *American Sociological Review*, 25:161–171.

Haan, N. (1978). Two moralities in action contexts: Relationships to thought, ego-regulation and development. *Journal of Personality and Social Psychology*, 36:286–305.

Haan, N., Weiss, R., and Johnson, V. (1982). The role of logic in moral reasoning and development. *Developmental Psychology*, 18:245–256.

Hoffman, M. L. (1976). Empathy, role-taking, guilt and development of altruistic motivation. In T. Lickona (Ed.), *Moral development and behavior*. New York: Holt, Rinehart and Winston.

Hoffman, M. L. (1982). Affect and moral development. In D. Ciccetti and P. Hesse (Eds.), *New directions for child development. Vol 16: Emotional development*, San Francisco: Jossey-Bass.

Keller, M. (1984). Resolving conflicts in friendship: The development of moral understanding in everyday life. In W. M. Kurtines and J. L. Gewirtz (Eds.), *Morality, moral behavior, and moral development*. New York: Wiley Interscience.

Keller, M. (1985). *The role of perspective taking in the construction of meaning*. Paper presented at the symposium "The Social Constitution of Meaning in Interpersonal Communication," Bad Homburg, West Germany, December.

Keller, M., Eckensberger, L., and von Rosen, K. (1989). A critical note on the conception of preconventional morality: The case of Stage 2 in Kohlberg's theory. *International Journal of Behavioral Development*, 12:57–69.

Keller, M., and Reuss, S. (1984). An action-theoretical reconstruction of the development of social cognitive competence. *Human Development*, 27:211–220.

Keller, M., and Reuss, S. (1988). Development of negotiation strategies in an interpersonal moral conflict situation. Paper presented at the First International Conference on Human Development and Counseling Psychology, Porto, Portugal, July.

Kohlberg, L. (1976). Moral stages and moralization: The cognitive developmental approach. In T. Lickona (Ed.), *Moral development and behavior*. New York: Holt, Rinehart and Winston.

Kohlberg, L. (1984). *Essays on moral development. Vol. 2: The psychology of moral development*. San Francisco: Harper and Row.

Macmurray, J. (1979). *Persons in relation*. Atlantic Highlands, NY: Humanities Press.

Moir, J. (1974). Egocentrism and the emergence of conventional morality in preadolescent girls. *Child Development*, 45:299–304.

Piaget, J. (1965). *The moral judgment of the child* (M. Gabain, Trans.). New York: Free Press. (Original work published 1932)

Selman, R. L. (1976). Toward a structural analysis of developing interpersonal relations concepts: Research with normal and preadolescent boys. In A. Pick (Ed.), *Tenth annual Minnesota symposium on child psychology*. Minneapolis: University of Minnesota Press.

Selman, R. L. (1980). *The growth of interpersonal understanding*. New York: Academic Press.

Shantz, C. U. (1983). Social cognition. In P. H. Mussen (Ed.), *Handbook of Child Psychology. Vol. 3: Cognitive Development*. New York: Wiley.

Thornton, D., and Thornton, S. (1983). Structure, content and the direction of development in Kohlberg's theory. In H. Weinreich-Haste and D. Locke (Eds.), *Morality in the making*. Chichester, UK: Wiley.

Youniss, J. (1980). *Parents and peers in social development*. Chicago: University of Chicago Press.

Youniss, J. (1982). Die Entwicklung und Funktion von Freundschaftsbeziehungen. In W. Edelstein and M. Keller (Eds.), *Perspektivität und Interpretation*. Frankfurt: Suhrkamp.

Youniss, J., and Volpe, J. (1978). A relational analysis of children's friendship. In W. Damon (Ed.), *New directions for child development. Vol. 1: Social cognition*. San Francisco: Jossey-Bass.

Moral Balance: A Model of How People Arrive at Moral Decisions

Mordecai Nisan

Moral decision refers to the individual's final choice of how to act in a given situation; it is thus distinguished from "moral judgment," an impersonal judgment as to how one ought to act in a given situation. Internalization approaches to morality, like learning theory, tend to reduce moral judgment (how I ought to behave) to moral decision (how I choose to behave), while the cognitive developmental approach tends to do the opposite—to reduce moral decision to moral judgment. According to my analysis, each of these processes constitutes a separate reasoning process. This paper examines the process of making a moral decision through analysis of moral conflict and its resolution from a cognitive psychological perspective.

In this approach, moral conflict is conceptualized as a conflict between reasons rather than behavioral tendencies. Analysis of moral behavior suggests that, within the framework of the moral attitude (i.e., without rejecting morality), people commonly allow themselves some deviation from what they believe is prescribed by an "ideal," impersonal moral judgment. They accept the dictates of a moral framework, but in a limited manner. In short, they allow themselves a measure of what they consider immoral behavior. The leverage to do this stems from judgment from the perspective of personal identity. This perspective grants an unavoidable right to assign special status to one's personal projects (Williams, 1981), on the one hand, and to one's natural weaknesses and limitations, on the other. All these are perceived not only as given features of one's identity that cannot be disregarded, but also as essential features of that identity and therefore as legitimate bases for reasons for action. At the same time, the concept of identity also ensures the status of the moral consideration, which is a major component in that identity. A person aspires to maintain a proper identity in terms of moral behavior—proper, but not necessarily perfect. Limited deviations from the moral may be perceived as not seriously damaging one's identity.

In light of the above, I offer a model of moral decisions, "the moral balance model," that suggests that people calculate a sort of moral balance for themselves on the basis of all their morally significant actions within a given time span. This balance represents a quantitative weighing of commissions and omissions based not only on impersonal dimensions, like the amount of harm inflicted, but also on personal considerations, like the amount and nature of the loss or gain to the actor. The moral balance is compared to a personal standard of "minimal morality" that the individual accepts as personally obligatory. A moral decision in a given situation is based not only on the individual's evaluation of the planned action, but also on his or her moral balance and "acceptable level of morality."

The test of the suggested model is in its plausibility, its contribution to and enrichment of our observations and distinctions in the domain of morality, its ability to provide a reasonable and consistent explanation of various phenomena, and its ability to suggest new hypotheses. This paper may be read as a primary examination of the model using these criteria. While it does not deal with all aspects of the model, nor with all the problems and questions it raises, it demonstrates the breadth and complexity of the subject.

Moral Conflict

Moral conflict—as defined here—emerges in the wake of moral judgment. A moral conflict can arise only after one has reached the conclusion that one ought to do A, although at the same time one tends to do B, and that the two acts are incompatible. In most cases the individual is aware of what the moral point of view prescribes—not to steal, for example—but sometimes it is more difficult to arrive at a moral judgment. In such cases, one is faced with a moral dilemma, requiring one to weigh the various arguments and reach a final judgment. After making this judgment, one may be faced with a conflict. This conflict, so vividly described by philosophers and other writers, concerns not the way one ought to act but rather how one chooses to act.

Moral conflict of this nature has been the principal object of research in learning theory and psychoanalytic theory. From the current cultural viewpoint (in the West, at least), this conflict is viewed as a struggle between good and evil inclinations— between an egotistic desire to satisfy personal wants, innate and/or acquired, and a moral tendency directed toward personal restraint and consideration of others (a tendency that is at the center of the socialization process). These tendencies have been conceived in a mechanical manner, i.e., as impulses of varying strengths, contingent upon the conditions fostering each. According to this approach, immoral behavior is explained by the relative weakness of the moral tendency. Cognitive versions of these theories have allowed cognitive factors to mediate and affect the strength of the impulse, occasionally even resulting in a cognitive manifestation of it, but not to play a constitutive role in it. Accordingly, the resolution of the conflict is perceived as a mechanical one, based on the relative force of the two competing tendencies.

If the conflict is mechanical, the resolution should not be difficult—victory to the stronger. How is it, then, that the conflict often persists? Miller's (1959) work on conflict has suggested an ingenious answer, based on the idea that the relative strength of each tendency is a function of the distance from the goal, and thus a region of conflict is generated. According to this theory, moral conflict is seen as a psychological struggle between two behavioral tendencies rather than between opposing intentions.

Cognitive developmental theory has barely touched on the subject of moral conflict. Since the moral point of view is considered obligatory and as overriding other considerations (cf. Frankena, 1973), one would expect a correspondence between moral judgment and moral choice. However, discrepancies between judgment and behavior cannot be ignored. How are they to be explained? A parallel can be drawn from irrational behavior: if the individual recognizes the superiority of rational judgments, how can irrational behavior be understood? The explanations of the cognitive school lean toward conceiving it in terms of an erroneous perception of the situation, stemming either from lack of knowledge, a low stage of moral judgment, or various cognitive biases (e.g., Sykes and Matza, 1957). In all these cases, the assumption is that the behaving individual mistakenly believes that his or her behavior is proper.

More intensive research into the cognitive processes of moral judgment, as well as a growing awareness of the need to explain discrepancies between judgment and behavior, have focused attention on moral conflict. The disparity between judgment and behavior has led to what I present as a distinction between a moral dilemma and its resolution through moral judgment on the one hand, and a moral conflict and its resolution through moral decision, on the other. These two distinct processes match components 2 (figuring out what one ought to do) and 3 (deciding what one actually intends to do) in Rest's (1984) scheme of morality. A distinction of this sort seems also to have been made by other researchers, among them Kohlberg and Candee (1984) and Schwartz and Howard (1981).

The "paradox" that university students who make moral judgments of Stages 3 and 4 on Kohlberg's scale come to engage in immoral behavior of the sort described by Milgram, Latane, and Zimbardo (see Brown and Herrnstein, 1975) has brought Kohlberg recently to speak about an intermediary stage that falls between moral judgment and behavior. Following Blasi (1983), Kohlberg and Candee (1984) speak of a judgment of responsibility, that is, of the extent to which one considers a behavior as strictly obligatory, which is described as an aspect of the stage-developing moral structure. From this point of view, the growing sense of responsibility involves "discounting of excuses or quasi-obligations" and a "growing concept of moral freedom and autonomy" (p. 534), a description that suggests that the judgment of responsibility belongs to the family of cognitive explanations of immoral behavior in terms of excuses. Hence, the person who chooses to act "immorally" is said to focus on a "quasi-obligation," disregarding a higher, overriding obligation, and to believe that it is proper in this case to perform the immoral act.

While the introduction of judgment of responsibility into the moral process may resolve the "paradox" described by Brown and Herrnstein, it does not work for the type of conflict situation we are dealing with here, where one is fully cognizant that one's behavior is improper (and that one is responsible for it). Moreover, as it is described by Kohlberg and Candee, the judgment of responsibility does not suggest any substantive rule; it does not specify, for example, the conditions under which one tends to feel and take responsibility. Rather, it is presented as an aspect of the developing moral structure, so that the higher one's stage level, the more one tends to assume responsibility—across the board. This description does not fit an essential feature of the type of conflict and decisions to which I am referring, namely, where the individual perceives the intended behavior as an exception, so that by the deviating in this one case the individual does not relinquish his or her moral identity. It is not thus an issue of more or less responsibility across the board, but a conflict about clear deviation in a specific case.

A distinction between two phases of judgment was also suggested by Schwartz and Howard (1981) in their model for altruistic behavior, which is anchored in social learning theory. They distinguish between the activation of a norm and the behavioral decision. This decision comes to resolve a conflict between a tendency generated by a moral norm and tendencies generated by personal interest of different sorts. This type of conflict is expected to be resolved by a "cost-benefit" process, where the cost includes the price paid for one's moral deviation. However, this formulation describes both the conflict and its resolution in mechanical terms. The conflict is between opposing forces, and the characterization of one force as moral has no particular significance. The resolution of the conflict has no unique features and does not derive from any particular principle. This formulation is related to the theoretical framework used by Schwartz and Howard, in which cognition is a mediating variable but not a factor that creates reasons for behavior and thus has an independent effect on it.

The approach I develop in this paper sees moral conflict as a contest between two reasons for behavior. While I do not deny the existence of a conflict between forces, of the kind described in learning theory and psychoanalytic theory, I claim that it often comes to be represented in the individual's mind and becomes part of a conflict between alternative actions, i.e., reasoned behaviors. This conflict is resolved on a deliberated and rational basis. When a conflict is resolved through the relative strength of two contesting forces, this is not a moral decision but rather impulsive behavior. Although upon occasion the distinction between a considered decision and impulsive behavior may be blurred, incontrovertible examples of both types of decision do exist. In any case, the issue is conflict between various considerations, which is resolved in a deliberated rather than an impulsive manner. It is my belief that this type of conflict and resolution is not rare in the ethical life of the individual.

Moral conflict can arise only after an "ought" judgment has been made, a judgment that has its roots in the moral point of view. The conflict is therefore between a moral viewpoint and an amoral one, which I shall call a personal point of view. This characterization of the conflict returns us to that proposed by learning theory, except that here each tendency is ostensibly given the status of a consideration, a conscious or quasi-conscious reason for action. This difference, however, alters fundamentally the entire concept of the conflict. Most significantly, conflicts between two considerations are not resolved in a mechanical fashion through the relative strength of the forces involved, but rather by a decision principle. The principle may perhaps be quantitative in content, as suggested by utilitarians, but it is not quantitative by nature. The resolution of a conflict between two opposing considerations cannot be the direct outcome of a quantitative interplay, though it may be mediated by a quantitative principle. Rather, the resolution involves a *choice* between alternatives. Moreover, a decision principle implies a judgment outside the immediate situation, according to an independent standard. Thus, it is expressed not through behavior, when actual forces are in conflict, but through judgment, when the confrontation is between considerations that integrate representations of these forces—and the resolution, provided it is systematic, can only come about on the basis of the principle. Our knowledge of both the moral decision principle and of the moral conflict is still scant, and there is clearly room for new proposals to suggest directions for further research. The model I suggest below, after first presenting a general background, is such a proposal.

The Status of the Amoral Viewpoint

I shall examine first the nature of the forces that are involved in a moral conflict. It should be made clear at this point that the following analysis is descriptive rather than normative. A psychological analysis of moral decisions may not, however, disregard the basic feature of moral considerations, i.e., their being perceived as obligatory and overriding. A cognitive view of moral conflict brings us face to face with a problem that has already been mentioned: the moral conflict I described is between a moral and an amoral consideration; however, a moral reason invalidates the conflict from the outset, as the moral consideration is perceived as taking priority over all others. This feature is not a philosophical invention; it is part of human intuition. The uniqueness of a moral prohibition, what distinguishes it, in the eyes of the beholder, from other reasons for action, is that it is perceived as a restriction that is binding on behavior and takes precedence over selfish tendencies (Nisan, 1984). If this is true, it would seem to rule out the possibility of a conflict between moral and amoral *considerations*, since the moral standpoint must take priority. However, as is clear from an analysis of true moral conflicts and decisions, the individual does experience a conflict between considerations. Analysis of moral conflicts suggests that, in addition to and concomitant with the moral considerations, individuals also raise considerations that they perceive as amoral, relating to their personal viewpoints, and moreover that their decisions sometimes tend, with their full awareness, to be not moral.

This characterization of a moral conflict and moral decision serves as my point of departure. From this I derive the basic assumption that, while a moral consideration is perceived as having a priority over other types of reasons for behavior, it is not perceived as taking *absolute* precedence over the personal, amoral consideration. In other words, even when conflicting with a moral consideration, the personal viewpoint can be perceived by the individual as "legitimate" to a certain extent, i.e., as not completely overridden. (I would like to reiterate that this is a psychological claim, rather than a philosophical one of the sort suggested, e.g., by Foot, 1972.)

While this view would seem to contradict the notion that the moral stand takes precedence over personal inclination, there is no contradiction from a psychological perspective. While one can discern the impersonal moral viewpoint and recognize its priority over personal considerations, this does not rule out the possibility that one can also recognize the existence of a personal viewpoint that should be taken into consideration, even if it is likely to contradict the moral judgment. The inference is that in the psychological reality of the individual, the moral viewpoint must also be subject to restrictions, which I have referred to as "limited morality" (Nisan, 1985). These restrictions have a special character, as we shall soon see, that reflects and preserves the perceived priority of the moral consideration. I assume that the individual is cognizant of the logical contradiction of such a stand, while fully aware that this implies no psychological contradiction. The logical contradiction is inevitable and derives from the inherent nature of the moral requirement, which is an idealized demand. Without this contradiction, there would be no moral requirement as we know it.

The socialization process stresses the moral viewpoint, perceived as weaker, opposed to human nature, and worthy of support. This emphasis sometimes conceals the fact that in real life the personal viewpoint is also perceived as legitimate. Indeed that viewpoint (e.g., in the form of the principle of personal utility) forms the core of the behavioral sciences, from economics to psychology. Only when moral considerations exist is the personal viewpoint overridden (at the level of judgment) by the moral one; and it is reasonable to assume that this is not unrestricted.

A wide range of human behavior discloses, upon analysis, that the individual considers the personal viewpoint as both significant and legitimate in the moral conflict. A prime example of this is supererogation. By definition, such behavior is considered good and even praiseworthy, but not obligatory, and its absence does not entail disgrace. Philosophically, supererogation is perceived as a special domain—one relating mainly to imperfect duties. Psychologically, however, the supererogatory conflict can be compared to the moral conflict. Both involve a confrontation between the moral and personal viewpoints. Moreover, there are many situations where it is impossible to differentiate clearly between the domain of morality, which entails obligation, and the domain of supererogation. An example of this is helping someone in trouble. An examination of supererogatory behavior reveals that the personal standpoint is taken by the individual as having "legitimate" status. One who refrains from helping others is not only likely to regard the personal consideration as preferable to the moral one, but also to feel that such a preference is justified. This the individual may do on the basis of intuitive thinking similar to that proposed by philosophers (Heyd, 1982). The important point, as far as we are concerned, is that one sees one's personal considerations as rightful; not merely no less than other considerations, but indeed, more so. Such attitudes are apparent in early childhood and continue into adulthood, although in a more sophisticated and complex form. Thus, it would seem that people set a limit to the privileges and demands of the moral viewpoint, a limit that derives from the perception of their personal rights.

The psychological distinction between supererogation and obligation is not clear-cut. One may feel that one's decision to refrain from helping another implies a preference for personal over moral interest. However, the same may be true of "perfect duties," or prohibitions. There seems to be a whole range of behaviors involving a specific prohibition that is nevertheless overridden by personal interests of various kinds. Mosenzon, an Israeli writer, relates a story of a kibbutz shepherd who sold goats belonging to the collective in order to buy paints for his own use. The shepherd justified his theft, which he was aware constituted a moral aberration, by his personal interest. In a meeting of the kibbutz members, he insisted that painting was as vital to him as bread, thereby claiming that human existence—which is certainly perceived as a legitimate reason for action—is not a mere matter of physical survival, but also the actualization of personal interest, which constitutes a legitimate and justified consideration in a moral conflict.

Self-actualization (and realization of personal projects [Williams, 1981]) may be perceived as a consideration within the moral domain, at least in certain cases. However—what is more pertinent to the present argument—it is often perceived otherwise. In many cases considerations of self-actualization or loyalties are perceived as different from, and indeed in opposition to, moral considerations, so that the final decision in favor of the personal consideration is perceived as deviating from ideal morality.

But my claim goes even further. I submit that the right granted by an actor to a personal consideration as overriding a moral one is not limited to "high" values, like self-actualization and loyalties, but may be extended to personal values of a "lower" type, such as cannot be included in the moral domain without losing the essential distinction of this domain. The expression of this right is in the form of a measure of freedom that one believes one can allow oneself in regard to the requirements of the ideal morality. In research in which we asked respondents to describe petty crimes they had committed and to explain why they had done so, we were supplied with cases of lying, copying during exams, taking books without permission, and so on, which were attributed to various degrees and types of self-interest, from "it meant a lot to me" to "too much was at stake" to "I can allow myself to sin this little bit." The picture arising from these responses is that the right of the personal consideration is not necessarily found in the positive value of such a consideration but may also derive from the burden of the moral demand and the individual's difficulty in obeying it. It is as if the individual claims, "I have a right to sometimes let myself go; you can't expect me to be a saint, especially when the weakness is shared by all human beings." This claim, too, belongs to the perception of personal identity—not of the identity aspired to, but of that which is perceived as given, even if it reflects a weakness.

It should be emphasized that we are not dealing here with akrasia or weakness of will (cf. Mele, 1985). Individuals disclose weakness of will when they not only *know* (i.e., have judged) that they ought to behave in a certain way but also *decide*—all things considered—to do so, and yet do not carry out their decision. Weakness of will thus relates to slippage in a specific situation. In contrast, in the case I am describing the individual indeed knows that one ought to act in a given way, but nevertheless *decides* not to take this route. Thus, the deviation is in the phase of decision rather than in the phase of action. Furthermore, the deviation is not an isolated unintended event but rather represents a general approach to morality, based on the perception of the general nature of humans, demanding, as it were, allowances to personal gratifications. Indeed, while in some cases the subjects indeed tended to "neutralize" their transgressions (Sykes and Matza, 1957), viewing them as justified and in effect not immoral, in many cases they clearly viewed the behavior as immoral and referred to it not as a "slippage" but as a planned "allowance." Such perceptions are not peculiar to deviants. Our research suggests that they reflect broader attitudes, although doubtless there are large individual (and cultural) differences in the content and range of their practical application.

The above can be summarized as suggesting two continuums in regard to moral allowances. The first concerns the type of the allowance, ranging from those relating to the supererogatory domain to those that clearly belong to the domain of moral obligation and prohibition. The second continuum relates to the type of the personal consideration that is taken as a reason for the transgression, ranging from the right to "self-fulfillment"—in the sense of higher values and aspired identity—to the right to partly surrender to human weakness and to instinctual gratification.

From the above one cannot infer that a personal consideration is a precursor to general moral license. Indeed, the notion of allowance presupposes acceptance of the moral system and the intention to maintain one's moral identity. Moreover, there are certainly limits and restrictions to the perception of personal interest as legitimate. Studies on seriousness of crimes (e.g., Sebba, 1984) suggest that people perceive a difference between the theft of paints by an artist, to whom art is of prime importance, and the theft of paints by someone who wishes to paint his or her warehouse. Similarly, we intuitively feel that there is a difference between stealing the paints from a factory or stealing them from another artist. As to types of behavior, a distinction can be drawn between that which can cause serious harm to others and that which causes relatively little injury. The restrictions of the extent to which the personal aspect is seen as legitimate require further theoretical and empirical research. In any case, the existence of such restrictions only serves to emphasize that personal interests of many types are perceived as reasons for allowance in moral decision-making.

The Resolution of Moral Conflict

The moral conflict under discussion here differs from that commonly discussed in psychological literature; in addition to the cognitive element mentioned above, its characterization of the nature of the forces involved in the conflict is different. In other words, the conflict is not between reason and impulse, the good and evil inclination, or good and bad tendencies; it is between two values based on two types of positively perceived tendencies, one relating to personal interest and the other relating to justice and appropriate social behavior. Although one of the tendencies is perceived as overriding in principle, both are considered appropriate and justified. Naturally not all moral conflicts are of this type. There are instances in which the amoral and/or the moral tendency do not undergo the process of deliberation described above. However, our concern here is with the conflict of deliberation, in which each tendency is represented by a consideration and perceived as legitimate, and with how such conflicts are resolved. I shall argue that resolution of the conflict between the impersonal and the personal value is based on a principle involving the maintenance of an "acceptable level of morality," which rests on a quantitative moral assessment of the individual's behavior.

The natural resolution of a conflict involving two values or tendencies that differ qualitatively but are both considered legitimate is according to the relative importance or value attached to each. In the case of moral conflict, the operation of such a principle requires the following elements: (1) evaluation of the moral value of the action, which may be positive or negative; (2) evaluation of the personal, amoral value of the action, which again may be positive or negative; and (3) a metaevaluation that compares the moral and personal elements on the basis of a common scale of values.

All this is fine when the two values are perceived to have equal status, and where a common standard for their evaluation exists. In this case, preference is given on the basis of their evaluation on the common standard. However, in our case, the moral value is known to take precedence over the personal value. Moreover, there is the problem of whether a common standard can be found—the problem of the incommensurability of different values (as the strength of the emotional reaction to each value, along the lines of Schwartz and Howard's [1981] cost-benefit theory, does not constitute a *principle* on which to base a decision).

The precedence of the moral value must be expressed in the decision principle—it cannot allow a resolution in accordance with the "weightier" value, disregarding the special status of the moral value. I suggest that the resolution adopted is a compromise that is anchored in the moral value. Individuals set a "moral" minimum below which they will not go, but at the same time allow themselves a certain fulfillment of the personal value, even at the expense of the moral one. This decision, I suggest, is based on a question of the following type: Given the overall circumstances of this situation (including the personal value), can I allow myself, in terms of my "moral minimum," to commit a transgression as serious as this? Such a resolution is by no means unequivocal, but it seems appropriate to most moral conflicts. According to this suggestion, the moral value is indeed the starting point for a moral decision, expressing the preferred status of the moral consideration.

Such a resolution can be termed "moral satisficing," along the lines of Simon's (1957) satisficing principle. In Simon's principle, satisficing stems from the individual's inability to process suitably all the information required to reach the optimal, rational decision, thereby forcing him or her to settle for a lower, but still acceptable level of benefit. In our case, by contrast, the satisficing springs from a need to consider and satisfy personal values that conflict with the moral value. References to this kind of motivational satisficing can be found in March (1978) in relation to rational behavior, but these refer to the need to submit to temptation rather than to considerations perceived as legitimate.

The type of resolution I have presented suggests a general scheme for moral decisions. However, there are two glaring shortcomings. First, this scheme completely overlooks the time dimension. It is reasonable to assume that behavior is assessed not merely for itself, but also in its relation to past or possible future actions. This omission is obvious when we speak of supererogatory behavior. It is clear that one's decision to stay on in a plague-ridden town will take into account the time factor: what has one accomplished so far and what does one intend to accomplish in the future? The questions involved are obviously related to the time dimension: have I already done enough, from my point of view? This brings us to the second shortcoming, which is more basic. The general scheme relates to actions and not to people. True, an assessment of the moral value of an action is impersonal; but the moral decision is not. Let us again take an example from the domain of supererogation: the individual does not ask whether "one" is allowed to leave the plague-ridden town, but rather: "Do I feel that I should leave the town?" These two shortcomings lead us to a more complex model of moral decisions, which I have called "moral balance." This model retains the basic features of the scheme first proposed—individuals set "moral" standards below which they will not fall, but also allow themselves moral deviation—adding to it a broader description of that moral standard. Such a description can be confirmed or discredited by empirical observations, and may have repercussions on various theories in the field of the psychology of morality.

Before turning to a more systematic presentation of the model, I shall discuss a pertinent question: Does the process of moral decision, as suggested here, entailing a self-allowance to deviate, hold for people in higher stages of moral judgment? This question may be asked from both theoretical and empirical viewpoints and the issue is obviously a broad and complex one. In the present context, however, I shall restrict my comments to the primary question of whether the structure of reasoning in the highest stages of moral judgment, according to Kohlberg, allows for the possibility of allowance.

As described here, the concept of allowance refers to a behavior that one decides to undertake on the basis of reasons that one perceives as personal, even though one considers this behavior a moral deviation. This process presupposes, so it seems, an agent who perceives the distinction, and even contradiction, between moral and personal considerations. Such a distinction, however, does not seem to apply to the highest level of moral reasoning. At this stage there seems to be an overlap between judgment from moral and personal points of view. What may appear as allowance to deviate may actually be based on reasoning and judgment in an inclusive framework, which is one with the moral framework and in which personal considerations are defined in ethical terms. This is perhaps what underlies Kohlberg and Candee's (1984) expectation that in the highest stage of moral reasoning there will be a full consistency between moral judgment and moral choice.

This is true, however, only for reasoning at the very highest stage, which occurs rarely. In lower stages, and even in Stage 5, there seems to be a distinction and a distance between moral and personal judgments. This is reflected in the analysis by Kohlberg, Boyd, and Levine (this volume), which shows, for example, that in Stage 5 the individual reasons in terms of fixed and given rights rather than in terms of the general principle of respect for people. This suggests that even at Stage

5—and certainly at lower stages—moral reasoning does not constitute an all-inclusive judgment, but is rather one of several considerations. Thus, as long as the different considerations are not completely integrated, the way is indeed open to an allowance to deviate in the strong sense suggested above—i.e., acting with full recognition that the behavior is improper yet choosing to let a personal consideration override a moral one.

While there are no direct empirical data linking the stage of moral judgment to self-allowance to deviate, extant data do shed some light on this issue. In the study mentioned above, which asked university students (likely to be at Stages 3 and 4) to describe their own moral deviations and their perceptions of such deviation at the time of its performance, many subjects presented cases of self-allowed deviation. In another study we presented the model of moral balance to a group of 20 social scientists and asked them if they could recall in their own recent behavior clear cases of deviations of the type described. More than 60% of these people, some of whom were likely to be at Stage 4 and probably even higher, replied affirmatively. I may thus conclude, with high certainty, that the model does apply to people at the conventional stages (i.e., most of the adult population), and very likely to people at Stage 5 as well.

The Moral Balance Model

The central thesis of this model is that the moral standard set for oneself is related not to the gravity of a specific action, but to one's moral balance, i.e., the assessment of one's current moral status. An evaluation of moral status is based on the sum of morally significant actions recently undertaken by the individual, over a given period of time. The basic assumption is that one wishes at all times to maintain one's moral status on a level that one considers satisfactory. A central consideration in one's decision to undertake or refrain from taking a morally significant action is whether this behavior would lower one's perceived moral status to an unacceptable level. The model is presented in the form of assumptions, each of which relates to a specific element of the model.

General assumption: The ideal moral judgment for a situation

The moral dimension is a central one in the individual's process of assessing the rightness of actions, performed or planned. This moral assessment may be immediate or involve a dilemma. In either event, the final moral judgment is perceived as objective, impersonal, and categorical—it determines whether the action is permissible, prohibited, or obligatory. I shall call this "the ideal moral judgment."

The moral weight of an action

Actions perceived as morally significant are assessed along a quantitative scale, as more or less good or bad. Thus, for example, one can assume that a large contribution to charity is assessed as "better" than a smaller contribution, or that intentional *serious* harm to another is assessed as worse than intentional *slight* harm. The criteria for such an assessment will not be discussed here.

Overall moral balance

When faced with a moral decision, one tends to assess oneself on the moral scale based on the sum of morally significant actions one has undertaken over a given time prior to the assessment. The level of such as assessment, which alters with each moral action, is what I call the individual's "moral balance." I assume, therefore, that the individual has a single moral balance, something akin to an overall self-assessment along a good-bad continuum, which is over and above the morally significant actions he or she has performed.

The wish to maintain a high moral balance

Morality, or acting according to what is right, is an important component of the individual's identity as well as a significant factor in self-evaluation. Assuming that people wish to preserve their identity and improve their self-image, it follows that they also wish to attain and maintain a high level of "morality," or a high moral balance.

Justification for choosing personal values over moral ones

People's sense of identity includes, among other things, their personal values: their needs, goals, and plans, both clearly defined and ambiguous, both long and short range. The satisfaction of personal values is often in conflict with the moral value, which is other-oriented rather than self-oriented. Identity and self-evaluation are a function of the extent to which individuals satisfy and actualize their personal values. Therefore, out of a recognition of their limited time and resources, individuals come to the realization that their personal values are justifiably significant factors in moral decisions. Such an awareness implies (psychologically) that, within certain boundaries, there is room for choosing personal values over moral ones, or that deviation from an ideal moral standard is both proper and justified. In other words, the moral balance one wishes to maintain does not necessarily have to be, and perhaps cannot be, the highest attainable.

Setting an acceptable, obligatory level of morality

The compromise that arises out of the above is to set an acceptable level of morality, which the individual must not fall short of but which is nevertheless lower than the ideal. The acceptable level sets the minimum required by the moral identity of the individual, while leaving room for the fulfillment of personal values. It follows that all things being equal, the higher the moral balance—for example, after a series of good deeds—the greater the likelihood that one will allow oneself to deviate (or refrain from good deeds). Conversely, the lower the moral balance—for example, after a bad deed—the greater the likelihood that one will not allow oneself to deviate and/or will consider it incumbent upon oneself to do a good deed. (As mentioned earlier, however, some deviations are unthinkable, whatever one's moral balance.)

Empirical Support for Some Elements of the Model

The model is supported by the results of interviews and questionnaires administered to people of varying ages, ranging from adolescence to middle age. The subjects, who maintained anonymity, were questioned about transgressions they had committed, their evaluations of these transgressions, and their feelings afterward. The majority of the subjects admitted to having committed "minor" transgressions at a greater or lesser frequency. Of greater pertinence to our study, they admitted that both at the time of commission and while answering the questionnaire they were aware that these were wrong acts, which should not have been performed; that they were not the result of irresistible impulses; that due to their performance they "compromised" their consciences; and that at times, after committing these acts, they felt the need to apologize and improve themselves. Nevertheless, subjects did not feel that they were "evil." Rather, they believed they had allowed themselves a temporary lapse from their moral framework.

These findings are consistent both with common sense and with several of the aforementioned assumptions: that there exists an ideal moral judgment, which one perceives as impersonal and obligating; that one permits oneself limited moral deviations, as a form of compromise with one's personal interests, while recognizing their wrongness from an ideal point of view; that one strives to maintain a measure of moral balance from which one would not want to slip, so that a considerable decrease in balance produces an uncomfortable feeling; that this uncomfortable feeling is connected only with the evaluation of one's *temporary* state but not with the more stable aspect of self-evaluation—i.e., after performing a wrong act, one does not define oneself as evil but rather perceives oneself as being involved in a "bad" situation—of having a low moral balance.

Alongside these personal responses, I conducted several controlled studies that, on the whole, offer support for my model. I will briefly discuss two kinds: one dealing with the evaluation of goodness and badness of acts, and the other investigating the assumption that one's moral balance affects one's decision to perform a good or bad deed in a given situation.

As was to be expected, both children and adults evaluated morally significant acts according to degrees of goodness or badness. This type of evaluation was perceived by them as natural, and much consistency was revealed among subjects. Two variables that affect act evaluation seem directly related to the assumptions mentioned above. The first is the amount of temptation present at the time the act was committed. The more the transgression was a result of temptation, the more the subjects tended to diminish its seriousness. Thus, for example, stealing money from mother to buy ice cream was evaluated as less serious when children saw all of their friends licking cones than when they did not. This effect was not due to their perceiving themselves as losing control of their actions. Rather, the level of temptation affected the evaluation of the act by becoming a *consideration* in determining their personal needs or interests. It should be noted that the ice cream example involves an apparently "low," drive-like need, yet even the presence of a temptation of this sort led to a perception of the transgression as less serious (and consequently—we may infer—the children will more readily permit themselves to commit this transgression).

The second variable relates to the importance of the reason for the deviation. Thus, for example, I found that copying on a test to ensure acceptance into a science club was perceived as less "bad" when done by a child planning to be a science researcher than by a child who had no special interest in the club. In the same vein, theft of a record by a sworn music buff was perceived as less severe than theft by one with no special inclination toward music, and telephoning from work was considered less serious when done for an "important" personal plan, such as the purchase of an apartment, than when done for an "unimportant" need, like a casual conversation with a friend. In all of these cases, the independent variable (the importance and nature of the personal value derived from the transgression) influenced the evaluation of the seriousness of the transgression, but not its perception as something wrong. The subjects generally agreed that the behavior was wrong, but they felt that it was "less wrong" when the personal value involved was "important" than when it was "unimportant."

Indirectly, these studies support several of the aforementioned assumptions. They suggest that a subject evaluates transgressions and good deeds according to a quantitative scale; that the individual takes into consideration the personal value at stake in the act (as a result of which the seriousness of the transgression is affected); but also that this personal value does not cancel the definition of the act as wrong.

A second group of studies investigated a "stronger" assumption of the model—that the moral balance influences the individual's tendency to decide to do a good or bad deed in a given situation. My model suggests that, other things being equal, those who have committed a good deed will feel less obligated to do an additional one and thus will allow themselves more liberty to deviate; and conversely, those who have committed a bad deed will feel a greater obligation to do a good deed that chances upon them, and will allow themselves less liberty to deviate again.

The second part of the hypothesis is supported by a number of social psychological studies (Rosenhan et al., 1981). Subjects who thought that they had caused harm to others, whether intentionally or inadvertently, or those who felt guilty, were more willing to volunteer for altruistic activities than subjects in a control group. These findings, which have been subject to various interpretations, are consistent with and well explained by the moral balance model. A more complex finding, which is consistent with my model, is that people who have sinned and are given the chance to confess show less of a tendency to volunteer to do good deeds than others who did not have the opportunity to confess (Harris, Benson, and Hall, 1975). However, these findings, like those mentioned earlier, relate to the moral balance in terms of behavior and not in terms of a decision principle.

Two recent studies (Horenczyk, 1984; Nisan and Horenczyk, in press) have directly examined the issue of moral balance in terms of judgment. The first included a sample of 242 seventh-grade students who read ten stories, each of which described a boy who performed a good or bad deed and, a few days later, was faced with the dilemma of whether to commit a transgression or to volunteer for a good deed. Examples of good deeds are returning a lost wallet and volunteering to help crippled children; examples of transgressions are stealing a book from a store and lying to mother. In some of the stories the past deed was similar to the deed about which the child was about to decide, in others it was not. The subject was requested to answer one of the two following questions: (1) "What do you think the child finally decided?" or (2) "In your opinion how serious was the behavior of the child in this situation?," with a five-step scale for the answer. Each subject answered Question 1 for one half of the stories and Question 2 for the other half. As expected, in all of the stories (except one, which will not be discussed here) the subjects predicted a greater probability for performance of the good deed by one who had previously done a good deed, and the inverse for one who had done a bad deed. This evaluation is based on a trait model. While an actor tends to attribute his or her behavior to reasons and situational causes, observers tend to attribute it to a stable personal trait (Jones and Nisbett, 1971), an attribution that seems to dominate their cognitive evaluation of the situation. Thus, one who did a good or bad deed is perceived as possessing the trait of doing good or bad, and therefore is expected to act accordingly in the future. However, when these same subjects were requested to evaluate the severity of the deed, they gave the opposite response. In all ten stories the transgression was perceived as more serious when committed by one who had previously committed a transgression than by one who had previously done a good deed. These results apply both to the stories in which there existed a similarity between the previous act and the new one and to those stories in which the two were different.

Horenczyk's findings, which show that morally significant acts are evaluated also against the background of the individual's previous behaviors, i.e., his moral balance, support our model. On the basis of findings (Nisan, 1979) that the more serious an act is evaluated as, the less one's willingness to perform it, we may conclude that when a person's moral balance is high (after performing a good deed or refraining from evil), there will be a greater willingness to commit a transgression or refrain from doing a good deed, and vice versa.

The second study was designed to further clarify this question. Each of the 271 seventh-grade participants read four two-part stories. In the first part of the story, two out of the following three character types were described: a good person (who always helps others or generally refrains from immoral acts), a bad person (who regularly refrains from helping others or regularly transgresses), and an ordinary person. The second half of the story described a temptation situation faced by the hero: the temptation to steal a book from a store or to refrain from helping an elderly person when rushing to a football game. After reading each story the subject was requested to answer two questions. For half the stories, the questions were: (1) Which of the two characters described (e.g., the good and the bad one, or the good and the ordinary one, or the bad and the ordinary one) was more likely to succumb to the temptation? and (2) To which of the two characters would you be more inclined to permit commission of the transgression? In the other half, it was mentioned that both characters committed the transgression and the subject was asked: (1) Which of the two do you think felt guiltier? and (2) Which of the two do you think *should* have felt guiltier? There were six versions of the questionnaire, which included all possible combinations of stories, characters, and questions.

The findings revealed the trends predicted by the trait model on the one hand and the moral balance model on the other. The subjects predicted a high probability of transgression by the bad person and a low probability of transgression by the good person. They also predicted a greater chance of guilt feelings by the latter and a smaller chance by the former. These results reflect the tendency of an observer to attribute behavior to stable traits, as mentioned before. The feeling of guilt is perceived as part of this trait: one who is accustomed to doing evil is perceived as lacking guilt, while one who generally does not transgress is perceived as feeling guilty following a bad deed. On the other hand, subjects were more inclined to permit transgressions by a good person, who is unaccustomed to doing bad deeds or accustomed to helping others, than by an ordinary or bad person. Similarly, they thought that the bad person *should* feel guiltier and the good person less guilty. These results, which support the moral balance model, were obtained both in the helping scenario and the stealing scenario, although the effect was stronger in the former. The model seems then to fit supererogatory behavior better than avoidance of transgressions, but it applies to, and predicts, the latter type of behavior as well.

The results support my model, provided that judgments concerning others reflect those that individuals would make about themselves. This assumption is indeed part of the overall conception of moral decision as connected with judgment and principles that, by definition, are generalizable and not oriented to a specific situation or person. By this I do not, of course, deny the possibility that one may decide differently about oneself than one would about others, just as there exists a gap between moral judgment and moral behavior. These differences would result from various motivational factors that are bound to cause distortion and bias in perception, reasoning, and behavior.

Further Clarification of the Model

In this section I shall reflect on a central topic of the suggested model—the "composition" of the moral balance. These reflections invite empirical research, whether via interviews or through controlled studies.

As mentioned, the moral balance is based upon the total moral weight (positive or negative) of an individual's morally significant acts. The question arises as to whether all such acts are included within one general balance (the "inclusive" hypothesis), or whether the moral balance is composed of several specialized moral balances, whether broad, such as for positive acts or transgressions, or more limited, such as for wrong behavior toward one's spouse or crimes against the state (the "differential" hypothesis). My results support both hypotheses. On the one hand, consistent with the inclusive hypothesis, people who have transgressed exhibit a greater tendency to help others in need. On the other hand, consistent with the differential hypothesis, people who have regularly helped others exhibit a greater tendency to refrain from extending additional help than to commit transgressions. Indeed, in spite of the great temptation to suggest that the greater the amount of good deeds that people perform, the freer they will feel to sin (righteousness, as it were, compensating for crime), this cannot be claimed without reservations. It seems that there are also various kinds of specialized moral balances, especially those oriented toward specific behaviors.

Another question involves the area and limits of the range of acts accumulating in the moral balance. The central area of this range seems to be clear: those positive acts and transgressions about which there is a consensus from a moral point of view. One can speculate about possible extensions of this range, for example, the time dimension. What time range is perceived as relevant to the calculation of moral balance? As temporal distance from an act increases, its emotional impact on the individual decreases (Ekman and Lundberg, 1971). It is reasonable to assume that good or bad deeds that were committed a long time ago lose their weight in the overall moral balance. If that is the case, what is the shape of the curve of decrease in act weight as a function of time? And is this curve similar in both positive acts and transgressions? Another question concerning the time dimension relates to the future. It is not too wild a speculation to claim that one is apt to allow oneself a moral deviation on the basis of a promise to oneself to correct the balance in the future. In a tentative study I found that high school students were more willing to allow a deviation by one who was planning to help people in distress than by one about whom no information of this sort was reported. In this example the protagonist had already made a formal commitment to perform the positive act; however, it is possible that one makes such a commitment to oneself and thus "borrows" on one's balance and allows oneself to deviate.

A second possible extension involves the contents of the acts. As already mentioned, the clear and prime components of the moral balance are positive moral acts and moral transgressions. But may other acts, which are not purely moral, also be included—for example, positive and negative religious acts, contributions to people and state (such as prolonged military service or even a dedicated political service)? These ideas derive from some popular conceptions and a few paltry observations. Some religious people do not distinguish between religious and moral norms, and in the absence of this distinction we would expect a unified moral balance for both. A balance of this sort could lead such individuals to be more exacting in those duties between person and God and to allow themselves more liberties in those duties between person and person. Perhaps this is what the prophet was referring to when he criticized the people for offering sacrifices with tarnished hands. Parallel to this is the possibility that people involved in activities that greatly contribute to society (the state or the people) will attribute to themselves a high moral balance and allow themselves extra liberties in the area of personal morality. King David's sin with the wife of Uriah was not a matter of self-actualization, but probably a liberty he took to consciously deviate in light of his strong balance, based primarily on his contribution to the people. Analysis of people's responses to the excesses of their leaders or of others who have contributed to society reveals two opposing patterns. On the one hand, the people expect such figures to be exemplary, while on the other they are sometimes willing to forgive them more than they would an ordinary person. The willingness to pardon certain people, ranging from military leaders to artists, can be explained in several ways. At times the suggestion of an expanded moral balance, which includes the factor of contribution to society, is probably the best explanation.

A third type of extension—but also a restriction—of the range of moral balance acts deals with the boundaries of the self. The acts relevant to one's moral balance are one's own acts. But it is possible that one's balance is influenced also by the acts of other people who serve as an extension of oneself— first and foremost the members of one's family. An interesting possibility within this context is the ramifications of a nation's crimes on the balance of an individual member. One can cite examples of individuals who feel personal guilt, or the need to perform personal expiating acts, because of crimes of a people or group. In all of these cases I am not referring to emotional feelings of discomfort, which indeed seem to exist, but rather to conscious and deliberate considerations concerning an individual's responsibility—considerations that can be conceptualized in terms of the moral balance.

Just as we can speak of an extension of the self, so too must we consider a "reduction" of self. One is apt to feel guilt for acts that one has committed unintentionally. On the other hand, one may shake off any guilt or "debt" in one's moral balance caused by acts perpetrated in "non-self" situations. This refers not only to coercive situations, but also to those connected with obeying authorities, conforming to society's demands, etc. One is liable to perceive one's behavior in these situations as behavior stemming from outside oneself, and thus will not consider them in one's moral balance. This is likely to be the case not only in momentary situations, such as the Milgram experiments, but also in more prolonged situations, such as military service.

The Moral Decision and Personal Identity: Concluding Remarks

The domain of moral behavior seems to be double-edged. On the one hand, it is perceived as a very personal domain: it is the individual alone who makes the moral decision out of an absolutely free choice. On the other hand, it is perceived as impersonal, possessing an objective status and applicable to everyone. This duality is clarified by the distinction between the moral judgment and the moral decision. Moral judgment, by its very nature, is indeed impersonal and is perceived as having no room for personal biases of any kind. This intuitive perception finds expression in the philosophical characterization of the moral viewpoint as judgment by an objective observer through a veil of ignorance (Rawls, 1971). This is a psychological truth concerning moral judgment, and it applies to the heteronomous judgment of the young child as well as to the autonomous judgment of the adult (Turiel, 1983). But judgment of the "ought" is only one side of the moral conflict; there are other considerations, which I have referred to collectively as personal ones. These raise the need for moral decision that is, according to my description, a very personal matter, not just because one is deciding by oneself, not just because the decision is determined by one's personal balance, and not just because each individual has his or her own unique experiences and lives in his or her own unique context—but primarily because the decision must be based on one's own choice. When setting an acceptable level of morality and deciding whether or not and how much to compromise, one cannot refer to any objective standard. These are decisions that no one else can make.

In our search for an inclusive conceptualization of the factors that influence the moral decision process we are led to the concept of personal identity. Personal identity has been suggested as the basis of moral motivation (Blasi, 1983); here I propose that it is also the basis of moral compromise. Interviews and responses to questionnaires have led me to conclude that people perceive the moral decision to be preceded by the right to preserve one's self, since it is their own personal choice. Totally relinquishing personal interests in favor of the moral value is perceived as implying, as it were, denial of self-identity. Personal decision in the sense suggested above allows a legitimate status for what I call the personal value. The concept of personal identity proposes, then, the following hypothesis: the more a moral decision involves personal value crucial to one's personal identity, the greater the moral concession that will be made, and this as a result of considered reasoning. This is how people perceive the case of Gauguin, who abandoned and neglected his family to devote himself to painting, or the moral conflicts of people with highly developed personal projects about whom Williams (1981) wrote. Preservation of their personal identity, of which their projects are a central component, demands of them, as it were, a moral concession. From here the way is open to making a moral concession for less grandiose and spectacular "projects," for example, the satisfaction of lowly interests and passions. Under special circumstances even gratification of passions could be perceived as a positive characteristic of one's personal identity. In other—probably most—cases, submission to one's passions is viewed as a "negative" characteristic of identity, but still part of it: "This is what I am; I possess this weakness. Accepting myself demands the making of a moral concession." Indeed self-definition is guided not only by the "ought" but also by the "is." Identity includes such elements as being a member of a certain family and nation, having a certain appearance, and indeed having certain attributes and weaknesses. This is the part of the identity that psychologists focus upon when they speak of the actual-I (as opposed to the ideal-I). In the framework of the moral balance, in which one strives not for perfection but for "satisficing," not for holiness but for reasonable morality, these aspects of one's identity will influence one's moral decision.

At the same time, personal identity also includes the moral value. This is the aspect that has received greater emphasis in the psychology of morality. Perception of one's personal identity is contingent upon the perception of the personal identity of others and their autonomous status. A sense of personal identity seems to imply—by a psychological necessity—a rational and objective moral judgment. This judgment acquires for itself the status of a necessary and preferred—but not exclusive—value in the framework of the personal identity. The anchoring of morality in personal identity provides it with a motivational basis, and from here derives the need for an "acceptable level of morality," beneath which one should not descend. This is primarily the obligatory aspect of the moral dimension, the limit that the personal identity sets on its behavior vis-à-vis others. But it seems that the moral value is likely to acquire for itself an "autonomous" status beyond this. There are people for whom the moral dimension is central to their identity. They will set for themselves a high acceptable level of morality, because this is how they preserve and express their personal identity. Their personal and moral values merge together, as it were. These are perhaps the "saints" of various levels, who act beyond the call of duty.

This description of the moral conflict and decision-making process is in accordance with two types of alienation that are connected with morality. Immoral behavior is likely to drag in its wake a sense of deviation from the self-identity—"it is not me who deviates in this way." This feeling will be sensed when the moral balance descends beneath the level that one sets for oneself as minimal. On the other hand, moral behavior, too, can cause a sense of alienation from one's personal identity— "It is not me who sacrifices so much of his personal values." This feeling will arise when despite a sufficiently high moral balance, the individual is led to make a very large personal sacrifice. The basic tendency to maximize the moral value encroaches on the personal "territory" more than necessary. These two forms of alienation, concerning the moral and personal dimensions of identity, do not harm the integration of the personal identity as long as they are not too extreme. This is due to the time dimension of the moral balance. Deviations to either side are perceived against the background of the individual's continuous existence, and they can be corrected or compensated for. This is the point at which moral balance and personal identity meet.[1]

Note

1. This study was supported by a grant from the United States–Israel Binational Foundation, Jerusalem. I would like to thank Bill Puka and Tom Wren for very helpful comments on an earlier version of this article, and Helen Hogri for her editorial assistance.

References

Blasi, A. (1983). Moral cognition and moral action: A theoretical perspective. *Developmental Review*, 3:178–210.

Brown, R., and Herrnstein, R. (1975). Moral reasoning and conduct. In R. Brown and R. Herrnstein, *Psychology*. Boston: Little Brown.

Ekman, G., and Lundberg, U. (1971). Emotional reaction to past and future events as a function of temporal distance. *Acta Psychologica*, 35:430–441.

Foot, P. (1972). Morality as a system of hypothetical imperatives. *Philosophical Review*, 81:305–316. Reprinted in P. Foot, *Virtues and vices and other essays in moral philosophy*. Berkeley and Los Angeles: University of California Press, 1978.

Frankena, W. K. (1973). *Ethics*. Englewood Cliffs, NJ: Prentice-Hall.

Harris, M. B., Benson, S. M., and Hall, C. (1975). The effects of confessions on altruism. *Journal of Social Psychology*, 96:187–192.

Heyd, P. (1982). *Supererogation: Its status in ethical theory.* Cambridge: Cambridge University Press.

Horenczyk, G. (1984). *Moral balance: An empirical examination of a model for moral decision.* Master's thesis, Department of Psychology, The Hebrew University of Jerusalem.

Jones, E. E., and Nisbett, R. E. (1971). The actor and the observer: Divergent perceptions of the causes of behavior. In E. E. Jones, D. E. Kanouse, H. A. Kelley, R. E. Nisbett, S. Valins, and B. Weiner (Eds.), *Attribution: Perceiving the cause of behavior.* Morristown, NJ: General Learning Press.

Kohlberg, L., and Candee, D. (1984). The relationship of moral judgment to moral action. In L. Kohlberg, *Essays on moral development. Vol. 2: The psychology of moral development.* San Francisco: Harper and Row.

March, J. G. (1978). Bounded rationality, ambiguity and the engineering of choice. *The Bell Journal of Economics,* 9:587–608.

Mele, A. R. (1985). Self-control, action and belief. *American Philosophical Quarterly,* 22:169–175.

Miller, N. E. (1959). Liberalization of basic S-R concepts: Extensions to conflict behavior, motivation and social learning. In S. Koch (Ed.), *Psychology: A study of a science* (Vol. 2). New York: McGraw-Hill.

Nisan, M. (1979). Judgments of seriousness of transgressions. Unpublished manuscript, School of Education, The Hebrew University of Jerusalem.

Nisan, M. (1984). Perception of morality, conventions, values and personal preferences. Unpublished manuscript, School of Education, The Hebrew University of Jerusalem.

Nisan, M. (1985) Limited morality: A concept and its educational implications. In M. W. Berkowitz and F. Oser (Eds.), *Moral education: Theory and application.* Hillsdale, NJ: Lawrence Erlbaum.

Nisan, M., and Horenczyk, G. (in press). Moral balance: The effect of prior behavior on decision in moral conflict. *British Journal of Social Psychology.*

Rawls, J. (1971). *A theory of justice.* Cambridge, MA: Harvard University Press.

Rest, J. R. (1984). The major components of morality. In W. M. Kurtines and J. L. Gewirtz (Eds.). *Morality, moral behavior and moral development.* New York: Wiley Interscience.

Rosenhan, D. L., Salovey, P., Karylowski, J., and Hargis, K. (1981). Emotion and altruism. In J. P. Rushton and R. M. Sorrentino (Eds.), *Altruism and helping behavior.* Hillsdale, NJ: Lawrence Erlbaum.

Schwartz, S. H., and Howard, J. (1981). A normative decision making model of altruism. In J. P. Rushton and R. M. Sorrentino (Eds.), *Altruism and helping behavior.* Hillsdale, NJ: Lawrence Erlbaum.

Sebba, L. (1984). Crime seriousness and criminal intent. *Crime and Delinquency,* 30:227–244.

Simon, H. (1957). *Models of man.* New York. Wiley.

Sykes, G. M., and Matza, D. (1957). Techniques of neutralization: A theory of delinquency. *American Sociological Review,* 22:664–670.

Turiel, E. (1983). *The development of social knowledge: Morality and convention.* New York: Cambridge University Press.

Williams, B. (1981). *Moral luck.* Cambridge: Cambridge University Press.

Moral Responsibility and Moral Commitment: The Integration of Affect and Cognition

Helen Haste

In the *London Times* of August 4, 1988, the eminent journalist Bernard Levin wrote about the breakthrough in the use of pig transplants into humans:

My first feeling on reading about the latest "breakthrough" was one of revulsion, indeed of horror. Beware of first feelings, the doctors involved would say. . . . No, say I; trust those first feelings, for in these matters they are overwhelmingly likely to be right. And there is a reason for that likelihood. There are impulses in us which come direct from a level far deeper than reason, and wise men and women will pay heed to what leaps across the rational gulf, because it comes from the ultimate repository of moral truth.

Why, and how, do we always know when we are doing wrong, even when we continue to do it? . . . Reason, later, finds arguments to back up that truth (or, too frequently, to deny it), but that extraordinary and inexplicable moral gyroscope which we all have in us will bring us back into balance if we will only let it.

Levin describes a common moral experience, an immediate affective reaction that appears to precede cognitive analysis of the situation. In explaining the experience he invokes a sort of "moral instinct" ("call it soul, call it spirit, call it the subconscious, call it conscience, call it a packet of prawn-flavoured potato crisps"). He recognizes that, conventionally, such a response conflicts with the acceptable rationality of cognitive moral reasoning—and therefore has to be justified and given legitimacy.

In this chapter I explore some routes to moral commitment. Commitment is characterized by the ways that the individual appraises the situation. I argue that it has three elements: *vision*, the interpretation of an event or situation in a wider social or moral context; *efficacy*, the belief that one is personally able (alone or with others) to do something about the situation; and *responsibility*, the belief that one is personally obligated to take action. One path to commitment depends upon level of moral reasoning. Commitment arises out of an understanding of moral issues within a context of social justice, respect for persons, and responsibility. This understanding, and particularly the commitment of the self to action, is characteristic of postconventional—especially Stage 6—reasoners. A second route to commitment involves a significant experience, a "triggering event" that creates a powerful affective response such as Levin describes, and precipitates a moral crisis. In the resolution of this crisis the individual gains new moral (or political) perspectives, a new sense of personal agency, and a shift in perceived role and responsibilities. A third path to commitment is usually found among people who come from a background where activism or public responsibility was taken for granted. They grew up with a sense of efficacy (as part of a group if not by themselves) and a framework for interpreting the world in moral or political terms. These people remember events that consolidated their awareness of increasing personal responsibility, or marked a qualitative progression in the degree of commitment, but they do not define these as major life changes.

These three paths are subjectively different experiences, but they all culminate in the individual becoming *morally engaged*. Do we require different theoretical models to explain the three paths to commitment? There has been no space in Kohlberg's cognitive model for an affective experience as the primary impetus to moral insight and motivation; the assumption of the cognitive model is that reasoning and reflection upon the situation or issue generates a judgment of moral wrongness, and that this, for some individuals, may lead to the engagement of individual responsibility. Built into this model is the assumption that there is a gap between judgment and action that may or may not be bridged, and that the moral responsibility and moral action consistent with "commitment" require a high level of moral reasoning. Yet it is clear that the other paths to commitment do not require a high level of moral reasoning. Also, those who reach commitment via a personal crisis or the consolidation of long-term orientation to responsibility do not seem to suffer from akrasia—the gap between judgment and action; in fact they experience their commitment to action as inevitable, even compelling.

I shall explore several case studies that reflect different degrees of commitment and different routes toward it. Some people experienced an initial moral crisis. Others do not recall a triggering event but they do describe events or incidents that made them aware of, or crystallized, their sense of personal responsibility.

Sandra is seventeen, an ordinary British teenager. On a visit to a French family, she had an experience that made her question the eating of meat, and she became a vegetarian. Lenny is an American, a Midwesterner from a conservative background. As a graduate student in England, he became caught up in campus protest in 1968 and experienced a powerful metamorphosis of his thinking; he returned to the United States a committed radical activist. Helen is the mother of five children, and a midwife; a moment of sudden insight about the effects of nuclear war set in train a series of activities that eventually led her to dedicate herself full-time to protest against the siting of Cruise missiles in England. As a young and self-confident lawyer, Gandhi went to southern Africa to practice; he rapidly encountered the ignominy of racial prejudice, and began his long career of activism by organizing the local Indian community.

These four people all experienced a crisis accompanied by powerful affect. Reflecting upon their experience, they constructed a moral dimension of the situation. Each of them made a moral decision; to a greater or lesser extent, they felt they personally had a responsibility to act. All these moral crises changed lives, but to differing degrees. Sandra's new moral commitment would have created minor changes in her family's domestic planning; Gandhi's substantially affected the history of India. Sandra moved a small step down a road to taking personal moral responsibility for her beliefs, whereas Gandhi went through many changes before he finally gave his life to the movement.

My other case histories are of people whose commitment is not associated with the memory of violent personal changes, but with crystallization of an existing perspective. Emily is a dedicated peace activist, and has been involved in peace work since her adolescence in the nineteen-thirties. Quietly and consistently, she has been a member of local groups wherever she has lived, in Britain and abroad. Justine Wise Polier is a lawyer who has campaigned for child care provision all her professional life, and worked to change fundamental attitudes in this field. Judianne Densen-Gerber set up a drug treatment center in New York but has always found herself at the center of causes. All these women have a low threshold for moral outrage, and a sense of inescapable obligation. Although they did not recall conversion experiences or crises, there have been turning points in their lives that consolidated an existing predisposition, qualitative steps in engagement.

The Definition and Justification of Commitment

I have defined "commitment" as a state in which the individual has become engaged morally in an issue or situation, to the extent of feeling an unusual degree of personal responsibility for making change, and believing that he or she can be effective in doing so.

Vision is the individual's perception that the situation involves moral issues, and that there are wider implications and contexts of those issues. Anyone can see that a man beating a horse is causing suffering to the animal, but to see the broader moral implications of a repressive institution or to question the legitimacy of authority requires a cognitive leap, a capacity to see the individual act of injustice as part of a wider problem of social institutions. Vision is a cognitive process, and a higher level of moral and cognitive complexity is more likely to facilitate such vision. On the other hand sometimes vision comes from seeing simple things differently, making connections where connections did not formerly have significance. This need not require sophisticated ethical analysis or insight; I know of a 4-year-old who refused to eat meat because she had learned to regard animals as her friends, and she wouldn't eat her friends. Not all children take this moral position, even though they possess the concept of animals as friends, the objection to eating one's friends, and the knowledge that meat is dead animals, but this child happens to have had that particular moral "vision."

Efficacy has two parts: believing one *can* be effective, and knowing *how* to be effective. The latter is mainly a matter of appreciating how to effect action. Believing that one can be efficacious requires not only a habitual response or predisposition to personal involvement, but also a conviction of the *legitimacy* of one's personal action; not only is a certain action right, but *one's own* action is both right and necessary.

Responsibility varies. Some rare individuals give up much in their lives in order to direct their energies to the cause. Their belief that they are personally responsible requires that they give themselves wholly to the service of those aims. In such cases, responsibility is the action extension of efficacy. For others, the investment of personal efficacy is more circumscribed—the voice raised in protest at the appropriate moment, the regular contribution of time or money: the responsibility is to aid the group rather than to commit oneself wholly.

Commitment in the sense that I am using the term seems characterized by certainty and conviction, a lack of doubt that is not only a matter of belief but also contributes to the motivation associated with commitment. While there may be blocks to the enactment of committed responsibility there seems to be a lack of akrasia, the motivational problem expressed as "I ought to, but . . ." It seems to be a characteristic of commitment that the motivation to act is not so much a sense of obligation as a sense of compulsion. To understand what it is that gives these individuals the certainty that they are right, and creates the compelling motivation to carry their conviction through, we must explore the psychological processes by which they arrive at such a level of efficacy, responsibility, and vision.

But there remains the problem of how a commitment may be judged to be morally justified. For this we must consider the argumentation invoked by the individual; paradoxically, we may be pushed into a situation in which the very intensity and extremity of the psychological processes is the legitimation for the moral basis of the commitment. For example, we may make the assumption that Stage 6 reasoning has such an extensive range of rational and moral functions that we cannot fault the moral logic even if we disagree with a particular moral conclusion. As yet, no one has documented an example of a morally objectionable Stage 6 (or even Stage 5) person, so the logic of "the moral point of view" stands. But if we take the perspective exemplified by Levin at the beginning of this chapter, that moral intuitions have a deep truth status, we cannot be so confident that all who act according to passionate conviction based on "moral intuition" are exempt from the judge's doubts.

Commitment both fascinates and disturbs. The person who has no doubts about the right course of action provokes uneasiness; has this person a wisdom that others lack, or merely the simplicity of the blind fanatic? It is the oldest of clichés that the good, the bad, and the mad all believe themselves to be the saviors of the human race; thus we must devise some criteria that exclude Hitler, McCarthy, and probably Savonarola, and include Martin Luther King, Mother Teresa, and maybe Albert Schweitzer. It is on the basis of a definition of what counts as "moral" that we will decide whether the commitment is good and right; the criteria accepted in Western society tend to be based on rational ends like nonpartisan concern for the human race as a whole and the implementation of justice and mercy, using means that do not cause gratuitous harm.

An example that illustrates the issues of both psychological and moral justification is Bernard Williams's (1981, pp. 20–39; cf. Williams, 1985, esp. pp. 174–196) discussion of Gauguin. Williams finds Gauguin fascinating because he made the decision to leave his wife and family (breaking a conventionally recognized, and undoubtedly felt, moral obligation) in order to pursue his personal destiny as an artist in Tahiti—a sense of obligation of a different sort that clearly imposed a powerful motivating force. From the point of view of the judge, how can Gauguin's decision be justified morally? From the point of view of Gauguin himself, how can he know that a decision of such magnitude is right?

Williams places great weight in his analyses of all moral issues on the importance of *feeling a moral obligation;* it is not enough for him that a rational conclusion about "rightness" can be arrived at. Gauguin meets this criterion; he felt an overwhelming sense of obligation to leave his family and pursue his artistic destiny. But there remains still the problem of how Gauguin would justify his overwhelming sense of obligation. The point about this example, as I understand Williams, is that the affect, the sense of personal destiny involved in going to Tahiti, is subjectively experienced as *prior* to the need for justification; indeed, it is the subjective compulsion that creates the moral conflict in the first place. There is no case of akrasia here, it is a straight conflict between motivations.

So the "Gauguin problem"—at least according to Williams— is that one comes to a realization that a particular action is right, something that one feels compelled to do even though it may conflict with other moral obligations. The Gauguin problem has much in common with the accounts of moral commitment that I have described, and poses very much the same problems. We have to give credence to the subjective compulsion of Gauguin's decision; as judges, we are a little unsure about the ultimate morality of Gauguin's decision because its justification rests upon an evaluation of the moral importance of fulfilling talent. As Williams points out, would we feel the same if Gauguin's project had failed? It is less difficult in the case of Luther or other moral reformers who felt a similar compulsion and also made a commitment that changed the direction of their energies. There our reservations are not about the moral rightness of their cause, but about whether single-minded conviction may obscure judgment about the consequences of one's actions, or neglect consideration of others' points of view.

Thus while arguing that there must be a sense of moral obligation inherent in the making of moral decisions, we are loath to grant all cases of subjective moral obligation the status of being "moral" without looking carefully at "objective" justifications. Nevertheless, we can recognize that there are distinctive psychological characteristics of moral commitment, the subjective states associated with it and the mechanisms of decision-making involved. These are substantially different from the model implied by "normal" rationality, where reasoning generates an obligation and the individual must then summon the motivation to carry out that obligation.

A particular example of the problem is discussed by Flacks, namely, the "public-private" conflict. Flacks (1983) distinguishes between decision-making in the "private" world of daily life and in the "public" world of history. Most people confine their moral activity to the private sphere, even though they consider they have the democratic right to some consultation with regard to decisions made in the public sphere that concern them. People who become involved in political activism move from the world of private morality to the world of public morality. Those who make the shift from private to public must be willing to take risks and to subordinate everyday life to their sense of social responsibility.

The conflict operates at several levels. The first is in values: Flacks points out that most of the framework for morality as conventionally understood is in terms of the sorts of obligations we have in the private domain, yet at the same time our culture values more highly the commitment and idealism of those who take on social responsibility—especially where this involves going against pressures to conform. A second and very concrete conflict is the one such as Helen John faces; by taking on public responsibility she is not fulfilling the routine responsibilities, the "private" morality, of everyday motherhood, and she may even be inflicting pain on her family either through emotional withdrawal or causing them embarrassment.

For anyone involved in "public" responsibility, there is a tension between interpersonal responsibilities and public obligations. But the conflict may be deeper; the principles governing the public commitment may lead the individual to adopt a way of living that involves others without their full consent. Gandhi has been extensively criticized for attempting to make his family collaborators in his activities even though it caused them distress (see Gilligan, 1982; Howard, 1986). At the very least this may be seen as unreasonable and inconsiderate, but it may also place the committed person in a moral paradox; Gandhi's behavior to his family can be seen as contravening his own principles of justice, as well as principles of caring and interpersonal responsibility that might have been less salient to his personal moral schema. Andrews (personal communication) has argued that by devolving the responsibility for domestic organization onto her daughter Helen John was contravening her public principle of feminism, recreating for her daughter the very oppression that she herself had escaped.

There is a broader question of whether commitment and the widening sphere of personal responsibility necessarily mean that "the personal becomes political." Flacks argues from his data on long-term activists that public morality depends on two moral perspectives, a capacity for autonomous moral judgment and antiauthoritarianism, and a capacity for taking responsibility for the social consequences of one's actions or for giving priority to the collective over the personal. These capacities can originate in higher levels of moral reasoning, because the individual can understand the specific event in the wider social context and the relationship between the individual and the social. But they may also be the heritage of long-term association with family or social group in which "public" responsibility is commonplace even if understood at a "concrete" level. In either case, the progression toward moral responsibility seems to go hand in hand with an appreciation of the wider context; as one extends one's desire to right the moral wrong, so one sees that the moral wrong does not exist in isolation from a social context. In this sense, the personal does become "political."

Finally, there is the question of value bias. The examples I have chosen mostly reflect progression toward a greater public responsibility on moral issues that have a left-wing political dimension. This is partly a consequence of history; the material available on commitment comes from the active causes of recent years, which have tended to be liberal-left in orientation. There is an extensive debate about whether higher-stage reasoning necessarily generates liberal-left rather than conservative moral arguments (Kohlberg, 1980a; Broughton, 1986; Weinreich-Haste, 1986). The omission of right-wing exemplars of the path to moral commitment does not reflect any pre-judgment about the moral superiority of left-wing commitment, but it does restrict the extent to which we can assume that the psychological processes of progress toward commitment are the same irrespective of the political orientation of the commitment. The community of moral-reasoning scholars still awaits the data that will establish whether a Stage 5 or 6 conservative differs fundamentally from a liberal at the same stage.

The Sequences of Events in Commitment

The differences between the three paths to commitment lie in the precipitating conditions and initial sequences; once the individual has made the transition into public responsibility, there seem to be few differences in vision and efficacy. One path involves a significant experience, a "triggering event" that engages the individual and precipitates a moral crisis. Many writers on moral and political activism find that respondents recall some event in which they gained a sudden moral or political insight, experiencing an alteration of perspective and a shift to agency (e.g., Frank and Nash, 1965). The affect may be aesthetic, like the disgust or revulsion felt by Sandra's reaction to the methods of butchery and the bloodiness of the meat on her plate, or Bernard Levin's reaction to pig transplants. It may be associated with personal threat, as in the case of Helen John, or an affront to pride, as in the case of Gandhi. This is the first stage in the sequence, and notably, it remains a vivid memory decades later.

The second phase of the sequence is the translation of this affective experience, invoking an adequate "explanation," making sense of it. The need to provide an explanation of the affective experience seems to be a crucial factor in the development of moral crises, and the explanation that is evoked sets the direction of the subsequent resolution process. As we noted, Bernard Levin immediately ascribed a fundamentally moral source to his affect. But Levin, and Sandra and Helen John, could all have evoked a different kind of "rationality" and decided that their immediate reactions were not legitimate—in some way "silly" or overreacting—and thus invalidated the experience.

If the affective response is taken seriously and the explanation includes a moral dimension, this generates "moral" affect, for example moral outrage or compassion. The combination of moral affect and locating the incident in a moral context seems to be the spur to action—Sandra gave up eating meat, Helen John took the opportunity to join a march against Cruise missiles, Gandhi set up an organization of Indians in southern Africa.

The next step is group involvement: this provides social support for efficacy and also a shared definition of the situation that legitimates one's changing perspectives. For many people, this phase in the sequence is the end state; they enter a plateau of regular group activity and the constant affirmation of their view of the situation, without an especial personal responsibility to go beyond the agreed and consensual action. But for some people, a crucial qualitative change occurs when the group's goals are frustrated, when the enthusiasm to create change, the shared efficacy, and the vision are undermined by failure—through opposition or the sheer nonresponsiveness of the government or the public at large.

The second path to commitment involves gradually increasing involvement and sense of personal responsibility: the individual appears to gain vision, efficacy, and commitment without the catalyst of a major crisis. These people remember events that consolidated their commitment, or marked a qualitative progression in the degree of commitment, but they do not define these as major life changes. They tend to come from a background where social, moral, or political activism, and public responsibility, were taken for granted. They grew up with a sense of efficacy (as part of a group if not by themselves) and a framework for interpreting the world in moral or political terms. For them, the point of change is to group involvement; they identify a subjective shift from a long-standing realization that things need to be changed, to a recognition that they themselves can be part of that change process; it is an internalization of agency and control.

The third path to commitment, through cognitive appraisal, depends on level of moral reasoning rather than on an affective crisis or a background of commitment (cf. Kohlberg and Candee, 1984; Haan, Smith, and Block, 1968; McNamee, 1978). Commitment arises out of cognitive recognition of the context of the moral issue, and the association of such understanding with a sense of one's own personal responsibility for action. These are characteristic of postconventional moral thought. The available evidence suggests that responsibility initially precipitates action by the individual, but then leads the individual to seek collaborative means to achieve the desired ends; as level of moral reasoning already equips the person with the capacity to see the wider social and political context of the issue, the effect of group involvement is to strengthen efficacy rather than to elaborate or extend the definition of the situation.

The Explanation of Commitment

Many psychological and philosophical analyses of morality assume the problem of akrasia. Given that I know what I should do (whether this knowledge comes from my reason, a tendency to a habitual response of "duty," or my reaction to an immediate situation), how do I translate it into action? The concept of "ought" is ridden with an assumption of motivational reluctance or conflicting demands. Kohlberg's focus on the cognitive processes involved in moral judgment assumes a gap between cognition and action; action has to be explained either by additional motivation or something like "will" that overcomes inertia.

Kohlberg offers some explanation of commitment in his analysis of how "responsibility" is inherent in the higher stages of moral reasoning; the higher the individual's moral stage, the more the key individual in the situation is perceived to have a responsibility to act consistently with the moral choice made. Thus, progressively through the stages, individuals see themselves as being more responsible in the situation, and increasingly integrate interpretation of the moral issue with a commitment to action.

So the cognitive developmental framework defines responsibility in terms of greater *differentiation*—in cognitive understanding and the appreciation that one is an *agent* in a situation in which one is involved—and greater *integration*—the coming together of moral judgments and judgments about the responsibility for action. There is convergence of objective reasoning and subjective involvement and responsibility. Evidence in support of this comes from the work of Haan, Smith, and Block and that of McNamee; in McNamee's study, for example, the "subjects" were ostensibly participating in a psychology class for which they were getting credit. An apparently freaked-out "stooge" appeared, requesting psychological help that the "professor" teaching the class refused, so the stooge appealed to the waiting students. People saw their responsibility to help in terms of their moral stage; lower-stage reasoners did not even feel they had a responsibility, higher-stage reasoners felt they had, and indeed acted upon it at the cost of getting credit for the class.

Responsibility is experienced in this context as obligation upon the *self* to act; it carries the energizing role conventionally ascribed to affect, but without the implication of an affective dimension. However, affect was not measured in these studies, so any mechanisms that might have come into play in coping with it, or in the translation of affect into cognition, were not explored. The results as they stand demonstrate a prima facie role for cognition as the origin of one's perceived responsibility and therefore imply that it is limited by cognitive structure.

However, the process of consolidation and integration that is characteristic of movement to higher stages of reasoning also occurs between what Kohlberg has called Type A and Type B reasoning within a stage; the more advanced Type B reasoning is exemplified by the elaboration and extension of concepts, but within the same stage structure. This theoretical development makes sense of the evidence that not all people who act with responsibility in accordance with their beliefs are postconventional reasoners. Indeed, all actors whose reasoning was below Stage 5 used Type B thinking. This extends the range of people who can be expected to take responsibility, but the model still proposes that rational reflection and cognitive appraisal are the precursors of engagement and subjective responsibility.

"The moral point of view" is fully developed in Stage 6 thought, and responsibility is an integral part of moral decision-making, experienced as incumbent upon the individual. The moral point of view receives its fullest discussion to date in the chapter in this volume by Kohlberg, Boyd, and Levine, and also in Habermas's chapter. Kohlberg and his colleagues have extended the definition of Stage 6 in response to the criticisms of Gilligan (1982) and to the somewhat different perspective of Habermas (1983, 1985, and this volume). Two developments have taken place. First, the original definition of the highest stages in terms of justice reasoning has been extended to include "benevolence." Second, there has been development of the social and dialogic implications of "ideal role-taking"—a concept that has always been fundamental to Kohlberg's work but has hitherto largely been interpreted in an individualistic way.

The inclusion of "benevolence" is partly a concession to Gilligan's argument that caring and responsibility for others, as moral principles, were absent from a model based on justice; the revision is not the addition of a further dimension but the subsuming of both justice and benevolence under a broader category, "respect for persons." This is described as an "attitude"—in other words a response tendency, a form of moral action, a way of relating to people. Both benevolence and justice are perspectives or orientations, frameworks for moral reasoning. Both can be the basis for generating personal responsibility. It is important to recognize that benevolence per se does not necessarily imply affect; Gilligan's own perspective, and Kohlberg's modification of principled morality to include benevolence, focus on an orientation or set of principles for judgment, not on affective response.

Kohlberg always considered Meadian ideal role-taking to be a fundamental psychological process in moral reasoning, and expansion of role-taking ability to be the basis of developmental change (Mead, 1934; Kohlberg, 1984; Noam, Kohlberg, and Snarey, 1983). The essence of Stage 6 is the capacity for "moral musical chairs," that is, the ability to take the perspective of all interested parties in the situation. This has parallels with Rawls's (1971) "original position." In the work on "just communities" Kohlberg (1980b) demonstrated that role-taking is stimulated and facilitated by social interaction and dialogue; nevertheless he continued to treat conceptual role-taking essentially as an individual cognitive act.

Habermas was attracted to Kohlberg's theory of moral development partly because the changing range of perspectives implied in the developmental stages fitted well with his "development of communicative competence." He saw it as a model of the development of rationality in a context of increasing understanding of the dialogic process (see Habermas, 1979, and this volume; Schmid, 1982). Through perspective-taking and the search for consensus, the individual arrives at ideal rationality. Habermas differentiates the "performative" from the "constructive"—the former implying communication of concepts and the intention to share meaning with a view to arriving at a consensus, the latter being more a matter of individual, private rationality.

I would argue that Kohlberg's earlier definition of ideal role-taking was in Habermas's terms "constructive": the essentially social psychological element of shared communication is lacking. Habermas emphasizes the importance of the cultural context in which concepts are discussed and dialogue takes place, and the role of dialogue or shared meaning in the construction of a rational outcome. His influence has altered the overindividualized, solitary perspective-taking of Kohlberg's earlier position to something in which dialogue is integral. A disposition to enter into dialogue is now an essential part of the "moral point of view," and the procedure of discourse, not only individual cognitive perspective-taking, is necessary to achieve the sort of consensus that is the aim of the moral point of view. Thus the social element of argumentation and the recognition of the need for conflict resolution, not merely the exercise of empathic imagination, are becoming part of the definition of Stage 6 processes. This development clearly reflects the influence of Habermas, though in his own chapter in this volume he argues that it has not gone far enough.

But in the present formulation of "the moral point of view" there is still a problem with "responsibility" as I am using the concept; it requires a shift from an essentially cognitive appreciation of the situation to an involvement that imposes upon the individual the obligation to take action. As Habermas points out, having respect for persons does not necessarily mean that one becomes concerned about their welfare; this is part of his criticism of Kohlberg's efforts to include benevolence along with justice under the umbrella of respect for persons. Discourse—in contrast to imaginative role-taking—does allow for communicating a need for action on behalf of the interests of the other, but one still has to explain the psychological processes involved in feeling an obligation to carry out the wishes of that other.

The absence of an affective dimension to Kohlberg's theory limits its use for understanding an affective response, but the model can explain why some of the ways of making sense of affective experience, and reconstructing the event in moral terms, are more successful than others in generating responsibility. The higher the stage of moral reasoning that the individual has reached, the more resources that can be drawn upon to make sense of the experience, and the more extensive the range of implications than can be conceptualized. It is, for example, easier for a higher-stage thinker to invoke a scenario of social change that locates a problem in a historical context or a social institution.

An Alternative Model

To find a suitable model for dealing with affective moral crisis I shall turn to a field of psychological research not normally associated with morality—coping with stress and risk. Both stress and risk are the consequence of an untoward event impinging on the life of the individual. The individual has a choice about how to interpret such an event, and the interpretation evoked will define the extent of risk or threat and also the psychological resources available for dealing with it. The options for interpretation will be derived from culturally accepted ways of responding to stress, interacting with individual styles of response and coping strategies.

Lazarus (1966; Lazarus and Folkman, 1984) originally described a model of the relationship between affect and cognition in the appraisal of threat; more recent developments in cognitive psychology, especially the definition of "schemata," have provided a language for extending the cognitive aspects of Lazarus's model.

Lazarus identified three phases in coping. Affect is the response to first perceiving threat or stress. This phase is *primary appraisal. Secondary appraisal* follows; this organizes both the perception of the situation and the potential for acting to diminish or deal with the threat. What is the actual nature of the threat (or other stimulus)? What resources do I have to deal with it? Identifying the threat involves making sense of the situation, marshaling interpretive resources. But secondary appraisal also includes considering how to deal with the affect— to suppress it or to channel it to effective motivation. Finally, secondary appraisal includes reviewing possible action—avoidance, confrontation, negotiation.

The third phase is the process of *reappraisal,* in which the situation is reconsidered in the light of the resources evoked in the secondary appraisal, and in which the mechanisms for dealing with the threatening stimulus come into play—reevaluating the actual threat, taking action to avoid or confront it, suppressing the noxious affect, and so forth.

A major feature of this model is that it treats affect as an experience that, though interpreted and altered by cognition, is not separate from it. Secondary appraisal does not remove affect and replace it with cognition, but translates the original affect into a different affect; what was fear may become anger, what was anxiety may become turned into the drive to resist. There is constant interplay of affect and cognition. Cognitive models of moral reasoning locate the cognitive analysis first, and postulate motivation as arising either out of the cognition, or from independent sources. In Lazarus's model the affective element has a primary role—primary both temporally and in terms of its significance as an experience. The model allows us to recognize that affect can be taken seriously as a valid form of knowledge; this is the subjective experience described by Levin in the opening of this chapter. It also makes sense of the conviction that Gauguin felt, and that Williams considers to be a significant part of moral experience.

The cognitive elements of Lazarus's model have been considerably enriched by recent developments in cognitive psychology. The idea of "schemata" originated fifty years ago in the work of Bartlett (1932), as an explanation for the role of meaning in memory; it has been revived by information-processing models that recognize that people have complex plans, lay theories, and scripts for action. A "schema" is in essence a script, strategy, or image that is familiar through frequent contact, or through its usefulness to the individual in making sense of experience. In confronting novel and unfamiliar events, people make parallels with what they see to be similar experiences. For example, in a risk situation people invoke familiar and easily accessed images or information for assessing risk and for conceptualizing its solution; thus the highly publicized event (like dying in an air crash) is erroneously believed to be more probable than less publicized events (like dying from an accident in the home) (see Slovic, Fischoff, and Lichtenstein, 1981). Schemata are part of the cultural repertoire, but a particular schema will be selected by the individual because of its usefulness, availability, or the extent to which it fits in with one's general world view—including making for comfort and reassurance.

The concept of schema is useful for extending the process of appraisal that Lazarus describes. It is clear from Lazarus's own work on stress and threat, from studies of response to nuclear threat, and from the case studies of triggering events that the initial experience of affect is powerful and distressing (Haste, 1989). It needs to be made sense of and, as it is usually unpleasant, to be coped with (or defended against). One may cope with the experience either by focusing on the affect itself or by focusing on the problem that elicited the affect. The process of secondary appraisal involves drawing on schemata for making sense and for providing scenarios for action.

I divide schemata into several types. First, there are those concerned with the belief that one can, alone or with others, take action, have some *agency*—or that there are bodies and institutions within society that can take such action. Second, there are schemata associated with *explanations of causality*, accounting for the event that causes the distress—for example, one will invoke different schemata to explain an explosion if one is standing by a quarry, in the center of Belfast, or in the middle of a tropical storm. Thirdly, there are schemata, or scenarios, for *the kind of action that can be taken under the circumstances.* Fourthly, there are schemata that might be termed *personal "self-evident truths,"* including values or principles, axioms that act as a baseline in the selection of other schemata: the belief that the USSR is an evil aggressor will predicate certain schemata about the effectiveness, possibility, and desirability of disarmament; the belief that equality is a preeminently desirable goal is going to affect one's explanations for racial discrimination and the scope of actions one deems necessary.

These are broad categories, and indeed so broad that there is a danger that every cognitive action can be described in terms of a schema. But the strength of the concept is that it allows for a model of complex and integrated cognitive activity, even in response to a sudden and unexpected event. Such responses are as it were a "library" built up over the individual's experience and drawn from the culture that the individual inhabits. One may lack a particular schema because it is simply not available in one's culture, because it is not valued by that culture and therefore has either been rejected or simply ignored, or because the immediate social context makes the schema socially inappropriate. In the ethos of machismo the scenario of non-violent protest is irrelevant; in Britain I do not need to remember the basic rules of survival in the cold of Minneapolis. But the individual may also fail to take on a particular schema through ineffective cognitive processing or lack of motivation.

The schemata that are central to the arguments of higher stages of moral reasoning may in theory be "available" to everyone in the sense that they exist in the public domain and are the object of public discussion. However, individuals interpret such schemata according to their current level of reasoning. For example, the basic schema that punishing the offender sets an example to others is understood at all stages, but it is supported by different arguments at different stages and will be interpreted accordingly (Turiel, 1966). But some higher-stage schemata are not widely accessible, because they demand more complex cognitive structure than the lower-stage reasoner possesses; they are not therefore "available" at lower stages of moral reasoning. Arguments that depend on a complex understanding of social and economic forces (such as those that require the "prior-to-society" perspective underlying postconventional reasoning) will not be part of the repertoire of lower-stage thought. The concept of "being responsible" in the sense of having a duty is certainly not confined to higher-stage thought, but the concept that perceiving a need lays upon one the personal responsibility to act does appear to be a higher-stage schema arising from the understanding of the location of the individual actor in the social context.

Rorty (1983) has argued that deliberation is what we do when rules and principles do not apply; he sees this as a hermeneutic process, making sense and interpreting. Translated into the terms of this chapter, deliberation is what happens when a primary affective experience creates a crisis of meaning because it cannot be explained according to the usual repertoire of schemata. Rorty argues that at this point we supplement "principles with vocabularies that mark out morally relevant features of the situation" (p. 173). A key question for explaining commitment is how far a crisis situation—the experience of novel and unpleasant affect—can be resolved by the invocation of existing schemata, and how much the experience requires the seeking of new schemata. In most of the examples I draw upon the events are remembered as experiences of change and development. The description of the event includes reflection on successive changes in schemata concerning the situation, and the search for more complex explanations. There are sudden changes in crisis situations, and slower and less dramatic processes of crystallization and the consolidation of responsibility among the group of long-term activists.

Lazarus's model proposes that primary affective experience is rationally reconstructed, made sense of, and in the process changed into a different kind of experience with which the individual can cope. In resolving a moral crisis, an affective experience is made sense of by being rationally reconstructed in moral terms, which eventually results in the individual taking a wider perspective on the social, moral, and sometimes political issues and becoming motivated to greater involvement.[1]

In this framework, I see the sequence of engagement and commitment following a "triggering event" as follows: experience of affect in response to a stimulus, explanation of that affect that translates the situation into a moral issue, arousal of "moral" affect, consideration of possible action, seeking of social support that confirms or develops the emerging schemata about the issue and the individual's role and responsibility in it. Subsequent escalation of commitment follows from the thwarting of action plans. Let us now consider the case studies in detail, in accordance with the proposed model.

The Analysis of Moral Engagement: Sandra

Sandra has progressed the shortest distance. Her account reflects just the first few steps toward engagement and commitment. The triggering event for Sandra was witnessing the slaughtering of meat while in France. Now obviously Sandra was aware that the meat on the table at home had once been living flesh, but she had no affective reaction to this knowledge, and even if she had a moral schema associated with animal rights, it was not something that engaged her.

S: I'm a vegetarian. It started when I went to France. I lived in a butcher's for two weeks. It was then that I realized how you kill things and cook things and that it was a matter of conscience whether I should eat meat or not. I don't eat any at all now. That's the biggest conscience thing I've ever done.

I: What was the situation that made you change your mind?

S: The fact that they cooked meat on the outside and it's burnt and you cut it open and it just sort of bleeds. That put me off for a start and that wasn't really anything to do with conscience, it was the actual idea of it.

It is important that Sandra's initial affective response was *aesthetic*. She felt revolted by what she had seen of the slaughtering process, and she was sickened by the French method of cooking meat. This aroused strong affect, but it was not at that point a *moral* affect. At this point a number of options were open to her. Many girls in her situation would have responded with a form of compartmentalization or *denial*—the French are different from us and have nasty ways of preparing food. Or she could have engaged in *affective catharsis*—made a joke or horror story out of it to relate to her friends at home.

Instead she began to make sense of her experience, to think. She reflected cognitively upon her affect; she looked for a schema to legitimate her revulsion. She began to see meat-eating as a moral issue and an issue on which she could exercise some personal responsibility.

S: When I came back to England I still couldn't eat meat because I just couldn't think of actually eating an animal, especially the way in which they are killed. If you're in a survival position then it's slightly different. But like farming is an industry where it just goes through and they're just killing all those animals, then I think that's wrong.

I: Why do you think it's wrong?

S: Because the animals themselves haven't really had a life. We're just breeding them to kill them. I just can't face eating something like that which has been killed in that way and hasn't had its own life.

Her initial affective response therefore engaged her, but as a consequence of appraising the situation in moral terms the nature of her affect changed; she began to experience *moral affect*. Her reaction, "I just can't face eating something like that which has been killed in that way and hasn't had its own life," is no longer an aesthetic response, it is a *moral feeling*, arising from the moral cognition—invoking schemata concerning the right of humans to kill animals, quality of life as an axiomatic value, and the additional excepting scenario of the survival situation. She has also a schema of her own efficacy; she has in fact done what she sees herself able to do and taken the responsibility not to eat meat herself.

Sandra's moral stage of thought at the time of her interview was 3/4. The moral schemata she invoked, the arguments of justification, reflect the resources available to that level of moral cognition to make sense of her initial affect. But had she not experienced the initial affective engagement, I argue, she would not have perceived the situation as one in which she had any responsibility at all, *even though* she already possessed the potential knowledge of the facts of meat preparation and probably even the schemata associated with animal rights and the moral dimensions of meat production.

Sandra has begun to take action that expresses her responsibility for her newly salient schema about animal rights. She has not yet sought social support, nor experienced the legitimation and confirmation of her schema through a group.

The Analysis of Engagement: Helen John

Helen John has gone considerably further down the path to commitment and engagement than Sandra. Helen John was one of the pioneers of the protest against the siting of American Cruise missiles at Greenham Common in Berkshire. This protest encampment on the perimeter of the airbase first came into existence in autumn 1981. It was a women-only protest, and the women argued that their action was feminist as well as antimissile. There were normally about thirty women living on the site, but these numbers swelled from time to time by large demonstrations—for example, when many thousands of women encircled the entire nine-mile fence. Some women who occupied Greenham Common gave up family or professional life or both for the protest; others made brief visits. The Greenham Common protest began with a march, planned to last ten days, from Cardiff to the airbase—a distance of about 100 miles. However, the indifference and trivialization by the press, and the response of the authorities, led to escalation of the protest and to the decision by some of the women to remain.

Helen John had been a supporter of the Labour Party and the Campaign for Nuclear Disarmament in the early 1960s. This background equipped her with certain schemata about dealing with nuclear threat, interpreting political issues, and the means for being efficacious in protest. The events she describes caused her to reflect upon these past schemata and reevaluate their usefulness. The "triggering event" for her was a sudden insight about the consequences of nuclear war for an area of land that she felt close to:

I was driving on my way through beautiful scenery in Wales where I live and it suddenly occurred to me how this would all be altered in a nuclear war. And it just stopped me dead in my tracks. I couldn't keep on driving, I had to stop and I felt really physically very unwell. And I was crying. I sat for about three-quarters of an hour before I could continue the journey. I was scared sick, really scared. And then I felt terribly angry that any lunatic could put so much fear and pressure on people. And I knew that the fear I was experiencing was minute compared to so many other people's fears.

Her immediate affective response was fear; in seeking to make sense of this fear her first schema concerned the people responsible for allowing the threat to exist, the "lunatics," and this translated her response into anger. The secondary appraisal also altered her perception of the nuclear issue:

I was one of those people who knew about nuclear weapons for years, and put it into the backs of their minds . . . because we were assured that we had enough nuclear weapons to stop any country attacking us. The deterrence theory lulled me into a false sense of security for years. And it was on that particular day driving into Builth that I realized that this was nonsense and that we are now moving into a stage not thinking of defending the country against the Russians, but that we are preparing for a nuclear war.

The change in her schemata was the immediate effect of her making sense of her affective experience. She also changed her perception of her own efficacy and the role of protest:

I think it was on that particular day that I realized you could actually stop this happening if you put some effort into it. And I think that day changed me a lot.

She may be reconstructing too neatly when she locates all those changes within the one day, but subjectively she perceives the whole series of events as a single psychological experience— the initial affect, the translation of this into a moral affect through the invocation of schemata that located the issue in a wider context, and the emerging schema of personal efficacy. However, this was only the first "change" that she identifies. The process continued; when she read about the proposed Greenham march she decided to join it; she saw this as part of her increasing sense of personal efficacy, and increasingly as her own responsibility.

My own understanding of the situation grew daily and my determination to make *my* contribution to stop it grew daily.

You make a decision that you will no longer cooperate with a system that is designed to kill other people. [new schema]

Prior to that I had never seen the value of marching anywhere. It didn't seem to achieve anything. But I was sufficiently worried on this particular issue to go on the march, and make my own personal statement. And it was during the course of this march that I changed. [changing schema]

The situation escalated when the marchers decided to stay at Greenham indefinitely. This was a qualitative leap in engagement for Helen; first, the actual decision was a recognition that she was making a commitment:

The moment it was suggested [to stay on] I knew that I wanted to take that initiative. It was completely right for me. And it was also really the very first totally independent decision I had made for myself in twenty years. Because I wasn't going to consult my husband or any other person. It had to be my own decision.

Second, she identified what she felt to be a special personal responsibility as a consequence of her schemata about the issue and the action needed:

I remember Douglas [her husband] saying to me very clearly, there must be other women who haven't got five children who can do what you're doing. But it's not true; there's only one of me. Nobody can do exactly what I'm doing in the way I'm doing it. Only I can do that. Every individual has their own contribution to make in the way they uniquely can make it.

In joining the group march initially she gained efficacy and legitimated her interpretation of her moral response to her affective experience. At this point, the responsibility was to make her voice heard, to express her moral objection. Later she felt a responsibility personally to make change. That occurred for Helen at Greenham itself; suddenly it then became her own responsibility to continue the protest. The schema of personal efficacy was also associated with changes in her schema of herself as a woman; making an autonomous decision would change her own definition of herself.

She also recalls how she had reconstructed some basic moral premises; she did not change her schemata about the rule of law but the boundaries and goals of its application:

I was very apprehensive about breaking the law because I believe in upholding the law; that's why I'm trying to uphold a moral law.

She regarded serving a prison sentence as an acceptable consequence of her protest.

There is not enough information in the interview to make confident statements about Helen's previous stage of moral reasoning, especially as the material is retrospective reconstruction. Much of her current thinking about responsibility, morality, and principles suggests Stage 5 reasoning: her memory of how she thought before, particularly about the mechanisms of social change, the role of law, and the principles that governed her family and professional life, sound like Stage 4 or even Stage 3/4. But it is clear that there was a progression in the complexity of her moral thought.

A similar realization of her changing interpretation of a basic value occurred with regard to her family role, and what she was "giving up" to participate in the peace camp:

I do not think the word sacrifice is a good one because I haven't sacrificed anything. I'm safeguarding a lot. I am defending the life of my children. Very selfishly. I have cut myself off from one way of life in order to preserve the very things I care about.

Helen's perception of her responsibility in those areas has changed. The shift is the recognition that she must do the preserving, the safeguarding, in the public rather than the private domain.

In Helen John's case history the progression starts with reactive affect, cognitive reflection to make sense of it, moral affect arising from the schemata that are invoked to do that, and a series of cognitive transformations that eventually place her own responsibility for action at the center, rather than the periphery. This case illustrates Flacks's argument about the "public-private" conflict. The quoted passages show that Helen recognizes the need to justify her resolution of the public-private conflict, her shift from "private" to "public" responsibility.

Flacks's distinction alerts us to the schemata the individual uses to interpret the situation as private or public, and how a resolution of the conflict is found. But he also describes the progressive shift from the private to the public domain. For Helen John the progression to public responsibility happens with the successive reconstructions of her perceived responsibility; she also finds schemata to subsume the private in the terms of the public—concepts that were part of her "private" vocabulary like "law-abiding," "caring," "responsibility," "safeguarding," and even her "duty as a mother" have become translated through her "public" schemata of social responsibility into a public arena and into her public roles and responsibilities.

Helen John had some schemata of public morality and social responsibility from her earlier political experience; she strengthened her developing schemata about the present issue through group support on the march and later at the peace camp. The transition from a private to a public morality was the outcome of her own increasing awareness of the nuclear issue, and her efforts to make sense of the implications. In her reconstruction of her own conflicts she translated the schema of her private morality into the schema of a public morality.

The Analysis of Engagement: Lenny

Both Sandra's and Helen John's accounts are retrospective. My third case study comes from Kohlberg's longitudinal sample, and consequently there are data from a series of points before, during, and after the events that were significant in the engagement process.

Kohlberg's longitudinal study covered twenty years, a turbulent period of American history, when the draft was an everpresent threat. Lenny came from a conservative background. In his early teens he expressed conventional Republican values and took some part in political life under his father's influence. Between the ages of seventeen and twenty he began to question his father's values, and gradually moved leftward:

Lenny (age 20): I believe in the Republican standpoint, but you have to look at the particular leader that is saying it. I mean I don't believe any longer. I used to; in the beginning I was a Republican more or less [as a result of] indoctrination and I was gung ho Goldwater and all this in '64 [the year of the previous interview]. I went to the Convention and all this, but since then I've changed to moderately liberal and I would say I'm more the Javits, Rockefeller type.

I: What changed you from Goldwater?

L: The fact that once I started taking some college courses in economics and you can actually see that some of his policies were just completely ridiculous, and as soon as you get away from this one set opinion that dominated our area, as soon as you get professors in the college, they give you another side . . .

He is describing cognitive reconstruction; at this point he has reached Stage 4(3) moral reasoning, and the beginning recognition of alternative perspectives is consistent with this level of cognitive structure. The recognition of the need for new schemata is expressed in his acceptance of his professors' alternative perspective. By his next interview, three years later, Lenny has reached 4(5) moral reasoning and has experienced several major life crises involving both affect and cognitive reconstruction:

Lenny (age 24): I started to come out of the [home suburb] conservative environment and gradually by the time I was a senior I'd become what you would call a contemporary liberal American. Before that time I had been a Goldwaterite and very conservative, exhibiting the effects of the community. . . . When I went away to London I really became radicalized, it was a very turbulent year there. The London School of Economics was closed for 25 days, and the British authorities blamed it on American students.

I started to do some work under Professor X in political sociology and all of a sudden I saw things not in terms of being harmonious, but I saw a lot of conflict going on in society and I started to think about it in that perspective. What was violent and what was in terms of being quieter. And then I came back and taught in the inner city for a year, and I was further radicalized.

Lenny's Stage 4 thinking recognizes more complex perspectives on social issues. In the previous extract his undergraduate cognitive development was extending the complexity of his existing conservative political schemata; now he is changing his basic premises.

The period at the London School of Economics was a crisis situation for him. The influence of the professor, and a peer group that was actively constructing new ways of thinking, provided him with new, radical schemata to make sense of the events, and also gave him the personal schema of himself becoming a radical—diametrically opposed to his earlier identity as a conservative. The sit-in at the School was for Lenny a "triggering event," a shock, and in resolving it he identified himself as one of the American students whom he saw the authorities as "blaming"—making him responsible. One new schemata for making sense of his response was the realization of violent and conflictful undercurrents in society that he had previously not recognized.

When we were growing up most of the time we spent our summers going to military conventions. . . . It was just incredible, the whole idea of the service and the military and the whole idea of capitalism. . . . In college we started questioning and we knew what kind of reaction we would get . . . and then I got . . . more passionately committed in a position, one I thought I really realized when I was in London.

I decided when I got back that since I wanted to take some time off and since I didn't want to serve in the army, I could effectively serve both objectives by becoming a teacher. I did. At that time, [the city] had a deficit of teachers, and I didn't have any educational courses but I went down to the Board of Education and I was assigned to the inner city schools.

Lenny reconstructed, at different points in time, events that were important in his progression to public responsibility; the initial London School of Economics experience, the doubts it raised, and his reconstruction of political ideas. However, Lenny did not become a particularly committed activist; he moved some way toward public moral responsibility in rejecting the draft and working in deprived inner city areas. He reached the point of locating individual activity validly and legitimately within a wider context, which put upon him some responsibility to be involved in action. He gained support from a peer group for his changing perspectives and new schemata for appraising the political and moral world, but he never moved as far toward public commitment as Helen John did.

The Analysis of Engagement: Gandhi

For the final case history involving "triggering events," I have selected one event in the life of Gandhi, the point at which he shifted from "private" to "public" responsibility. Many accounts of Gandhi's life rely on his autobiography, which was written many years after his youth, and in which full rational reconstruction must be assumed. However, Robert Howard (1986) has researched other material, including letters, that are contemporary with the events. Howard has constructed an account of Gandhi's moral stages of reasoning over his life on the basis of such sources, and in particular has analyzed the transitions between stages and substages. Of necessity I am going to be very selective from so much material.

There are certain background points to be made in order to draw attention to cultural differences between Gandhi and the Western case studies, in particular regarding assumptions that can be made about moral life and goals. The schemata available to the growing Gandhi differed from those in the West. Howard points out that Indian culture places more emphasis on family ties and life and fulfilling of roles. The making of vows is an important basis for establishing commitment to a particular behavior.

Autonomy of judgment is less encouraged than in the West. The concept of taking many sides on an issue is central to Jainism, whereas in Western society it emerges rather late in the individual's moral development as both an ideal and as praxis. Finally the renunciation of material things is a normative characteristic of later periods of life; it is part of the "normal" goal of increasing wisdom, rather than as in the West a rare choice associated with puritanism or mysticism.

Gandhi grew up in an atmosphere of strict principles. His adolescence was, according to his later accounts, filled with deliberate confrontation with temptation, striving for asceticism and setting himself strict guidelines for his own behavior—particularly concerning cleanliness and vegetarianism. Initially these constraints were imposed by vow-taking, but later—Howard argues as a manifestation of his transition to Stage 4 thought—on the basis of worked-out principles. He was therefore very preoccupied with *private* morality, and with the pursuit of purity. He was trained as a lawyer in England, after a childhood and youth in India.

The incident with which I am concerned is the well-known train journey through Natal, where he had traveled as a representative of his Indian law firm—and where he encountered racism, first with regard to the wearing of a turban, later when he traveled first-class on the train. The conductor told Gandhi to travel in third class; he refused and was put off the train.

I went and sat in the waiting room. . . . It was winter and . . . severely cold. My overcoat was in my luggage but I did not dare ask for it . . . lest I might be insulted and assaulted once again so I sat and shivered. There was no light in the room . . . sleep was out of the question. . . . I begin to think of my duty. Should I fight for my rights or should I go on to Pretoria without minding the insults and return to India after finishing the case? The hardship to which I was subjected was superficial—only a symptom of the deep disease of color prejudice. I [reached the decision that I] should try, if possible, to root out the disease and suffer hardships in the process. Redress for wrongs I would seek only to the extent that would be necessary for the removal of color prejudice. This resolution somewhat pacified, then strengthened me but I did not get any sleep.

These words were written over fifty years after the event; Gandhi remembers still vividly the humiliation and shock. It is striking that, like Helen John and others who experienced triggering events, he recalls so clearly both the affective experience, and the reconstruction process—which he remembers as happening very fast.

It was not at first a "moral" response; he describes the process of making sense of the experience, which translated his interpretation into moral terms. He asked himself what his "duty" was. For someone so imbued with private morality it is perhaps not surprising that the first schema he invoked was one associated with private morality. This rapidly shifted to responsibility in the public domain when he considered the social implications of color prejudice. He directed his attention to the underlying conditions that had given rise to his ignominy, and in so doing, brought upon himself the responsibility for public action; he spent the following year organizing the Indians of southern Africa into an effective political pressure group. Gandhi identified that night as the point at which his active non-violence began; an interesting feature of this sudden precipitation into public morality and social responsibility was that, even at the age of twenty-three, he was convinced that he was peculiarly equipped to deal with the situation. He wrote *at the time* that he felt "inexperienced and young, and therefore quite liable to make mistakes. The responsibility undertaken is quite out of proportion to my ability." Nevertheless, he still felt, "I am the only available person who can handle this question."

Like Helen John, Gandhi's schema of his own efficacy changed as part of his making sense of his experience. Both of them recall the experience that recognizing the problem as one in which they were involved made them feel motivated to take responsibility to act. In neither case can this be explained by very high stage reasoning; Howard considers that Gandhi was still at that point within Stage 4 thought, and I consider this is likely to be the same for Helen John.

Gandhi of course experienced many more transitions in his moral and political career; he developed or took on board many new schemata for moral and political explanations—and indeed for living; he adopted Ruskin's ideals of goodness and labor and established a communal farm. Each new schema was part of the extension of his perception of his (and his followers') relationship to the political and moral world. But the first major schematic shift was the move out of a rule-defined privatized world.

Gandhi as a young adult entering Stage 4 reasoning had a schema of British power in India derived from a rule-based, law-abiding analysis that was pro-British in its conclusions; Helen John used to accept the deterrence schema; Lenny had moved quite comfortably from a Stage 3 version of conservatism to a more elaborated Stage 4 version. Each greatly altered these schemata as a result of crisis, personal engagement, and a new sense of efficacy. For none of my examples can the shift to a new moral insight and personal responsibility be adequately explained solely by their stage of moral reasoning and a purely cognitive analysis of the situation; the cognitive processes that led to taking responsibility were activated out of a need to understand the affective involvement. But level of moral reasoning set the bounds of the resources available to them to make sense of their experience.

Subsequently their moral reasoning became more complex, as they developed a wider perspective of the issues and their responsibilities. As Gilligan (1982; Blackburne-Stover, Belenky, and Gilligan, 1982) has demonstrated, the way in which a personal moral crisis is resolved depends on one's level of reasoning; the extent to which the resolution leads to cognitive development depends on the success of the resolution. The cases I have selected are of course all of people for whom the resolution was a growth stimulus.

The Moral Careers of Long-Term Activists

People who emerge as activists out of long-term immersion in a schema of social responsibility and efficacy often remember significant moral events in their families' lives that caught their early imagination, and they remember periods of particular awareness. They identify the time when they switched into a different perspective and took responsibility; they do not recall this process as a major life change so much as a change in gear. We therefore must look for the foundations of the relevant schemata in their lives prior to the event, as well as observing how their schemata changed when they moved from the periphery to the center of action.

Molly Andrews (1988; see also Andrews, 1987, 1989) specifically contrasts the experience of lifelong left-wing activists in British social movements with the model of the "triggering event" as a path to public responsibility. Her respondents were young adults in Britain during the interwar years—a time rife with left-wing political activity and analysis. It was not the mere fact of the historical events that radicalized them, but rather the way they made sense of, and connected themselves to, the events. Their awakening consciousness was a consequence of the interaction between the circumstances of their own lives and the historical and political context.

The CP and the left of the Labour Party and the socialist groups would hold their street corner meetings and they would spell it out, night after night wherever the corner, their corner, they were speaking. You was listening to a fellow talking in your own working class way of talking. So you could relate what they was saying to your own experience.

Such immersion provided schemata for people to make sense of their condition. Initial radicalization, in the form of participating in a hunger march, strike, or demonstration, was an empowering experience: they came to see themselves as exercising some control over their own lives and over their social environment. By engaging in political activism, they were fighting back. Andrews emphasizes that there was often concurrently the experience of a new schema for explaining their situation, and a schema that gave them a sense of efficacy, shifted the control to themselves:

It was a sudden illumination, that you saw a pattern to life, and you understood how life operated. It wasn't chaotic as you kept thinking . . . you didn't rely on a god who would put things right . . . it was the scientific approach to life . . . an understanding, and illumination so that you could cope with life and you had something that showed you how it worked and that you could take part in that.

Part of the changing schema of efficacy is an understanding of the role of organization, the power of the group. For Andrews's respondents, the discovery of organizations, as well as entering them, gives the individual efficacy and provides a schema for social change. In contrast to the experience of these lifetime social activists, it would appear that in the case of moral crisis the shift to some sense of personal responsibility and efficacy may precede organizational involvement; the response is "I must do something; what can I do? Who is doing something?" The power of the group is often a new idea for people who have hitherto lived in a world of private morality.

Andrews argues that her respondents became radicalized through a process of crystallization. Such crystallization is a realization of one's own responsibility, applying to oneself the schemata of efficacy and the political and moral contextualization of the issues that have hitherto been "out there." My case history of this type of engagement is a British woman who has been a lifelong peace activist. Emily was 68 at the time of my interview with her. She was born in a rural seaside town and became a teacher after university. She married a teacher, who was a conscientious objector during the Second World War. They lived in England, raised a family of three, and recently spent several years in Africa. She is, and always has been, a member of the United Reformed Church. On the moral judgment interview she demonstrated Stage 4/5 reasoning.

Emily has always been actively involved in several organizations, pressure groups associated mainly with peace but also with remedying injustice.

You can't have peace if there's injustice, so they're really all linked.

Her main activities are demonstrating, leafletting, and disseminating information; her house has also been open to all kinds of people in need, from Jewish refugees during the war to visitors from Eastern bloc and Third World countries.

Emily's memories of her early years are of "immersion" in an ethos of public responsibility and left-wing politics, and the role model of activist relatives.

My father was very actively engaged in politics. We used to travel about Dorset a lot, and I saw the poverty of these beautiful Dorset villages. He used to tell me about them, and I was brought up on the story of the Tolpuddle Martyrs. . . . He was a very active Trade Unionist. He was in business and he saw the conditions of the shop assistant, and he was very active in the formation of a strong branch of USDAW [the retail trade union]. He used to tell me stories about the way employers would force their assistants to be dishonest, to make profits. . . . He'd got a passionate concern for the underdog.

She made the shift from being an onlooker to being part of the action at the time of the Ethiopian War and the Peace Ballot:

I can remember the Secretary of the League of Nations Union coming to school to talk about it, and he'd been collecting signatures, his eyes were red with fatigue. . . . This was the first time I can remember feeling that I was concerned, and there was something that could be done about it. . . . This was quite a distinct feeling; before that, I was an onlooker, after that, I wanted to do something. So as soon as I got to university, two years later, I got involved with the activities.

Although she does not describe this as a crisis or triggering event, she retains vivid memories both of her own feelings and such incidentals as the red-eyed fatigue of the speaker. Several activities expressed her newfound efficacy: she became involved in peace groups, and made a commitment to peace even though by then it was obvious that war was inevitable; first the Spanish Civil War, later the Second World War.

The Peace Pledge Union, I joined that. I had to work out that basically I'd got to stick to the peace witness, even though we were going to have years of war. Because at the end of it we had to go on again.

We can see from Emily's history the processes by which she moved from being, as she put it, an "onlooker" in public responsibility to being a participant. By joining several social groups she gained personal efficacy and affirmation of her schemata of working for peace and justice. This continued, with a slight letup when she was tied with small children, and took on different elements as the situation changed, but within the same basic schema. It was natural that when the Greenham peace camp was set up she became a frequent visitor.

That her efficacy was tied up with a certain kind of activism is evident from her feelings about the Korean War and its aftermath:

I think the Korean War had a very depressing effect on me. . . . I think when you've got small children, you think what sort of future they're going to have—you're very vulnerable—and I was cooped up at home with nothing but the housework and the children. So when the Aldermaston March started, I cheered up and felt that that was something that we could get going on again, and we went to the first one.

Emily found her main goals—peace and justice—in her late teens, and at the same time found both her own efficacy and the scenario for putting it into practice. She did not experience further crises or major changes, but sustained her public responsibility and commitment throughout, making adjustments to changing conditions. In Africa it was impossible to be involved in peace work or in any protest against the government directly, but she worked for Amnesty International and she also took on aid issues that she construed as a part of her justice schema.

It is impossible to judge Emily's level of moral reasoning at the time of her first involvement. Her present level of moral reasoning contains much postconventional structure and also many components of what Dittmann-Kohli and Baltes (1989) describe as "wisdom"; she has a subtle and integrated system of interpreting her role and responsibilities, and has recently begun to integrate feminism into her perspective. It is clear that her engagement and moves toward commitment arose from the consolidation of taken-for-granted schemata, interpreted in the terms of her current stage of reasoning, not from an exceptionally high moral stage. Her present interpretation of social and political issues is consistent with the structure of her moral reasoning.

I would argue that for people like Emily, as well as Andrews's respondents, moral reasoning stage neither precipitates personal responsibility nor provides the resources for new ways of interpreting a situation, but instead mediates the interpretation of the already-available schemata of public responsibility and social analysis; as development progresses, the understanding of these schemata deepens and extends, and wider perspectives are appreciated.

I shall conclude my examples with two women who were interviewed by Gilbert and Moore for their book *Particular Passions* (1981). Each illustrates an interesting aspect of the process of commitment. Each had, like Emily, a family background in which public responsibility was taken for granted. Each also describes a particular period of her life when she was drawn into social action, in which she came to a realization of her responsibility, accompanied by a changing or consolidating schema of how the immediate situation fitted into a wider perspective. This was the beginning of their conscious commitments. There are no data on moral reasoning for these examples.

Justine Wise Polier is a lawyer who has been instrumental in making major change in the practice of family courts in the United States, and is committed to improving the condition of children. The crystallization of her own sense of responsibility, the point at which her personal efficacy became engaged, was when she worked in a factory after graduating from college and saw the condition of the textile workers before unionization. Her factory experience consolidated and made real the tendency toward public responsibility that her background had given her. It required her to interpret the situation; she developed schemata that gave her a theory to account for injustices, and for ways of eradicating them. The experience gave her a schema of efficacy at the time, and pushed her to acquire the greater efficacy of becoming a professional lawyer. But her memories of childhood show how immersed she had been in public responsibility; her family was

involved in many social problems and battles for social justice, whether it was for blacks or Jews or Armenians. . . . People concerned with similar problems always gathered [at our home].

She remembers a particular event; her father, a rabbi, invited some New York neighbors to meet an eminent black artist.

A very distinguished-looking, white-haired man turned to my father and said, "Rabbi Wise, you cannot expect me to sit down with a colored man for dinner." My father responded politely, "Oh, I'm so sorry. May I take you downstairs and help you get your coat." I remember . . . my father helping the gentleman on with [his coat] and saying "Good night." Somehow this strange flashback reminds me of values; the strength, the courtesy and the absolute unyielding on matters of principle that I have come to value very very much.

It is interesting that she does not think of herself as a crusader:

I don't think of myself as a crusader, just a hard-working old drayhorse. I would think crusaders are much more sure of their positions. Unfortunately, if you've learned to look at both sides of things, life gets more complicated.

This seems to be a distinction between responsibility born of affective crisis, and responsibility born of a habit of public morality. The former is indeed accompanied by a sense of "rightness" and conviction, the latter by a sense of participation in an established social process, alongside others.

My final example is someone who did experience a "triggering event," but after many years of public responsibility. Judianne Densen-Gerber is not part of a social movement, nor does she appear to have sought the legitimization of her changing schemata by an activist group. She found personal efficacy within her work as a psychiatrist, and her shift to public morality came out of a sense that her personal integrity was involved in taking responsibility for things that she had begun. She describes having a predisposition to moral outrage, and she comes from a background of activist women:

I became involved in challenging child prostitution and child abuse . . . because my work showed me things from which I could no longer hide. In 1969 Walter Vandermeer died of a heroin overdose shortly after his twelfth birthday. All his life he had been horrendously abused and neglected. My husband, Michael, was the New York medical examiner on the case. He came home from the death site in a Harlem hall bathroom with a little T-shirt and he threw it down . . . it was a size eight! A picture of Snoopy on the front said, "I wish I could bite someone to relieve my nervous tension." I looked at this T-shirt and grasped this child's tragedy.

Denial didn't seem a possible defense mechanism because I had been profoundly influenced by a scholarship I won in 1952 to study restoration and reconstruction after World War II. In Europe, I talked to the Germans about the Holocaust, the camps and the atrocities. One after another, they defended themselves by repeating, "We didn't know." I suppose in my work the thing that happened is that I kept hearing of these denials. Once you knew a certain problem, you had the choice of not facing the reality and walking away, or squarely facing an issue no matter how difficult or unpleasant.

She had a particularly explicit and well-developed schema concerning strategies for dealing with stress—unsurprising perhaps in a psychiatrist. The experience with the boy's death extended an already existing sense of responsibility, pushed her further into a commitment that already existed and that some years earlier had made her take action, feeling an inescapable responsibility.

I have never looked for an issue. It literally hit me on the head. I never sought a cause. They've always knocked on my door. I started Odyssey House in 1966 because a group of my drug-addicted patients wanted to be drug-free. Previously I'd promised them that if they kept the faith I wouldn't abandon them. So when New York's Metropolitan Hospital turned them out, they appeared on my doorstep. I did not have an ethical choice . . . I had given my word, and therefore my own sense of integrity was involved.

Judianne Densen-Gerber expresses, particularly well and in language that is consistent with the argument of this chapter, the mechanisms by which people deal with moral crisis, finding a resolution of the affect and drawing upon a range of schemata to translate their response into moral affect. Unlike Justine Wise Polier she feels she is a crusader and she expresses "moral outrage"; it is this that also seems to distinguish those who have gone through a moral crisis from those who have switched more smoothly from efficacious onlooker to efficacious participant.

Conclusions

In this chapter I have explored different paths to moral commitment, and I have considered how useful a model of moral reasoning can be for explaining them. The logic of a cognitive developmental model is that moral commitment arises out of a level of reasoning high enough to integrate the perception that a moral issue has a social context, the recognition of the potential for individual action, and personal motivation to take such action. The limitations of such a model are, first, that it restricts commitment to the higher stages of moral development; second, that it places cognitive appraisal processes as prior; and third, that motivation is seen as a separate process from recognition of a moral issue. While there is evidence that the gap between moral judgment and moral action is less in the higher stages of reasoning, and that a sense of personal responsibility does follow from cognitive appraisal, it seems adequate as an explanation only for certain kinds of engagement and commitment.

Subjective accounts of the process of moral commitment indicate at least two other major types of experience. In the case of moral crisis, powerful affect is the primary experience, initially engaging the individual. This is followed by a process of cognitive reconstruction in which the individual substantially changes his or her perspective of the issues, and his or her own potential agency in relation to them. This process integrates affect and cognition in relation to the issues; the individual emerges not only with a cognitive appraisal that reflects considerable change from the state prior to the experience, but also with strong motivation to take action. Furthermore, the evidence does not suggest that such processes require a high level of moral reasoning.

The third path to moral commitment is through long-term immersion in an environment where public responsibility is taken for granted, and the individual has access to perspectives that locate moral issues in a broad social context. In this path there is a greater emphasis on cognitive processes and the cognitive dimensions of the reappraisal in which one moves from being an "onlooker" to becoming a participant—taking oneself the responsibility that one has observed among others. But even here it appears that it is access to schemata of responsibility, rather than individual construction of the moral problem, that precipitates the shift from private to public responsibility. Again, though the evidence is limited, it does not appear that a particularly high level of reasoning is required.

I argued that we have the option of differentiating moral commitment that can be explained through a cognitive model, and moral commitment that is outside the purview of such a model, requiring other theoretical perspectives. There is a traditional conflict between models of morality that take affect into account and those that do not; one solution is a division of the psychological territory that is to be colonized by the theory. Instead I have proposed a model that offers an account of the process of moral crisis and its resolution, drawn from the work on stress and coping that has a long tradition of integrating affect and cognition. I have argued that the concept of schema that is integral to this model necessarily incorporates

levels of moral reasoning—even though this is not yet acknowledged in that body of literature.

A schema is in essence a widely available theory or scenario
that may be understood differently at different levels of cognitive complexity (within certain limits). Thus the schema invoked to account for a powerful affective experience will reflect
the level of moral reasoning of the individual; this will have an
effect on what form the resolution of the crisis takes.

The individual who has always been exposed to the expectation that people take public responsibility, have efficacy, and
perceive the social context of moral issues may grasp these
concepts at an age or stage when they are only comprehensible
in concrete terms; one may move from the status of onlooker
to participant while still only having a concrete level of moral
reasoning.

I have illustrated the application of this model with case
studies of people who experienced crisis, and people who experienced the crystallization of responsibility out of long-term
immersion. Such case studies demonstrate the operation of
engagement and commitment, and the mechanisms of appraisal in the process of developing changing perspectives on
efficacy and the moral issue itself. I have also attempted to
confront the problems of defining "commitment" without falling into the trap of identifying commitment with moral excellence. It is a logical consequence of the cognitive developmental
model that if commitment and responsibility are only construed as the outcome of the highest stages of moral reasoning,
then they are necessarily unimpeachable. Other theoretical
perspectives may also give the same validity to convictions that
arise from affect. My concern has been to explore the psychological mechanisms by which commitment, responsibility, and
efficacy are arrived at; ultimately I consider that the excellence
of a cause cannot be judged on the basis of the psychological
processes through which it becomes espoused.[2]

Notes

1. The development of Lazarus's model through the elaboration of cognitive schemata
has many parallels with Eckensberger's action theoretical model for aggression as a

motive state. Eckensberger argues that the sequence starts with an action barrier that gives rise to an affective response or motive state. Attributions about the action barrier, about the individual's capacity to act, and about the responsibility for the action barrier then modify the affect. The probability of action depends on this cognition-affect interaction. A feature of Eckensberger's model that exactly parallels ours is that the cognitions are both about the individual's role as causal agent and efficacious actor, and about moral dimensions of the situation—the latter being dependent on the individual's moral stage. (See Eckensberger and Emminghaus, 1982.)

2. In the development of the ideas in this chapter I wish to thank, for stimulating discussion and friendship, the following people: Howard Gruber, who started me on this particular train of thought; Ann Colby, Bill Damon, Tom Wren, and Molly Andrews for many exciting agreements and disagreements; Beverly Halstead, for being committed in all sorts of ways. And, for so much, Larry Kohlberg.

References

Andrews, M. (1987). The perception of moral conflict in the lives of several lifetime social activists. Paper presented to the British Psychological Society: Social Psychology Conference, Oxford.

Andrews, M. (1988). Making history: Political activists and the historical context. Paper presented to the British Sociological Association, Edinburgh, Scotland, March.

Andrews, M. (1989). *Lifetimes of commitment: A study of socialist activitists*. Doctoral dissertation, Cambridge University, Cambridge, England.

Bartlett, F. C. (1932). *Remembering*. Cambridge: Cambridge University Press.

Blackburne-Stover, G., Belenky, M. F., and Gilligan, C. (1982). Moral development and reconstructive memory: Recalling a decision to terminate an unplanned pregnancy. *Developmental Psychology*, 18:862–870.

Broughton, J. M. (1986). Kohlberg's contribution to political psychology: A negative view. In S. Modgil and C. Modgil (Eds.), *Lawrence Kohlberg—Consensus and controversy*. London: Falmer Press.

Dittmann-Kohli, F., and Baltes, P. B. (1989). Toward a neofunctionalist conception of adult intellectual development: Wisdom as a prototypical case of intellectual growth. In C. W. Alexander and E. Langer (Eds.), *Higher stages of human development*. New York: Oxford University Press.

Eckensberger, L. H., and Emminghaus, W. B. (1982). Moralisches Urteil und Aggression: Zur Systematisierung und Präzisierung des Aggressionskonzeptes sowie einiger empirischer Befunde. In R. Hilke and W. Kempf (Eds.), *Aggression: Naturwissenschaftliche und kulturwissenschaftliche Perspektiven der Aggressionsforschung*. Bern: Huber.

Flacks, R. (1983). Moral commitment, privatism and activism: Notes on a research program. In N. Haan, R. N. Bellah, P. Rabinow, and W. M. Sullivan (Eds.), *Social science as moral inquiry*. New York: Columbia University Press.

Frank, J. D., and Nash, E. H. (1965). Commitment to peace work. *American Journal of Orthopsychiatry*, 35:106–119.

Gilbert, L., and Moore, G. (1981). *Particular passions: Talks with women who have shaped our times.* New York: Clarkson Potter.

Gilligan, C. (1982). *In a different voice: Psychological theory and women's development.* Cambridge, MA: Harvard University Press.

Haan, N., Smith, M. B., and Block, J. H. (1968). Moral reasoning of young adults. *Journal of Personality and Social Psychology,* 10:183–201.

Habermas, J. (1979). *Communication and the evolution of society.* Boston: Beacon Press.

Habermas, J. (1983). Interpretive social science vs. hermeneuticism. In N. Haan, R. N. Bellah, P. Rabinow, and W. M. Sullivan (Eds.), *Social science as moral inquiry.* New York: Columbia University Press.

Habermas, J. (1985). Philosophical notes on moral judgment theory. In G. Lind, H. A. Hartmann, and R. Wakenhut (Eds.), *Moral development and the social environment.* Chicago: Precedent Publishing.

Haste, H. (1989). Everybody's scared, but life goes on: Coping, defense and action in the face of nuclear threat. *Journal of Adolescence,* 12:11–26.

Howard, R. W. (1986). *Mohandas K. Gandhi: A biography of moral development.* Doctoral dissertation, Harvard University Graduate School of Education, Cambridge, MA.

Kohlberg, L. (1980a) The future of liberalism as the dominant ideology of the West. In R. W. Wilson and G. J. Schochet (Eds.), *Moral development and politics.* New York: Praeger.

Kohlberg, L. (1980b). High school democracy and educating for a just society. In R. Mosher (Ed.), *Moral education: A first generation of research.* New York: Praeger.

Kohlberg, L. (1984). *Essays on moral development. Vol. 2: The psychology of moral development.* San Francisco: Harper and Row.

Kohlberg, L., and Candee, D. (1984). The relationship of moral judgment to moral action. In L. Kohlberg, *Essays on moral development. Vol. 2: The psychology of moral development.* San Francisco: Harper and Row.

Lazarus, R. (1966). *Psychological stress and the coping process.* New York: McGraw Hill.

Lazarus, R., and Folkman, S. (1984). *Stress appraisal and coping.* New York: Springer.

McNamee, S. (1978). Moral behaviour, moral development and motivation. *Journal of Moral Education,* 7:27–31.

Mead, G. H. (1934). *Mind, self, and society.* Chicago: University of Chicago Press.

Noam, G., Kohlberg, L., and Snarey, J. R. (1983). Steps toward a model of the self. In B. Lee and G. Noam (Eds.), *Developmental approaches to the self.* New York: Plenum Press.

Rawls, J. (1971). *A theory of justice.* Cambridge, MA: Harvard University Press.

Rorty, R. (1983). Method and morality. In N. Haan, R. N. Bellah, P. Rabinow, and W. M. Sullivan (Eds.), *Social science as moral inquiry.* New York: Columbia University Press.

Schmid, M. (1982). Habermas' theory of social evolution. In J. B. Thompson and D. Held (Eds.), *Habermas: Critical debates*. Cambridge, MA: MIT Press.

Slovic, P., Fischoff, B., and Lichtenstein, S. (1981). Perceived risk: Psychological factors and social implications. *Proceedings of the Royal Society of London*, 17–34.

Turiel, E. (1966). An experimental test of the sequentiality of developmental stages in the child's moral judgments. *Journal of Personality and Social Psychology*, 3:611–618.

Weinreich-Haste, H. (1986). Kohlberg's contribution to political psychology: A positive view. In S. Modgil and C. Modgil (Eds.), *Lawrence Kohlberg—Consensus and controversy*. London: Falmer Press.

Williams, B. (1981). *Moral luck*. Cambridge: Cambridge University Press.

Williams, B. (1985). *Ethics and the limits of philosophy*. Cambridge, MA: Harvard University Press.

Beyond Freud and Piaget: Biographical Worlds— Interpersonal Self

Gil G. Noam

As long as the ego is cut off from its internal nature and disavows the dependency on needs that still await suitable interpretations, freedom, no matter how much it is guided by principles, remains in truth unfree.

—*Jürgen Habermas*

For those who work toward a deepened understanding of social development, self, and identity, the theories of Lawrence Kohlberg and Jürgen Habermas are, I believe, essential. Though more customary, perhaps, are the insights of William James (1890), Erik Erikson (1950), and more recently Jane Loevinger (1976) into this complex and ill-defined psychological terrain, I will argue in this essay that Kohlberg's and Habermas's frameworks offer radical philosophical and psychological reconstructions.

The dialogue between these men continued for well over a decade. This book is testimony to the many theoretical sources they and their colleagues shared. Philosophical discussions about logic and telos in moral development were central to their thinking; the question of how the moral domain relates to a broader theory of self and identity was a challenge to each. However, no formal discussion developed to clarify the issues surrounding the concepts of self and identity. In this chapter I write about these important domains and show how we can learn from both Kohlberg and Habermas and the theoretical traditions they embraced: symbolic interactionism associated with Baldwin (1906) and Mead (1934); modern psychodynamic ideas, especially the approaches of Sullivan (1953) and Erikson (1950); and the cognitive developmental theory of Piaget (e.g., 1936/1952).

Kohlberg's and Habermas's innovative ways of integrating these and other traditions provide new possibilities for tracing the developmental trajectory of self and uncovering relationships between moral judgment and action and between productive and problematic psychological adaptations. They have provided the critical insights necessary for theory transformations. The work of molding a new perspective of self, one beyond Freud and Piaget, is left for others to accomplish.

For almost fifteen years I have worked toward a new theoretical framework that simultaneously builds on and gives rise to structural developmental investigations and in-depth clinical developmental observations. In this essay, I organize the presentation of this ongoing exploration and theory transformation around three themes:

1. I describe a new framework that combines symbolic interactionism, cognitive developmental principles, and modern psychoanalytic ideas. I show that these traditions cannot be eclectically pieced together, but must provide a larger context in which a new synthesis of self theory can emerge. This synthesis produces a view of the self as (a) emerging from social interactions as well as (b) from the interiorization of these interactions, (c) creating a consistent experience and understanding of internal and interpersonal relationships, and (d) giving a biographical pattern to the self's evolution across time.

2. I argue that many insightful and creative psychoanalytic ideas about biography remain insufficient for the new theory because they reduce fundamental structures of biography to early childhood experiences (i.e., repetition compulsion of childhood trauma, unresolved oedipal conflicts, etc.). In contrast, the cognitive developmental theories have introduced a conceptual road map of the continued developmental transformations throughout life. These transformations are not defined in terms of behaviors, adaptations, or age-salient tasks, but by an underlying structure of knowledge and meaning.

But there, too, we find ourselves in need of new theoretical ideas, since Piaget's psychology has introduced no language for the biographical dimensions of self. In cognitive theory the self is a generalized logic, also called the "epistemic self," where a multitude of individual and collective life experiences are condensed into a few ideal developmental types or stages. It is essential to bring the epistemic subject into dialogue with the person who molds experiences into a pattern of life both lived and unfolding. Toward this end, I pursue a path where cognitive developmental and psychoanalytic thinking are not merely "used" or placed in closer proximity, but instead undergo important transformations. The outcome of this transformation—in which a new, broadened social developmental frame is provided—I call the theory of biography and transformation.

3. This theory introduces two structures of self: "schemata" and "themata." Schemata refer to the cognitively anchored processes of *self complexity*. Schemata stand in the tradition of Piagetian psychology and address the transformations of the knowing and experiencing self. Themata refer to a second structure of the self's organization. They contribute to typical ways we explore, understand, and relate to the world, but their systematic nature emerges out of important events and interactions that have produced a biographical pattern. Both structures shape a person's outlook on life and motivate behavior. Both structures, and their complex relationship to each other, are at the heart of this theory of social development. The developmental implications of the theory for clinical research and practice have been elaborated elsewhere (e.g., Noam, 1986a, 1986b, 1988a, 1988b, 1988c). This essay will address conceptual concerns regarding the self, ending with a discussion of how developmental constraints occur even under the influence of principled moral reasoning and advanced self-complexity.

Moral Judgment and "Causality of Fate"

In general, Kohlberg and Habermas hold similar theoretical positions on the self (or what Habermas sometimes refers to as self identity or ego identity [see Habermas, 1979]). But their work also reveals important differences, especially in the status ascribed to unconscious and irrational processes. The complexity of both theorists' work suggests a paper just on the similarities and differences of their views and on the influence they had upon each other.[1] In the context of this essay it is only possible to draw on some of their central ideas pertaining to the self.

It is widely known that Kohlberg viewed the theory of moral judgment as a general, cognitive developmental reconceptualization of social development. He discussed the fundamentals of his position in two essays, "Stage and Sequence" (1969/1984) and "From Is to Ought" (1971/1984), both of which attest to the paradigmatic nature of his work. Not only was philosophy to play a central role in psychology, but moral development was to enlighten new ways of studying the more general domain of social development. In order to detail structural distinctions and the practical implications of moral development, Kohlberg focused on the psychology of moral judgment and on educational interventions during the last decade of his life. As his essay in this book demonstrates, he also continued to elaborate on the philosophical underpinnings of his theory.

Central to Kohlberg's earlier work was his concept of the self and those processes that ensure its birth and development (i.e., internalization, imitation, identification, and idealization). In "Stage and Sequence" he outlined the relationship between moral judgment and the broader domain of self. He posited a fundamental unity of personality organization and development that he called ego and self; in the presence of various strands of social development (psychosexual development, moral development, etc.), he stated, we can make a common reference to a single concept of self in a single social world. In that essay he also contrasted the cognitive developmental approach to imitation and identification with the social learning theory and psychoanalytic approaches. Kohlberg's essay contains, to my mind, the most thoughtful and innovative ideas written on these topics. I think it is fair to state that all of the recent social cognitive theories of stages and of the self (e.g., Blasi, 1983; Kegan, 1982; Damon and Hart, 1982; Noam, 1985) are elaborations of the ideas Kohlberg outlined in 1969.

These early insights into the workings of the self remained peripheral, however, to Kohlberg's later pursuits. He regretted that he had not followed his earlier intuitions. For example, shortly before his death he wrote:

Following Piagetian structuralism's focus on the rational-epistemic subject, Kohlberg's approach has ignored (a) moral content of development as opposed to structure, (b) moral motivation as opposed to moral reasoning, and most fundamentally, the existence and function of a moral self. (Kohlberg and Diessner, in press).

Despite his overall neglect of this important developmental line, he initiated a collaboration to clarify similarities and differences between his own work and that of other contributors to the study of self. In 1982 and 1983, Kohlberg, Snarey, and I conducted an ongoing discussion of this topic. We published two detailed accounts that not only compared Loevinger's theory of ego development and Kohlberg's stages of moral judgment, but also distinguished between structural and functional theories of the self (Noam, Kohlberg, and Snarey, 1983; Snarey, Kohlberg, and Noam, 1983). We concluded that an adequate theory could not be established solely from within the Piagetian paradigm, since the self also evolves from functional life tasks, processes of attachment, and styles of coping and defense. I began to specify some of these issues (e.g., Noam, 1984, 1985), which in turn led to the constructivist framework discussed in this chapter.

Kohlberg's educational interventions provided another impetus for his thinking on the self. He observed that the study of moral conduct required not only a theory of moral judgments (what he called "deontic" judgments about rights, duty, and justice), but also a theory of responsibility. For Kohlberg, the moral actor was in need of an additional set of judgments regarding the responsibility to act according to the deontic judgments. This interest in moral responsibility, sensibility, and action led him to develop ideas on the moral self. In accordance with Loevinger, Erikson, and neopsychoanalytic character psychologists (e.g., Peck and Havighurst, 1960), Kohlberg stated that the subjective experience of moral commitments forms a unity with moral behaviors. He defined this unity as the moral self.

Kohlberg's greatest inspiration in his work on the self was Baldwin, but he was also influenced by a number of psychoanalysts. Even though he rejected orthodox Freudian drive theory, he found many points of convergence between himself, Erikson, Sullivan, and other neopsychoanalytic thinkers. Mostly he searched for—and found—the cognitive-structural parallelism between his own stages and those of the psychoanalytic theorists. But as a psychologist steeped in empirical research, he would not subscribe to many psychoanalytic notions untestable by empirical methods. At the same time, he shared with psychoanalytic psychologists the use of hermeneutic text interpretation. This procedure directs attention to an underlying text that places individual stimuli, behaviors, and understandings into systematic relationships to each other. Psychoanalysis and Kohlberg both were worlds apart from the behaviorist orientation so thoroughly in control of American psychology at midcentury. But in Kohlberg's view, the unconscious in psychoanalysis did not follow strict criteria for text interpretation. Thus, his use of psychoanalysis for self theory was mostly through the work of Erikson (e.g., 1950), for Erikson had transformed a theory of drives and the unconscious into psychosocial tasks and identity.

Accepting Erikson's life cycle theory, however, led Kohlberg to dismiss prematurely the important questions raised by psychoanalysis. Rejecting the proposed solutions psychoanalysis offers, he simultaneously dropped some critical questions. For Erikson, identity was a complex result of convergent forces: individual life history, biological and social timetables, social environment, and the "historical moment." Kohlberg chose to focus on Erikson's stages, neglecting the important issues Erikson faced (and did not solve) about how earlier vulnerabilities, strengths, identifications, and life experiences become part of the makeup of later stages. Or, to put it differently, how it might be possible to have some childhood identifications resist the governance of the more mature developmental positions.

Habermas and Kohlberg are remarkably close in much of their thinking about the self. But in relation to this last issue— that the rejection of solutions offered by psychoanalysis does not need to lead to a rejection of the questions posed—we find important points of divergence. This can partly be explained by Habermas's ties to the Frankfurt School, so heavily influenced by psychoanalytic thought. As is widely known, Horkheimer, Adorno, Fromm, and Marcuse, all distinguished members of this circle of critical theorists, worked to bridge Marxist theory with psychoanalytic psychology (for a detailed overview see Jay, 1973). Habermas went considerably further than his teachers in addressing the newer developmental and social psychological theories (e.g., cognitive developmental psychology, as well as identity and role theory). He viewed psychoanalysis as an important ground against which the other theoretical developments had to be interpreted. I will return to the role of psychoanalytic thinking after describing more specific issues concerning Habermas's view of the self.

Habermas's starting point in discussing the self is the notion of ego identity, not the moral self. For Habermas, identity is the sociological equivalent of the ego or the self. It refers to the symbolic structures that create continuity and consistency across different social contexts and social interactions in accordance with the biographical nature of the person. He defines ego identity as proving itself

in the ability of the adult to construct new identities in conflicting situations and to bring these into harmony with older superseded identities so as to organize himself and his interactions—under the guidance of general principles and modes of procedure—into a unique life history. (1979, pp. 90–91)

Habermas views identity as following a developmental path from "natural identity" to "role identity" and finally to "ego identity." He and his colleagues viewed moral judgment structures as important dimensions in this sequence and as simultaneously sharing a common underlying structure with ego identity, that of "role-taking" (Döbert, Habermas, and Nunner-Winkler, 1977). Thus, identity and self encompass broader developmental dimensions than the moral domain. Identity and self include the tension between universal stages and the uniqueness of the one life. In addition, for Habermas self and identity include typical patterns of adaptation, coping, and an array of defenses. They also involve ways to communicate competently in an ever more complex radius of social interactions.

Again, we can see important parallels in Kohlberg's and Habermas's thinking. For Kohlberg, too, the self shares with moral judgment an underlying structure of role-taking. But the Kohlbergian self is less concerned with coping and defense, or with communication and superseded identities.

We now return to the role of psychoanalysis. For Habermas (1971), psychoanalysis not only provides important dimensions for a theory of self, but more importantly it provides a non-positivistic psychology and a hermeneutic method. Like Kohlberg, Habermas criticizes Freud's original model of hydraulic energy distribution (drives). But in contrast to Kohlberg, he reinterprets central psychoanalytic dimensions from the perspective of his own general theory. Two theoretical formulations relevant to our topic of the self emerge. First, Habermas reconstructs psychoanalysis as an example of systematically distorted communications. Second, he introduces psychodynamic principles into his formulation as an important contributor to principled moral judgment and emancipated action by the self.

What Habermas calls "rational reconstruction" of psychoanalytic thought builds on Lorenzer's (1970) influential theory of language destruction (*Sprachzerstörung*). Habermas suggests the existence of two separate forms of symbolic structures. One is based on the rules of a shared linguistic system. The other is prelinguistic, distorted, and part of what he calls a "corrupt text." The former is part of the explicit communication between therapist and client—it is "public"—while the latter is removed from public communication. It is part of what Freud called the "internal foreign territory."

Habermas sees psychoanalysis as possessing a powerful method of producing enlightenment through self-reflection: actions and nonverbal behavior of a person belie what is expressively stated, even though they are the expressions of the subject. Habermas states that "their symbolic character, which identifies them as split-off parts of a symbolic structure, cannot be permanently denied. They are the scars of a corrupt text that confronts the author as incomprehensible" (Habermas, 1971, p. 219). He describes rules through which the private communication becomes "public" (communicated). Through therapy systematic distortions are traced back to two developmentally separate stages of symbol organization. In other words, a previously inappropriately symbolized text becomes *re*symbolized; in the process it becomes reappropriated as a formerly lost part of the self.

Habermas's reinterpretation of this basic psychoanalytic idea leads us to an essential difference in emphasis between himself and Kohlberg. In Kohlberg's model and in his use of psychoanalytic ideas only one symbolic structure is of interest: the symbolic and rational one. In the process, I believe, he lost the other, developmentally separate stage of symbol organization. That Habermas keeps this second dimension of self alive ends up providing him with a significantly larger radius of exploration than does Kohlberg's stage conception.

The analysis of the self, for Habermas, can occur in a systematic way not only because we have theories of the "epistemic self" so ingeniously traced by Piaget and Kohlberg, but also because the self follows what he calls a "causality of fate." In the tradition of Hegel, he distinguishes "causality of fate" from "causality of nature." Causality of fate is biographical in the sense that motives, meanings, and actions are laid down in a life history and are filtered through the symbolic organization of the mind. This inner world of self does not follow laws of nature, but is "an invariance of life history that can be dissolved by the power of reflection" (McCarthy, 1978, p. 201).

The belief in our ability to overcome this "causality of fate" places ego identity in a dominant position in Habermas' overall theoretical considerations about autonomy and emancipation. For Habermas the self's ability to resymbolize dimensions of the self that have not undergone reinterpretation follows cognitive scientific principles: the self's reflective powers produce possible understanding of and necessary emancipation from this less evolved "text."

In relationship to the moral domain, Habermas repeatedly states that principled moral judgment is an insufficient condition for freedom from conventions. He makes this point most poignantly in a passage also used as an epigraph to this essay:

As long as the ego is cut off from its internal nature and disavows the dependency on needs that still await suitable interpretations, freedom, no matter how much it is guided by principles, remains in truth unfree in relation to existing systems of norms. (Habermas, 1979)

Had Habermas and Kohlberg engaged in a discussion about the self and its role in moral development, this complex statement could have served as a starting point in clarifying their similarities and differences.[2] Instead, this passage provides us with a starting point of a different kind: it raises the question of how we can overcome decades of studying morality and self as phenomena disembodied from their own history and internal nature.

Since Kohlberg dedicated his work to a cognitive view on moral judgment, many points made by Habermas regarding the self do not appear central to Kohlberg's work. But the fact that Kohlberg needed to postulate a "moral self" to create a more unified view on moral judgment, moral behavior, and responsibility shows that the issues discussed above await serious consideration. First steps have been taken by reviewing contemporary theories and returning to the insights of Baldwin and Mead (Noam, Kohlberg, and Snarey, 1983). But in the meantime, problems implicit in Kohlberg's theory have become a great deal more pronounced in models that expanded Piaget's and Kohlberg's ideas to dimensions of ego, personality, and faith. These theories not only demonstrate the usefulness of Kohlberg's model beyond moral judgments, but also reveal the problems of structural theory of social development.

Structuralists' Expansion into New Domains: Ego, Personality, and Faith

Piaget's brilliant insights into the development of intelligence created entirely new approaches to social development and social cognition. After the initial excitement over the usefulness of cognitive theory for moral and social development, stages were introduced for almost all psychological domains. In the midst of what Loevinger once called the "mushrooming of stage theory," Kohlberg insisted that few of these theories provided "hard" criteria for structural change. He elaborated that a theory is hard only when a precise distinction can be drawn between structure and content and between competence and performance. Structures, he said, have to form an invariant sequence independent of cultural influences, and stages must represent hierarchical integrations that involve increased differentiation and integration. Kohlberg was convinced that his theory was organized by hard-stage criteria of what he called justice structures. Inspired by Kohlberg and other cognitive thinkers, a variety of social cognitive theories of self were introduced (e.g., Blasi, 1983; Broughton, 1978; Damon and Hart, 1982; Noam, 1985; Selman, 1980; Rogers, 1987). These theorists examined self dimensions organized around concepts such as self-understanding, self-representation, and self-other differentiation. Despite considerable differences (e.g., self as a unitary process or consisting of physical, psychological, and social subdomains; use of different theory traditions and research tools, etc.), the developmental descriptions remain strikingly similar across theories.

Some investigators have taken the Piaget-Kohlberg paradigm into a different direction. They have moved away from hard stage-principles in order to address broad dimensions of personality, faith, and ego development (e.g., Fowler, 1981; Kegan, 1982; Loevinger, 1976). In the process, what was for Kohlberg and some self theorists a strictly defined social cognitive focus has become a more loosely defined frame of thinking and feeling, judging and acting, and intimacy to persons or to an ultimate Being. What began as a circumscribed developmental sequence has been transformed into a developmental metaphor—a notion of evolution and growth that somehow incorporates self, life, or religion.

Kohlberg labeled these approaches "soft-stage theories" since they refer to the content and function of personality rather than to structures of cognitive operations. They refer to "the individual's reflections upon the self's psychology" (Kohlberg, 1984, p. 243) and are self-constructed individual theories rather than structural forms of reasoning. Even though the distinctions these theories offer are "soft," it can be useful to explore a set of theoretical propositions to their limits. In the process, however, we run the risk that the phenomena studied cannot be "held" by the principles used. This, in fact, has occurred and has remained unrecognized.

Fowler (1981), for example, expresses his indebtedness to Piaget and Kohlberg for their basic developmental principles, which provide him with a structural theory of faith. He transcends the cognitive structures when he describes faith in terms of such diverse dimensions as intuitive knowledge, self, personality, emotions, and what he calls a "logic of conviction." He also includes the ecstatic, imaginative, and symbolic "unconscious structuring processes," "personal knowing and acting," "bounds of social awareness," "locus of authority," and "form of world coherence." He introduces these dimensions into his stage theory as important extensions of the "rationalistic" Piaget-Kohlberg models.

But while he and other soft-stage theorists incorporate so many noncognitive processes and dimensions into their stage definitions, he simultaneously assumes that the basic Piagetian principles outlined above—the distinction between structure and content, stage sequentiality, hierarchical integration and differentiation, and so on—continue to apply. Despite his focus on the "life map," Fowler does not discuss the changes in the Piagetian paradigm needed to account for all these new dimensions.

This important issue confronts us also in Loevinger's and, more recently, Kegan's work on ego and personality development. In an earlier publication (Noam, Kolhberg, and Snarey, 1983), my colleagues and I showed that Loevinger's stage model includes both structural and content dimensions. Loevinger defines stages of ego development partly in terms of structures, but equally important are psychological functions and motives pertaining to self-enhancement, coping, and defense. For example, the self-protective stage (Delta) is characterized primarily by an interpersonal style that functions to defend the self and less by the structures used at that stage to understand the world. This has led to repeated criticisms that Loevinger's ego stages are not guided by an underlying logic (Habermas, 1979; Broughton and Zahaykevich, 1977). Without that logic, it is difficult to justify a sequence of hierarchical stages. What makes one stage higher, more mature, more adequate, more adaptive, or better than another? Thus, it remains unclear why Loevinger chooses a Piagetian model over other possible developmental theories to account for the mixture of structural, functional, and motivational elements that are part of her stages.

Loevinger posits an indivisible ego simultaneously engaged in what she calls impulse control, interpersonal style, conscious preoccupations, and cognitive functioning. In contrast, and from a stricter structural perspective, there is evidence that the different domains are governed by separate substructures. What Loevinger calls the "cognitive style" facet of ego development points to the subdomain defined by Piaget's stages of cognitive or logical operations. "Interpersonal style and self-concerns" corresponds to the subdomain described as perspective-taking (Selman, 1980), and "impulse control and character" overlaps with the moral judgment domain. Research has shown these domains to be related (i.e., that there are necessary but not sufficient relationships between cognition, perspective-taking, and moral development), but there is no empirical support for the idea that all developmental domains are necessarily organized identically. Thus, to arrive at a unified stage score, Loevinger is required to use mathematical techniques (i.e., the ogive rule) rather than hermeneutic methods because people often show considerable stage scatter when testing on her sentence completion instrument. Given these results, and given that Loevinger stresses that empirical observations rather than underlying logical definitions led to many of the stage distinctions, it is unclear why a unitary stage model was introduced to describe the many dimensions characterizing ego development.

Kegan (1982) introduced a set of similar ego stages and argued for a structural logic underlying each stage. For such a goal to be achieved, it is essential that a basic psychological function be defined that can then be traced through its structural reorganizations. Only this clearly defined psychological function (in Kohlberg's work it is justice structures) allows for a structural reconstruction of stages and transitions. Without the definition of this function it is impossible to explore the difference between what is taken as structure and what is taken as content.

Kegan introduces subject-object relationships as the unifying functional force in his model. He states that all other cognitive stage models are organized by this "deep structure." But why should the development of impulses (Stage 1), of needs (Stage 2), of interpersonal relationships (Stage 3), of an ideological self-system (Stage 4), or of an intersubjective process (Stage 5) be united by one function? In fact, it is more parsimonious and closer to research findings to assume that each one of these processes is in itself a psychological function and has its own developmental line (e.g., impulse control, pursuit and negotiation of needs, development of intimacy, of autonomy, etc.). Any one of these processes exists throughout the lifespan and undergoes important developmental transformations.

Furthermore, because there is no definition of a function, the subject-object relationship does not tell us why we should include some developmental processes and exclude others. Is it not possible to argue that there is a transition from "being one's trust" to "having one's trust"? This would be in line with Kegan's subject-object distinction of "having" at the new stage what one "is" at the previous stage. Nothing about the definition of a subject-object function would preclude a switch from a stage definition of impulses as used by Kegan to the Eriksonian notion of trust. Similarly, any number of psychological processes, such as self-esteem, creativity, group affiliation, and so on, could be inserted at any stage and be viewed as part of subject-object differentiation. For example, what criteria would be used to support or reject the claim that at a given stage a crucial transition was occurring from "I am my creativity" to "I have my creativity" or "I am my self-esteem" to "I have my self-esteem"? There is nothing about the function of subject-object relationships that would prevent the inclusion of these dimensions or the exclusion of many possible others. In summary, the logical relationships between different stages can only emerge if the function is defined in ways that remain meaningfully tied to a given construct. This is not the case in Fowler's, Loevinger's, or Kegan's work.

It might appear that we are engaging in tiresome academic debates with little import for further development of theory or practice, but I have found it essential in my theoretical, empirical, and clinical explorations to deal with these issues. If one wants to pursue empirical investigations and clinical practice based on theoretical constructs, questions about the relationship between phenomena studied and the use of a paradigm become essential. We have learned from psychoanalysis and behaviorism how problems in underlying theory lead to stagnation and inadequate clinical treatments. In contrast, important progress has always been accompanied by rethinking the organizing paradigm. For example, the transition from classical psychoanalytic theory to attachment theory was accompanied by a transition from drive theory to an ethological perspective. Erikson's and Sullivan's new developmental formulations were heavily influenced by an emerging anthropologic-environmental paradigm. Similarly, cognitive behavior therapy has fundamentally transformed the traditional Skinnerian paradigm. This form of fundamental theory transformation has not occurred in the Piagetian theories described above. There, the basic model has remained in place only to be "filled" with ever more issues, dimensions, processes, and content.

The result of this attempt to simultaneously unify a multitude of psychological processes while using a cognitive-structural framework has been an unnecessarily restricted view of human development and personality functioning. Interestingly, this restriction came to the fore when an increasing number of investigators began to apply structural ideas to clinical contexts (for an overview see Noam, 1988d). Piagetian theories were used not only to stage the many dimensions of personality, but also to give organization to clinical problems and psychopathology. Of course, there is good reason to expect a relationship between a person's social cognitive level and typical forms of distress as well as coping. What is experienced as dangerous and upsetting has a great deal to do with how a situation is evaluated and what strategies are deemed useful in response. This hypothesized relationship between social development and clinical issues, in fact, has produced one of the most vital and exciting new applications of the Piaget-Kohlberg paradigm. It has also, however, helped uncover basic weaknesses of the paradigm, necessitating an important step in formulating a new theory. Interestingly, the need for a theoretical shift became most apparent when we analyzed those Piagetian theories that had moved furthest away from the hard-stage cognitive-conceptual dimensions. I have discussed this shift in detail in earlier publications (Noam, 1988a, 1988b, 1988c), and so here will only address two central points.

The first issue goes to the heart of the "architecture of structuralism"—the idea that each new stage integrates all earlier structures and synthesizes them as content into a new form. Clearly, the "hard-stage" Piagetian principles were used well beyond any of the original purposes intended. For example, Piaget had stated repeatedly that in his view personality dimensions are not organized by structural principle, but consist of many complex and contradictory processes. It is, I believe, helpful to consider this position and loosen our hold on prescribed stage principles, because we are in need of a less restrictive model.

The second issue relates to these theorists not having transcended the generalized, epistemic self. When we pursue the growth of personality and the course of life, we need to infuse fresh insights into those personal meanings that give life coherence—"biography." The focus on the epistemic self has not produced necessary knowledge—in fact, it has systematically screened out the issue of biography. Both points taken together underscore, again, that addressing new psychological domains requires not only theoretical addition, but qualitative transformations of the underlying framework.

Let us explore the first point regarding structure. I have argued that as more and more content has been included in the ego, faith, and personality theories, there is little reason to assume that a stage change would reorganize and transform all diverse aspects of self and personality. A new and more complex image of relationships, for example, does not necessarily go hand in hand with better impulse control. Or a more complex view of personal identity may coexist with an impoverished and unevolved perspective on faith. Even within a more limited and defined developmental dimension (e.g., constructions of important interpersonal relationships) it is quite possible that discrepancies in developmental perspective exist. Seeing, knowing, and committing, Fowler tells us, are the "stuff" stages are made of. But don't we see those things we have confronted and explored differently from those we have never encountered or have shied away from? And don't we often remain committed to persons and meanings even when we are capable of more mature commitments and understandings? Skepticism of unified self, personality, or faith structures also comes from the more circumscribed cognitive realm, where studies show that some cognitive capacities can transform while others do not (e.g., Fischer, 1980).

I suggest that we recognize the research of Heinz Werner (1948), who demonstrated that a person can structure internal and interpersonal realities simultaneously in hierarchically more and less differentiated and integrated ways. Within the Piaget-inspired stage models of ego and personality, this view has been eliminated, since coherence is forced onto data even when discrepancies are manifest. The final common empirical pathway in all structural measurement is a stage assignment. Instead of taking unified organization of diverse functions for granted, we need to understand also the inconsistencies both *among* cognitive, emotional, and behavioral systems and *within* developmental subdomains (e.g., cognition, morality, perspective-taking).

That structural ideas have been extended beyond their categorical limits becomes even more evident around the role of the epistemic self. I have mentioned earlier that the Piaget-Kohlberg self is defined in terms of universal structures of intelligence and justice. We have also seen that Kohlberg himself was aware of the limitations of the epistemic self for understanding morality, especially when it came to issues of motivation, responsibility, and action. The primary focus on the epistemic self is even more misplaced when we deal with broadened psychological domains studied by the above theorists. This is because a great deal of the ego, self, personality, and faith structures are intricately tied to motivation, perceived responsibilities, and what Habermas calls "causality of fate." Let me elaborate upon this point.

As a way to overcome mechanistic theories of behavior and trait, Loevinger introduced the idea that developmental stages account for qualitatively new styles, or "conscious preoccupations." Fowler and Kegan follow along the same lines when they use the term "making meaning" to define the organization of self, emotions, relationships, commitments, and so on. For them each stage has a "different story to tell," the structure expresses itself in a new narrative. In other words, a qualitatively different story or narrative emerges at each of the five or six stages and their transition points. The narrative exists in a few forms of underlying meaning applicable to all in our culture and across the world. This "story of the stage" is a new version of the old epistemic self.

However, as we have moved from cognition to social cognition and now further into the dimensions of ego, personality, and faith, it is hard to conceive of "the person" as the stage (Basseches, in press). For we are told that the new theoretical focus is not just a form of reasoning but the person's essential "being-in-the-world"—ontology as well as ontogeny. However, a generalized, epistemic self is not the center of a person's *being*. The person, the life's story, or the evolution of the self's important meanings cannot be captured by a stage position. Instead, we need to address the self rooted in the specific experiences that shape a person's life. Only then can we hope to create an appropriate theory where the structural dimensions find their appropriate applications. In such a theory the self integrates a unique set of experiences within biographical patterns available in a given society with tools provided by the developing epistemic self.

One important stumbling block facing those who search for an encompassing perspective has been what Döbert (in this volume) appropriately calls the "content phobia" of investigators in the Piaget-Kohlberg tradition. The unique experiences, as well as the typical biographical paths, are considered mere content in comparison to structure, which provides what one can call the "royal road to the conscious." In analyzing moral judgment theory and research, Döbert argues that the Piagetian indifference to content has exacted a significant price. In my view it led to two problems. Some shied away from exploring new phenomena by restricting the cognitive model to intellectual development. Others embraced a form of "structural imperialism" where almost any new content was viewed as grist for the structural mill. Both approaches share the same problem. They neglected more fundamental questions: When we place cognition in the broader domain of self and personality, do we need to transform our understanding of what we have taken as structure and content? By drawing new distinctions, can we uncover other structuring activities of emotion, cognition, and action that have before been viewed as content?

It is my view that cognitively based theorists have overlooked the central structuring activities of the self by defining the epistemic self as the sole representative of structure. In the process, I believe, the cart was placed before the horse, life history became content to the structure of the epistemic self. Said differently, the five or six generalized perspectives that define ego or faith development were viewed as the organizing principles of that which "makes meaning" in a person's life. Epistemology replaced life history. But as I applied Piagetian ideas to research on the life course and to clinical questions, I became convinced of the power of another narrative—a biographical one. We cannot consider it a Piagetian structure in any strict way, but it reveals a pattern, produces meanings, and provides typical motivations. Biography is not necessarily organized by the most mature social cognitive structure of ego, self, personality, or faith, but it must be viewed as other than content in a Piagetian sense. To call it content is misleading since it is coherent, systematic, and also *organizes* action, cognition, and emotion.

More recently, others have also expressed their doubts about the adequacy of cognitive structural interpretations in the study of lives. Bruner (1986), for example, states that while we know a great deal about a paradigmatic mode of thinking (organized by cognitive, logical, mathematical, and scientific principles), we still know little about what he refers to as narrative structure. This structure, he states, follows the logic of a story line about "the vicissitudes of human intentions." Parks (1986) remains within the Piagetian distinction between structure and content but expands "content" to include guiding images that give shape to a person's self and faith. These positions also return us to Habermas and his ideas on the self.

As mentioned earlier, Habermas states that (1) a theory of self requires dimensions of biography since the unique experiences of one life symbolize the generalized patterns that span across lives, and (2) a focus on biography necessitates an understanding of ways in which earlier selves become incorporated and integrated into the present self organization. We still lack a specific proposal for a theory that details the relationships between transformational and biographical dimensions of self. Habermas states that the earlier resolutions of developmental crises are critical for whatever present-day solutions the self has available. But beyond this rather general idea, neither he nor anyone else has provided a way to systematically relate biography to the self's epistemic organization.

Even Erikson, who combines an interest in early development with a commitment to the developing ego's changing psychosocial tasks, neither systematically describes nor adequately explains their influence upon each other. He asks for further exploration to accomplish this important goal (Erikson, 1968). Similarly, many who have empirically studied the relationship between early development and adult psychological and psychiatric outcome have suggested necessary model-building to help guide research (e.g., Stroufe and Rutter, 1984).

To accomplish this model-building I found it necessary to go beyond "applying structural theory" and to add even more content to already existing stage descriptions. Thus, I began to work toward a new developmental and constructivist approach. This large project required three main steps. The first step was to depart from the overinclusiveness of soft-stage theories and to specify those underlying operations of the self that can with justification be defined in cognitive developmental and structural terms. I explain these operations as a developmental sequence of self complexity resting on the "deep structure" of self perspectives.

The second step was to define a method for studying those configurations of meaning and experience that form a different, albeit related, unity of psychological organization from that formed by structural stages. I chose the term "biography" for this exploration because it is not excessively burdened by previous uses in psychology. Biography expresses that many experiences and relationships have coalesced into some pattern; that the diverse threads that contribute to a tapestry of life generate form and coherence across time and place. I do not define biography in the literary sense, as a genre of writing about a person's past, although I believe that we theorists and researchers can learn a great deal from the novelist's portraits of life in time.

Having established two organizing principles of the self it became essential, as a third step, to place them into relationship with each other. This step was and continues to be the most challenging one. We cannot turn to any existing developmental theory for the answers. Exploring this new relationship will provide an essential and missing key to studying the self processes that constrain and enhance development. We will begin to understand what constitutes the developmental capacities that are at the root of altering the "causality of fate"—not once, but at each point of transformation. Simultaneously, we can learn about those processes that contribute to incomplete generalizations or fragilities in developmental progress, or to developmental arrest. Of course, biological predisposition, physical constitution, and social and historical conditions all contribute to a person's development. Among these variables, I focus on the essential meanings people attribute to themselves and their important relationships.

The Theory of Biography and Transformation

Fundamental processes of self development

Like Piaget and more recent contributors to social cognitive psychology (e.g., Broughton, 1978; Selman,1980; Harter, 1988), Kohlberg and Habermas were influenced by Baldwin, Mead, and the Chicago school of symbolic interactionism. Throughout their lives, Baldwin and Mead searched for a broad and imaginative account of all mental development, including emotions, creativity, morality, religion, and the self.[3] I will touch upon only three of their major ideas that have proven invaluable in formulating the theory of biography and transformation: (1) the self is fundamentally social; (2) the self is organized by an underlying organization of "role-taking"; and (3) the self is based upon internalizations.

1. *The social construction of self* For Baldwin and Mead all experience of self is social, willful, and reflective. Both writers believe that the child is not born with a self but rather derives a self from interactions with others—individuals, groups, and social systems. This thinking gives rise to the idea of the self as a "social structure," or translated into contemporary language, a "social construction." According to Baldwin and Mead, selfhood implies a "Me" or self-consciousness that emerges out of viewing the subjective—the "I"—from the perspective of other selves, groups, or systems. Mead, in fact, points out that "the individual experiences himself as such, not directly, but only indirectly, from the particular standpoints of other individual members of the same social group, or from the generalized standpoint of the social group as a whole to which he belongs" (Mead, 1934, p. 138).

This idea is critical, since most other psychological traditions have led us to view the self as a more isolated, independent, and autonomous entity without real reference to its basic social and interpersonal nature. Freud, for example, viewed the ego primarily as an inhibitor of biological drives and linked it only tenuously to the "object world."

The theory of biography and transformation represents a departure from those theories that locate the self primarily as an internal structure or identity abstracted from the continuous experiences of interpersonal relationships. Like Baldwin and Mead, I view the self not as a weak (ego) rider of a powerful (id) horse, but rather as a basic, organizing principle of interpersonal relationships. The self not only emerges from relationships but is continuously expressive of them. Thus, the construction of self is always a function of the self's relationships to others and should be explored and systematically studied "interpersonally."

"Interpersonally" does not necessarily mean that the only way to study the self is by observation of its transactions with others. Still, many family and small-group researchers have demonstrated that relationships can be studied in this manner. I have found it equally important, however, to define the interpersonal self by the ways a *person constructs* his or her involvement—past and present—in important relationships. This includes how a person feels enhanced by others, offers support, and engages in and resolves conflict. Furthermore, such construction includes those interactions that are viewed as important, satisfying, and reciprocal. Most importantly, it gives definition to how a person expresses intimacy and autonomy.

Defining self, self-esteem, or the "self's treatment of itself" in purely intrapsychic terms creates major problems. Such an approach reinforces the view of the self abstracted from the self's fundamental social nature. Instead, I find the essential categories of self development in what Buber so eloquently described as the "I and thou," the *interrelationship* between self and other. Thus, I believe that in order to understand and study the self, we need to observe the self's experience and its understanding of others and itself in important relationships. In this way, we also find the key to important dimensions of psychopathology and the healing potential of psychotherapy.

The recent theoretical contributions to studying the development of self, relationships, and care have helped refocus our attention to the interpersonal dimensions of self (e.g., Kohut, 1977; Gilligan, 1982). We need to understand, however, how the interpersonal self continues to transform well beyond childhood and in what ways its development represents a general human process, even in the face of important gender differences. These ideas together with the foundation provided by Sullivan (1953) and the advances in Piagetian theory allow for new principles of the interpersonal self. To uncover structural and developmental underpinnings of the interpersonal self, the construct of role-taking and social perspective is critical.

2. *Development of role-taking and social perspective* For Baldwin, self and others exist only through role-taking and engage in continuous role-taking activities. That is, they engage in activities that lead to an understanding that the other is both like and unlike the self and that the other responds to the self in complementary expectations and communications. Role-taking

refers to the idea that knowledge and meaning are constructed in the living exchange between self and others. Those who view role-taking as a purely cognitive process should realize that it involves sharing—a form of social cooperation and co-operative activities between the other and the self. Because the group and "the other" exist before the birth of the self there must be social sharing and cooperation as a motivating force in the self's evolution.

We find here a more positive theory of motivation for the self's development than in traditional psychoanalysis (i.e., drive, drive reduction, and defense). The theory of biography and transformation posits a basic motivation for social coop-eration and interpersonal conflict resolution. White's influen-tial motivational principle of "mastery" (White, 1963) thus emerges with new meanings. The self's needs for intimacy and autonomy, for closeness and distance, for the establishment and reorganization of boundaries, require permanent negoti-ation. The self's development always progresses in relationship to a mastery of these interpersonal processes. While role-taking provides basic principles to order these diverse psychological dimensions, much work remains to tie the general and abstract principles to specific processes of the interpersonal self's development.

3. *Processes of internalization* The importance of internalization in the development of self is prominent in Mead's and Bald-win's theories. The child's self and the child's knowledge about others grow simultaneously. In Baldwin's theory of the "bipolar self," what is called self is an incorporation of what earlier was called other. This notion makes internalization a fundamental process in self development, an idea also found in the influ-ential developmental and social theory of Vygotsky (1986) from which I have drawn. Throughout his work, Vygotsky relates culture to individual development. One quotation crystallizes his position on self: "We are aware of ourselves, for we are aware of others, and in the same way as we know others; and this is as it is because in relation to ourselves we are in the same position as others are to us" (Vygotsky, 1979). Vygotsky viewed the intrapersonal processes as internalized interper-sonal relationships. For example he writes: "Each function in

the child's cultural development appears twice: first on the social level and later on the individual level; first between people (interpsychological), and then inside the child (intrapsychological)" (Vygotsky, 1978). These ideas bring him into close proximity to the symbolic interactionists.

For Mead and Baldwin, imitation and identification are ways in which internalization occurs. These processes have been reviewed in detail in another publication (Noam, Kohlberg, and Snarey, 1983). For the purposes of this chapter, it is important to remember only that the symbolic interactionists view internalization as part of the normal and continuous exchanges between parents and children as well as among peers. It is not a response to frustration or loss as it has been in primarily classical psychoanalysis.

While I have found myself in agreement with this more positive and health-oriented understanding of internalization, I have found that an encompassing self theory also has to address typical negative consequences of internalization. It has been my observation that critical and self-attacking voices are little more than internalized interaction patterns that continue to exist in the self. For this purpose the history of social interactions and their internalizations—presented not as an account of what "once really was" but as a *living biography* of important relationships—becomes extremely relevant to our explorations.

We begin to enter uncharted territory when we expand the general principles introduced by Baldwin and Mead in the direction of a lifespan-transformational and biographical self. How are we to understand from a social developmental point of view the role of internalized relationships? Is there a living biography of self-other relationships that continues to shape the person's choices, experiences, and self-understandings? If so, how does this biographical dimension of self relate to the development of role-taking and new internalizations throughout life? To try to answer these questions we must trace simultaneously the developmental line of self-other complexity (schemata) and a biographical structure (themata). The three basic ideas presented above—the social construction of self, the development of role-taking and social perspective, and the processes of internalization—define and unite the two structures of self.

Schemata: Self perspectives and development of self complexity

Out of the principles just mentioned, I have formulated a developmental line of self-other complexity. It always represents the developmentally most mature side of the self. Through continuous assimilation and accommodation between the organism and the environment the self is challenged to establish increasingly more complex views about itself and important others. These self schemata are not only related to thought, although their development is made possible by advances in the cognitive realm. At each new developmental position typical affects, meanings, and motivations emerge. Each stage brings out new strengths and opportunities to rework past vulnerabilities. But each new system of self complexity can also lead to new weaknesses or to more complex forms of old maldevelopments. For that reason I do not assume that higher stages of self complexity are better, truer, or more mature psychological adaptations. For example, self complexity can be applied in the service of self-deception. Nonetheless, the hierarchical ordering of self complexity points to the potential of a lifelong transformation of the ways we view ourselves and important others.

Past publications have discussed this stage description in some detail (e.g., Noam, 1988c; Noam et al., in press) allowing here for a brief summary. My view on self complexity builds on an underlying logic of what I term *self perspective*. This term conveys that the theories of Baldwin, Mead, Kohlberg, and Selman on role-taking and social perspective have been of great value to my own work. Especially helpful has been Selman's (1980) operationalization of these concepts through a variety of developmental studies on the evolution of perspective-taking in childhood and adolescence. However, he as well as others who have employed a role-taking or social perspective approach (e.g., Chandler, 1973; Flavell, 1977) have not taken the necessary step of developing an explicit theory of self. I introduce the term "self perspective" to refer to those aspects of social perspective-taking that make up the underlying logic of the interpersonal self.

This approach contrasts with that of Loevinger and Kegan. As mentioned before, Loevinger has not defined an underlying organizational system that gives developmental coherence to her ego stages. Kegan has done so, but has introduced categories that supposedly organize not only the ego and the self but most other developmental domains (e.g., intelligence, morality, perspective-taking, faith, etc.) under the heading of subject-object differentiation. I have described the arguments against such a strategy earlier. In contrast, I view "self perspective" as a domain-specific psychological function that serves to understand the specific issues of self development (and not those of moral, intellectual, and faith development, etc.). The brief descriptions that follow show that the stages of the interpersonal self parallel, rather than incorporate, Kohlberg's and Piaget's domains.

The first stage is defined by what I term *subjective-physical self perspective*. This perspective on self and other permits no consideration of the other's interests and desires as different from the self's. There is an emerging awareness of the distinction of physical and psychological characteristics in people, but actions are mostly evaluated in terms of physical consequences. Impulsive responses are typical and feelings are expressed in action language. Strength is the emerging ability to distinguish between fantasy and reality, to pursue wishes and desires by translating them into directed action, to show strong will, and to demonstrate an independent curiosity. These strengths are in part based on achievement of object constancy, on the knowledge that the other continues to exist even when separations occur. The weakness is an emphasis on wish fulfillment, seeing others as suppliers and being dependent on them. This self perspective gives rise to a dichotomous view of being or acting good or bad. In the process, the self hides from or submits to powerful authority figures that can inflict physical harm or punishment.

The *reciprocal-instrumental self perspective* gives rise to the possibility of defining the self's interests and goals as separate from the intent of others. Conflicting interests between self and other are usually resolved through instrumental exchange. The person can step out of the concrete bounds of the self, thus creating two-way reciprocity. This perspective also changes the internal perspective-taking ability. There is now the conceptual distinction between the outer appearance of the "public self" and the "inner hidden self." This creates the possibility of planned deception through which the self can impose its boundaries. Conflict usually does not lead to submission or impulsive action, but to self-protective assertion of control. The positive outcome is the mastery of the instrumental world, the ability to control feelings and to concentrate on tasks. The limitation of the reciprocal-instrumental stage is the isolation of two exchange partners whose relationship is not primarily guided by trust and altruism but, rather, by self-interest. This often leads to opportunism, exploitation, and manipulation.

With the *mutual-inclusive self perspective* a person understands others in relationship and this understanding is coordinated through a generalized perspective. The person experiences different points of view according to the Golden Rule of seeing reality through the eyes of another person. This perspective creates the context for altruistic actions and for surpassing the bounds of self-interest. Attitudes and values are seen as persisting over time, often leading to stereotypes like "I am that kind of person." These self-traits in addition to the new internal perspective lead to more complex self-observational capacities. The limitations of this stage, however, are an overidentification with the views of the other and the dangers of conformist social behavior. It is crucial for the self to be liked and appreciated in order to feel a sense of esteem. Typical feelings of low self-esteem and a proneness to experience depression and anxiety are linked to a sense of abandonment and feeling "lost in the world."

The *systemic-organizational self perspective* makes possible the distinction between the societal point of view and the interpersonal one. Multiple mutual perspectives can be integrated into a broader systems view. When the self takes a systemic perspective on relationships, the communication between people is seen as existing on a number of levels simultaneously. Individual relations are interpreted in terms of their place within a larger system of consciously defined roles and rules. System-maintenance of the self becomes the hallmark of this stage. The person views the self as having control over his or her destiny. It is also the point, however, at which one realizes the existence of parts of the self not easily managed by the system's control—conscious or unconscious. The societal perspective also brings out strong motivations of achievement, duty, and competition. The limitation of the systemic self-other perspective is the attempt to overcontrol self and other, to reflect on social relations too much in terms of power, role, and status, and to take so many perspectives on self and other that obsessive-compulsive indecision can result.[4]

Like the soft-stage theorists discussed earlier, I was at first intrigued by the possibility of capturing a real-life "developmental narrative" by applying a structural stage analysis. However, each time I pursued such a path, I ended up forcing clinical material or research interview data into ill-suited categories. Frequently, I ended up viewing central information as mere content, even though I could see that, in fact, it had unifying and structuring power. Alternatively, I grouped the material into given stage definitions, at which point the descriptions began to resemble loosely connected amalgamations of traits, experiences, processes, and functions—an action I criticized earlier. I realized that I was about to confuse the *most complex side of the self* with the *entirety of the self*, as soft-stage theorists in the Kohlberg tradition have done and continue to do.

For example, a detailed story told in an interview about a passionate relationship to work and discovery might "earn" a subject the evaluation of being "Stage 4." But what are the specific meanings of this passion? What biographical issues is the person reencountering? What is being worked out, or worked into the present-day organization? I began to value these questions rather than to treat them as "leftovers" or contents to the all-important structure. This meant to describe those aspects of the past that remain alive in the present and to coordinate those meanings with a continued developmental transformational view of self. I found that biography is not only a reconstruction at each new stage of self complexity, but that biographical dimensions also influence the shape, dynamics, and continued fate of developmental stages.

Themata: Biographical structures of self

Many have struggled with the issues of thematic continuities in life history. Of course, most importantly, Freud's discovery of the repetition compulsion opened entirely new ways of understanding the role early experiences play in character formation and continuities of psychopathology. Influenced by this discovery others have followed in outlining basic psychological issues, styles, or themes that organize adaptations to life (e.g., Adler, Jung, Bowlby, etc.). More recently these organizers of life history have been referred to variously as narratives, metaphors, scripts, life projects, or working models. While clinicians and literary theorists have with some ease applied these ideas, empirical investigations have been slow in coming. Nonetheless, there is now a growing body of research. Csikszentmihalyi and Beattie (1979), for example, have conducted a study on "life themes," defined as hierarchical affective-cognitive systems composed of a central existential problem. Another example is provided by the research, begun by Murray and pursued by many, on fantasy productions using the Thematic Apperception Test.

Despite significant differences in terminology, definition, and research strategy all these theoretical, clinical, and research perspectives share in a conviction that life themes organize a multitude of life experiences into key interpersonal or intrapsychic patterns. These patterns form for individuals a basic frame of reference that is used to understand, explore, and respond to reality. Beyond these unifying convictions however, the development of theory and research has been hindered by important conceptual shortcomings. Many theorists in the psychodynamic tradition have yet to embrace a lifespan-developmental approach and thus interpret themes as emerging early and retaining their early, unaltered form.

The issues arising out of locating thematic and narrative origins have led to interesting recent debates in psychoanalysis. In growing numbers theorists view the reconstruction of life history not as a return to a "real past" but to the narrative construction of a fitting metaphor (e.g., Spence, 1982; Stern, 1985). While these approaches strengthen a psychoanalytic strand of constructivism and facilitate innovative discussions, we find in these contributions no language for the systematic transformations of biographical constructions at different positions of the lifespan. Thus, we find little help from previous work when we establish a bridge between thematic continuities and transformations in self organization.

We now turn to the view provided by the theory of biography and transformation. The theory posits that despite situational variability and powerful developmental discontinuities each person has core issues that help organize the many events, relationships, and contexts encountered in a life. Because of the basic organizing nature of these themes, I view them as biographical structures and call them "themata." Gerald Holton has used the term with a different connotation to describe themes in the history of scientific discoveries. In the present context, themata refer to life themes that create a frame of knowing, experiencing, and relating in the ongoing relationship between person and environment. They further convey four points: (1) that multiple life experiences are organized into key interpersonal and intrapsychic patterns of adaptation; (2) that these patterns can be described and defined in terms of some basic existential themes; (3) that they have a certain enduring quality, spanning time and space; (4) that they contribute to the organizing of behavior, cognition, and affect.

This last point especially calls attention to the incomplete position of constructive developmental perspective and soft-stage theories in which only the most complex self organization is viewed as having structuring power. Themata cannot be relegated to mere "content" since they provide structuring frames on our basic ways of knowing the world. To deepen our understanding of themata I will return to the principles of the self and address the notions of construction, internalization, and the interpersonal self.

Themata are constructions of meanings about the self's evolution, not objective accounts of life history. Every new clinician or researcher makes the discovery that it is impossible to predict the qualitative or quantitative effect of certain events on patients or research subjects. One learns that it is the meanings people attribute to these events that make them formative, powerful, or traumatic. And only those meanings that have an enduring quality should be labeled as biographical. For that reason, I use the term *living biography* in contrast to lived life history. "Living" conveys that these constructions still shape a person's way of being. Once they have become *history* they have been reflected upon, worked through, and have lost their organizing power. This leads us to the second issue, that of internalization.

The reason biography continues to shape experience long after original events have occurred and social environments have ceased to exist is that experiences and actions become internalized. Interestingly, this is the same process through which schemata get established. Schemata, however, are defined by generalizable logic of knowing, understanding, and role-taking. Thematic structures are concerned with internalization of specific relationships and relationship patterns. These relationships are specific, their affective valences and cognitive understandings are tied to meanings transmitted through the generations, to family constellation and life circumstances.

For this reason it is natural to assume that themata refer to one life rather than to many. Since internalization and social construction are always part of the relationship between self and others in friendship, family, and community, themes emerge individually. They are the stamp of identity as important as the name, making the one life different from all others. Living biography is a personal expression of the meanings of one life lived and unfolding. Nonetheless, there are generalizable patterns. From each life, one can generalize to the many lives that solidly embed the individual in his or her cohort and the historic moment. From each life one can also generalize to the epistemic structures.

Uncovering the relationship between the specific and the general, the biographical self and the epistemic self, makes this work particularly challenging. The theory of biography and transformation posits that early life history does not just get replayed. Thus, we can rarely find life history that is not also filtered through the self's most mature developmental position. There is also no expression of the self that exists in a vacuum, abstracted from its genesis. Each level of organization requires its own descriptions and explanations. The two structures have their own shape and properties, yet each structure affects the other. The experiences in one structure will reframe experience of the other. Each frame is incomplete and thus we are required to focus on both for an encompassing view of self.

There are two main ways in which themata can produce constraints in development and interact with more complex self positions. I call the first "encapsulations" and the second "problem pathways." These are discussed in greater detail in Noam 1986a, 1986b, 1988b, 1988c.

Encapsulations are old meaning systems that are guided by the cognitive and affective logic that governed at the time the encapsulation occurred. Prone to significant distortions, internalized earlier environments and important others often become tied to powerful meanings and strong emotions. Persons remain loyal to them even when they are not adaptive and create a great deal of pain and conflict in the self. Often the loss involved in detachment from them is experienced as greater than the gains anticipated in development. If the present interpersonal world provides opportunities for transformation, a partial transformation can occur, one that does not generalize to all aspects of the self and is the source of encapsulations.

The assertion that individuals can develop in some areas only, functioning consequently at multiple developmental levels, is in line with some of the findings of recent neo-Piagetian research (e.g., Fischer, 1980). Most explanations of development asynchrony state that the limited generalization of transformation is due to a lack of opportunity to try new skills. From the perspective of the self, I am suggesting an additional interpersonal interpretation for the discrepancies: internal relationships can keep a person from experimenting with possible new situations and responses. This is why, for example, impulse control or the ability to delay needs does not necessarily reach mature levels even when an understanding of interpersonal relationships may have done so.

The model of encapsulations does not correspond with psychoanalytic fixation theory. Even when aspects of the self do not join the overall thrust of development, it is essential to understand the continued developmental path of the self and to view what is left behind always in relation to the more mature self positions. Furthermore, fixations refer to early experiences, and encapsulations can occur at any developmental level throughout life. Finally, I view the overassimilative activity as a process that returns us not to a real past but rather to a living biography.

Encapsulations are concepts less concerned with momentary regressions than with systematic ways of viewing self and world. They are tied to themata in that biographical views have become basic in guiding belief systems. Used in this context, a belief is a meaning system that is not truly tested against an external reality but follows an internal logic less developed than the most mature stage of self complexity. In therapy, testing, or in-depth interviews it usually becomes quite apparent that even though certain beliefs do not hold up to close scrutiny, they still exert a strong hold over the person. Continued development of the themata will influence these basic beliefs, but a great deal of the energy that is needed to maintain these less differentiated thoughts and feelings cannot be subsumed under the most mature aspect of the self.

Depending on the developmental level the encapsulations are associated with, they can be more "physical" (based on magical thinking, focused on the body-self and images of bodily survival during physical separations), "concrete action oriented" (based on a view of the self as an agent that acts on the world or needs to manipulate the world deceptively to achieve need gratification), or "psychological" (a state where needs are expressed in symbolic form around identifications with others).

While encapsulations refer to hierarchical discrepancies in the self, *problem pathways* refer to maladaptive themes that have undergone developmental transformation in line with the maturation of self complexity. Under the pathway model, the negative biographical themes are being transformed to ever more complex levels. They help us understand how it is possible to be at more complex developmental positions and yet be less adapted. With greater developmental self complexity comes the possibility for greater complexity of negative self-image and more internalized and toxic self-hate.

For example, when the individual is at the mutual-inclusive stage, we expect to see themes of self-definition through group membership. We further expect concern about other's acceptance of self. In contrast, at the reciprocal-instrumental stage we can expect to find preoccupations that reveal a need for concrete control and mastery. There is a thematic focus on behaving in consonance or discordance with other's rules placed on the self. There is generally an orientation toward people as either "being on my side" or "curtailing my freedom." But these themes must not be understood as a function of the continued evolution of the self alone.

For a person at the mutual-inclusive stage, it is important to determine whether the concern for acceptance by others is fueled by a theme that the self will be abandoned and is not worthy of love. Similarly, it is necessary to explore whether the person at the reciprocal-instrumental stage believes that there is no possibility for intimate relationships because earlier experiences have been hurtful. In that case, the need for concrete control is linked to a belief that giving up control will lead to abandonment. Thus biographical themes become transformed but continue on a problem pathway.

Conclusion

This paper introduces a new framework that owes a great deal to the innovative work of Kohlberg and Habermas. It presents a number of ideas that provide the necessary steps toward new theory development. I have shown that Kohlberg's and Habermas's far-reaching contributions have implications not only for the moral domain but also for social development and for a theory of self. However, with regard to the self Kohlberg and the social cognitive school remained too closely tied to the specific shortcomings of Piaget's paradigm. In the process, the epistemic subject became the sole representative of self, leading to a loss of central biographical and life historic dimensions. While Kohlberg recognized this problem, it was exacerbated by those who tried to fix it: the structural theorists of self, ego, personality, and faith. Hard-stage principles were inappropriately transferred to soft-stage domains. Not only were structural categories overstretched by myriad biological, technological, or psychological dimensions and processes, but the self remained an epistemic unit existing in five or six stage varieties. As a consequence, the biographical self, the person's core evolution of meaning-making, got lost even further.

We saw that Habermas's ideas about identity and ego autonomy provide important building blocks for a broadened social developmental theory of self. While he is strongly influenced by the cognitive developmental model, he brings in a rationally reconstructed psychoanalysis that provides a more encompassing and truer account of the relationship between moral development and ego identity. He places the epistemic subject into a context where personal identity and "causality of fate" play a critical role in determining the relationship between autonomy and moral judgment. However, his few writings on this topic have produced neither an encompassing theory of self nor specific approaches to studying the relationship between a biographical component in personal identity and the general principles of the epistemic subject.

First steps in this direction have now been taken. The approach described in this chapter creates a wider constructivist lens by relating qualitative reorganizations of self to essential biographical themes. This approach, along with research and clinical observations, can create the new insights needed to revitalize structural theory. For example, we can point to the relationship between moral judgments and moral actions. Despite the great deal of thinking and research that has gone into this relationship (see Blasi, 1980, 1983), we still know very little. As long as exploration is not furthered on moral judgments as part of the meanings they hold in a person's life, we will not progress significantly. To do so requires an appropriate theory of self.

In building a new frame we recast Freud's observations about the repetitive nature of biography and free them from unnecessary reductions to early childhood. We simultaneously redefine Piaget's disembodied and epistemic subject. By doing so, we are not only going beyond Freud and Piaget but simultaneously returning to their great observations, and to the profound insights on the self generated by the symbolic interactionists almost one hundred years ago.

Notes

1. McCarthy (1978) provides a good introduction to Habermas's complex theory. There is, as yet, no comparable introduction to the entirety of Kohlberg's work.

2. This passage introduces consciousness and freedom as central dimensions in moral and self development. Here I can only point to the important discussion of this question by Blasi (in Loevinger, 1976). He argues that structuralist theory has a limited ability to address self-consciousness and freedom since these dimensions of psychological or social structure are by definition conceptualized as aspects of a whole. Thus notions of autonomy and postconventionality need to be tied to conceptualizations of consciousness and freedom *from existing structures.*

3. Detailed descriptions of Baldwin's developmental account can be found in Noam, Kohlberg, and Snarey (1983), and Kohlberg, Hart, and Wertsch (1987)

4. The empirical validation of this construct has been of great importance as a corrective to this theoretical proposal. My colleagues and I have introduced a method of empirically evaluating the various self-complexity positions based on a clinical-research "self interview" (Noam et al., in press). This measure now makes it possible to explore in great detail self-complexity in typical and atypical development.

References

Baldwin, J. M. (1906). *Social and ethical interpretations in mental development.* New York: Grune and Stratton.

Basseches, M. (in press). Toward a constructive-developmental understanding of the dialectics of individuality and irrationality. In D. A. Kramer and N. J. Bopp (Eds.), *Transformation in clinical and developmental psychology.* New York: Springer Verlag.

Blasi, A. (1980). Bridging moral judgment and moral action: A critical review of the literature. *Psychological Bulletin,* 88:1–45.

Blasi, A. (1983). The self and cognition. In B. Lee and G. Noam (Eds.), *Developmental approaches to the self.* New York: Plenum.

Broughton, J. (1978). The development of concepts of self, mind, reality, and knowledge. In W. Damon (Ed.), *New directions in child development. Vol. 1: Social Cognition.* San Francisco: Jossey-Bass.

Broughton, J., and Zahaykevich, M. (1977). Review of J. Loevinger's *Ego Development. Telos,* 32:246–53.

Bruner, J. (1986). *Actual minds, possible worlds.* Cambridge, MA: Harvard University Press.

Chandler, M. (1973). Egocentrism and antisocial behavior: The assessment and training of social perspective-taking skills. *Developmental Psychology,* 9:326–332.

Csikszentmihalyi, M., and Beattie, O. V. (1979). Life themes: A theoretical and empirical exploration of their origins and effects. *Journal of Humanistic Psychology,* 19:45–63.

Damon, W., and Hart, D. (1982). The development of self-understanding from infancy through adolescence. *Child Development,* 53:841–864.

Döbert, R., Habermas, J., and Nunner-Winkler, G. (1977). Zur Einführung. In R. Döbert, J. Habermas, and G. Nunner-Winkler (Eds.), *Entwicklung des Ichs.* Cologne: Kiepenheuer and Witsch.

Erikson, E. (1950). *Childhood and society.* New York: Norton.

Erikson, E. (1968). *Insight and responsibility.* New York: Norton.

Fischer, K. W. (1980). A theory of cognitive development: The control and construction of hierarchies of skills. *Psychological Review,* 87:477–531.

Flavell, J. H. (1977). *Cognitive development.* Englewood Cliffs, NJ: Prentice Hall.

Fowler, J. W. (1981). *Stages of faith.* New York: Harper and Row.

Gilligan, C. (1982). *In a different voice.* Cambridge, MA: Harvard University Press.

Habermas, J. (1971). *Knowledge and human interests.* Boston: Beacon Press.

Habermas, J. (1979). Moral development and ego identity. In J. Habermas, *Communication and the evolution of society.* Boston: Beacon Press.

Harter, S. (1988). Developmental and dynamic changes in the nature of the self-concept. In S. Shirk (Ed.), *Cognitive development and child psychotherapy.* New York: Plenum.

James, W. (1890). *Principles of psychology.* New York: Holt.

Jay, M. (1973). *The dialectical imagination: A history of the Frankfurt School and the Institute of Social Research, 1923–1950.* Boston: Little Brown.

Kegan, R. (1982). *The evolving self.* Cambridge, MA: Harvard University Press.

Kohlberg, L. (1969). Stage and sequence: The cognitive-developmental approach to socialization. In D. Goslin (Ed.), *Handbook of socialization, theory and research.* New York: Rand-McNally. Reprinted in Kohlberg (1984).

Kohlberg, L. (1971). From is to ought: How to commit the naturalistic fallacy and get away with it in the study of moral development. In T. Mischel (Ed.), *Cognitive development and epistemology*. New York: Academic Press. Reprinted in Kohlberg (1984).

Kohlberg, L. (1984). *Essays on moral development. Vol. 2: The psychology of moral development.* San Francisco: Harper and Row.

Kohlberg, L., and Diessner, R. (in press). A cognitive-developmental approach to moral attachment. In J. Gewirtz and J. Kurtines (Eds.), *Moral development*. Hillsdale, NJ: Erlbaum.

Kohlberg, L., Hart, D., and Wertsch, J. (1987). The developmental social self theories of James Mark Baldwin, George Herbert Mead and Lev Seminovich Vygotsky. In L. Kohlberg (Ed.), *Child psychology and childhood education*. New York: Longman.

Kohut, H. (1977). *The restoration of the self*. New York: International Universities Press.

Loevinger, J. (1976). *Ego development*. San Francisco: Jossey-Bass.

Lorenzer, A. (1970). *Sprachzerstörung und Rekonstruktion*. Frankfurt: Suhrkamp.

McCarthy, T. (1978). *The critical theory of Jürgen Habermas*. Cambridge, MA: MIT Press.

Mead, G. H. (1934). *Mind, self, and society*. Chicago: University of Chicago Press.

Noam, G. (1984). *Self, morality, and biography: Studies in clinical-developmental psychology*. Doctoral dissertation, Harvard University, Cambridge, MA.

Noam, G. (1985). Stage, phase, and style: The developmental dynamics of the self. In M. Berkowitz and F. Oser (Eds.), *Moral education: Theory and application*. Hillsdale, NJ: Erlbaum.

Noam, G. (1986a). Borderline personality disorders and the theory of biography and transformation (Part 1). *McLean Hospital Journal*, 11:19–43.

Noam, G. (1986b). The theory of biography and transformation and the borderline personality disorders: A developmental typology (Part 2). *McLean Hospital Journal*, 11:79–105.

Noam, G. (1988a). A constructivist approach to developmental psychopathology. In E. D. Nannis and P. A. Cowan (Eds.), *New directions in child development. Vol. 39: Developmental psychopathology and its treatment*. San Francisco: Jossey-Bass.

Noam, G. (1988b). The self, adult development and the theory of biography and transformation. In D. Lapsley and C. Power (Eds.), *Self, ego and identity*. New York: Springer Verlag.

Noam, G. (1988c). The structural theory of biography and transformation: Foundation for clinical-developmental therapy. In S. Shirk (Ed.), *Cognitive development and child psychotherapy*. New York: Plenum Press.

Noam, G. (1988d). Self-complexity and self integration: Theory and therapy in clinical-developmental psychology. *Journal for Moral Education*, 17:230–245.

Noam, G., Hauser, S., Santostefano, S., Garrison, R., Jacobson, A., Powers, S., and Mead, M. (1984). Ego development and psychopathology: A study of hospitalized adolescents. *Child Development*, 55:184–194.

Noam, G., Kohlberg, L., and Snarey, J. (1983). Steps toward a model of the self. In B. Lee and G. Noam (Eds.), *Developmental approaches to the self*. New York: Plenum Press.

Noam, G., Powers, S., Kilkenny, R., and Beedy, J. (in press). The interpersonal self in lifespan-developmental perspective. In R. Lerner, P. Baltes, and D. Featherman (Eds.), *Lifespan development and behavior* (Vol. 10). Hillsdale, NJ: Erlbaum.

Parks, S. (1986) Imagination and spirit in faith development: A way past the structure-content dichotomy. In W. Dyksta and S. Parks (Eds.), *Faith development and Fowler*. Birmingham, AL: Religious Education Press.

Peck, R. F., and Havighurst R. (1960). *The psychology of character development*. New York: Wiley.

Piaget, J. (1952). *The origins of intelligence in children*. New York: International Universities Press. (Original work published 1936)

Rogers, L. (1987). *Developmental psychopathology: Studies in adolescent and adult experiences of psychological dysfunction*. Doctoral dissertation, Harvard University, Cambridge, MA.

Selman, R. L. (1980). *The growth of interpersonal understanding: Developmental and clinical analyses*. New York: Academic Press.

Snarey, J., Kohlberg, L., and Noam, G. (1983). Ego development. *Developmental Review*, 3:303–338.

Spence, D. P. (1982). *Narrative truth and historical truth: Meaning and interpretation in psychoanalysis*. New York: Norton.

Stern, D. N. (1985). *The interpersonal world of the infant: A view from psychoanalysis and developmental psychology*. New York: Basic Books.

Stroufe, L. A., and Rutter, M. (1984). The domain of developmental psychopathology. *Child Development*, 55:17–29.

Sullivan, H.S. (1953). *The interpersonal theory of psychiatry*. New York: Norton.

Vygotsky, L. (1978). *Mind in society*. Cambridge, MA: Harvard University Press.

Vygotsky, L. (1979). Consciousness as a problem of psychology of behavior. *Soviet Psychology*, 170:29–30.

Vygotsky, L. (1986). *Thought and language*. Cambridge, MA: MIT Press.

Werner, H. (1948). *Comparative psychology of mental development*. New York: International University Press.

White, R. (1963). Ego and reality in psychoanalytic theory: A proposal regarding independent ego energies. *Psychological Issues*, 3:1–210.

Contributors

Augusto Blasi is a professor in the Psychology Department of the University of Massachusetts at Boston. His research interests and principal publications are in the areas of moral cognition, the development of self-identity, and the relationship between responsibility and behavior.

Dwight R. Boyd is Associate Professor in the Department of History and Philosophy of Education, Ontario Institute for Studies in Education (Toronto). His publications and current research lie at the intersection of moral philosophy, developmental psychology, and philosophy of education, with particular reference to the role of the teacher and to issues of gender and multiculturalism.

Rainer Döbert is Privatdozent at the Institute for Sociology at the Free University of Berlin and Research Fellow at the Wissenschaftszentrum Berlin. He has published books and articles on religious evolution, as well as on moral and ego development. He is presently engaged in a research project on the ethical dimensions of the science-value connection.

Wolfgang Edelstein is Professor at the Free University of Berlin and Co-director of the Max Planck Institute of Human Development and Education (Berlin). His research is in the interface of development and socialization in the areas of cognition and sociomoral development. He has published numerous books and papers in scientific journals in developmental psychology, sociology, and education.

Jürgen Habermas is Professor of Philosophy at the University of Frankfurt am Main. He is the leading representative of the Frankfurt School, whose social theory over the last decades has been largely shaped by his writings on philosophy, sociology, linguistics, and psychology. His work on discourse ethics was especially influential on, and influenced by, the cognitive developmental theory of Kohlberg.

Helen Haste is Lecturer in Psychology at the University of Bath in England. Her publications and current research deal with the nature and interrelationships of moral, political, and social development, as well as the relationship between career and values, the social psychological aspects of sex roles (especially the nature and effect of stereotyping), and the social image of science.

Monika Keller is a developmental psychologist and research fellow at the Max Planck Institute of Human Development and Education (Berlin). Her main research area is developmental psychology, specifically social cognitive and moral development. She is the author and editor of books on the development and socialization of social cognition, and has published articles in Germany and America on social cognition and moral development.

Lawrence Kohlberg was Professor of Education and Social Psychology and Director of the Center for Moral Education at Harvard University until his death in 1987. His cognitive developmental approach to socialization and moral judgment is one of the most important contributions of the latter half of this century to social psychology, influencing not only psychologists but also numerous philosophers, educators, and social scientists.

Charles Levine is Associate Professor in the Department of Sociology at the University of Western Ontario. His recent publications and research interests focus on the structural basis of Kohlberg's theory, relations between Kohlberg's and Erikson's work, and adolescent socialization.

Mordecai Nisan is Professor of Educational Psychology in the School of Education at the Hebrew University of Jerusalem. His main publications and research interests have to do with moral development and behavior, human motivation, and self-control.

Gil Noam is a clinical psychologist in the Department of Psychiatry in the Harvard Medical School of McLean Hospital, and Director of Evaluation Research for its Hall-Mercer Children's Center. His research interests and publications are concerned with the relationship between cognitive development and psychoanalytic theory, social interaction, self-interpretation, and communicative discourse.

Gertrud Nunner-Winkler is a sociologist and research fellow at the Max Planck Institute for Psychological Research (Munich). She has published several books and articles on educational sociology and, with R. Döbert, on adolescence crisis, identity formation and moral development, the development of suicide understanding, the problem of judgment and action, and the question of female morality. She is presently engaged in a research project on the development of moral understanding and moral motivation in early childhood.

Bill Puka is Associate Professor of Philosophy at Rensselaer Polytechnic Institute. His doctoral work at Harvard was a blend of philosophy and psychology. His publications include studies of Rawls's moral philosophy, as well as various critiques and defenses of Kohlberg's theory of moral development and Gilligan's conception of caring. He was a Congressional Fellow of the American Philosophical Association, working as legislative aide on issues of economic democracy and employee ownership.

Ernst Tugendhat is Professor of Philosophy at the Free University of Berlin, where he teaches philosophy of language and moral philosophy. He has published numerous books and articles in English and German on these and other philosophical topics.

Thomas Wren is Professor of Philosophy at Loyola University of Chicago, where he teaches moral philosophy and philosophical psychology. He has published books and articles on these topics as well as on moral motivation, the philosophy of human action, and a variety of historical figures including Spinoza, Hume, Macmurray, and Kohlberg.

Index

Abortion, 21, 31, 33, 103, 104, 116, 117
Activism, 316, 317, 322–325, 342, 347–354
Adler, Alfred, 389
Adorno, Theodor W., 366
Affect, and cognition, 22, 315–356
Agapeism, 194
Aggression, 356n1
Akrasia, 24, 293, 317, 319, 321, 326
Alexy, R., 250n1
Allport, Gordon W., 25
Altruism, 25, 203, 221n4, 287, 303, 387
  and care, 194
  as a moral domain, 44, 49
  motives of, and moral motives, 84, 263, 264
Andrews, Molly, 323, 347–348, 351
Apel, Karl-Otto, 228, 234, 245, 249
Aretaic ethics, vs. deontological, 22, 32
Aristotle, 25, 238, 247
  ethics of the polis, 238–239
  neo-Aristotelianism, 226
  theory of justice, 81–85
  virtue conceptions, 194
Aron, I. E., 149n4
Aronfreed, Justin, 26
Assimilation and accommodation, 22, 385
Attachment, 364, 374
Attanucci, Jane, 194
Attitudes, 132, 137
  objectivating vs. performative, 137–140, 143–146, 149n5
Attribution theorists, 25
Authority, and obedience, 43, 45, 48–49, 65, 255, 264, 277

Autonomy
  and justice, 192–193, 201–203
  and moral agency, 163, 165, 167, 229–230
  as a moral ideal, 94, 134
  and self development, 368, 382, 395, 396n2

Baier, Kurt, 158
Baldwin, James Mark, 360, 365, 369, 396n3
  theory of the self, 380–385
Baltes, Paul B., 351
Bandura, Albert, 26
Bartlett, F. C., 332
Basseches, M., 377
Baumrind, Diana, 51
Beattie, O. V., 389
Behaviorism, 27, 80, 374
  neobehaviorists, 20, 27, 28
Belenky, Mary F., 347
Beneficence, 43, 65, 67, 154, 264
Benevolence (care), 49, 84–85, 111, 115–118. See also Care, and responsibility ethics; Gilligan, Carol; Justice and benevolence
Benhabib, S., 149n4
Benson, S. M., 303
Bentham, Jeremy, 34n2
Berkowitz, Marvin W., 138
Bernhardt, Michael, 16
Bertram, H., 13
Biography, 73, 122, 238, 242, 247
  and the self, 360–396
Blackburne-Stover, G., 347
Blasi, Augusto, 25, 29, 30, 38, 48, 129, 395

Blasi, Augusto (cont.)
  and personal identity, 310, 363, 370, 396n2
  and personal responsibility, 31, 286
Block, J. H., 326, 327
Blum, Lawrence, A., 39, 255, 264
Bovet, Pierre, 13, 256
Bowlby, John, 389
Boyd, Dwight R., 129, 149n4, 153, 158
  with Kohlberg and Levine, 151, 228, 234, 297, 328
Bridgeman, D., 47
Broughton, John M., 39, 138, 323, 371, 380
  on Gilligan, 264, 280
  as a "soft-stage" theorist, 93
  theory of self, 370
Brown, Roger, 286–287
Bruner, Jerome, 378
Buber, Martin, 382
Bundesministerium für Jugend, Familie und Gesundheit (BMJFG), 117
Burton, Roger V., 25

Calley, William, 29, 103
Candee, Daniel, 103
  with Kohlberg, 16, 29–30, 60–61, 102–103, 286–287, 297, 326
Care. See also Gilligan, Carol; Justice and benevolence
  Lyons's scoring system, 195
  and responsibility ethics, 42, 49, 165–166, 176, 182, 184–185, 192, 265
Categorical imperative, 111–112, 172, 228, 230, 235, 242
Cattell, R. B., 25
Chandler, M., 385
Character, 34, 94, 211, 220, 236, 372
  formation and psychopathology, 389
  neopsychoanalytic psychologists, 364
Characterological research, 80
Cognition and affect. See Affect and cognition
Cognitive behavior therapy, 374
Cognitive conflict, 140
Cognitive dissonance, 23
Cognitive processes (cognitive operations), 24, 153, 165, 286
Colby, Anne, 113, 125n, 138, 186, 221, 269, 277
Commitment, 122. See also Moral commitment
  development in friendship, 255–280
Communication theory, 244
Communicative action, 233, 235, 245
Communicative competence, 329

Complementarity thesis, 139–143
  vs. identity thesis, 135–136
Consensus, 86, 114, 122, 329
  and dialogue at Stage 6, 152, 153, 162–165
  and ideal reciprocal role-taking, 167–168, 170, 238
  and the moral point of view, 175, 179, 229
  and validity claims, 137, 247
Constructivism, 49
Contractual agreement, 229–230
Cooperation, principle of, 201
Coping and defense, 115, 364, 366, 367, 371
Craig, R. P., 149n4
Critical theory, 194, 366
Cross-cultural decision-making, 217, 219
Csikszentmihalyi, Mihaly, 389
Cultural validation
  of schema, 333
  of Stage 6, 142, 189–193
Culture, and self development, 383–384

Damon, William, 39, 42, 45, 91, 363, 370
  and friendship understanding, 257–259
Deontic judgments, vs. responsibility judgments, 30–33, 364
Deontological ethics, 93, 177, 202, 207, 220, 228, 244, 364
  vs. aretaic, 22, 32
  vs. utilitarian approach, 225, 236–240
Deontology-teleology debate, 210
Descartes, René, 52
Desert, principle of, 75, 91, 95–97
deVries, B., 195
Dialogue
  and ideal role-taking, 153–180 passim, 187–188, 234, 329
  peer, 13
Diessner, Rhett, 364
Differentiation and integration, 326–327, 370, 371
Discourse, standards in friendship, 273, 275, 279, 280
Discourse ethics, 228, 235, 243–249, 250n7, 329
  and procedural justice, 86, 89
  procedure of, 329
  and universalism, 105–106, 113–114, 121–123
DIT (Defining Issues Test), 58
Dittmann-Kohli, F., 351

Döbert, Rainer, 71, 91, 115, 116, 118, 366, 377
  with Nunner-Winkler, 76–77, 116
Downie, R. S., 166
Drive theory, 365, 374, 383. *See also* Freud, Sigmund; Psychoanalysis
Dworkin, Ronald M., 231, 238, 250n1

Eckensberger, L. H., 76, 265, 278, 356–357n1
Edelstein, Wolfgang, 255
Ego, 360, 368, 381, 391. *See also* Identity; Self
  and Alter, 233
  defenses, 26, 383 (*see also* Coping and defense)
  development, 54, 73, 76, 78, 190, 369–380, 386 (*see also* Kegan, Robert; Loevinger, Jane)
  identity, 363
  psychologists, 25
Egoism, 264
Egoists, rational, 225, 229–231
Einstein, Albert, 3
Eisenberg, Nancy, 264. *See also* Eisenberg-Berg, Nancy
Eisenberg-Berg, Nancy, 43. *See also* Eisenberg, Nancy
Ekman, G., 307
Ellsberg, Daniel, 103. *See also* Pentagon papers
Emler, N. P., 25
Emmet, D., 257
Emminghaus, W. B., 357n1
Empathy, 202, 234, 242, 247, 263, 264
Engels, Friedrich, 51
"Epistemic self." *See* Self
Epistemology, 149n7
Equality, 157, 160, 177, 179
  justice operation of, 75, 82, 94–96, 153
  principle, 91
Equilibration, Kohlberg's model, 183, 190, 207, 215
Equilibrium
  interpersonal, 77
  reflective, 16–18, 23, 29, 33, 230
Equity, justice operation of, 75, 82
Erdynast, A., 207
Erikson, Erik, 73, 360, 364, 365, 374, 379
  notion of trust, 373
Euthanasia, 85, 98, 101, 103, 158–159. *See also* Moral dilemmas
Externalism, 26–28
  vs. internalism, 15–34 (*see also* Moral motivation)
Eysenck, Hans J., 25

Faith, 369, 386, 395. *See also* Fowler, James W.; Religion
  Fowler's stage theory of, 370–379 passim
Festinger, Leon, 23
Fingarette, Herbert, 26
Fischer, Kurt W., 376, 392
Fischoff, B., 332
Fishkin, James, 163
Flacks, R., 322–323, 340–341
Flavell, John H., 106n1, 385
Folkman, S., 330
Foot, Philippa, 9, 290
Formalism, 51, 53–55, 65. *See also* Structuralism
Formalist ethics, 66, 99, 226, 228
Foucault, Michel, 74–75
Fowler, James W., 54, 373, 376–377. *See also* Faith
  as a "soft-stage" theorist, 93, 187, 370–371
Frank, J. D., 324
Frankena, William K., 39, 154
  on moral motivation, 19–20
  on the moral point of view, 161, 163, 285
Frankfurt School, 366
Freud, Sigmund, 24, 25, 40, 73. *See also* Psychoanalysis
  Freudian Id, 75
  and self development, 360–396
Friendship, 62, 255–280
  vs. authority relations, 264–265
  Damon's levels of, 257–259
  developmental understanding of, 257–261, 269–272
  and moral reasoning, 266–276
  vs. parent-child relations, 255–256
  Selman's levels, 258–259, 263, 276–279
"From Is to Ought: How to Commit the Naturalistic Fallacy and Get Away with It in the Study of Moral Development" (Kohlberg), 133, 363
Fromm, Erich, 194, 366
"Functions." *See* Structure-content distinction

Gandhi, Mohandas, 179, 189. *See also* Moral exemplars
  and moral commitment, 317, 322–325, 344–346
Gauguin, Paul, 310, 320–321, 331
Geiger, T., 110
Gender differences. *See* Sex differences
Generalizability, 46
  and universalizability, 119
Gert, B., 83–85, 87, 89, 99, 118–120

Gibbs, John C., 39, 113, 138, 221, 250n3
Gilbert, L., 351
Gilligan, Carol, 39, 182, 190, 322, 328, 347, 382. *See also* Care; Benevolence; Justice and benevolence
care and response ethics, 42–43, 192–200, 202, 237, 264, 265, 280
and relativism-universalism controversy, 109, 111, 115–118
"self-description" interview, 193
as "soft-stage" theorist, 54–55, 93, 187
Golden Rule, 158, 164, 263, 387
and Stage 6, 172–173, 175
"Good life," the, 47, 114, 122, 164, 238, 247
Goodman, Nelson, 34n1
Gouldner, A., 262
Grice, G. R., 43, 45

Haan, Norma, 39, 43, 66, 266, 326–327
Habermas Jürgen, 39, 188. *See also* Discourse ethics
concept of rational reconstruction, 59–60
concept of value, 97–100
on justice and solidarity, and Stage 6, 224–250
on morality and justice, 80, 84, 86, 88, 90–91, 220
and the moral point of view, 328–330
and moral universalism, 71–106, 109, 113–14, 119, 121–122, 124
and the relation between psychology and philosophy, 66, 133–137, 140–141, 143–144, 149n3, 149n5
and the self, 360–362, 365–369, 371, 376, 379–380, 394–396n1
Hall, C., 303
Halstead, R., 149n7
Hare, Richard M., 119
Harris, M. B., 303
Hart, Daniel, 363, 370, 396n3
Hart, H. L. A., 82, 83–85, 88, 99–100
Harter, Susan, 380
Hartshorne, Hugh, 80
Haste, Helen, 315, 332. *See also* Weinreich-Haste, Helen
Havighurst, Robert J., 364
Hegel, Georg W. F., 226, 237–238, 368
Heinz dilemma, 85, 96, 103–105, 113, 121, 137
and Stage 6, 154–178 passim, 208–210, 213, 215–217
Hermeneutics, 33, 334, 367, 372
in Kohlberg's approach, 136, 365
and social science, 119–120

Herrnstein, Richard, 286–287
Hersh, S., 16
Hewer, Alexandra, 52–54, 66, 113, 134–136, 140–141, 182, 199
Heyd, P., 291
Hobbes, Thomas, 225, 226, 229
Hoffman, Martin L., 264
Hogan, Robert, 25
Holstein, C. B., 43
Holton, Gerald, 390
Horenczyk, G., 303–304
Horkheimer, Max, 366
Howard, J., 286–287, 295
Howard, Robert W., 322, 344–346
Hume, David, 21
Hutcheson, F., 18
Hypothetical imperative(s), 4, 6, 9

Ideal community, 245, 246
Ideal reciprocal role-taking, 112–113, 328–330. *See also* Role-taking; Perspective-taking
Habermas on, 228, 233–236, 238, 240, 242, 250n8
and Stage 6, 153–180 passim, 212
Ideal types, 255, 270
Idea of a Social Science and Its Relation to Philosophy, The (Winch), 38
Identification, 234, 364, 384
Identity, 10, 360, 375, 391. *See also* Ego; Self
Erikson's theory of, 365
Habermas's theory of, 362, 365–366, 395
Mead's views on, 243–244
and moral balance, 283–284, 287, 293–294
and moral decisions, 299–300, 310–312
Illustrations on the Moral Sense (Hutcheson), 18
Imitation, 363, 384
Indian widow-burning dilemma, 117–118, 123–124
Information-processing models, 332
INRC group, 74, 77, 106n1
Intelligence, 369, 376
Intentionality, 147
Interests, and moral stage structures, 261–263
Internalism, 22–26
vs. externalism, 15–34 (*see also* Moral motivation)
Internalization, 363, 381, 383–385, 390, 391
Isomorphism claim, vs. identity claim, 135. *See also* Complementarity thesis
"Is-ought" gap, 129–149

Jainism, 344
James, William, 360
Jay, M., 366
Johnson, J. A., 25
Johnson, V., 266
Johnston, Kay, 194
Jones, E. E., 304
Jouard, Sydney, 25
Jung, Carl Gustav, 389
  self-disclosure theory, 25
Just community, 220, 328–329. *See also*
  Moral education
Justice
  Aristotle's, Kohlberg's, and Rawls's the-
    ories of, 81–83
  distributive, 82–83, 85, 86, 214, 216,
    239
  meritocratic, 208–210, 213
  and morality, 42, 47, 49, 51, 65, 67,
    80–86, 90, 97
  procedural, 86–90
  reciprocal, 182
  retributive, 85–86
  social, 221n3, 221n4, 316
  and solidarity, 224–249
Justice and benevolence (care), 42–43,
  55, 264–266, 280
  Habermas on, 228, 237–239, 241–244,
    248
  and moral commitment, 323, 328, 330
  and the relativism-universalism contro-
    versy, 84–85, 111, 115–118
  and Stage 6, 153–158, 163, 169, 177,
    182, 192–203, 206–207, 210, 218, 220
Justification, principle of, 228

Kant, Immanuel, 8, 33, 51–52, 72, 225,
  226, 247
  deontology and Stage 6, 201, 202,
    206–210, 220
  hypothetical imperative, 4
  influence on Kohlberg, 39, 237–241
  and internalism, 17–18, 21
  moral self, 188
  and respect for persons, 185
  rights and duties, 111–114, 119, 151,
    172–173
  and social contract tradition, 189, 228–
    231, 233
  theory of action, 233
  theory of law, 239
Kegan, Robert, 54, 93, 363
  ego and personality development, 370–
    373, 377, 386
Keller, Monika, 77, 255–279 passim
King, Martin Luther, 179. *See also* Moral
  exemplars

Kohlberg, Lawrence, 16, 125n, 158, 249,
  250n2, 250n6, 323
  vs. Aristotelian ethics, 81–83
  and friendship understanding, 258,
    261–265, 269–270, 276–280
  vs. Gilligan, 193–200, 237–244, 247,
    248, 264, 328
  on ideal reciprocal role-taking, 164,
    168, 173, 216–218, 233, 234, 236,
    242, 250n8, 328
  longitudinal sample, 153, 341
  metaethical assumptions, 53
  and moral action, 60–61, 102–103
  and moral education, 220, 363
  morality as justice, 42–43, 80–86, 90–
    97, 114–115, 256
  on moral judgment and action, 28–31,
    33, 297, 326–327
  and moral motivation, 18, 23, 316
  and the philosophy-psychology rela-
    tion, 38–39, 51–56, 65–66, 129–130,
    132–144, 149, 149n3, 149n4
  on responsibility judgments, 286–287,
    326–327
  and the self, 264, 360–396 passim
  and Stage 6, 13, 151–180, 182–221,
    224–226, 228
  and structuralism, 54, 71–106
  and universalism, 109, 112–113, 121,
    123, 124
Kohut, Heinz, 382
Korean dilemma, 86, 87, 176–177, 205,
  221n4, 247. *See also* Moral dilemmas

Langdale, Shari, 194
Latane, B., 286
Lazarus R., 330–332, 334, 356n1
Lempert, W., 91
Levin, Bernard, 315–316, 320, 324, 331
Levine, Charles G.
  with Kohlberg and Boyd, 228, 234,
    297, 328
  with Kohlberg and Hewer, 52–54, 66,
    113, 134–136, 140–141, 182, 199
Lewin, Kurt, 25
Liberty, principle of, 176
Lichtenstein, S., 332
Lieberman, Marcus, 221
Lifeboat dilemma, 159–162, 164, 173,
  176, 205, 238, 247
Life cycle theory. *See* Erikson, Erik
Life history. *See* Biography
Lincoln, Abraham, 179. *See also* Moral
  exemplars
Lind, Georg, 80
Loevinger, Jane, 73, 360, 377, 386,
  396n2. *See also* Ego development

Loevinger, Jane (cont.)
  as a "soft-stage" theorist, 54–55, 93,
    364, 369–373
Logical entailment, 19, 20–22, 33, 35n3,
  35n4. *See also* Internalism; Moral
  motivation
Logic and Psychology (Piaget), 106n1
Lorenzer, Alfred, 367
Lukacs, Georg, 51
Lundberg, U., 307
Luther, Martin, 163, 321
Lyons, Nona, scoring system for care,
  195

McCarthy, Thómas, 149n5, 250n3, 368,
  396n1
McDougall, William, 24–25
MacIntyre, Alasdair, 39, 46
Mackie, J. L., 3
Macmurray, John, 39, 264
McNamee, S., 326–327
MacPherson, C., 194
March, J. G., 296
Marcuse, Herbert, 366
Marx, Karl, 39, 51, 52, 194, 366
Maslow, Abraham H., 194
Matza, D., 286, 293
May, Mark A., 80
Mead, George Herbert, 243, 360, 369,
  380–385
  and ideal role-taking, 232–233, 235,
    240–241, 328
Mele, A. R., 293
Memory, 27
Metaethics, 15–34, 53, 183
Mikula, G., 91
Milgram, Stanley, 29, 286, 309
Miller, D. L., 91
Miller, N. E., 285
Milo, R. D., 34n2
Mischel, Walter, 26
Moir, J., 265
Moore, G., 351
Moore, G. E., 15
Moral action (behavior), 38, 41–49, 64–
  65, 80, 102, 180. *See also* Moral
  judgment–moral action relation
  and moral commitment, 315–356, 364
  and moral decisions, 283–312
Moral adequacy, 135, 152, 213–214,
  218, 220
  hierarchy of, 54, 60, 63, 66, 219
  and Stage 6, 183, 184, 192, 200, 207
Moral argumentation, 114, 148, 234–
  235, 245–246, 329
Moral balance, 283–312

Moral beliefs, 27, 29
Moral commitment, 315–356, 364
  liberal vs. conservative political orienta-
    tions to, 323–324
Moral conflict, and moral decisions, 283,
  284–298
Moral consciousness, 13, 75–78, 80, 88,
  100, 102–103, 250n2
Moral crisis, and moral commitment,
  315–356 passim
Moral decisions, 100–106, 283–312, 322,
  328
  in friendship understanding, 266–269,
    272, 274, 276–280
Moral dilemmas, 116, 122, 286. *See also*
  Euthanasia; Heinz dilemma; Indian
  widow-burning dilemma; Korean dilemma; Lifeboat dilemma
  and content issues, 61, 86, 101, 103,
    106, 113, 118–120, 265
  vs. Gilligan's methodology, 193–194
  as justice problems, 81, 92–93, 189,
    211–213
Moral duties. *See also* Obligation
  imperfect vs. perfect, 111–112, 114,
    119, 264–265, 291
  natural, 83, 85, 87, 89
  prima facie vs. actual, 119
  and rights, and Stage 6, 183–221
    passim
Moral education, 149n1, 219, 220, 363,
  364. *See also* Just community
Moral exemplars, 179–180, 186
Moral feelings (moral emotions), 7–8, 12
Moral insight, 316, 324
Moral intuitions, 87, 88, 90, 91, 135,
  141, 226, 227, 230, 320
Morality
  vs. conventionality, 43–45 (*see also* Tur-
    iel, Eliot)
  psychologically defined, 38–68
  vs. skills, 59
  type vs. general, 196–198
Moral judgment (reasoning), 34, 53, 56,
  84, 115–116, 132, 146, 197. *See also*
  Moral judgment–moral action relation; Stages of moral development
  and friendship understanding, 266–
    277
  and moral conflict, 284–286
  and moral motivation, 21–25
  and the moral point of view, 232, 235,
    236
  as normative, 133–134
  vs. responsibility judgments, 29–33
  and self development, 362–369

Moral judgment interview, and scoring system, 28, 42, 113, 125n, 134, 139, 186, 189, 193, 207. *See also* Moral dilemmas; Research methodology
Moral judgment–moral action relation, 41–42, 60–61, 64–65, 67, 361, 369, 395
and moral commitment, 316–317, 326, 354
and moral conflict, 286, 297, 306
and moral motivation, 18–19, 24–26, 28–31
Moral Judgment of the Child, The (Piaget), 22
Moral motivation, 13, 15–34, 231, 263, 316, 364, 376, 383. *See also* Externalism, vs. internalism
and moral commitment, 326, 331, 333, 335, 354, 355
and personal identity, 310
and responsibility, 319–321
"Moral musical chairs." *See* Ideal reciprocal role-taking
Moral nihilism, 109–110, 111, 123–124
Moral orientations, 42, 94, 111, 115–118, 123–124, 196, 225. *See also* Justice and benevolence
Moral point of view, 27, 53, 60, 125n, 307, 320
and friendship understanding, 259, 273, 278, 279
Habermas's views on, 225, 226, 228–236, 241–242, 249
and moral conflict, 284–285, 288
and moral decision-making, 328–330
and Stage 6, 151–180
Moral principles, 21, 27, 58, 122, 256, 263
competition among, 90–92
liberal-egalitarian, 183, 210, 212
role of at Stage 6, 158–163, 178–179, 214
vs. rules, 225, 232, 240, 250n1
Moral relativism, 161
and universalism, 71–106 passim, 109–124
Moral "satisficing," 296, 311
Moral self, 188, 274, 278, 364, 369
Moral standards, 261, 266, 267
Moral types (A and B), 327
Moral understanding, 38, 45, 58, 60
Moral values, 42, 59, 60, 115, 119
and conceptions of morality, 53–54
Habermas's concept of, 97–100
in Kohlberg's theory, 113–114, 121, 134, 174, 178–179, 212

and moral commitment, 322–323
vs. nonmoral, 110
vs. personal, in moral decision-making, 292, 294–296, 300, 310–311
Moral "voices." *See* Justice and benevolence; Moral orientations
Much, Nancy C., 42
Murdoch, Iris, 39
Murray, Henry A., 389
My Lai massacre, 16, 29, 103

Nagel, Thomas, 16, 18
Nash, E. H., 324
Naturalistic fallacy, 133–134
Natural law, 51, 229, 238, 240
Nicomachean Ethics (Aristotle), 81
Nisan, Mordecai, 283, 289, 290, 303, 304
Nisbett, R. E., 304
Noam, Gil G., 328, 360–396 passim
Nozick, Robert, 208–210
Nucci, Larry, 47–48, 57
Nunner-Winkler, Gertrud, 76–77, 115, 116, 366

Obedience. *See* Authority, and obedience
Obligation, 8–9, 64, 67, 83, 85, 89, 245. *See also* "Ought"
development of in friendship, 255–280
and moral commitment, 319–322, 327, 330
and moral motivation, 19, 22, 28
personal vs. ultra, 43, 45–49, 65
quasi-obligations, 286–287
vs. "special obligations," 188, 221n4
and Stage 6, 151, 178, 213, 220, 221n3
vs. supererogation, 203, 218, 248, 291, 293
Oedipal conflicts, 361
Ontogenesis, 67, 90, 109, 140
Oresick, R. J., 48
"Original position," 86, 89, 229–232. *See also* "Veil of ignorance"
and Kohlberg's ideal reciprocal role-taking, 112, 164, 216–217, 328
"Ought," 3–13, 184, 226, 237, 288, 326. *See also* "Is-ought" gap; Obligation

Parks, Sharon, 378
Parsons, Talcott, 97
Particular Passions (Gilbert and Moore), 351
Peck, Robert F., 364
Peer relationships. *See* Friendship
Pentagon papers, 103
Perry, Thomas D., 160

Perry, William G., 54, 93, 187
Personal interests, vs. moral interests, 291–292, 294
Personality, 23, 47, 92, 363
and structural theories of self, 369–380, 395
theorists, 24, 26
Personologists, 25
Perspective-taking, 59, 267, 329, 372. *See also* Role-taking
and self development, 376, 387
Selman's stages of, and friendship understanding, 258–259, 278
Pflicht, 8
Phenomenalism, 57–61
Piaget, Jean, 22–24, 28, 62, 77, 92, 187
INRC group of operations, 106n1
morality as justice, 42–43
and moral respect, 13
neo-Piagetian research, 392
and self development, 360–396
and structuralism, 38, 73–75, 93–95, 224, 364, 375–378
and unilateral constraint, 255–256, 277
and values, 99–100
Pierce, Charles Sanders, 245
Plato's theory of the good, 23
Problem-solving, 206, 207, 214, 218
Procedural ethics, 225–226, 239, 246, 248
Promise-keeping, and friendship understanding, 269–278
Psychoanalysis, 40, 60, 285, 288
and the self, 360–396 passim
Psychopathology, 24, 374, 382, 389
Psychosexual development, 363. *See also* Freud, Sigmund
Psychosocial tasks, 379
Puka, Bill, 182, 183, 199
Habermas's response to, 224, 226, 228, 237, 239–240

Rationality, 51, 59, 134
and cognitive moral reasoning, 315, 322, 324, 329
and universalism, 120–121, 124
Rationalization, 40
Rational reconstruction, 59, 65, 90, 367
and the "is-ought" problem, 134–136
and postconventional morality, 180, 226, 227
Rawls, John, 34n1, 39, 80, 85, 191, 225, 238
concept of person, 250n5
influence on psychologists, 51–52
on morality and justice, 82, 91–92

and the moral point of view, 228–232, 234
"original position," 164, 216, 328 (*see also* "Veil of ignorance")
procedural justice, 86–89
psychological laws, 12–13
reflective equilibrium, 17
and social justice, 221n3
"veil of ignorance," 118, 164, 229–230, 309 (*see also* "Original position")
Rawls-Nozick debate, 208–210
Rechtslehre, 239
Reciprocity, 75, 77, 82, 95, 96, 387
and friendships, 255–280 passim
and Stage 6, 153, 207
Reinforcement, 26, 38
Religion, 58, 187, 191, 307–308, 370. *See also* Faith; Fowler, James W.
Research methodology (measurement issues), 34, 50, 55, 60, 72, 100, 193–195, 227, 249. *See also* DIT; Gilligan, "self-description" interview; Lyons, scoring system; Moral dilemmas; Moral judgment interview
Respect, and "respect for persons," 11, 13, 297, 316, 328, 330
"equal respect for all," 94, 177, 228, 238, 242
and Stage 6, 152–180 passim, 185, 201, 202, 203, 204, 210–212
Responsibility, 95–96, 309, 364, 369, 376
and friendship understanding, 256, 276–280
judgments, 23, 28–33, 34, 286–287
moral, and moral commitment, 315–356
and Stage 6, 156–157, 183, 210, 212, 213, 218–219
Rest, James R., 39, 42, 58, 286
Reuss, S., 257, 266, 269, 279
Reversibility, 75, 168, 207, 215–219, 221n4
Rogers, Laura, 370
Role-taking, 49, 75, 77, 78, 94, 106n3, 184, 191. *See also* Ideal reciprocal role-taking; Perspective-taking
the reversibility criterion, 216–218
and self development, 366, 367, 381, 382, 386, 391
Rorty, Richard, 334
Rosenhan, D. L., 303
Ross, W. D., 119
Rules, 78, 86, 88, 89, 100
conventional vs. moral, 44–45
and friendship understanding, 265, 266, 277, 280

and ideals, 83, 84, 85
and principles, 225, 232, 236, 240, 249, 250n1
Ruskin, John, 346
Rutter, Michael, 379

Sanctions, 6, 7
internal vs. external, 7, 9–10, 12
Sandel, Michael, 226
Scalon, Thomas M., 228, 231–232, 235
Scheler, Max, 226
Schemata
and moral crisis, 331–335, 355–356
self structures, 362, 384, 385–389, 391
(*see also* Themata)
Schmid, M., 329
Schwartz, Shalom H., 30, 286–287, 295
Sebba, I.., 294
Self, 10, 32, 33, 54, 92, 264, 327. *See also* Ego; Identity; Moral self
"connected" vs. "individuated," 115, 118
ideals of, 257, 265
and moral balance, 308–310
theory of biography and transformation, 360–396
Self-actualization, 194, 292, 308
Self-affirmation, 10, 12
Self esteem, 10, 12, 13, 373, 382, 387
Self-fulfillment, 293
Self-realization, 51, 73, 114, 242
Self-respect, 13, 94
Self structures, 384, 385–394
Self-understanding, 370, 384
Selman, Robert L., 261, 370, 372, 380, 385
and friendship understanding, 257–259, 263, 268–269, 276–279
Sex differences, 43, 115–118, 193, 194, 382
Shantz, C. U., 257
Shweder, Richard A., 39, 42
Simon, H., 296
Simpson, E. L., 190
Sittlichkeit, 237
Skinner, B. F., 40, 109, 374
Slovic, P., 332
Smetana, Judith, 47, 57
Smith, M. B., 326–327
Snarey, John R., 142
with Kohlberg and Noam, 328, 364, 369, 371, 384, 396n3
Social cognition, 78, 369
"descriptive" vs. "prescriptive," 256–257, 261, 266–267, 268

Social contract
vs. role-taking model, 231–234, 246
theory of, 89, 152, 178–179, 189, 226, 229, 263
Social conventions, 43–45. *See also* Turiel, Eliot
Socialization, 27, 118, 163, 234, 243, 285, 290
Social-learning theory, 18, 26–27, 283, 285, 287–288, 363
Social psychology, 20, 25, 26, 27, 91, 234
Sociobiology, 25
Solidarity, 256, 259
and justice, 224–249
Speech community, 136, 243
Spence, D. P., 390
"Stage and Sequence" (Kohlberg), 363
Stages of moral development, 75, 136, 138–139, 297. *See also* Moral judgment (reasoning)
conventional, 103, 124, 151, 185, 249, 262, 298
and ego development, 371–373
and friendship understanding, 256, 261–266
and moral commitment, 315–356 passim
postconventional, 13, 78, 98, 101–105, 124, 151, 224–228, 248–249, 262, 316–351 passim, 362, 367, 368, 396n2 (*see also* Stage 6)
preconventional, 103, 256, 261, 265
Stage 4½, 250n2
Stage 6, 13, 125n, 133–135, 142, 146, 151–180. *See also* Postconventional stages
and moral commitment, 320, 324, 328–329
responses to Kohlberg's conception of, 182–220, 224–249
vs. Stage 5, 153, 174–180, 204–206, 219
Stern, D. N., 390
Strawson, P. F., 12
Stroufe, L. A., 379
Structuralism, 29, 39, 41, 49, 53–56, 66, 183, 188–189, 364, 375
vs. functional theories of self, 364, 370, 372–373
and "functions," 73, 74, 76, 79, 83, 99, 101–102
"hard" vs. "soft" structural stages, 54–55, 92–94, 187, 369–395 passim

Structure-content distinction, 21, 67,
71–106, 113, 225, 227–228, 241, 364–
390 passim
Sullivan, Edmund V., 39, 51, 190
Sullivan, Harry Stack, 360, 365, 374,
382
Superego, 24
Supererogation
and friendship, 255–256
and justice vs. care, 203, 213, 218, 264
and moral balance model, 293, 296,
306
vs. obligation, 203, 218, 248, 291, 293
Sykes, G. M., 286, 293
Symbolic interactionism, Chicago School
of, 360, 361, 380, 384
Sympathy, 7–8
and Stage 6, 153, 165–170, 175–177,
242–243

Taylor, C., 46
Taylor, P. W., 167
Telfer, E., 166
Themata (biographical structures of
self), 362, 384, 389–394
Thematic Apperception Test, 389
Theory of Justice, A (Rawls), 80
Thomist ethics of goods, 238
Thornton, D., 261–262
Thornton, S., 261–262
Thought experiments. See Ideal recipro-
cal role-taking; "Original position"
Traits, 24, 25, 154, 377
vs. moral balance model, 304, 305
Trevethan, S., 195
Tugendhat, Ernst, 3, 7, 11, 90, 148
Tulving, E., 27
Turiel, Eliot, 39, 42, 309, 333
social conventions vs. moral domains,
43–45, 47, 57

Unamuno y Jugo, Miguel de, 25
Unilateral constraint, 255, 258, 263, 265
Universal discourse, 233, 235. See also
Discourse ethics
Universal heteronomy, principle of, 28
Universalism, universality, 51, 53, 67,
125n, 185
Habermas on, 229, 231, 238, 241–244,
246
and moral relativism, 71–106 passim,
109–124, 125n
Universalizability, 21, 46, 56, 65, 75, 84,
112, 230, 233
vs. generalizability, 119
and Stage 6, 153, 165, 168–169, 170–
173, 175–177, 204

Utilitarianism
vs. deontological approach, 185, 196,
201–209 passim, 225–226, 236–240
notion of justice, 91, 92, 94, 159, 175,
177, 196, 248
Utility, principle of, 238

Validity claims, 59, 137–138, 140, 234,
245, 247
and Habermas's concept of value, 97–
99
Values. See Moral values
"Veil of ignorance," 112, 118, 230, 309.
See also "Original position"
Vernunft, 8
Virtue, 95, 154
and justice, in the theories of Kohlberg
and Aristotle, 81–83, 87
and Stage 6, 194, 203, 204, 214, 220
Volpe, J., 260
von Rosen, K., 265, 278
Vygotsky, Lev S., 383–384

Walker, Lawrence J., 194, 195
Watergate scandals, 103
Weber, Max, 78, 97–98, 100, 110
Weinreich-Haste, Helen, 323. See also
Haste, Helen
Weiss, R., 266
Werner, Heinz, 376
Wertsch, James V., 396n3
Western individualism, 189–190
White, Robert W., 383
Wiggans, Grant, 194
Will, 88, 202, 229, 239, 326
heteronomy of the will, 18
rational will formation, 231, 234, 235,
245–247
Williams, Bernard, 34
on Gauguin, 310, 320–321, 331
and personal projects, 283, 292, 310
Wilson, John, 149n1
Winch, Peter, 38, 41
Wisdom, 351
Wollheim, Richard, 26
Wren, Thomas E., 26, 30

Youniss, James, 39
on peer relationships, 255, 257, 264–
265, 269

Zahaykevich, M., 371
Zimbardo, P. G., 286

Studies in Contemporary German Social Thought
Thomas McCarthy, General Editor

Theodor W. Adorno, *Against Epistemology: A Metacritique*

Theodor W. Adorno, *Prisms*

Karl-Otto Apel, *Understanding and Explanation: A Transcendental-Pragmatic Perspective*

Richard J. Bernstein, editor, *Habermas and Modernity*

Ernst Bloch, *Natural Law and Human Dignity*

Ernst Bloch, *The Principle of Hope*

Ernst Bloch, *The Utopian Function of Art and Literature: Selected Essays*

Hans Blumenberg, *The Genesis of the Copernican World*

Hans Blumenberg, *The Legitimacy of the Modern Age*

Hans Blumenberg, *Work on Myth*

Susan Buck-Morss, *The Dialectics of Seeing: Walter Benjamin and the* Arcades Project

Helmut Dubiel, *Theory and Politics: Studies in the Development of Critical Theory*

John Forester, editor, *Critical Theory and Public Life*

David Frisby, *Fragments of Modernity: Theories of Modernity in the Work of Simmel, Kracauer and Benjamin*

Hans-Georg Gadamer, *Philosophical Apprenticeships*

Hans-Georg Gadamer, *Reason in the Age of Science*

Jürgen Habermas, *On the Logic of the Social Sciences*

Jürgen Habermas, *The New Conservatism: Cultural Criticism and the Historians' Debate*

Jürgen Habermas, *The Philosophical Discourse of Modernity: Twelve Lectures*

Jürgen Habermas, *Philosophical-Political Profiles*

Jürgen Habermas, editor, *Observations on "The Spiritual Situation of the Age"*

Jürgen Habermas, *The Structural Transformation of the Public Sphere: An Inquiry into a Category of Bourgeois Society*

Hans Joas, *G. H. Mead: A Contemporary Re-examination of His Thought*

Reinhart Koselleck, *Critique and Crisis: Enlightenment and the Pathogenesis of Modern Society*

Reinhart Koselleck, *Futures Past: On the Semantics of Historical Time*

Harry Liebersohn, *Fate and Utopia in German Sociology, 1887–1923*

Herbert Marcuse, *Hegel's Ontology and the Theory of Historicity*

Guy Oakes, *Weber and Rickert: Concept Formation in the Cultural Sciences*

Claus Offe, *Contradictions of the Welfare State*

Claus Offe, *Disorganized Capitalism: Contemporary Transformations of Work and Politics*

Helmut Peukert, *Science, Action, and Fundamental Theology: Toward a Theology of Communicative Action*

Joachim Ritter, *Hegel and the French Revolution: Essays on the* Philosophy of Right

Alfred Schmidt, *History and Structure: An Essay on Hegelian-Marxist and Structuralist Theories of History*

Dennis Schmidt, *The Ubiquity of the Finite: Hegel, Heidegger, and the Entitlements of Philosophy*

Carl Schmitt, *The Crisis of Parliamentary Democracy*

Carl Schmitt, *Political Romanticism*

Carl Schmitt, *Political Theology: Four Chapters on the Concept of Sovereignty*

Gary Smith, editor, *On Walter Benjamin: Critical Essays and Recollections*

Michael Theunissen, *The Other: Studies in the Social Ontology of Husserl, Heidegger, Sartre, and Buber*

Ernst Tugendhat, *Self-Consciousness and Self-Determination*

Mark Warren, *Nietzsche and Political Thought*

Thomas E. Wren, editor, *The Moral Domain: Essays in the Ongoing Discussion between Philosophy and the Social Sciences*